The Genesis of the Civil War in Somalia

The Genesis of the Civil War in Somalia

The Impact of Foreign Military Intervention on the Conflict

Muuse Yuusuf

BLOOMSBURY ACADEMIC
LONDON • NEW YORK • OXFORD • NEW DELHI • SYDNEY

BLOOMSBURY ACADEMIC
Bloomsbury Publishing Plc
50 Bedford Square, London, WC1B 3DP, UK
1385 Broadway, New York, NY 10018, USA
29 Earlsfort Terrace, Dublin 2, Ireland

BLOOMSBURY, BLOOMSBURY ACADEMIC and the Diana logo are trademarks of
Bloomsbury Publishing Plc

First published by I.B. Tauris in Great Britain 2021
This paperback edition published by Bloomsbury Academic in 2023

Series design by Adriana Brioso
Cover image: Marxist Ethiopian forces with a Russian T-54 tank guard quantities of captured
Somali rifles, Ethiopia. (© Keystone/Getty Images

A catalogue record for this book is available from the British Library.

A catalog record for this book is available from the Library of Congress.

ISBN: HB: 978-0-7556-2709-7
PB: 978-0-7556-4241-0
ePDF: 978-0-7556-2711-0
eBook: 978-0-7556-2710-3

Typeset by Deanta Global Publishing Services, Chennai, India

To find out more about our authors and books visit www.bloomsbury.com
and sign up for our newsletters

Contents

Preface

As a young man growing up in Mogadishu in the 1970s, the author vividly remembers how he was mobilized by endless nationalist and revolutionary songs of the 'socialist' cult of General Siyad Barre's military regime and how state media used to broadcast them to prepare the public for the liberation of the occupied territories, particularly the Ogaden region. Like many other young people, the author was made to sing these revolutionary songs, praising leaders of the socialist/Marxist world such as Engels, Marx, Lenin and also General Siyad Barre.

Although the author was too young to understand the complexity of Cold War politics, one thing he can recall was the way in which the military regime mobilized the public and organized rallies either to denounce what it described as forces of 'imperialism' which were perceived as an obstacle to Somali peoples' self-determination or to praise 'progressive socialist forces' which were described as helping the Somali peoples' struggle for freedom. Also, in those days, to see Soviet-made military hardware in Mogadishu was the norm and not the exception. Indeed, the nation was very much a pro-socialist alliance country.

Then in the early 1980s the author secured a job at the United Nations office in Mogadishu. The work experience made him feel disheartened by the shortcomings of the United Nations' developmental and humanitarian projects and how they were not really making much difference to the local people. Indeed, a high percentage of project budgets returned to bank accounts in developed countries as salaries to staff from those countries. The remaining percentage either ended up as salaries to local staff or as corruption to government ministries run by government officials with vested interest in the projects.

At the time the author could not understand why this was happening because of his lack of theoretical understanding of the working of international development and its impact on the third world. From early 1990s the author immersed himself in the theoretical world of international relations. For example, he began to understand that third world countries were at the periphery of a world political structure that was dominated by the developed nations, a system that exploited poor countries and sucked their resources.

More importantly, theories about Cold War politics and superpower rivalries in the third world helped him understand why Soviets and Cubans were friends of Somalia at one point only to become bitter enemies at another point, and why Somalia was defeated in the Ogaden conflict and lost the war. With that humble background in international relations the idea of writing a book about the impact of world politics on his native country was always at the back of his mind.

Then events in 2006 propelled the author to write the book. Ethiopia, a historical enemy, supported by the United States, another superpower in pursuit of its 'war on terror', invaded Somalia. The author felt that the military intervention was wrong and would only inflame the situation, considering how other military interventions, such as the military intervention in 1992 led by the United States, failed to help reconstitute the failed Somali state.

If people ask the author, 'What he wants to achieve from publishing this book?', he wants to tell the world the story of how Somalia, a homogenous society that speaks one language and practises one religion, found itself torn apart by some huge global political events that were beyond its control, or in other words to help people read the history of the Somali civil war through the lenses of world politics and their impact on the conflict.

Acknowledgements

The author acknowledges people and organizations which helped him survive through those lonely and emotionally draining years when he was writing the book. Many thanks to Helen, Angus, Marek, Kevin, Barry, Thomas, Isterlin, Chris, Jackie, Jayanti and Alina for their support and friendship, and of course staff at the British Library for allowing him to use library facilities.

The author cannot express in words the depth of his gratitude to Prof. Stephen Chan, OBE, former dean of the Faculty of Law & Social Sciences at the School of Oriental and African Studies for his support of the manuscript. Special thanks go to Prof. Gaim Kibreab for his companionship at the British Library and Prof. Vivienne Jabri of King's College University for her guidance and support. Also, the author is grateful to Tomasz Hoskins, the commissioning editor and Nayiri Kendir at I.B. Tauris/Bloomsbury, the publisher and of course Dr Lester Crook, editor at Sword and Pen publishers for supporting the manuscript.

The author dedicates this book to people who have been affected directly or indirectly by the ongoing civil war throughout its different phases from the late 1970s.

Introduction

The ongoing civil war in Somalia with its different stages has shocked both analysts and ordinary people because no one, except a few scholars, has ever imagined a homogenous society like Somalia could ever disintegrate and descend into anarchy and civil strife. Piracy, mass people displacement, famine, terrorism, extremism and threat of secession are the lenses through which the world sees and describes Somalia.

Scholars and analysts have all been struggling to explain the genesis of the conflict. There are the anthropologists and historians who explain the conflict through Somalis' ancient clan system, which they believe divides them into rival clans unable to govern themselves under a modern state structure.[1] To this group, the collapse of the post-colonial state into clan-based fiefdoms is confirmation of their long-held argument that clan is the most determinant factor in Somali societies' political and socio-economic life. There are also the modernist and transformationist scholars who argue that despite clan being a salient factor, it is simplistic to use clan as the main explanatory method of the conflict and that there are other socio-economic and political factors, which need to be considered, for example competition of the ruling class and petite bourgeoisie over resources of the state.[2] To this group, the traditional Somali clan system is not destructive as the anthropologists tend to describe it, but a positive social system based on kinship supported by a mixture of traditional customary laws, Islamic faith and social moral values.

There is a third group, mainly the Western media, which, since the outbreak of the civil war in 1991, has been arguing that violence and anarchy constitute the foundation of Somali culture, and that political intolerance is the norm, which leads to perpetual violence.[3] These allegations are refuted by Somali scholars, such as Dr Afrah and Dr Samatar[4] who argue that violence and political intolerance are not inherent in Somalis' traditional social structure.

Although the scholars have valid points, this author would take a different approach in explaining the genesis of the Somali predicament. It will be argued that the defeat of the Somali National Army in the 1977 Ogaden war between the Republic of Somalia and Ethiopia at the hands of a foreign military superpower, former Union of Soviet Socialist Republics (USSR), was a turning point, which unleashed dynamics, forces and a sequence of events that ultimately led to the gradual disintegration of the country. After losing the war, Somalia experienced political unrest, huge refugee problems, entrenched dictatorship and revival of an atavistic divisive clan politics leading to the civil war, as the following chapters will illustrate. Indeed, while the USSR military intervention saved Ethiopia from disintegration at that historical juncture, it precipitated the collapse of the Somali state and the subsequent civil war. This fact has not been fully appreciated by scholars when they analyse the genesis of the civil war. Put simply, the evil monster jumped off the wagon of the Ogaden debacle and most of the later events were/are consequences of the humiliation and loss of national pride that the nation has suffered.

Although scholars have recognized the Ogaden debacle as a watershed in Somali history, and have highlighted its immediate impact, there is not much literature written on the long-term impact of the debacle on the Republic from 1977 to the present day in a systematic and coherent way. For example, there is hardly any serious study that shows how the debacle precipitated entrenched dictatorship, which led to the civil wars in the 1980s and the collapse of the Somali state in 1991 and then the ongoing civil war. And that was, of course, followed by the failure of the foreign military intervention in 1990s, and the current war on terror with its militaristic foreign military intervention and how this has given the conflict a religious dimension.

This book not only offers a full account of what went wrong during the entrenched dictatorship of General Siyad Barre's rule and the subsequent virulent clan conflict, it goes beyond mainstream conventional discourse of the conflict as rival clan militia fighting over meagre resources and territories. Indeed, by recognizing the impact of foreign power military interventions in Somalia from the fourteenth century, including colonial wars in the nineteenth century, the twentieth-century Cold War and the present-day war on terror, on the initiation and perpetuation of the Somali tragedy, the book attempts to partially exonerate Somalis from the 'blame the clan' game that the clan-based discourse places on their shoulders and their social order.

The book, as much as it is a history of the civil war and its different stages, also offers a military history and recounts various military operations starting from the fourteenth century to the present-day wars either fought by (1) Somalis against foreign military powers, (2) foreign powers fighting among themselves over control of the Somali nation, (3) the Somali state fighting against its own people and (4) Somali clans fighting in civil war scenarios, including current religious wars.

Despite the obvious gloomy picture of the conflict with its colossal human and economic costs and as Somalia is described as a failed state, the book will narrate some positive news that have come out amid the ruins and will describe how Somalis with their resilience and survival skills have thrived despite unimaginable obstacles and have achieved some impressive socio-economic results.

Breakdown of chapters

Chapter 1 will analyse the historical background of the Ogaden war, starting from the fourteenth-century religious wars between Somalis and Ethiopians, to the partition of Somali clans' lands by colonial powers in the nineteenth century. And finally the rise of Somali nationalism leading to independence and Somali governments' efforts in liberating the missed territories, which led to the Ogaden war in 1977.

Chapter 2, as the Ogaden war was one of the biggest and bloodiest conflicts in Africa at the time, will analyse how the war was executed, dividing it into two phases: the first phase in which Somalia won the war, and the second phase in which Somalia was defeated. The chapter will particularly examine the critical role that superpower rivalry in the Horn of Africa played in dictating the outcome of the conflict. It will be argued that Somalia lost the war not because of an Ethiopian or even African army, but by the combined forces of a USSR-led international coalition. Indeed, while the foreign intervention saved Ethiopia from disintegration at that historical juncture, it precipitated the collapse of the Somali state and the subsequent civil war. This is a fact that has not been fully appreciated by scholars when they analyse the genesis of the civil war. They tend to see the Ogaden conflict as a historical narrative without analysing its long-term impact on the country. They also tend to evaluate the Somali conflict as an isolated phenomenon, mainly using clan factor analysis, without paying greater attention to the impact of that historical event on Somalia, especially how the Ogaden disaster led to entrenched dictatorship, which then resulted in civil wars as the subsequent chapters will demonstrate. This is what makes this book different as it explains the Somali conflict not only through the clan discourse but by recognizing the impact of foreign intervention as a factor in its own right.

Chapter 3 will describe how the military regime, having lost the war together with its dream to liberate and unite the Ogaden region with the Republic, introduced repressive measures in the country's socio-economic and political institutions, which resulted in endemic corruption and bad governance leading to entrenched dictatorship. The exploitation and manipulation of divisive clan politics by the regime alongside repressive political measures and subsequent first civil wars in the northern regions will be exposed. It will be highlighted as missed opportunities, for example, President Siyad Barre not resigning after losing the war in order to allow much needed political reforms and how this could have saved the country from what was to come. New information, which reveals how the dictator nearly resigned after the Ogaden debacle, a fact not known to many Somalis or observers, will be revealed.

The chapter will also argue that as much as the military regime was to blame for the Somali tragedy during the dictatorship, armed rebel groups terribly failed too to save the country from the looming catastrophe because of deep divisions within these groups along clan lines, the lack of vision and their preference of military force as a means to achieving political objectives over political dialogue.

The role of Cold War politics in prolonging the military regime's tenure of power and how superpowers abandoned the Republic to collapse once it lost its strategic importance in the post-Cold War era will also be analysed. It will be argued that the international community left Somalia to collapse without providing much needed leadership in pre-conflict resolution or mediation through this transitional period from Cold War to post-Cold War era. This is because Somalia was not high priority on the world agenda and the international community focussed its attention in helping the socialist block (the collapse of former USSR and socialist states) go smoothly through that painful transitional period of world politics.

Chapter 4 will narrate the ugly face of the second phase of the civil war, which followed the collapse of the dictatorship and central government in 1991, and how destructive forces of vindictive clan politics, bad leadership, warlordism, personal ambitions and rivalries and competition over limited resources reduced the proud Republic to merely clan fiefdoms fighting over resources, a scenario that is similar to the European explorers' description of the nineteenth-century Somalia, where a traveller required clan protection to travel from A to Z. The chapter will explore leadership failures in the post-1991 period in which Somali leaders failed to rise above clan politics, which caused unspeakable atrocities, horrific clan cleansing and the balkanization of the Republic.

It will also highlight the international relations' dimension of the conflict, particularly the United Nations' military intervention in the early 1990s. It will be argued that although it saved hundreds of thousands of people from starvation, the UN mission known as the United Nations Operation of Somalia (UNOSOM) failed to stabilize the country. The chapter will expose political blunders and leadership failures by both Somali and UNOSOM leaders, and how these mistakes reduced the ambitious nation-building mission to no more than a city-based manhunt project in which Admiral Jonathan Howe, UN's representative in Somalia, became Sheriff of Mogadishu, hunting down a renegade warlord, General Mohamed Farah Aideed, in what seemed like a classic wild-west movie. Certainly, the UNOSOM debacle destroyed the ambition and vision of the UN secretary general Boutros Boutros Ghali and President Bill Clinton of making the UN a nation-building and peace-enforcer organization in the post-Cold War era.

Chapter 5 will analyse actions taken by different Somali stakeholders as the conflict unfolded as a coping mechanism or as an instrument to assert new socio-political realities and rights. For example, to explain how the rise of new political communities (e.g. Somaliland and Puntland) out of the ashes of the civil war have created new communal identities and loyalties, as they offer opportunities as well as challenges. The chapter will demonstrate how low-cost locally driven reconciliation initiatives by Somalis succeeded in resolving local conflicts (e.g. Somaliland, Puntland, etc.) while other reconciliation programmes led by the international community failed in reconstituting a viable Somali state, and how the internationally led initiatives became a top-down process dominated by armed factions and warlords. The lack of real ownership of the process by Somalis and a foreign-driven agenda by stakeholders adamant to creating a Somali central government in a pressurized time-framework were the predominant and towering characters of these reconciliation conferences, which failed to end the conflict.

Chapter 6 will explain the Somali conflict in the context of 9/11 and the global war on terror, and how this huge global political event has precipitated further disintegration of Somalia not only into clan fiefdoms but also along religious sects. It will be argued that the war on terror changed the Somali predicament from a clan-centric conflict to a religious one. Indeed, while the 1991–2000 conflict was mainly about warlordism, factionalism and clans fighting over control of resources and territories, the post-2001 conflict took a religious dimension, which has bitterly divided Somalis along ideological lines. As well as lineage division, Somalis are now deeply divided along religious sectarian lines as never before.

It will be revealed how events leading up to the Ethiopian invasion of southern Somalia in 2006, which radicalized Somalis and resulted in the rise of radical Islamists, such as Al-Shabaab, had all the hallmarks and similarities of the circumstances leading up to the Iraq War in 2003 and how the Bush administration colluded in the Ethiopian invasion.

Despite the obvious gloomy picture of the conflict with its colossal human and economic costs, Chapter 7 will narrate some positive news amid the ruins and will describe how Somalis with their resilience and survival skills have thrived despite unimaginable obstacles. Indeed, with limited resources, Somalis have made remarkable progress in some socio-economic sectors, and ironically, some of Somalia's human developmental trends may have been improving amid the prevailing lawlessness and anarchy and are better than the pre-war period.

The chapter will also make some recommendations as to what needs to happen if Somalia is to recover from the current political turmoil and regain its prestige in the international arena.

The historical context of the Ogaden war

The Ogaden region

The Ogaden region, where the conflict took place, covers around 370,000–400,000 square kilometres with an estimated population of about 4–5 million[1] who are mainly ethnic Somalis from the Ogaden clan and other Somali clans. The region is also known by Somalis as 'Soomaali Galbeed', 'western Somalia', a term preferred by Somali nationalists. It has borders with Somalia to the north, east and south; Ethiopia to the west; Djibouti to the north; and Kenya to the south-west. It is a semi-arid plateau with an average annual rainfall of 350 millimetres or less. The region suffers from frequent droughts, for example, in 1984–5, 1994 and 1999–2000.

At present, the region is internationally recognized as an autonomous province in Ethiopia that falls within that country's sovereignty, and it is the ninth state of Ethiopia's ethnic-based federal structure. The region is the poorest in Ethiopia, but it is rich in natural resources – copper, gas, petroleum and gold.[2]

However, Somalis have territorial claims over the province and believe that the region has always been part of Greater Somali nation, and that Ethiopia expropriated it by force, supported by European colonial powers which also divided the Somali nation into five regions: British Somaliland Protectorate in north-west regions, Italian Somali colony in north-east, central and south-western Somalia, the Ogaden region in Ethiopia, the Somali region in north-east Kenya and French Somaliland in present-day Djibouti.

Somalis have never accepted the division of their nation. Their determination to liberate Somali territories stirred awareness of strong nationalism as it shaped their foreign policy and relationship with their neighbours and outside world. They fought wars to liberate the occupied territories during colonial times and after Somalia's independence in 1960.

Following is an overview of Somali clans' wars with Ethiopia, the colonial division of their nation and the rise of Somali nationalism leading to the 1977 Ogaden war.

Holy wars of Imam Ahmed Gurey

As early as the thirteenth century, Somalis participated in holy wars between Abyssinian Christian Kingdoms (now Ethiopia) and a loose confederation of Islamic Arab states in the Horn of Africa, such as Ifat, Dawaro, Bale and Hadiya states. It was after the defeat of Muslim forces under the leadership of Saʿd ad-Din of the Walashma Arab dynasty, ruler of the Ifat state, in 1415 by the Abyssinian emperor Negus Yeshaq (1414–29) that the name 'Somali' was recorded for the first time in an Abyssinian song, celebrating the emperor's victory over Muslims. In that song, Somalis were mentioned as among the defeated foes. Saʿd ad-Din was killed on an island off the coast of Zeila town in Somalia.[3]

After the Ifat sultanate had disintegrated, Muslim power declined for some time. However, in the second decade of the sixteenth century the Adal emirate which was one of the oldest and most famous Muslim emirates and was once part of the defeated Ifat sultanate, became the base for another wave of holy wars between the Abyssinian Christian Kingdoms and Muslim emirates. The Adal emirate acquired a new leader by the name of Ahmed ibn Ibrahim Al-ghazi, born c. 1506, better known as Ahmed Gran (Axmed Gurey), or the left handed, after he had overthrown the Walashma dynasty rulers. The Imam was a famous warrior who took up the religious title of Imam in order to wage a holy war against the Abyssinians.[4] The Somali clans in the Ogaden and north regions, mainly Daarood and Dir clans, fell under the control of the Adal sultanate based in Harar town in present-day Ethiopia. After raising an army of Somalis and ethnic Afars, the Imam and his army, supported by Turkish forces (the Ottoman Empire), conquered most of Abyssinia, including Abyssinian highlands, in less than ten years.

The Imam's victory did not last long and in 1542 the Abyssinian emperor, Galawdewos, with the help of Portuguese forces decisively defeated his army. Imam Ahmed Gurey was killed in fighting near Tana Lake, and with his death, the Adal emirate collapsed.[5]

Presence of and interference by foreign superpowers played a crucial role in the conflict, and, as mentioned earlier, the warring parties had sought foreign support; for example, Turkish military support enabled the Adal state to conquer Abyssinia, whereas the Portuguese helped Abyssinia to defeat the Adal state.

Somalis played a remarkable role in the conquest of Abyssinia by Muslim states in the Horn of Africa. It is, however, unclear the extent to which Somalis were part of these states and whether they were under their jurisdiction. This is because some other ethnic groups, such as Afars, were part of the Muslim states. Furthermore, Somali clans did not traditionally come under formal centralized state structure until their independence in 1960. Nevertheless, it would appear Muslim states had exerted some influence over Somalis because some Somali coastal towns like Zeila and Berbera in the north-west region of present-day Somalia had flourished during their reign.[6]

Although Imam Ahmed Gurey was related to Somalis by marriage and united Somali clansmen, mainly Daarood and Dir, under his leadership during his holy wars, historians debate over his ethnic identity.[7] However, Somalis considered him as one of them, and he became a folk hero and the first significant Somali national hero character. Indeed, the Somali government erected a statue in Mogadishu to honour the Imam.

Colonial powers divide the Somali nation

The Somali coastal towns along the Indian Ocean and the Red Sea were a passageway for trade centres in Africa and Asia from Egypt to the Arabian Peninsula and far places like China as early as the tenth century and well before that. The coastal zones attracted foreign powers' attention, including the Ottoman Empire, Arab and Muslim emirates and Portugal, which from 1499 to 1518 looted and destroyed coastal towns, such as Mogadishu, Berbera, Zeila and Baraawa. It was, however, in the nineteenth century when Somali coastal towns attracted European colonial powers' attention and their infamous but fateful scramble for Africa.

British involvement in northern Somali coast began in 1825 after what became known the incident of Mary Ann, a British brig, which was blundered off the Berbera coast by Somalis and the British blockage of the coast until 1833.[8] However, it was after the annexation of the port of Aden in Yemen by Britain in 1839–40 that Britain's interest in the region grew stronger. The British interest was for logistical reasons because Britain needed continuous supply of meat to feed its soldiers at the Aden garrison to protect its trade route to its Indian colony. Indeed, the Aden garrison was entirely dependent on meat supply from Somali clans' livestock in north-west regions of the Somali nation.[9] Hence, British colonial administrations signed treaties with Somali clans in north-west regions as they had been doing since 1827.

Furthermore, after the British explorer Richard Burton's visit to the Horn of Africa in 1854 and the opening of the Suez Canal in 1869, realizing the strategic importance of the Somalis coastal towns to its international trade routes, the British established the Somali Coast Protectorate in north-west regions, which later became known as the British Somaliland Protectorate. The colony was administered by the India Office in London from 1884 to 1898 and then by the Foreign Office until 1907 when the Colonial Office in London took control of the colony.

That British adventure was followed by France which in 1859 signed treaties with the Afar people to get access to the small port of Obock in the Red Sea north of present-day Djibouti as a trading route. It continued its territorial ambition and after entering further treaties with the Somali clan of Isse and other arbitrary 'colonial border treaties' with Britain, France annexed Jibuti (Djibouti) to its colony. Because of colonial rivalry to control the Red Sea, Britain closed the port of Aden in Yemen to French shipping, and as a consequence of this France built a coaling station for its Suez bound ships at Djibouti, which became the official capital of the French colony in the region.[10] By 1916, France built a railway connecting Djibouti to Addis Ababa in Ethiopia, thus completing its domination. The new French colony became known as the French Somaliland.

The French adventure was followed by Italy with its colonial efforts in East Africa and Somalia starting from Foreign Minister Pasquale Mancini's colonial expansion programme from 1885 to acquire new settlements and commercial interests to enhance his country's economic interests.[11] By 1885, Italy conquered Massawa in Eritrea, and gradually occupied Ethiopia and Somalia, sending Antonio Cecchi, an Italian explorer, to explore the Juba river and Somalia. These exploration missions led to protracted negotiations with the sultans of the Zanzibar sultanate, which was occupying the coastal region of Benaadir in southern Somalia. In the first instance, Italians failed to acquire commercial access to the coastal towns, such as Brava, Marka, Mogadishu and particularly the Kismayo port because of intense colonial interests by Britain, France, Germany and Arab emirates and states.[12] By 1893, Italy consolidated its power in Somalia, and the Benaadir ports came under Italian control after it was granted a lease of these ports by the Zanzibar sultanate with the help of the British.[13]

The Filonardi Company, owned by Vincenso Filonardi, an influential Italian in East Africa and the first Italian consular in Zanzibar, was deployed in southern Somalia and was used as a tool of indirect rule by the Italian government. In addition to these treaties with other colonial powers in the region, in this early stage of colonization Italians also used a mixture of force and treaties with Somali clans, kings and sultans, such as sultans of Obia, Alula and Geledi, to conquer Somali territories.

By 1923, Italy realized its final conquest of Somalia after the Italian fascist government of Benito Amilcare Andrea Mussolini (29 July 1883 to 28 April 1945) had ordered occupation of all Somalia by force. This was a departure from the peaceful occupation of Somali territories. From there on Italy pursued its policy of forced occupation, which led to armed resistance movements across the country.

One of these revolts was the Barsana revolt, in which Sheikh Hassan Barsana, a spiritual leader of the Barsana people, a sub-clan of Gaaljecel of Hawiye clan family in southern Somalia, led an armed campaign against the Italian fascist government under its governor of Somalia, Maria Cesar De Vecchi. The Barsana revolt was the first resistance against the fascist government's policy of disarming Somali clans by force, hence the Barsana clan taking the honour of becoming the first to oppose the Italian fascists.[14] The Italians put down Sheikh Hassan Barsana's revolt after a series of battles involving the two parties. The spiritual leader was captured and later died in prison in 1927.

While the first wave of dividing the Somali nation by European powers was underway, the Abyssinian empire was extending its influence and domination from the Ethiopian highlands in what was the beginning of the Ethiopian imperialism in the region.[15] Even before he became an emperor, the Ethiopian emperor, Menelik II, born on 17 August 1844 and baptized as Sahle Maryam, had conducted military campaigns in order to conquer Somalis and other ethnic groups, such as Oromos and Afars. He captured the city of Harar in 1887, killing its Muslim ruler Abdallah Muhammad whom, according to a message to the British colonial administration at Aden in Yemen, Menelik regarded as the successor (embodiment) of the late Muslim conqueror Imam Ahmed Gurey. Menelik saw the defeat of the Muslim ruler as vindication of Christian sovereignty.[16]

Menelik consolidated his power and assumed the title of King of Kings and was enthroned King on April 1889 after the death of King John of Tigre, another rival king, who was killed in 1889 in fighting with the Mahdists of the Sudan at the battle of Galabat. He made Addis Ababa his empire's power base. The new emperor concluded the Uccialli (Wichale) Treaty in 1889 with Italy, which had already consolidated its power in the Horn and occupied Eritrea. The treaty allowed Ethiopia to be part of the European powers club, known as the Brussels General Act, and to import weapons as a Christian state.[17]

It was around that time when Menelik wrote and sent his famous circular letter to European colonial powers in 1891 defining the ancient boundaries of Abyssinia. In the circular, he claimed large parts of the Somali nation, including the Ogaden region and northern regions as part of his kingdom; he also warned European powers that his kingdom would not stand by while they divide the Horn among themselves.[18]

Under the Uccialli treaty, Ethiopia was supposed to be an Italian protectorate according to the Italian understanding of the treaty. However, Menelik disputed that interpretation and renounced it in 1893. This led to the Ethiopian–Italian war, in which Italy was defeated at Adowa in 1896. That victory marked a turning point for the Ethiopian empire because it was the first time that an African country had defeated a European colonial power, and most importantly, the victorious Menelik finally asserted his country's sovereignty and independence, thus continuing with his territorial expansion and empire building.[19]

Menelik's military expeditions did not stop at the Ogaden and northern regions of the Somali nation. Using Harar as his base, his forces penetrated deep inside southern Somalia, which was an Italian colony, as far as the Benaadir coast to Luuq at the Juba river and Bal'ad town on the Shabelle river[20] just a few kilometres from Mogadishu. Motivated by the need to feed his hungry army, droughts and also to extract taxation from Somali clans and to occupy their territories, Menelik forces brutally raided Somalis, committing atrocities, which included skinning men alive, cutting off private parts of boys and women's breasts, dead heads piled up as pyramids and virgins killed and their guts examined for omens.[21] The looting of livestock was rife, and between 1890 and 1897, about 100,000 head of cattle, 200,000 camels and 600,000 sheep and goats were looted from Somalis.[22] This was huge wealth at the time and would have had a devastating economic impact on Somalis who depended on livestock as their main economic source. Menelik died on December 1913 having asserted his country's hegemonic power in the Horn.

While partitioning the Somali nation, colonial powers and Ethiopia concluded treaties between themselves to demarcate their frontiers and spheres of influence, thus legitimizing their arbitrary action. For example, the 1891 and 1894 Anglo-Italian treaties in which the Ogaden and Haud regions changed hands between the two powers. And more crucially, the 1897 Rodd[23] Treaty with Ethiopia, in which the British returned the Haud area, part of the Somaliland British Protectorate, to Ethiopia. This is because Britain wanted to ensure Ethiopia's goodwill and neutrality in its war against the Mahdist rebellion in Sudan. Also, Britain was not prepared to defend the 1894 border treaty, which put the Haud region in British sphere, as this meant incurring higher costs and taking on powerful Ethiopia, which was exerting its hegemony and authority over Somali territories.[24]

The Rodd treaty had the following implications for Somalis. First, Britain handed the Haud region, an important grazing area for Somali clans, to Ethiopia. Second, it abandoned protection treaties it had signed earlier with Somali clans that were meant to protect them from Ethiopian raids and to represent their interests. Third, the British colonial administration did not arm Somalis to defend themselves against harassment and intimidation by the Ethiopians. Fourth, the treaty was a betrayal of trust because Somalis had not realized that an important grazing land had been arbitrarily handed over to their enemy without their consultation and knowledge. Indeed, the British failed to inform Somalis of the treaty with Ethiopia.[25]

After the British treaty with Ethiopia, the Italian government, weakened after it had lost its war with Ethiopia at Adowa[26] in 1896 and having failed to subjugate Ethiopia as a colony, followed suit and concluded the Menelik–Nerazzini protocol with Ethiopia, another boundary treaty negotiated by the Italian representative in Ethiopia, Cesare Nerazzini, to divide Somali territories among Italians and Ethiopians. The treaty was shoddy and confusing because Italians and Ethiopians had different interpretations of the boundaries they agreed to. The two countries attempted to resolve the border issue in 1908 eleven years after the first treaty but failed to reach a conclusive agreement.[27]

The arbitrary and contradictory colonial treaties in the nineteenth and twentieth centuries[28] are the cause of much of the territorial and border disputes between Somalia and Ethiopia. This is because of the lack of clearly defined and demarcated borders, hence subsequent animosities between the two countries starting from the religious wars of Sayyid Muhammad Abdille Hassan.[29]

This is how Lord Rodd, the British official, who was instrumental in concluding the 1897 treaty with Ethiopia, remorseful of his government's actions in the nineteenth and twentieth centuries, eloquently described the imperial actions and how the division of Somali territories would remain a thorn in East Africa:

> if we had been interested enough . . . (and if the world had been sensible enough), all the Somalis . . . might have remained under our administration. But the world was not sensible enough, and we were not interested enough, and so the only part of Africa which is racially homogenous has been split into such parts as made Caesar's Gaul the problem and cockpit of Europe for the last two thousand years. And Somaliland will probably become a cockpit (battleground) of East Africa.[30]

Also, a Somali poet, Faarah Nuur, captured the nineteenth and twentieth centuries' colonial powers' relentless drive to conquer and divide the Somali nation without the awareness of Somalis of the implication of the imperial action, when he said:

> The British, the Ethiopians, and the Italians are squabbling, the country is snatched and divided by whosoever is stronger, the country is sold peace by peace without our knowledge, and for me, all this is the teeth of the last days.[31]

Indeed, and unfortunately, as of today the prophesies of the British official and the Somali poet seem to be unfolding in the Somali nation from Zeylac to Ras Kamboni and the country looks divided just like it was in the nineteenth century when colonial powers divided the Somali nation (see Figure 1: colonial division of the Somali nation).

Dervish resistance movement

The first wave of partitioning Somali territories and the expanding of the Ethiopian empire spearheaded by emperor Menelik provoked Somali nationalism and resistance movements. Sayyid Muhammad Abdille Hassan, who was born on 7 April 1856 in northern Somalia from a family from the Ogaden, a sub-clan of Daarood clan family,

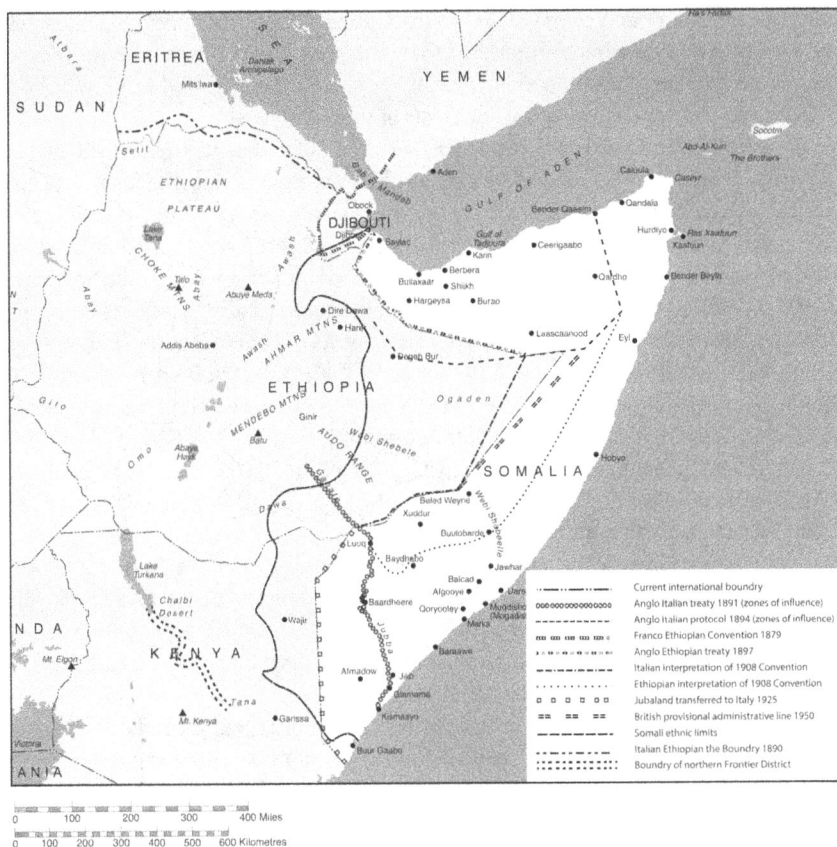

Figure 1 Colonial division of the Somali Nation. Source: Nelson Harold D 1982 Somalia a country study Washington DC American University. Thomas Lisle © 2021.

was one of the leaders of such movements. After finishing his Quranic studies, in search of further religious education, Sayyid travelled inside and outside Somalia, including Sudan, Kenya and the holy city of Mecca in the Hijas (present-day Saudi Arabia). In Mecca, he met Sayyid Muhammad Salih, founder of Salihiya, a Sufi order.[32] After falling under his influence, Sayyid embraced the Salihiya order and returned to British Somaliland colony to teach the new order to Somali clans in the north who mainly followed the Qadiriya order.[33] Sayyid did not like the introduction of foreign culture to his country, particularly what he perceived as European colonialism and un-Islamic activities.[34]

He spent two years in Berbera in the British Somaliland colony, but failed to convert many followers from the Qadiriya, another Sufi order practised in Somalia by many clans including Isaaq clans[35] who were happy with their order and by then had established commercial interests with the British colonial administration.[36] By 1898, Sayyid retreated to his clans' (Ogaden and Dhulbahante) hinterlands to pursue his teachings of the order to nomadic populations who were not influenced by foreign cultures. His oratory and poetry skills, important skills in an oral society like Somalia, had won him a large number of disciples and converts from other clans. In order to discourage traditional clan identities and loyalties, the Imam referred to his followers as Dervishes, a term applied to the adherents of the Salihiya sect.

The Imam's early insurgency was stirred after British authorities demanded Sayyid to surrender a convert accused of stealing a rifle from the British authorities. Initially, the British did not take him seriously, dismissing him as a religious fanatic, and nicknamed him the 'mad mullah' to deride him.[37] By 1899, Sayyid raised an army of 5,000 men and declared a holy war (jihad), a term used by Muslims to refer to holy wars against the British, and the Ethiopians who with their relentless raids were committing atrocities against the Somalis. His forces' first successful military operation was in August 1899 when they had seized Burao, a town not far from Berbera, the British colonial administration's headquarters, as his forces also raided settlements of other religious orders, which showed little enthusiasm for his call for jihad.[38]

Sayyid continued his resistance activities. By March 1900, his strong army of 6,000 men had seized an Ethiopian garrison at Jigjiga in the Ogaden region, and to show their strength they raided other Somali clans, looting camels. At this military engagement, his forces, widely known as the Dervish, proved to be formidable, and Sayyid established himself not just as a religious man but a political leader who was now the unchallenged commander of the Ogaden clan.[39] His status among other major Somali clans across Somalia rose, as he continued to urge them to form a common national front against the Christian colonial invaders.[40]

Between 1901 and 1904, the British assembled four military expeditions, comprising elements of Kings African Rifles, South Africans, Somalis, Indians and Ethiopians to capture Sayyid. However, the British suffered humiliating defeats by the Dervish, hence failing to capture Sayyid. Encouraged by the withdrawal of British forces from some parts of the British colony, by 1910, Sayyid was on a warpath, assembling a strong and well-trained army of 70,000 men, equipped with modern rifles. He had 10,000 cavalry, was able to manufacture his own gunpowder and bullets, and commanded the respect of 800,000 followers.[41]

Feeling invincible, the forces of the man who, for eleven years, had kept 10 Downing Street jittery attacked British led forces at Dul Madoobe in the British Somaliland protectorate in 1913, annihilating British forces. The battle was a turning point in Sayyid's insurgency because it was the first time that a British commander known as Richard Corfield was killed in what was a humiliating defeat to the British. After the humiliating defeat, the Dervish forces took the British commander's severed arm as a trophy to Sayyid, their master.[42] This was at a time when Sayyid's power was being felt across Somalia and East Africa. Indeed, British colonial authorities in Kenya and Uganda were concerned about the threat posed by his followers to the life of the former American president Roosevelt, who was visiting East Africa.[43]

That battle was a great victory for Sayyid as Prof. Said Samatar, a Somali historian, explained: 'it was a great morale booster for the Dervishes, no doubt about it, Corfield was a symbol – the British colonial man. In a sense it was a blow against colonialism'.[44] Indeed, Sayyid composed his famous victory poem: 'Adaa Koofiloow Jiitayoo Dunida Joogeyn' (you have died, Corfield, and you are no longer in this world) in which he taunts the dead British official,[45] calling him names and telling him that he will go to hell because he was an infidel.

The first British campaign against Sayyid was a failure and costly, as a journalist reporting about British failures at the time explained:

> In the archives of 10 Downing Street, London, is a dossier labelled 'Somaliland', a large part of which is made up of material dealing with Abdullah [Sayyid]. It is probably the most costly budget of material in the archives. It represents expenditure in the last eleven years of $50,000,000 and 5,000 lives and a mortifying, humiliating failure without a jot of compensation.[46]

After the First World War, the British government decided to take on the 'mad mullah'. Winston Churchill, then minister of war and air, who was earlier reluctant to engage Sayyid and argued for the reduction of the British colony in the region, was now convinced that air power was the only means to destroy Sayyid.[47] In 1920, the British, collaborating with Ethiopian and Italian forces, launched a coordinated military action of aerial, sea and land fronts against the Dervish movement.[48] The military campaign reached its climax when British warplanes bombed the movement's fortress at Taleh in the Nugal region of the north-west region of Somalia in what was one of the earliest uses of air power to defeat a nationalist insurgency. The Dervish were no match for such huge colonial onslaught, and after twenty years of defiance, the Imam, rejecting surrender, died on 21 December 1920 of natural causes (malaria or influenza) at the age of fifty-six.[49] With his death came the end of the Dervish movement.

Many Somalis consider Sayyid and his Dervish movement as the beginning of the Somali nation's liberation and resistance movements and hail Sayyid as their national hero and source of national pride and identity. In fact, the previous military government (1969–91) erected a huge statue in Mogadishu to honour him. However, Sayyid remains a controversial figure in Somali history because while some regard him as a national hero and founder of modern Somali nationalism,[50] others see him as a warlord and dictator who had committed atrocities against his fellow Somalis.[51] Others see him as someone whose importance in Somali history has been exaggerated to the disadvantage of other national heroes.[52]

Colonial powers' wars and birth of the Somali Youth League (SYL)

Another incident that shaped the future of the colonial powers' rivalry in the Horn was the Italian and Ethiopian war. Italians, to fulfil their ambition of subjugating Ethiopia as an Italian colony, which they had failed to do after the defeat at Adowa, provoked armed confrontation with Ethiopian troops at Wal Wal, a grazing area for Somali clans in the eastern Ogaden region in 1934. The United Nations attempted to mediate between the warring parties but failed. Italy, which by then had exerted its authority over the Ogaden and had strengthened its position as a colonial power in the

Horn, continued with its aggressive campaign against Ethiopia from Eritrea. Italians recruited about 40,000 Somalis in their war campaign against Ethiopia.[53]

By 7 May 1936, the Italian forces had taken over Ethiopia and occupied Addis Ababa, the capital city. Immediately, after entering the Second World War in June 1940, Italy declared war against Britain, and the Italian forces seized the British Somaliland colony, thus putting the Somali nation, including the Ogaden region, effectively under Italian occupation.[54]

In February 1941 the British launched a counterattack against Italians and within a month, Mogadishu, the Italian colonial administration's headquarters in the south, fell to the British forces. The British continued with their military operations until they seized nearly all the Somali territories, including the Italian Somaliland in the south, Somali territories in north-eastern Kenya and the Ogaden region, except the French Somaliland, which was still under French occupation. British forces also re-took Ethiopia from the Italians.[55]

It was during this time when the Somali nation, except Djibouti, was under British occupation, that the next stage of modern Somali nationalism found its voice. Somalis formed nationalist parties and organizations to liberate their nation from colonial powers. These included the Somali National League (SNL), the United Somali Party (USP) in the British Somaliland Protectorate and Hisbiya Digil & Mirifle or Hizbia Dustur Mustquil Somalia (HDMS) in the south-west region of the former Italian Somali colony.

However, the most prominent and leading party was the SYL established on 15 May 1943 in the former Italian Somali colony. Backed by the British colonial administration, which was against the return of the Italians to Somalia, the group wanted to liberate and unify all Somali territories in a Greater Somalia and was against Italian rule.[56] The thirteen founding members of the organization, who represented major Somali clans, promoted the concept of common Somali unity without regard to clan affiliation. The SYL became the base for modern Somali nationalism.

While modern Somali nationalism was taking shape, political events were moving fast at the international front. By the end of the Second World War in 1945, the Allied forces decided not to return the Italian colonies, including the Italian Somaliland captured during the war, to Italy. They delegated the responsibility for deciding the future of the Italian Somaliland over to the Four Power Commission, which consisted of Britain, France, the Soviet Union and the United States. The commission visited Mogadishu in 1948 to hear testimonies and collect representations from interested parties, such as the SYL and other movements. During the commission's visit, the SYL organized a public political rally in Mogadishu against the re-imposition of Italian rule in Somalia. The rally descended into riots after some pro-Italian groups tried to disrupt it. Fifty-one Italians and seventeen Somalis lost their lives in the incident.[57]

However, the commission went ahead with its mission and heard different political plans, including SYL representation made by some of its members, such as Abdullahi Isse and Haji Mohamed Hussein, who demanded unification of all Somali territories and full independence after a ten-year trusteeship supervised by an international commission. The commission reported its findings to the Allied

Council of Foreign Ministers and recommended a trusteeship plan that was in favour of the SYL's position.

Unfortunately, the Council failed to agree on the plan as each power suggested different plans. France and Soviets suggested Italy to return to its colony, while the United States favoured an international administration. The British foreign minister Ernest Bevin presented a proposal, which called for the unification of all Somali territories under a British-supervised trusteeship leading to eventual independence, provided Ethiopia would approve that. However, the British plan, which was closer to the SYL's vision, was rejected because the Council accused Britain of imperial expansionism at the expense of Italy and Ethiopia.[58]

The worst scenario for nationalist movements came to realization after the British had unilaterally and arbitrarily handed over the Ogaden region and Haud grazing regions to Ethiopia in 1948 and 1949, respectively, against Somalis' will. This meant effectively putting the much-disputed territories, particularly the Ogaden region back under Ethiopian jurisdiction despite fierce opposition by Somalis who had demanded the issue to be referred to the United Nations' General Assembly. The British action was a betrayal of nationalist movements' vision and trust in British authorities.[59]

As the Allied forces could not agree on the future of the Italian Somaliland, the matter was transferred to the United Nations, and in November 1949 the General Assembly decided to place it under Italian trusteeship for ten years, provided full independence was granted to the colony. Although SYL was against the return of Italian rule it accepted the trusteeship because the trusteeship, although managed by the Italians, guaranteed eventual independence before the end of 1960,[60] which was an advantage not enjoyed by many colonies.

Eventually, just before the end of the trusteeship period, the British colonial administration granted its colony, the British Somaliland Protectorate, full independence on 26 June 1960. This was followed by the independence of the Italian Somaliland on 1 July 1960 after ten years under Italian trusteeship. The two former colonies joined in formal union on 1 July 1960, forming the Somali Republic, the first modern Somali state. This left French Somaliland, which would achieve its independence on 26 June 1977, the Ogaden region and the Somali territories in north-eastern Kenya remaining under colonial occupation. The independence of the former colonies was, as some scholars put it, a 'bitter harvest' because Somalis had inherited 'dismembered nation' in which three Somali territories were still under occupation.[61]

The Republic and the issue of Greater Somalia

After independence, the Republic, faced with the difficult task of integrating two different colonial administrations[62] and an underdeveloped socio-economic post-colonial state,[63] had also to deal with the immense pressures of the pan-Somalism vision: the demand for self-determination and unification of all missing territories, a principle that was enshrined in the Republic's first constitution.[64]

The late prime minister Dr Abdirashid Ali Sharmarke articulated the grim situation that confronted the new Republic, surrounded by countries hostile to the ideals of Greater Somalia, when he wrote:

> Our misfortune is that our neighbouring countries with whom like the rest of Africa we seek to promote constructive and harmonious relations, are not our neighbours. Our neighbours are our Somali kinsmen (in Kenya, Ethiopia and French Somaliland) whose citizenship has been falsified by indiscriminate boundary 'arrangement'. They have to move across artificial frontiers to their pasturelands. They occupy the same terrain and pursue the same pastoral economy as ourselves. We speak the same language. We share the same creed, the same culture, and the tradition. How can we regard our brothers as foreigners? Of course we all have a strong and very natural desire to be united. The first step was taken in 1960 when the Somaliland protectorate was united with Somalia. This act was not an act of 'colonialism' or 'expansionism' or 'annexation'. It was a positive contribution to peace and unity in Africa.[65]

From the SYL struggle era throughout the democratically elected civilian governments (1956–69), pan-Somalism was a controversial issue that political parties and politicians promoted aggressively.[66] It determined governments' survival, as it shaped the Republic's foreign policy. For example, as a strong army was essential to achieving Somalia's irredentism claims, the Republic sought military assistance from the USSR to build a strong army of 20,000. This is because Western countries were reluctant to support Somalia militarily, particularly the United States which was an Ethiopian patron.[67]

The new Republic's first test on the pan-Somalism issue was the future of Somali territories in Kenya, or the Northern Frontier District (NFD), which was part of the British East Africa Colony. Prime Minister Dr Abdirashid Ali Sharmarke's government demanded self-determination for Somalis in the region through peaceful means. The British government, under pressure from both sides, Somalis and Kenyans who wanted to keep the region as part of Kenya, organized a referendum to ascertain whether residents preferred independence or to stay in as an autonomous province within independent Kenya. In a referendum, supervised by a Canadian general and Nigerian lawyer, overwhelming majority in the region, including non-Somali ethnic groups, voted for independence and union with the Republic.[68] Unfortunately, the British government in order to maintain its relationship with France and Ethiopia, both hostile to pan-Somalism, disregarded the outcome and decided to keep the region in Kenya within a federal structure to be worked out.[69] This arbitrary decision was another betrayal and blow to Somali unity. Under pressure from the public, Dr Abdirashid's government formally cut diplomatic relations with Britain on 12 March 1963 in protest against the arbitrary decision.

At the other border with Ethiopia, as Somalia rejected the 1954 Anglo-Ethiopian treaty in which Britain recognized Ethiopia's claim over the Haud region, within six months of independence, armed clashes, involving Somali and Ethiopian armed forces, occurred alongside the Ethiopian–Somali border. In 1961 inside the Ogaden region a massacre occurred in Dhagaxbuur town after some youths burnt down the Ethiopian flag and raised the Somali national flag. Ethiopian forces destroyed the town as hundreds of people were killed.[70] As resistance against the Ethiopian occupation had been gathering momentum since the 1940s, on 16 June 1963 the Ogaden Liberation Front (OLF), a resistance movement to oppose emperor Haile Selassie's attempts to legitimize occupation, was formed at Hoyado near Wardheer in the Ogaden region.[71] The new OLF's first leader was Garad Makhtal, an active politician once detained by the British in Mogadishu who handed him over to Ethiopia. He also worked with the SYL and received its delegation in the Ogaden region in order to help it set up offices there.[72]

In February 1964 the first modern war between the Republic and Ethiopia erupted after Ethiopia had accused the Republic of supporting the OLF. The fighting was brief, and the Somali forces of about 4,600 men were no match for the Ethiopian empire's 30,000 strong men with superior air power, which defeated them easily.[73] The war ended after mediation efforts by Sudan and the Organisation of African Union (OAU).[74]

At this stage of events since independence, the Republic had not only lost both the NFD region for an arbitrary colonial decision and the first modern war with Ethiopia, it had also found itself politically and diplomatically isolated. The Republic failed to convince the OAU that the Ogaden issue was a self-determination matter between an occupier (Ethiopia) and occupied people after Ethiopia had successfully presented the conflict as a border dispute between the two countries with Somalia being the aggressor, violating its territorial integrity.[75] Indeed, in July 1964, the OAU meeting in Cairo on the Somali–Ethiopia conflicts re-affirmed the sacredness of Article III, paragraph 3 of the OAU's Charter, which demanded member states to accept and respect inherited colonial borders.[76] This did not help the Ogaden cause and dashed any hope of presenting it as a self-determination problem riddled with history full of arbitrary decisions by colonial powers.

It was therefore not surprising that after the end of the war, Prime Minister Mohamed Ibrahim Egal's government, under pressure by the OAU's position on colonial borders, and after a treaty of defence signed by Kenya and Ethiopia against the Republic, adopted a détente policy towards the two countries in view of resolving disputes through negotiations.[77] This détente policy led to the normalization of relationship with Kenya and Ethiopia lasting until the 1977 Ogaden war.

In conclusion, lessons learned from the analysis included foreign powers' rivalry in the Horn of Africa and Somali coastal towns as early as the fourteenth century. Portugal and the Ottoman Empire supported Abyssinia (Ethiopia) and Muslim emirates/Somalis, respectively. Then colonial powers' division of the Somali nation into five regions was followed by the rise of Somali nationalism. In pursuit of the ideals of Greater Somalia, the Somali Republic went to its first post-independence war with Ethiopia in 1964 to liberate the Ogaden region, but was defeated. These historical narratives are a prelude to the 1977 Ogaden war.

The Ogaden war

One of the biggest conflicts in Africa

The 1977 Ogaden war was one of the biggest and bloodiest modern conflicts in Africa and probably the world's largest conflict at the time.[1] Scholars and historians trace the genesis of the conflict back to the emperor Menelik's occupation of Harar in the nineteenth century and his subsequent subjugation of Somalis under the Abyssinian hegemony, and of course the arbitrary imperial partition of the Somali nation, which led Britain to handing over the region to Ethiopia.[2] However, they also place immediate factors of the conflict in some events that happened in the Horn of Africa in the 1970s, including some socio-political and economic upheavals as well as Cold War superpower rivalry in the region.

Briefly highlighting the situation in Ethiopia, during 1972–3 drought had hit the Wallo and Tigray regions in Ethiopia and over 200,000 people had died.[3] Because of the failure of emperor Haile Selassie's economic reforms, and the famine, the Ethiopian empire was under the grip of some huge socio-political and economic upheavals.[4] Labour unions and other social forces were demanding political reforms amid mass demonstrations. After its defeat in Eritrea, a region that was fighting for independence from Ethiopia, the morale of the Ethiopian armed forces was low and some units mutinied.

On 28 June 1974, army representatives met in Addis Ababa and established what they called Dergue, an advocacy military committee for better terms and conditions for their units. General Aman Andon, an Eritrean by origin, became the leader of the committee. However, the group split into two factions because of disagreements over whether or not to overthrow the emperor and also how to resolve the Eritrean issue. One faction, led by General Andon, was in favour of resolving the Eritrean issue peacefully, while the other led by Colonel Mengistu H. Mariame opposed it. This power struggle resulted in the death of Andon while resisting an arrest attempt by the other group.[5]

After the emperor's attempts to improve the situation by appointing civilian governments had failed to resolve these massive problems and after various internal power struggles within the Dergue, Colonel Mengistu Haile Mariame emerged as the strong man. Emperor H. Selassie was deposed on 12 September 1974. This date, declared as the revolution day, was the end of Ethiopia's monarchy, which was a feudal-based land grabbing empire.[6] The military junta, led by Mengistu, became the winner and powerhouse after it had crashed other revolutionary movements by conducting what later became known as the 'red terror campaign'.[7] The Ethiopian empire with its diverse ethnic groups, an empire kept together by a feudal and monarchical system was at its weakest and fragile state.

Compared with Ethiopia, Somalia in the 1970s, although economically under-developed,[8] was politically stable and secure. The military regime, which had deposed the last democratically elected civilian government on 21 October 1969, was popular in Somalia and the public was behind it. Its 'hantiwadaagga cilmiga ku dhisan', or scientific socialism, ideology and developmental programmes were making progress. It had completed the very impressive mass literacy campaign (1974–5), and for the first time had successfully introduced the Somali language script officially. It had also managed successfully the 1974–5 droughts, the worst in Somalia's modern history at the time,[9] which meant resettling hundreds of thousands of people. Twenty thousand nomads died during the drought, and five million animals, half of Somalia's sheep and goats and one-third of its cattle perished.[10]

Furthermore, the Republic was militarily stronger. Supplied by the Union of Soviet Socialist Republics (USSR), Somalia had accumulated the largest military arsenal in the sub-Sahara Africa with 250 T-34 tanks, T-54/55 Soviet tanks and over 300 armoured personnel carriers.[11] Even though Ethiopia had armed forces as big as twice of Somalia's 23,000 armed personnel, the Somali tank force was three times larger than the Ethiopian one. The Somali air force of fifty-two combat aircraft, including twenty-four Soviet supersonic MiG-21s, was larger than the Ethiopian air force of up to forty aircraft.[12] Thus, political turmoil in Ethiopia combined with the military build-up in Somalia changed regional power balance in favour of Somalia,[13] which was feeling superior and confident politically and militarily.

By 1975 as disorder increased in Ethiopia and the military junta was struggling to consolidate its power, insurgency groups intensified their activities throughout Ethiopia. A newly revived Somali resistance movement called Western Somali Liberation Front (WSLF), committed to the liberation and unification of the Ogaden region with the Republic, completed its re-organizational and structural process. In January 1976, it elected a twenty-five-member committee and a leader at its conference in Balidogle – Yaqbadiwey inside the Republic.[14] By October 1976, its forces completed training and were already inside the Ogaden region, conducting military operations. The movement established its main training camp in Qoriley, dividing its forces in operational divisions, for example, the Gulweyne division in Afdheer and Godey; the Ahmed Gurey division in Jigjiga zone; the Duufan in the Jarer and Nogeb regions; the Iltire in Shinille zone and Yasin in Qorahay and Wardheer areas all in the Ogaden region.[15]

In addition to the WSLF another group called Somali-Abo Liberation Front (SALF), made up of non-Somali ethnic groups, such as Oromo and Arusi, was also already conducting military activities in Bale, Sidamo and Arusi in the south and west of Ogaden by 1977. This organization had closer links with and supported the WSLF's liberation objectives. However, there was confusion over the future of non-ethnic Somalis in SALF and whether they would claim independence on their own right or would be part of the Somali Ogaden region once the region was liberated as the WSLF would have liked.[16] Both organizations were supported by the Somali regime and were under its direct control.[17] Their manpower strength throughout the conflict was estimated at up to 63,200.[18]

On the other hand, inside Ethiopia, a separate liberation front called Oromo Liberation Front (OLF) was challenging the Ethiopian regime over the control of Oromia region in Ethiopia. This was in addition to different Eritrean liberation movements that were consolidating their grip over much of Eritrea having defeated Ethiopian armed forces.

As events unfolded, WSLF forces launched successful raids and captured territories including Hamaro, Barey, Elkare and Afdheer,[19] and by June 1977 it claimed control of 60 per cent of the Ogaden region.[20] Ethiopian forces launched counter-attacks, as the Ethiopian government accused the Somali government of supporting the WSLF and the involvement of its regular troops in military operations. Despite mounting evidence, the Somali government denied any involvement in the conflict. By then, the WSLF, whose forces were estimated at 6,000 personnel[21] was broadcasting its communiqués inside the Republic, claiming victories. A war between Ethiopia and Somalia was imminent.

Diplomatic efforts to avert the war

The Somali government tried to resolve the conflict through diplomatic avenues as early as the 1970s. The leader of the military regime General Mohamed Siyad Barre was not keen on a war and had been resisting direct support for the WSLF as demanded by the pro-liberation wing within his government who wanted to take advantage of the upheavals in Ethiopia.[22] This is because, first, President Siyad Barre's regime had endorsed the détente policy adopted by the previous civilian government and continued seeking resolution of the Ogaden issue through diplomatic means with Ethiopia within the OAU. Second, General Siyad Barre had predicted that, after the overthrow of Emperor Haile Selassie, Ethiopia would explode into chaos, implying that self-determination for the Ogaden region would be realized without bloodshed.[23] Third, the USSR, the main superpower supporting the Republic, had warned General Siyad Barre that it would abandon Somalia if his forces were to intervene in the Ogaden region.[24] Fourth, General Siyad Barre was going to be chair of the OAU soon and it would have been inappropriate to conduct a war while leading the organization.[25] Last, the argument that General Siyad Barre initiated the Ogaden war to deflect domestic problems is not strong because at the time his regime was popular enjoying relatively strong economy and social cohesion and his personal power base was firm.[26] General Siyad Barre recognized WSLF formally in 1975 after some of these diplomatic initiatives had failed.[27]

In addition, third parties attempted to mediate between the two states, including President Fidel Castro of Cuba's visit in Aden, South Yemen in March 1977 to get the two governments agree on a USSR-sponsored plan, under which the Ogaden region would have been granted local autonomy within Ethiopia in a loose socialist federal structure,[28] including South Yemen, Djibouti, Ethiopia and Somalia. However, both countries rejected the plan: Somalis sticking to their guns to realize the Greater Somalia dream, while Ethiopians were adamant in preserving their disintegrating empire. Somali nationalism proved more powerful than ideology as a scholar put it: 'If Somalia's espousal of progressive ideology (socialism) was eclipsed by the exclusivity of nationalism, the Ethiopians were equally trapped by their determination to "preserve the integrity of a discredited empire" ... the pull of nationalism proved more powerful.'[29]

In a transcript of a meeting between Fidel Castro and East German leader Erich Honecker on 3 April 1977, in which the Cuban leader was briefing the German leader about his efforts in resolving the Ethio-Somali conflict, Castro made clear how the Somali leader's strong nationalist views and what he described as his 'chauvinistic' attitude were obstacles to progressing the talks between the two parties. The Cuban leader described the Somali leader as 'nationalist and chauvinist' who saw himself as the 'wise man' while Mengistu was seen as 'quiet, serious and sincere leader'.[30] It is also clear from the transcript that the Cuban leader believed in and preferred the Ethiopian revolution and Mengistu's socialist credentials over the Somali leader's 'chauvinistic' and nationalistic attitude. He also perceived the Somali revolution as being sabotaged by imperialists and right-wing forces.[31]

In the transcript, the Cuban leader made it clear that he was going to support the Ethiopian revolution. Indeed, he did not hide his willingness to support Ethiopia militarily. Here is a quote of his own words in the transcript translated into English:

> In order to find the best solution we must think through this question calmly and thoroughly and consider it in terms of the overall situation of the socialist camp. Above all we must do something for Mengistu. Already we are collecting old weapons in Cuba for Ethiopia, principally French, Belgian and Czech hand-held weapons. About 45,000 men must be supplied with weapons. We are going to send military advisers to train the Ethiopian militia in weapons-use. There are many people in Ethiopia who are qualified for the army.[32]

After the failure of the mediation and other OAU-sponsored peace initiatives, by the summer of 1977, the conflict reached its peak and war was unavoidable. The strength of Somalia's regular and irregular forces was estimated at 50,000-strong army.[33] By then General Siyad Barre was not in complete control of the situation after some guerrilla forces had already penetrated deep inside the Ogaden region.[34] Therefore, the Somali government, which had already been supporting the insurgency, had little choice but to commit its regular forces to the conflict.

Once the war was underway, the Somali forces' performance was remarkable. By 25 July 1977 they captured Godey, which Ethiopians had resisted previous offensives by Somali forces, followed by the immediate fall of major towns and other areas, such as Shilaabo, Qalaafe, Qabridaharre, Wardheer, Aware, Dhagaxbur and Dhagaxmadow, to the Somali forces.[35]

However, the Somali forces suffered few setbacks. First, they failed to capture Dire Dawa, an important surfaced airfield available for Ethiopians for launching airstrikes in northern Somalia and northern Ogaden. At the Dire Dawa battle, Ethiopian forces repelled the Somali onslaught, consisting of one tank battalion and a mechanized infantry brigade supported by artillery units, with heavy losses. Second, at the battle of Jigjiga, the Somali forces lost over half of three tank battalions of over thirty tanks after they had tried to take over the heavily defended Ethiopian tank base there, although Somalis re-captured Jigjiga in their second attempt in mid-September.[36] Recapturing Jigjiga was the greatest victory for Somalis because this put them in a controlling position of the historical city of Harar, once emperor Menelik's headquarters. The final push for definitive victory was to overcome the Madra Pass, strongest position between Jigjiga and Harar, but this was hindered by heavy losses of tanks in previous battles combined with weaker Somali airpower and superior Ethiopian F-5 fighter jets.[37] Finally, by mid-September, the Ethiopian regime conceded that 90 per cent of the Ogaden region had fallen to the Somali forces.[38]

As towns and villages were being liberated, jubilations and celebrations broke out in the Ogaden region and across the Republic. This is how a Somali scholar, Abdi (2007) described the euphoria:

> The scene of jubilation and celebration that followed the liberation of the various towns across the region was indescribable. 'Thanks to Allah freedom has reached us at last', the people chanted. They had also shown their joy in action, but in different ways. Some of them laughed and danced wildly on the streets, while others prostrated more to Allah, thanking Allah for the mercy of freedom . . . The word 'Somali' was the symbol of the new pride in that it brought a new identity to the people as everything was 'Somalised': Somali government, Somali schools.[39]

As a teenager in Mogadishu at the time, the author can still vividly remember how the state media broadcasted non-stop nationalistic and patriotic songs to celebrate the victory, and how the overwhelming euphoria and ecstatic emotions gripped the county. At the time, the public feeling was we had finally liberated our brothers who had been under colonial domination since Menelik's occupation of Harar in the nineteenth century, or as Lewis, the British scholar described the nationalism fervour: 'Nationalist sentiment in the Republic, stimulated to an unforeseen degree by Somali literacy, had reached a climax. The fighting in Ogaden, in which many were directly and all indirectly involved, had become a national obsession.'[40]

While the Somali forces were achieving military success in the Ogaden region, as early as 1976 another important landmark regarding self-determination of the Somali people had happened in the Horn of Africa. Djibouti, the French Somaliland colony, had finally achieved its independence from France at midnight on 27 June 1977. Although Djibouti had not joined the Somali Republic in a union and this was a disappointment to supporters of the pan-Somalism vision, the Republic, however, welcomed the independence as victory over French colonialism and self-determination for the Somali people.[41] The situation in 1976–7 was better than the 1960s when the Republic had not only lost the NFD, the Somali region in Kenya and was defeated in the first modern war with Ethiopia, but was diplomatically isolated. At least in 1977, the Republic had won a war and celebrated the birth of another Somali nation.

USSR undermines Somalia war efforts

Unfortunately, because of superpower rivalry in the region euphoria proved premature. While the conflict was ongoing, other important global and regional factors had gathered momentum in the region, including a superpower changing sides in the conflict, which would change the course of the war and dictate its outcome.

Because of its strategic location, the Horn of Africa had always been a hotspot for foreign power interests and rivalry starting from Portuguese and Turkish presence in the fourteenth century to the European colonial powers' scramble for Africa in the nineteenth century, and of course Cold War superpower rivalry between the West and the USSR in the twentieth century.

US–USSR rivalry in the region started in the early 1950s after the United States had secured military base at Kagnew near Asmara in Eritrea, then part of the Ethiopian empire.[42] The United States had been paying the Ethiopian emperor, Haile Selassie, millions of dollars to keep its military facilities, and had even sponsored a UN resolution in December 1952, which made Eritrea province in federal Ethiopia so that the countries could remain one state where the United States could keep its military base.[43] Resolution, no. 390, was against another USSR proposal, which would have granted Eritrea full independence. The long-term American support might have even encouraged the emperor to annex Eritrea to Ethiopia in 1966 when he abrogated the 1952 Ethiopian–Eritrean Federation Act.[44] As history tells, the annexation provoked long and bloody secession wars by Eritreans until their independence on 24 May 1993.

At the time of the Ogaden conflict, the USSR was actively involved in Africa and the Red Sea. It had already acquired military bases at Hodeida port in Yemen and Berbera in Somalia, as well as other bases in Beira and Lourenco Marques in Mozambique and Port Louise in Mauritius.[45] The USSR was supporting liberation movements across Africa, and was seen as the leading anti-imperialist force against white minority rule in South Africa. It was already involved in other African countries such as Angola supporting other liberation movements.

On the Somali side, since independence, the Republic, a small country in need of credible army capable of liberating the occupied territories, had been seeking military aid from different sources, including China, Arab countries and the West. Western countries, including the United States, which was already Ethiopian ally, had been reluctant to supply arms due to concerns over what they saw as Somalia's aggressive irredentism policy in the region. However, the USSR was more than happy to support Somalia.[46] By 1963, the USSR lent US$32 million for military equipment to Somalia, and by 1969 some 800 Somali officers had been trained in Russia.[47]

After the military regime had seized power in 1969 and had embraced a socialist ideology, the relationship between the countries improved. They signed a treaty of cooperation in 1974, thus making Somalia the first African country to enter such agreement and the largest client for Soviet arms in black Africa. Immediately, the USSR deployed 1,500 Soviet advisers in the Republic, as 60 per cent of the nation's military officers received training in the USSR.[48] Finally, approval of the new relationship was confirmed when the USSR was granted a military base at the port of Berbera at the Gulf of Aden.

However, the friendship was strained during the Ogaden conflict due to events in the Horn in 1977. First, the relationship between the United States, Ethiopia's long-term military ally, and the Ethiopian military regime deteriorated because of President Jimmy Carter's administration's concern over human rights abuses in Ethiopia.[49] In April 1977, the Ethiopian military regime closed down the US military base at Kagnew in Eritrea, abrogating the 1953 friendship treaty with the United States. Mengistu, Ethiopia's military leader immediately visited Moscow in May 1977 and entered mutual cooperation agreement with the USSR. Second, to fill the power vacuum left by United States's partial withdrawal from Ethiopia and as it was already not happy with Somalia's involvement in the Ogaden conflict, the USSR switched its support to the Ethiopian side, accusing the Republic as the aggressor in the conflict. As part of the military deal, the USSR agreed to provide arms aid programme, estimated around US$400 million, and indeed over the following twelve months the Soviet military input would reach up to US$1 billion,[50] far greater than what it had provided to Somalia.

This immediate change of sides in the conflict might have been strategic decision by the USSR in the context of superpower rivalry in the region void of any national sentiment or sympathy with self-determination movements.[51] In other words, by abandoning the Ogaden cause, the USSR was running against its socialist principle of supporting liberation movements. Somali leaders, including General Siyad Barre, condemned the USSR's alignment with Ethiopia and accused it of arrogance with mentality of colonialism.[52]

However, President Siyad Barre and his government who needed an arms supplier were not prepared to let USSR–Somali relationship end so disastrously. To win back the Soviets, he visited Moscow in August 1977 at the height of the conflict and met the Soviet leaders. The visit was a failure and disappointing to say the least. The Soviet leadership made clear its disapproval of Somalia's incursion in the Ogaden region. Indeed, on 30 September 1977, the *New York Times* reported that Leonid I. Brezhnev, the Soviet leader, criticized Somalia for supporting Somali guerrillas who invaded Ethiopia. By October 1977 the USSR cut arms supply to Somalia, and decided to provide weapons to Ethiopia to thwart Somalia's invasion. By now it became clear to President Siyad Barre who, even before the Ogaden war, had already sensed Soviets preferred Ethiopia,[53] that they had deserted him.

Climax of the political deadlock between the two governments reached at boiling point on 13 November 1977 when the Somali government annulled the 1974 treaty of cooperation between the two countries. Although maintaining diplomatic ties, the Somali government withdrew the Berbera military base facility, as it repatriated 6,000 Russian personnel and their families.[54] The Somali government also severed diplomatic ties with Cuba, which was Soviet ally and proxy and would play a decisive role in the conflict. Although the Somali public welcomed the expulsion of the Soviets because of the USSR's betrayal of the Somali cause for supporting Ethiopia, the move was a risky strategy because there was no guarantee that the United States would replace the USSR's role as an arms supplier to Somalia.

USSR's immediate change of heart surprised observers and analysts, including the West. After all, Somalia had been a solid USSR client for a long time. Historians are divided on USSR's motivation for intervening in the conflict directly. Anyway, besides its geopolitical and strategic interest in the region, the USSR's action could be explained as follows.

First, it was suggested that Soviets and Cubans had embraced Ethiopian socialist revolution as more real and authentic than the Somali one.[55] Unlike Somalia, revolutionary forces in Ethiopian were perceived as grassroots and working-class forces fighting against entrenched feudal aristocratic system. In fact, Ethiopian leader, Colonel Mengistu was seen as having better revolutionary credentials than General Siyad Barre who was perceived as a chauvinist and nationalist who had no regard to socialism. Or to put it in another word Ethiopia was the 'valuable prize' compared to Somalia.[56] In a recent interview with Abdi Warsame Isaaq, Somali minister at the time, revealed how the Soviet president, Nikolai Viktorovich Podgorny, had told a presidential delegation in Moscow that in history there had never been a Muslim country and military government (like Somalia), which had really embraced and implemented socialism.[57] The Soviet leader made clear his country was going to support the Ethiopian revolution. This is how the British historian, Lewis (2002b), analysing the historical context under which Ethiopia had become USSR client, articulated:

> The long cherished Tsarist ambition of making Ethiopia a Russian protectorate, prominent at the end of the nineteenth century, when Russian arms and advisors had facilitated Menelik's conquest, and romanticized in the Ethiopian origins ascribed to the national poet Pushkin, had at least borne fruit. This happy outcome which in the nineteenth century was to have been achieved within the bosom of the Christian Church was now realized under the successor ideology of communism in circumstances strongly reminiscent of the Soviet Union's own revolutionary experience.[58]

In other words, if Russia's Christian Church in the nineteenth century failed to make Ethiopia a protectorate, Ethiopia was now a Russian client thanks to the communist ideology, which the Ethiopian leadership had embraced.

Second, the USSR could not support the Somali military adventure aimed at achieving irredentism claims because Soviets themselves feared irredentism claims by different ethnic groups within their country of multi-ethnic and religious composition,[59] which as it is known disintegrated into fighting ethnic fiefdoms after the USSR had collapsed at the end of the Cold War in the late 1980s and early 1990s.

Third and more importantly, the USSR was in a dilemma. If it had sided with the Republic, it would have been supporting the Somali adventure which was seen by Africans as aggression against neighbour's territorial integrity enshrined in the OAU's charter. Therefore, the USSR would have come across as a neocolonialist supporting an expansionist regime.[60] The USSR would have been unpopular in Africa, a continent it wanted to keep in its sphere of influence at a time when it was leading anti-imperialist movements adamant to see the end of the white minority rule in South Africa. It was therefore probably easier for the USSR to collaborate with Ethiopia, which was seen by Africans as a victim, defending its territorial integrity. Yet, the USSR wanted to keep both countries in the socialist block and indeed tried unsuccessfully to mediate between them.

US policy and its role in the conflict

The United States welcomed the Somali move of expelling Soviets and saw it as 'major step' towards its interests but continued its policy of non-supplying arms to either side while the conflict was still going on.[61] Inheriting previous US administrations' foreign policies in the region, President Jimmy Carter administration's role and conduct in the conflict could be divided into (1) its policy towards the two countries, (2) its policy concerning the USSR in a wider geopolitical Cold War superpower rivalry.[62] Despite Carter administration's efforts to wean off the Somali government from the Soviets by sending signals that implied its willingness to provide defensive weapons since 1976,[63] it was, however, not prepared to support Somalia militarily, particularly during the first phase of the conflict when the Somali government was denying any involvement in the conflict. The administration was not willing to assist until such a time when Somalia had withdrawn its forces from the region. This is how President Carter, in a recent interview thirty years after the end of the conflict, justified his decision to deny military aid to Somalia: 'I thought that Somalia should not be permitted to succeed in trying to take Ethiopia territory and I refused to give the Somali government any weapons.'[64]

However, the administration's occasional announcements of its willingness to provide defensive weapons were confusing and resulted in Somali leaders interpreting them as the administration's readiness to assist. An incident at a reception meeting, hosted by the US ambassador, Andrew Young at the UN in September 1977, involving Abdirazak Haji Hussein, Somalia's ambassador, and Richard Moose, assistant secretary of state for Africa in which the Somali official accused the Carter administration of betraying Somalia for refusing to supply arms,[65] revealed Somali officials' frustration and confusion over the messages. These conflicting messages might have even encouraged the Somali government to increase its activities in the Ogaden conflict and its subsequent decision to expel the Soviets,[66] hoping that the United States would step into the USSR's shoes, a decision that could have changed the balance of powers in the region. Indeed, the Carter administration was forced to deny that it had given Somalia the 'green light' to invade Ethiopia.[67]

In addition to its policy of not supporting the aggressor, the Carter administration wanted to resolve the conflict through political negotiations. Because seeking peaceful resolution was in line with President Carter's emotional commitment to resolving international disputes peacefully.[68] President Carter had even written to Somali and Ethiopian leaders, urging them to seek a solution through peaceful means. In fact, the United States proposed a UN-supervised referendum to settle the Ogaden conflict, though both sides rejected it.[69]

In the wider context of Cold War superpower rivalry in the Horn, despite ample evidence of the USSR and Cuban presence in Ethiopia, after the USSR had switched sides, the administration was reluctant to get physically involved in the conflict because of its commitment to resolving the conflict through dialogue and negotiation, but also because of incoherent policy towards the conflict due to division within the administration's policy makers/advisers: pro-regionalists versus pro-globalists.[70]

The administration pressurized the USSR and its allies through diplomacy to get out of the region, although this had never worked.[71] Also, despite existence of globalist ideologues within the administration, such as Zbigniew Brzezinski, a national security adviser, who advocated for an active role against the USSR expansionism, the Carter administration seemed to have been dominated by regionalist advisers, such as Cyrus Roberts Vance, secretary of state, who saw the war as a regional conflict to be resolved by Africans. The regionalists were also in favour of dialogue with the USSR.

More importantly American public opinion might not have supported the administration had it decided to intervene directly because of the 'Vietnam syndrome'. Equally, the administration believed that direct involvement and internalization of the conflict would have worsened the situation.[72] This is how Paul Henze, national security officer, in a memo circulated to Brzezinski expressed his views on direct involvement: 'I am extremely sceptical that here at home we would ever get support for active interventionist policy on the side of Somalia against the Soviets and Cubans in the Horn.'[73]

In summary, the Carter administration's role in the Horn during the first phase of the conflict was conducted in line with its long-term policy of seeing the conflict as a regional issue to be resolved through peaceful means. It would appear that the administration adhered to its overall policy of resolving through peaceful means, as it adhered to its human rights policy in the region at least in the first phase of the conflict.[74] Within the global superpower rivalry context, although the administration viewed the conflict through the Cold War lenses,[75] regionalists' view of the conflict within the administration had won the argument because Americans did not intervene directly in the conflict, although the same Carter administration would later change its policy for its strategic and national interests in the region.

Also, it is worth mentioning that although the Carter administration wanted to keep its relationship with both Somalia and Ethiopia, it saw Ethiopia as the more important ally in the Horn, and despite Ethiopia's relation with the USSR, the administration wanted to restore relationship with Ethiopia.[76] The Carter administration did not trust General Siyad Barre, the Somali leader, and described him as an 'old Somali camel trader in mentality' and 'wily Somali dictator'.[77] In other words, the two superpowers preferred Ethiopia.

The second phase of the war

The USSR's unexpected change of heart in the conflict triggered off second phase of the conflict as both sides entrenched in their positions. The USSR had already undertaken the largest shipment of military equipment and men in Africa. Indeed, Carter administration was surprised by the scale and the speed of the Soviet and Cuba assistance to Ethiopia.[78] This included shifting 225 planes (12 per cent of the entire Soviet fleet), 1,500 Soviet advisers and 10,000 Cuban troops and Yemeni forces, and the mobilization of the public in Ethiopia.[79] Other sources estimated the combined forces of the Warsaw pact in the conflict up to 500,000 and 500 tanks.[80] Indeed, the USSR's military input in Ethiopia from 1976 to 1980 was estimated at US$2 billion,[81] and by the end of the war Ethiopia had the largest and best-equipped military forces in sub-Sahara Africa; its forces could have occupied Somalia easily.[82]

Cuba, with its national and other revolutionary interests in the region at heart, was the most important partner with the Soviets in the conflict, and would play a crucial role in determining the outcome of the conflict.[83] Indeed, the Cubans had the largest troops estimated at 10,000–18,000, and under the political leadership of Mengistu, the Ethiopian leader, and his Soviet and Cuban masters, the overall commander of the military operation was a Cuban major general by the name of Arnaldo Ochoa, supported by a mixture of Ethiopian and Soviets generals.[84] The Ogaden conflict was the only time that Cubans and Soviets had ever conducted and agreed to a joint military operation, as confirmed by President Fidel Castro in an interview thirty years after the end of the conflict. Explaining the USSR–Cuban military adventure, which would dictate the outcome of the conflict, the Cuban president said: 'It was the only operation we conducted in full agreement with the Soviets. No such cooperation took place even in Latin America. Quite the opposite.'[85]

On the Somali side, from October 1977 to January 1978, 20,000 Somali forces were engaged in their last push to capture the historical city of Harar where nearly 50,000 Ethiopian forces supported by Soviet-supplier armour and artillery and about 11,000 Cuban troops, 1,500 Soviet advisers and Yemeni forces, were stationed.[86] By deploying this huge military equipment and personnel, the USSR wanted to end the conflict decisively.[87] And indeed the USSR intervention would prove to be the decisive factor in precipitating the Somali defeat. Unfortunately, the Somali forces were no match for this multinational force under the command of Soviet generals, Grigory Grigoryevich Varisov and Ivanovich Petrov, and within a few weeks of the fighting, major cities had fallen to the allies (see Figure 2: the Ogaden war operation, 1977–8).

In the second phase of the conflict, Somalia suffered heavy casualties, as 8,000 armed personnel, one-third of its pre-war army, killed; three-quarters of its tank force and nearly half of its aircraft destroyed.[88] It took less than a month for the multinational force to eject Somali forces from territories they had captured or liberated since the conflict started. Under pressure from the USSR-led military build-up and by the international community (i.e. OAU, UN, United States), the Somali government announced on 9 March 1978 withdrawal of its regular forces from the Ogaden region, hence the end of the conflict.

With that outcome, the Somali dream of liberating the Ogaden region from Ethiopia was aborted by the action of an interventionist global superpower. The Republic again found itself diplomatically and militarily isolated. Diplomatically, Somalia was an aggressor and forced to withdraw its troops; militarily she had not only lost its main arms supplier, the USSR, but had failed to secure military aid from the United States/ West except a few Arab countries.

One can only imagine the betrayal, humiliation and anger that President Siyad Barre and his government must have felt during these difficult times in the Republic's history. This is how Peter Bridges, the American Ambassador to Somalia at the time, described the mood of President Siyad Barre when the Soviets sided with Ethiopia: 'To add insult to injury, one of the Soviet commanders (of the battle) had earlier been Siad Barre's top military advisor in Mogadishu. A reliable resource told me later that no one had ever seen Siad Barre so enraged as when he learned this.'[89]

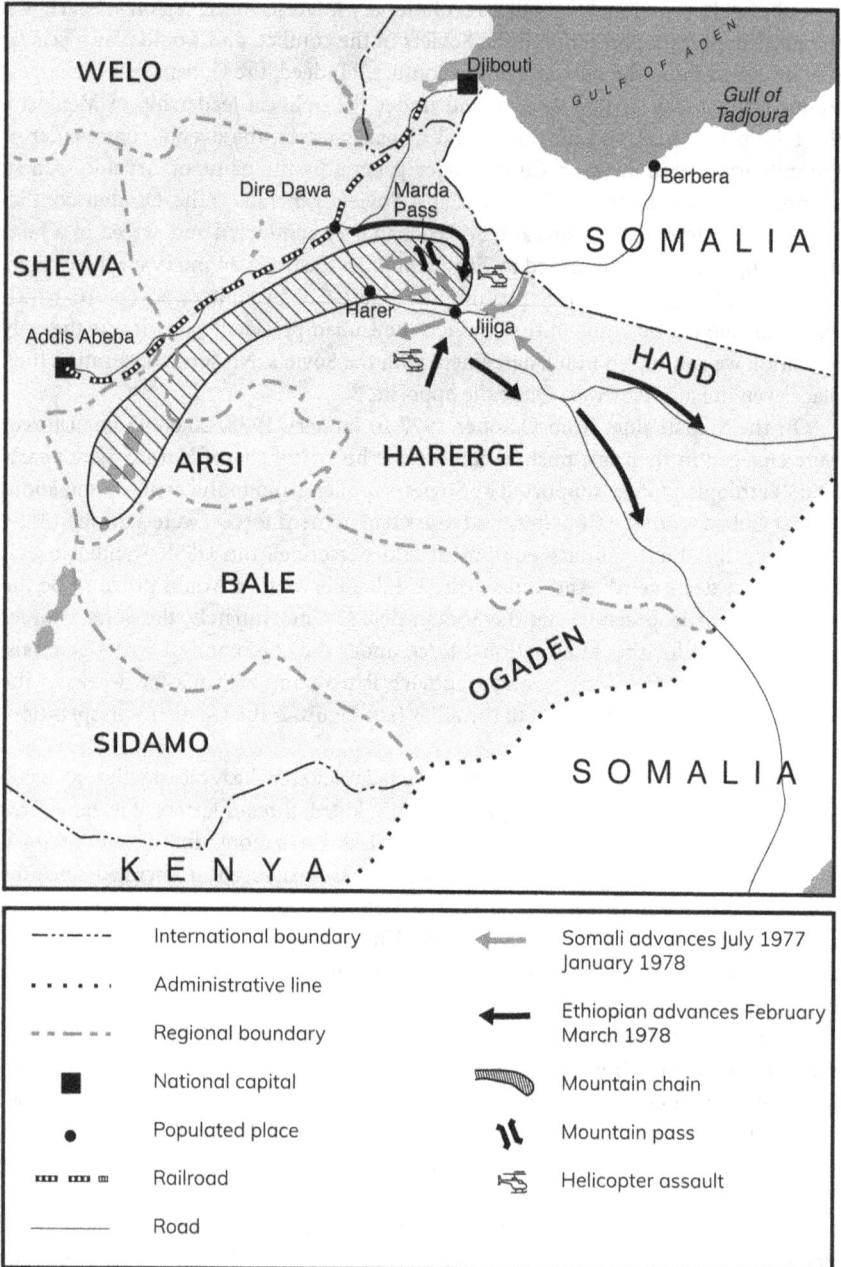

Figure 2 The Ogaden War 1977–8. Source: The Ogaden war operation 1977 to 1978. Source Ethiopia: A country study. Authors: Thomas P. Ofcansky laVerle Berry, Washington, DC, publisher Library of Congress 1993 page 312. Thomas Lisle © 2021.

It was the might of multinational forces led by an expansionist superpower, which had cornered the Republic, forced it to capitulate, and in a way denied Somalis of their long-held dream of liberating the Ogaden region from Ethiopian hegemony. Even with the help of the Soviets, Ethiopia could not have defeated Somalis in such a short time, as confirmed by Peter Chaplygin of the Soviet military mission in Ethiopia. Commenting on the role of the Cuban forces, he said: 'The Cuban troops in Ethiopia played a very important role. The Ethiopians could not have provided the military organization to destroy the Somalis in such a short period even with our help.'[90]

By 1981 with a 225,000 strong Ethiopian army[91] supported by massive 40,000 personnel from the communist bloc[92] the balance of power had changed drastically. Certainly, let alone Somalia being a threat to its neighbours, the multinational force could have occupied Somalia as confirmed by Peter Chaplygin in a recent interview when he said: 'Among the Soviet military we thought about occupying Somalia but the Soviet government was right not to allow this because it would have made our relations with countries like the United States, Great Britain and others more difficult.'[93]

Although origins of the Ogaden conflict stem from the historical events of the nineteenth and twentieth centuries and the 1970s political developments in the Horn, superpower rivalry had also played a decisive role in enticing ancient animosities and historical grievances. By flooding the Horn with huge military arsenal, superpowers encouraged the bigotry and intransigent attitude of the Ethiopian and Somali regimes, which resulted in the devastating conflict, in which thousands of people were killed and wounded.

Furthermore, the USSR's change of heart and the presence of a huge force from the socialist countries, although saved Ethiopia from total disintegration and collapse and restored its national pride,[94] it had, however, the opposite effect on Somalia. This is because the Ogaden defeat was one of the factors that would lead to the disintegration of the Somali state. The proud Republic, which had been spending high percentage of its national wealth since its independence on its armed forces[95] combined with its long ambition of liberating occupied Somali territories, was humiliated and suffered the worst defeat in its modern history. This was not by an Ethiopian or even African army, but by the combined forces of multinational forces under the command of superpower, which provided military input worth billions of dollars. This is how historians, lamenting on the defeat of Somali forces, described the situation: 'It took massive infusions of foreign expertise, troops and material to defeat the Somali army.'[96]

Consequently, the Republic was abruptly brought to its knees. This is because, as we will see in the following chapters, the Ogaden debacle would unleash short-, medium- and long-term destructive forces, factors and sequence of events that would ultimately cause the collapse of the state and subsequent civil wars, which is the main argument and raison d'être of this book.

Indeed, as pointed out by a political analyst, Somalia's international prestige, its national pride and resources were spent on the Ogaden venture, and once the war was lost, the Republic's national pride and vision was destroyed,[97] hence the collapse of the state.

In conclusion, the USSR intervention had saved Ethiopia from a humiliating defeat. But it had contributed to the collapse and disintegration of the Republic and subsequent civil wars as will be discussed in the next chapter.

Implication of the Ogaden defeat

Loss of human, financial and military resources

Since the official end of the Ogaden conflict in March 1978, humiliated by a superpower, the proud Republic faced immediate, medium and long-term insecurity, and political and socio-economic problems. Particularly as a government that lost the war, the task that faced the military regime was challenging and frightening.

The immediate loss of human life was huge with the death toll approaching 25,000 people,[1] thousands wounded or missing, compared to 6,650 Ethiopians, 400 Cubans and 100 Yemenis, although the number of the allied casualties was estimated at 20,000.[2] Other sources estimated the total loss of life in the whole conflict at 60,000.[3] The loss of human life was heavy for Somalia, a country with a population of just 4.3 million and 464,000 young males fit for military services at the time[4] compared to Ethiopia with a population of 27 million.[5] It would seem half of the 50,000 strong Somali forces[6] had perished in the conflict.

The loss of military equipment was also substantial for a poor and developing country like Somalia. Twenty-eight aircraft (half of the national air force), 72 tanks, 30 armoured personnel carriers and 90 vehicles were destroyed in contrast with the allied forces side's loss of 23 aircraft, 139 tanks, 108 armoured personnel carriers and 1,399 vehicles.[7] Other sources estimated that 60 per cent of the nation's military equipment was lost.[8] The loss of the military hardware from the Somali side would prove detrimental to the Republic's later defence capability for a country that not only had lost its main military suppliers, the USSR, and failed to attract other major supplier at a critical historical juncture, but also had no arms manufacturing capacity. This is how a scholar described the post-war military situation:

> The shortages of military hardware, inadequate maintenance, and unavailability of spare parts for what remained of Soviet-supplied equipment considerably limited the effectiveness of all elements. Units of the army, however, had been battle-tested in the Ogaden and were among the world's most recently experienced fighting forces.[9]

Unfortunately, the battle-tested armed force found itself not only in shortage of military equipment, but at the mercy of more powerful and vigorous Ethiopian army, heavily equipped with USSR military hardware. In hindsight, the Ethiopian armed forces and its allies had the military power and could have invaded and occupied Somalia if they wanted as mentioned earlier. Indeed, the change in balance of power was obvious in the aftermath of the Ogaden war, as Ethiopian forces launched airstrikes inside the Republic well into the 1980s in pursuit of Somali regular units and WSLF rebel fighters and also to support some Somali armed rebel groups, which were formed against President Siyad Barre's regime.[10] The Somali regime was so concerned about imminent Ethiopian invasion that it had considered arming the whole population to defend the country against any aggression by Ethiopia's 225,000-strong army.[11]

In addition to the loss of human life and military equipment, the financial burden of the conflict was high. A huge chunk of money from the public budget was spent, or to put it bluntly wasted in the conflict, thus putting pressure on the Republic's meagre resources and its underdeveloped economy. The pre-war 1975 government's ordinary defence expenditure was estimated at US$23 million, and by 1979 that figure jumped to US$94 million,[12] which was an increase of 75 per cent.[13] During the conflict, the government's ordinary per capita expenditure on defence had exceeded the combined budgets of education and health, which were US$7 per capita, and the per capita expenditure on defence continued to increase to US$17 after the war.[14]

Refugee burden

Besides the loss of human and other resources, the Republic had to cope with massive influx of displaced people as thousands of mostly ethnic Somalis, fleeing from the conflict, swamped the country. An estimated 1.3 million refugees were in camps, while additional 700,000–800,000 people, 90 per cent of them women and children were wandering.[15] Described as the 'refugee invasion' by Lewis (2002b), this mass displacement of people added 20 per cent more people[16] to the country's 4.3 million population. This would have short- and long-term problems, including social integration problems in a tribal society, insecurity and ecological problems.[17] For example, resettlement of refugees from the Ogaden in northern regions of Somalia would later on result in insecurity as President Siyad Barre, manipulating clan politics, would use refugees from the Ogaden clan, which is part of his Darood clan, to oppress Isaaq clans, the host community.[18] The 'refugee invasion' was burdensome on one of the poorest third world countries in the world with a fragile ecosystem plagued by intermittent droughts and floods, a country that had been reliant on food imports even in normal situations.[19]

Although the Republic had handled well the resettlement of victims of the early 1970s drought, this time it was less prepared for the Ogaden refugees because the post-Ogaden war Republic was a broken country, which had spent large portion of its scarce resources on the adventure. Furthermore, the Somali government did not have access to the helping hand of the USSR, which had assisted the Republic to resettle hundreds of thousands of Somalis during the 1970s droughts.

To deal with the refugee problem, the Somali government swiftly set up refugee camps in the country and formed a National Refugee Commission (NRC). Overwhelmed by the magnitude of the problem, the Somali government appealed to the international community for help in September 1979. It took six months before the United Nations High Commission for Refugees (UNHCR) was able to help,[20] hence putting strains on the country's meagre economic resources. Together with the government's efforts, the Somali public generously welcomed the displaced people by sharing their homes with them.

By the early 1980s there were forty refugee camps scattered across the country, each camp holding 3,000 to 70,000 displaced people[21] with annual cost of US$100 million[22] provided mainly by the international community because of the seriousness of the situation. Certainly, the Ogaden refugee problem was the biggest one in the world at the time, as confirmed by a senior government minister.

In his book, the Cost of Dictatorship, Ghalib (1995) eloquently articulated his clashes with President Siyad Barre over minister's determination to eliminate corruption within his ministry instigated by some of the president's Mareehaan clansmen, and how this resulted in the president's decision to transfer the refugee department from Ghalib's ministry to the NRC, a body created to manage the refugee crises.[23] The minister claims President Siyad Barre wanted to control the multi-million dollar refugee industry which he had already been fiddling with its figures (i.e. inflating the number of refugee population) to attract more aid. The president had even expelled representatives of aid organizations who opposed his refugee agenda from the country.[24] By then the Republic was almost completely dependent on international aid and food supplies for the Ogaden refugees or as Omar (1992) put it: 'Food assistance for refugees was used to keep the whole country afloat.'[25]

Political unrest: The 1978 military coup

On the political front, as a government that lost the war, the blame game went into full gear leading to waves of criticism and accusation and counter-accusation within the ruling elite or what Samatar (1988b) called 'the ruling petite bourgeoisie'.[26] After the retreat of the Somali National Army from the front, faced with the daunting task of eliciting battlefield reports from his generals, and answering criticism from disgruntled officers, General Siyad Barre met his generals in Hargeisa, the second capital city in the north-west region of Somalia. The generals aired their grievances over his leadership failure, including authoritarianism, incompetence and "clanism". And also operational shortcomings, for example, the lack of adequate air cover, and execution of officers who had evacuated Jigjiga because of a massive Ethiopian counter-offensive during the height of the second phase of the conflict when Cubans and Russians were heavily involved in the conflict.[27]

Another accusation against General Siyad Barre's leadership was his failures on political and diplomatic fronts,[28] particularly expulsion of the USSR at the height of the conflict without first securing alternative source of diplomatic and military support.[29] Lewis (2002b) commenting on the government's failures particularly on diplomatic and media fronts wrote:

There were ample grounds for criticism in this grim post-mortem. If the government had spent a minute fraction of its military budget on a professional public relations campaign it might have been easier to convince outsiders of the justice of the Somali case for self-government in the Ogaden. Sustained publicity over the years would have kept the issue alive in the public mind and made it more difficult for foreign governments (such as those of Britain and Italy) to forget their past involvements in the origins of the Somali–Ethiopian dispute.[30]

Having lived in Somalia during the conflict, the author still remembers how the few government-controlled media outlets never ceased talking up the rightness of the self-determination of Somali Ogadens. In hindsight as Lewis argued the government could have done more to publicize the Ogaden conflict as a self-determination issue at the international level.

Regrettably, by sacking Omar Arte Ghalib, a competent and popular foreign minister at the height of the conflict only to be replaced by the president's cousin, Abdirahman Jama Barre, an ineffective and inept civil servant[31] had failed the Ogaden cause. This bureaucratic change had ensured that the rightness of the Ogaden issue was not successfully sold to the international community, and the conflict remained border issue in which Somalia was seen as the aggressor. It is also obvious expulsion of the USSR without first securing alternative support was a failure because the United States did not step in to assist the Republic immediately after the expulsion of the Soviets. This lack of support combined with the massive USSR-led coalition force had precipitated the defeat.

During General Siyad Barre's visit to Hargeisa, seeking reports on the outcome of the war, some officers were reportedly executed by his order,[32] a man who, according to one of his ministers, was so controlling and authoritarian that no minister could take a decision no matter how trivial without his approval.[33] However, the execution was denied by Mohamed Ali Samatar, the then defence minister who described the alleged execution of eighty officers in Hargeisa as cheap propaganda.[34]

By then and after the Hargeisa meeting, the search for a scapegoat and bloodletting was unstoppable. Disgruntled with the president's conduct of the war and failure of his political leadership, a group of military officers staged military coup on 9 April 1978, which would be a turning point for the Republic. Within hours, government forces quickly crashed the coup, which was led by Colonel Mohamed Sheikh Osman 'Cirro' on the outskirts of Mogadishu. The ringleader, Colonel Abdullahi Yusuf Ahmed, long-term political detainee of General Siyad Barre and other thirty junior officers escaped to Kenya.

Lack of coordination, communication and logistical support were the main reasons for the failure of the coup, as confirmed by the ringleader in an interview with a Nairobi radio station in May 1978. The ringleader particularly mentioned that General Siyad Barre had concentrated the troops at the Somalia–Ethiopia border in the north,[35] which meant lack of a backup for plotters in the south. Furthermore, the coup leader, Colonel Cirro, perhaps fearful of the security and intelligence services knowing the plot, had hurried up the coup that was planned for 12 April, the Somali National Army's day.[36]

Straight away plotters were charged with treason under chapter 1 of law number 54 of 9 October 1970 and were tried at the National Security Court in Mogadishu, which dealt with political offences against state security. By September 1978 the court sentenced seventeen officers and civilians to death by firing squad for taking part in the coup, which according to the government radio 'was against the unity, peace and sovereignty of the Somali nation'.[37] Another forty-six officers and civilians received long-term sentences ranging from twenty to thirty years of imprisonment and confiscation of their properties. A brigadier general by the name Abdullahi Mohamud Hasan (Ma Tukade) was sentenced to twenty-eight years of imprisonment.[38] These sentences were typical harsh punishments that the most feared court in the land used to pass on crimes, ranging from murder to embezzlement, tribalism to anti-revolutionary acts.

On 26 October 1978 the convicted were taken to the Scuola Polizia (the police academy), which was Mogadishu's execution site. As the 'tradition' was, hundreds of frightened Mogadishu residents would have gathered on the top of a sandy hill, which overlooked the site, to watch the drama unfold. Residents would have learned the execution date from Radio Mogadishu, which used to play its notorious song: *Sama-diidoow* (plotters against security and stability of the state) with its chilling warning message of death by hanging to those plotting against the state, usually broadcasted just before any execution. Parading in front of spectators, the officers, described by the then defence minister as 'a small unit of lackey of foreign powers'[39] were quickly put to death by a firing squad.

With the execution of the officers, the coup, which was described by a diplomat in Mogadishu as 'ill-timed, ill-planned, ill-supported and tiny',[40] was over. The government survived and there was no major disorder or instability in major cities, such as Mogadishu or Hargeisa. Indeed, it is incredible how a government that lost the war survived and stayed in power for another twelve years, although costly and bloody. This is how Brigadier General Ahmed Suleyman Dafle, the man who once led the notorious National Security Services (NSS), described the mood of the regime's survival at the time in a recent interview thirty years after the end of the Ogaden conflict:

> When a government loses war, it normally falls, and for having survived and stayed in power for some time was exceptional and showed we were real strong men. President Carter in a meeting with President Siyad Barre at the Egyptian President, Anwar Sadat's funeral, made remarks on the Ogaden defeat, saying that for having survived after the debacle showed that we were strong and resilient people. . . . Let alone being honoured, our government should have collapsed.[41]

Some scholars, such as Lewis (2002b)[42] described the aborted coup as a clan revolt led by Majeerteen[43] officers. These scholars are anthropologists and historians, such as Laitin and Samatar (1987) and Lewis (1994a) who always tend to use clan as a major factor in explaining Somalia's problems, although this might not always be the case. However, before analysing clan dimension of the failed coup, here is an overview of Somalis' clan system and its role in their politics and socio-economic affairs.

An overview of the Somali clan system

Somalis are part of a south-eastern Africa Hamitic/Cushitic ethnic group, which also includes Oromo, Afar, Saho and Beja ethnic groups in Eritrea and Ethiopia. Despite being described as part of the Hamitic/Cushitic ethnic group, Somalis traditionally trace their genealogy to Arabian ancestry. They believe that Hiil, father of Sab and Samaale, the two ancestors or fathers of the Somali nation, was a descendant of Qureysh, an Arabian tribe and the tribe of the Prophet Mohamed. This genealogical tree is revealed through Somalis' oral tradition in which children are taught to memorize their genealogical tree, which sometimes goes back up to thirty named generations or ancestors. However, the ethnicity of Somalis is contested by historians and scholars, and their traditional claim of Arab ancestry and their relation to the Prophet are part of their efforts to assert their identity as Muslims[44] (see Figure 3 – Somali traditional clan structure).

Somalis, compared with other African countries like Ethiopia with its diverse ethnic groups that speak over seventy languages and practise over four religions, are ethnically and culturally one of the most homogenous societies in Africa, although there are a handful of non-ethnic Somali minority groups. Somalis practise one religion (Sunni-Islam) and speak one language, the Somali language divided into 'MaxaaTiri' and 'Af-Maay Maay' branches. But the puzzling question is then why such a homogenous society has failed to govern itself in a modern state structure since 1991?

To some scholars, the answer can be found in what they describe as Somalis' ancient kinship and segmentary lineage system, which they claim divides them into clan units. According to this view, politics of the Somali society are based on a belief in agnatic kinship *Xigto* through patrilineal blood ties, a philosophy which shapes the socio-economics and politics of the society.[45] The importance of kinship in the Somali society is illustrated through its oral tradition. One of the many proverbs includes the following: *Talo Tol la Diida Tagoog Jabay leedahay* which is translated as 'A limb is broken when the advice of agnatic kinsmen is rejected.'[46] Another proverb goes like this: *Tolkeeyda idila ama I nooleeya* which translates as 'My survival depends on my agnate kinsmen.' As the proverbs show, survival of the individual depends on their agnatic kinship, and those who dare to stand outside the circle are doomed to gloomy future.

Agnatic genealogical ties are not merely a family tree, recording historical descendants, but are reference points for the individual's socio-political and economic position in the clan system. The identity of a Somali is traced through recounting the genealogy of their clan. The question 'Where are you from?' exchanged by two strangers from different parts of the world is replaced by 'Whom are you from?' which means, 'Tell me which clan are you from?'[47]

The Somali kinship is organized through a clan structure. Clan family is the highest level of corporation in the segmentary structure. There are such four major clan families in Somalia, namely Daarood, Hawiye and Dir (descendants of Samaale) and Rahanweyn (descendant of Sab), Samaale and Sab being the two ancestors of the Somali nation. Kinsmen who want to count their ancestral genealogy to the clan family level may have to count roughly thirty named generations. Since a clan family is vast with a population

HILL

SAB · SAMAALE

DIGIL + MIRIFLE (REEWIN) (SDM) 2 factions

(Jidda, Dabarre Tunni, garre, Geledi

Sagaol (Iaway, Geelidle Yantaar, Hadama, Jilible, Hubeer

Siyeed (Eelay, Ieysan Eemid, Disow Maallan, Wiina

IRIR   Mayle   Yaabur   Gardheere   Maqaare   Garre   Gariire   Xammarre   Xariire

Xawadle   Hubeer   Dabarre   Garre

Gaaljecel   Dagoodi   Cawrmale

HAWIYE (USC) 2 factions · AJI

Karanle   Goorgarte   Gugundhabe   Jambeelle · DIR · Dangalo

Murusade   Hiraab   Badacadde   Ajuuraan

Mudulood   Duduble   Sheekhall   Harbarghidir

Doombiro +DARWOOD

Abgaal   Wacdaan   Moobleen   Ujajeen

Ogaadeen   Mareexaan   Harti   Awrtoble   Leelkas
(SPM)2   (SNF)   (SNDU)

Sacad   Saleebaan   Cayr   Saruur

Majeerteen   Dhulbahante   Warsangeli
(SSDF)   (USP)

Biimal   ISAAQ   Gadabursai   Ciise (Madoobe)
(SSNM)   (SNM)   (SDA)   (USF)

Cusman   Maxamuud   Cumar Max'mud   Clise Maxmud

H/awal   Garxijis   H/Jecel   Arab

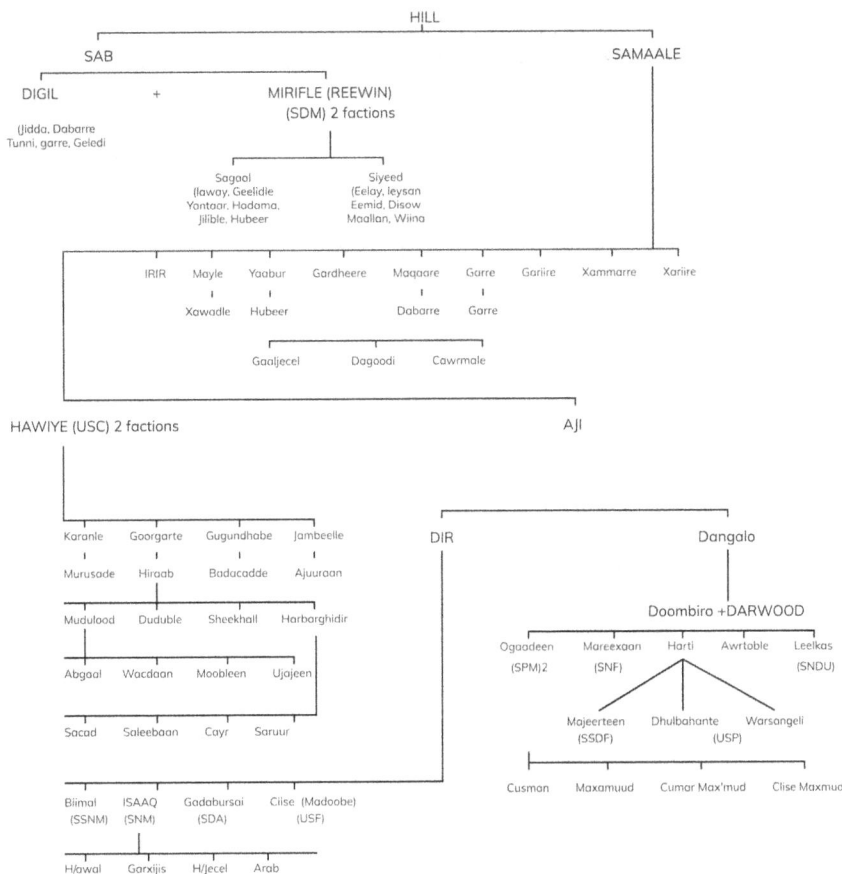

Figure 3 Somali Clan Genealogical System. Source: Ahmed Ali Jimale (1995). Day-break is Near, Won't You Become Sour? Going Beyond the Current Rhetoric in Somali Studies. The figure also shows rebel groups (SNM, USC etc,) and their affiliated clans. The figure is among other versions of the of Somali clan genealogical narratives. Thomas Lisle © 2021.

of about 500,000 to 1,000,000 people who rarely share a common territory, clan families do not act as a corporate political unity, which means they do not have political authority over the constituent sub-clans who trace their ancestral genealogy to it.[48]

The second level of the clan structure is the clan, which comes underneath the clan family. The genealogical span of this level is smaller than the clan family, around twenty named generations to a common ancestor, who is a descendant of the common ancestor of the clan family. Population at this level is estimated at 80,000–100,000.[49] Some clans, such as the agro-pastoralist clans in the south who have strong ties to the land as farmers, share common territory. This is a relative concept because some pastoral clans, such as those in northern regions, did not have strong ties to locality.[50] At this level of the clan structure, clans might act as a political corporate, but this concept is elusive and does not suggest clans have political authority over their constituent lineages or sub-clans.

The third level of the clan system is primary and secondary lineages that are branches of the clan. The genealogical span of this level is about six to ten named generations to a common ancestor who is a descendant of the clan ancestor. Population is estimated at 1,000–10,000 or even a few hundreds.[51] It is at this level of the segmentation where an important group called the *Diya-Paying* group is found. The group is constituted by an association of families related through patrilineal blood ties (*Tol*) and matrimonial ties (*Xidid*). More importantly, the group is bound together by a customary social contract (*Xeer*) that binds its members together for political, security and defence responsibilities. This group of a few hundreds to a few thousands is the most basic political corporate unit in the vast clan system in which an individual's political and socio-economic responsibilities are located. This collective group pays or receives blood compensation in cases of inter- or intra-clan conflicts which result in homicide, as it also resolves other social or criminal offences committed by its contracting members.

The Somali clan system is described by some anthropologists as decentralized and individualistic in which the individual rather than the group has always the ultimate power over their affairs. For example, even at the level of the *Diya-Paying* group, which is supposed to act as the government, clan leaders or elders do not have executive power over their kinsmen. Kinsmen can get away with murder as clan leaders cannot execute their power over them and their offices are nominal.[52]

The argument for decentralized authority and individualistic nature of the kinship system is supported by the exclusivity and particularistic nature of the segmentary social order, and how kinsmen call on this particularity to suite their particular socio-economic and political interests. Thus, 'we' as opposed to 'they' is invoked by kinsmen at any level of the segmentation, even within the *Diya-Paying* group. This exclusivity reaches to the point of 'I' as opposed to 'You'. Remarking on this particularistic character of the lineage system, a scholar writes 'the more closely they are related the more readily they unite, transiently, against others: 'myself against my brother, my brother and I against my cousin; my cousin and I against the outsider.'[53]

For anthropologists and other historians (Samatar and Lain, 1987; Lewis, 1994a), although Somalis are ethnically and culturally homogenous, it is their segmentary, individualistic and particularistic social order which is the culprit for their difficulties to govern themselves as a political unit, hence resulting in the disintegration of the Somali Republic into clan fiefdoms.[54]

For them, the divisive clan system remains the foundation for this pastoral society, and that primacy of lineage interest and its subdivision is reflected in all political levels in the modern Somali society as a nation-state. To them, one cannot explain Somalis' contemporary socio-economic and political realities without understanding kinship politics. Therefore, the Somali conflict is analysed through lenses of what they see as an unstable social order that either divides or unites Somalis according to contemporary prevailing socio-economic and political circumstances. Lewis (1994a), supporting his view of the supremacy of divisive kinship system in Somali politics and its responsibility for the collapse of the post-colonial Somali state in 1991, writes:

> At a more abstract level, the collapse of the colonially created state represents technically a triumph for the segmentary lineage system and the political power

of kinship. For better or worse, clanship has certainly prevailed, and the assertions of some Somali and non-Somali ideologues that clanship was an atavistic force doomed to oblivion in the modern world seem rather dated. Given then, that like nationalism, clanship is a human invention, is it in the 1990s basically the same phenomenon that it was in the 1890s? Linguistically the answer must be 'yes' since the same terminology has been employed throughout the recorded history of Somalis. Sociologically, the evidence also supports this view. Indeed, the argument of this book is that clanship is and was essentially a multipurpose, culturally constructed resource of compelling power because of its ostensibly inherent character 'bred in the bone' and running 'in the blood' as Somali conceptualise it.[55]

Traditionally, like many other tribal- or clan-based societies, there were inter- or intra-clan conflicts over control of resources or other reasons, for example, conflicts between Daarood sub-clans and lineages, or conflicts between Hawiye and Daarood clans. This is particularly the case given clans tend to co-habit and share territories and intermingle in their pursuit of meagre resources.

Since independence, clan identity and rivalry has played a role in the politics of the new Republic. During the civilian governments from 1960 to 1969, political parties and politicians sought support from their kinsmen, although some parties, such as the SYL tried to discourage clan affiliation. It is true that Daaroods followed by Hawiyes and Isaaqs dominated politics of the modern Somali state and had held most of senior government offices. This left Rahanweyns marginalized and at the bottom of the ladder.[56] During the military regime, the president of Somalia for twenty years was a Daarood until the collapse of the central government in 1991.

However, besides the anthropologists' approach, there is another school of thought pioneered by Dr Ahmed Ismail Samatar that criticizes the anthropological discourse. This school's main argument is to challenge the view that Somalis' ancient clan structure survived and remains intact throughout the many centuries that Somalis had been subjected to transformation since colonization.[57] It argues that although clan remains a salient factor other social strata (petit bourgeoisie, elite, traders and state class) had emerged since the imposition of colonialism, and it is the interaction of these forces that shaped the modern Somali nation-state. If one needs to explain the modern Somali society, one needs to take this transformation into account and not only the clan discourse.

This view disagrees with the characterization of the traditional Somali social order as divisive with unsustainable social and political institutions. Despite frequent feuding and constant competition over scarce resources by clans, the transformation school of thought describes the Somali kinship structure as a communitarian system with stable political and social institutions to govern the individual and community.[58] The social and political institutions were based on a basic Somali moral order which was supported by communal kinship upheld by customary law (*Xeer*) and Islamic law.[59] They disagree with the description of the traditional lineage system as segmentary and individualistic which makes the Somali 'ungovernable, associable species'.[60]

According to this group, problems in the kinship system arise when the male ego devoid of any kinship values and Islamic law degenerates into self-destructive, primitive and asocial, which leads to *clanism*, a perverted version of the kinship values.[61] To this school, although it accepts clan identity and rivalry have played a role in the ongoing conflict, political turmoil in Somalia is as a result of contemporary *clanism* politics dominated by state class, factional leaders and warlords devoid of any traditional kinship values, motivated by the pursuit of state power and lured by the availability of modern weaponry.[62] In other words, clan identity itself is not the cause of the conflict, but it is the role played by the ruling elite in mobilizing and using it as an instrument for political and economic gains. The argument here is that traditional Somali kinship was a useful tool to help Somalis organize their socio-economic and political realities, but that system has been perverted by contemporary ruling classes and elites.

The author agrees with the second school's analysis of the role of the kinship system in Somali society, which is an instrument used for good or bad. It is also fair to say that while other multi-ethnic and multi-faith countries exist in Africa and elsewhere and function as nation-states or state-nations, there is no reason why this ethnically and culturally homogenous society, despite the kinship system, could not hold together as one nation-state as it did for thirty years in its modern state, provided that other prevailing political and socio-economic circumstances at local, regional and global levels allow it.

A classic example of how prevailing world politics in the twentieth century did not allow Somalis to continue as one nation-state is the role played by the USSR in the defeat of Somalia in the Ogaden conflict. As this book will argue, the Ogaden debacle, instigated by the superpower, had precipitated the collapse of the Somali state and its disintegration into clan fiefdoms. Put simply, the evil monster jumped off the wagon of the Ogaden debacle and most of the later events were/are the consequences of the humiliation and loss of national pride, which the nation has suffered.

It is therefore a misconception to blame Somalis' social order as the culprit for the disintegration of the Somali state into clan fiefdoms as anthropologists would like to suggest particularly when other huge global forces had been working against this homogenous society.

Now let us return to the failed 1978 coup and whether it had a clan dimension. Unlike anthropologists, such as Lewis (2002b) who argue that the coup had a clan dimension, Samatar (1988b) while not dismissing clan as a salient factor argued that the coup was an expression of a wider public discontent over President Siyad's leadership failure during the Ogaden debacle and other socio-economic and political failings. In his opinion, while leaders of the coup were from the Majeerteen clan and the regime had been paranoid from a Majeerteen conspiracy to oust him even before the war, members of the same clan had held senior positions in President Siyad Barre's government, and therefore clan cannot be the sole determinant factor. Samatar, challenging the clan explanation of the coup, writes:

> While this view does not completely dismiss the role of primordial affinities in the emerging struggle over the state in Somalia, it is an attempt to go beyond any single determinism (*clan*) and consider the interaction of various factors – clanism and intra-class competition among them the Somali state class broke up, once more, into various antagonistic factions.[63]

Samatar (1988b) argued that because of the lack of any other independent public organizations that could have articulated the post-Ogaden public anger and frustration, officers of the coup within the military establishment were the plausible force capable of direct challenge to the military regime at the time.[64] To rephrase it, as there were no other independent political parties in the country, challenge within the military and security establishments was or would have been the only reasonable means of expressing discontent over the Somali predicament at a time when there was disgruntlement within the military establishment and the wider public.[65] This is to presume that the plotters, despite being dominated by Majeerteens, might have seen themselves as saviours in a country where the armed forces were held in higher prestige in the national life.[66] Indeed, in an interview with Colonel Abdullahi Yuusuf, the ring leader who would become the president of Somalia in 2004, articulated how he and other military officers from different clans plotted the coup well before the Ogaden debacle because they were dissatisfied with the military regime's socialist policies.[67]

The author agrees with Samatar's analysis of the coup as an expression of wider public discontent over political and socio-economic ills, which he articulated in his book. Furthermore, the author takes the debate back to a particular moment in the Republic's history in which the nation was vulnerable and fragile.

At the time of the coup, Somalia was at its weakest and lowest historical point. However, prior to the war, the country, despite some shortcomings, was politically stable, and the general public was united behind its leaders with a strong feeling of Somali nationalism and unity which disregarded clanism. The country went to war to liberate the Somali people from Ethiopia, a popular cause, but was defeated not by its enemy but by the combined forces of the USSR and its Warsaw alliance. The USSR-induced Ogaden debacle then disturbed the pre-conflict social and political equilibrium, national unity and harmony. Therefore, it was not unexpected that some political tension, such as the coup, had occurred.

Although its leaders were from one particular clan, this cannot simply be explained as clan revolt because there were other underlining socio-economic and political issues as Samatar explained in his book. And losing the Ogaden war was one of them. In addition, there were no popular clan uprisings in the Republic, except some reports of isolated disturbances in coup plotters' homeland.[68] And even in the case of the coup being a clan project, there was no support from traditional leaders for the plotters. The country was stable and united, and clan identity was discouraged through the concept of socialism. Even the Somali military regime, with its internal divisions, stayed put and was popular well into the 1980s, as another scholar put it: 'Although the government regime (which appears to have been held in high esteem among Somalis for several years after coming to power) may have been declined in popular favour, in 1981 there was no sign of broad-based, coherent opposition.'[69]

Any country in a similar stressful situation is probably bound to disintegrate into ethnic or religious fiefdoms. Compare the 1977–8 Somalia situation with Iraq in 2002 or former Yugoslavia in the early 1990s. Iraq, despite the Kurd issue and dictatorship, was once a united and stable nation, but that country descended into warring tribal and religious fiefdoms after its ethnic and religious equilibrium and harmony had been disturbed by the 2002 invasion of Iraq by the United States and its allies. Indeed, after the invasion, Iraq lost its relatively ethnic and religious harmony and balance, and descended into anarchy. The powerful Western countries have been struggling to mould this fractured country as one nation.

The situation in Somalia in 1978 was similar to the Iraqi situation in 2002 and the US invasion of the country. The socio-economic and political equilibrium in Somalia was disturbed by the defeat of Somalia by the USSR in the Ogaden war. In hindsight, it was a miracle that Somalia held together as one nation and did not collapse into clan fiefdoms at that critical historical moment just like Iraq had done after the US invasion, or as ex-Yugoslavia had disintegrated after the collapse of the socialist bloc, which disrupted its socio-political systems.

Indeed, if the Republic's survival immediately after the Ogaden defeat had shown anything, it had proved the resilience, strength and cohesion of Somalis as one social unit through their clan system, a structure that is often unfairly portrayed by anthropologists as divisive and fragile, which makes Somalis ungovernable without fully analysing other important political and economic factors alongside the clan dimension.

It took twelve years or so, although bloody and costly, before the Republic finally succumbed to the long-term impact of the USSR-induced Ogaden debacle, plunging the Republic into warring clan-based fiefdoms. Although Somalia descended into clan fiefdoms in the 1990s and anthropologists would use this as evidence of their belief that clan is the determinant factor in the Somali society, they often overlook or underestimate other factors that are behind its re-emergence, for example, the long-term impact of the USSR-induced Ogaden defeat, which is the thrust of this book's argument that the origin of the civil war is in the Ogaden debacle.

Although no one can deny the clan factor, these anthropologists often ignore that the Somalis lived in harmony and peace in major cities regardless of their clans since the 1960s. Indeed, Somali scholars accused some foreign academics of fuelling the conflict by using the divisive clan factor to the point of racism and xenophobia as Hitler and other fascists had categorized races.[70] The author agrees with the Somali scholars' point of view.

Missed opportunity for political reforms

Nonetheless, having survived as a nation-state after the Ogaden defeat, the Republic had missed a great opportunity for much needed political reforms during this time. Prior to the Ogaden debacle, President Siyad Barre, under pressure by the USSR, had already established the Somali Revolutionary Socialist Party (SRSP) in 1976, a move seen by some analysts as his wish of fulfilling his people's democratic aspiration, although he later retreated from the move towards democracy for fear of being rejected by the people.[71] However, others described the creation of the party as consolidation of power.[72]

Having lost the Ogaden war, the president could and should have resigned after admitting his government's failure under his leadership, thus handing power over to a new caretaker government or to members of his government, for example to the vice president, General Mohamed Ali Samatar, then a popular figure within the regime[73] and a likely successor.[74] After his resignation alone or with his government, the president could have operated behind the scenes as an honourable Somali elder and a leader with a positive role to play in seeing the Republic through one of its difficult times in its history. By this action, he could have achieved hero's status in the nation's history books, or he could have been elected president in fair democratic elections, as Mohamed Osman, former ambassador, observing the prevailing feeling at the time, explained:

> By now, it was widely held that it would have been better had President Siad relinquished power and let the people choose new representatives by election. Even those who blamed him for mismanagement of the country's affairs would probably have forgiven him if he had made the gesture to stand down. His popularity had been high among the masses during the early heady years of the Revolution. Had he conceded to hold elections for a parliamentary based on multi-party system, there was a fair chance he might have been elected with a thumping majority, thus legitimizing his authority.[75]

The possibility of General Siyad Barre relinquishing power was, for the first time, revealed by Mohamed Ali Samatar, former vice president and a senior member of the Socialist Party's Politburo, the highest political office. In a recent interview thirty years after the end of the Ogaden conflict, he mentioned that the president had offered to resign after the Ogaden defeat.[76] However, members of the Politburo rejected his offer because they had felt that leadership failure was a collective responsibility, and that they would either all resign or stay together. They also felt that the president was still popular and the public saw him as their leader, and therefore any move of resignation by the president would have been interpreted by the public as a plot and betrayal by members of the Politburo against him.

However, in the same interview, Osman Mohamed Jeelle, another senior minister, doubted the proposition and mentioned that he had never heard of anything like that. He also did not think General Siyad Barre was such a character who would have relinquished power easily.[77] General Siyad Barre's later behaviour of clinging to power at any cost seems to corroborate Osman Jeelle's statement. Regrettably, President Siyad Barre stayed put, hence plunging the Republic in entrenched dictatorship.

Entrenched dictatorship: 1978–90

After the 1978 coup, divisions within the military regime along clan lines became rife. The president, who was already paranoid of a Majeerteen plot and had been conducting campaigns against Majeerteen members of his government, was more nervous and paranoid than ever and perhaps 'relegitimated the language of tribe in Somali politics' as some scholars have put it.[78] After the superpower-induced Ogaden defeat, which disturbed the social order, increased factionalism within the regime had contributed to the president's paranoia. This means that he was not only to blame for the increased clan factionalism, but other wider clannish forces within the regime.[79]

By 1979 and as some opposition fronts were already formed abroad, the regime was conducting retaliations against its opponents. The security forces systematically destroyed water reservoirs in Majeerteen homelands in central and north-eastern regions to deny water to members of the clan and their herds. For example, in May and June 1979 an estimated 2,000 people died of thirst in these regions, as the security forces raped large numbers of women, and the community lost around 50,000 camels, 10,000 cattle and 100,000 sheep and goats.[80]

These indiscriminate atrocities against those associated with rebel groups would continue to be the regime's normal practice throughout its life span. As opposition against the regime grew stronger, the military regime became even more repressive and oppressive leading to entrenched dictatorship, whose structure was already in place. The following paragraphs highlight how the entrenched dictatorship structure had been evolving since 1969.

After deposing the democratically elected civil government in 1969, the Supreme Revolutionary Council (SRC), led by General Siyad Barre, built effective security, political and social institutions to control opposition; to eliminate tribalism, nepotism, favouritism and corruption, which they saw as obstructing its socialist-based principles of a just and fairer society. The SRC immediately disbanded civilian and democratic institutions: political parties, the parliament and the supreme court. At the same time it repealed the constitution and civic laws. It militarized state institutions from local to regional and central government, appointing military officers to important positions to ensure that ultimate power rested with the SRC. In addition, by embracing centralized socialist economy, the regime nationalized the economy particularly financial services and production industries.[81]

A NSS, set up after the military coup with the help of the KGB, the Russian secret service, was one of the intelligence gathering organizations outside the normal bureaucracy apparatus with a wide range of powers from investigative to detention. This powerful intelligence service, which was staffed by people loyal to President Siyad Barre and was headed by General Ahmed Suleyman Dafle, his son-in-law, played an important role in internal and external policy making, for example, it recommended promotion or demotion of government staff.[82] *Hangash* (*Hayadda Nabadgelyada Gaashaandhiga*), a military intelligence service, presidential body guards known as (*Koofi Cas*) 'red berets' also headed by Colonel Mohamed Siad Morgan, another son-in-law and a national security court, were set up to deal with crimes such as treason, murder, embezzlement of public money and tribalism.[83]

A people's militia known as '*guulwadayaasha*' or pioneers of victory, created in 1972 to fight laziness and anti-revolutionary forces, was another infamous tyrannical organization, which was the regime's long arm, or 'big brother'. Although it was outside normal security agencies, its forces mainly recruited from society's misfits could arrest and detain people, as it spied on the public.[84] The SRC also created orientation centres, which conducted all kinds of state-sponsored activities from public speeches and rallies to recruitment in order to indoctrinate the public about the regime's scientific socialism. The centres were also meant to undermine traditional family structure, the most sacred unit of society in order to control the private and public spheres.[85]

Despite the prominent role they played in social and economic development projects and in maintaining security, the above organizations and many others, such as women and youth organizations, were essentially repressive instruments, which came under General Siyad Barre's control.[86] Indeed, according to Laitin and Samatar (1987) the regime's greatest achievement in institution building was its security apparatus[87] under which citizens who were accused of anti-socialism, anti-revolution or anti-government, did not have access to fair justice and were imprisoned and tortured to death without a fair trial, as extra-judicial killings became common.[88]

More importantly, the SRC erected a personality cult around its leader, General Siyad Barre who was crowned as 'father of the nation' and 'teacher of the nation' among other titles. Adults as well as children were indoctrinated to sing 'Guulwade Siyad', the 'Victorious Siyad', song on a daily basis, and those who failed were punished with mixture of demotion, detention or other forms of punishment. A personality cult that was similar to socialist states of China and North Korea, or what Lewis (2002b) described 'the Maoist cult'[89] was created.

Despite some political reforms, such as the establishment of the SRSP meant to democratize politics, according to Samatar (1988) by 1978 General Siyad Barre's speeches and orders were the final source of authority.[90] Certainly, for some analysts, the organizations mentioned earlier were repressive and rubber stamp institutions.[91]

Early victims of the unfolding dictatorship structure were higher officials of the deposed civilian government, such as prime ministers who were arrested and left to rot in prisons without a trial from 1969 until the 1980s. Second victims of the dictatorship were some high-ranking officers, such as General Salad Kedie Gavere, Major General Mohamed Ainanche, Colonel Abdullahi Yusuf Ahmed and General Mohamed Farah Aideed who were either executed or detained after power struggle and an attempted coup within the SRC. Again this coup was interpreted by Lewis (2002b) as a clan rivalry while Samatar (1988b) saw it as a mixture of ideological and personality clashes within the SRC.

The author again agrees with Samatar's analysis that the clan was not the main reason for the attempted coup. This is because having deposed the civilian government because of tribalism, it would have been political suicide for the regime to be seen as a tribal institution in the early 1970s when it was vehemently pursuing its anti-tribalism campaign, using its 'scientific socialism' ideology as a unifying factor. Indeed, the word *Jaalle* or comrade was introduced to eradicate clan identities. Having lived in Somalia throughout the revolutionary era, the author can still vividly remember how Somalis regardless of their clan or regional differences lived in Mogadishu, the metropolitan city in peace and harmony, and how *Somalinimo* Somalism was the prevailing identity at the time.

Therefore, although no one can disregard the clan factor, earlier disagreements or plots within the SRC was a mixture of personality clashes and ideological differences within the SRC in which General Siyad Barre emerged as the strong man. In the power of the hindsight, clan dimension in Somali politics at the early years of the revolution was lesser factor, though it increased after the Ogaden defeat, which was induced by the USSR and its socialist alliance, which then disturbed Somalia's social and political equilibrium.

A group of clerics who openly opposed the regime's family law on gender equality in 1975 were the third victim of the evolving dictatorship. The law gave women equal rights to men, especially with regard to inheritance rights in a society in which under the Islamic Sharia a girl gets half of boy's share of inheritance. In accordance with this family law, killing a woman attracted the same death penalty as of that of murdering a man. This was a great leap forward from customary laws under which a murdered woman's relatives would have only expected to receive half of man's blood money. The clerics described the law blasphemous and contrary to Islam. This cleric-led dissent was probably the only open opposition to the SRC at the grass roots level in the 1970s when it was trying hard to reconcile its 'scientific socialism' with Islam. Ten of the clergymen or 'Sheikhs' were executed in 1975.

Introduction of the liberal family law and swift execution of clerics in the International Women's Year of 1975 was a decisive move by the SRC to confirm its secularist and reformist principles in a conservative Muslim country like Somalia.[92] Having consolidated its power, the SRC was in full control and stable throughout the 1970s until the end of the Ogaden war when the regime would descend into totalitarianism.

Education and gender equality for a just society?

However, things were not all about dictatorship and oppression. The SRC achieved some historical social and economic developments in the 1970s. Having overthrown what it described as corrupt and clannish civilian governments, the SRC announced a range of economic and social policies to create what it called a 'united and fair society'. Education was proclaimed as a key for achieving that goal, as President Siyad Barre explained it in one of his speeches:

> The key . . . is to give everybody the opportunity to learn reading and writing . . . . It is imperative that we give our people modern revolutionary education . . . to restructure their social existence . . . it will be the weapon to eradicate social balkanization and fragmentation . . . and there will no room for any negative foreign cultural influences.[93]

Improving literacy in a country with a literacy rate of 5 per cent,[94] the writing of the Somali language, free universal education, getting more girls into schools and creating higher education institutions became SRC's education policies.[95] By January 1973, the government decided to adopt the Roman alphabet as a script for the Somali language, which it declared the official language of communication, replacing foreign languages. The decision was a great departure from previous civilian governments' squabble over which script to adopt. However, it was not easy to reach the decision and the SRC had to sit on the project for a while. It created committees to discuss it because of disagreements within the rank of the regime over whether to adopt Latin, Arabic or other indigenous scripts.[96]

General Jama M. Ghalib, former government minister during the military regime, twenty years after the writing of the Somali language, revealed that the Chinese leader, Mao Zedong, might well have been the inspiration behind SRC's decision to adopt the Roman script. Ghalib (1995) mentioned that a Somali delegation on official state visit in China in 1971 met the Chinese leader. On that occasion, Mao Zedong, who must have been following the developments in Somalia, asked the delegation about progress on the issue of writing the Somali language. The delegation had no answer and the Chinese leader remarked:

> whatever you do, do not make the same mistake we made. After all these years, China is now considering transcribing its script into Latin in order to share technology with the advanced world.[97]

On its return to Somalia, the delegation mentioned Mao's remarks to the SRC, which then decided to adopt Latin, although the announcement was delayed until 1972. Ghalib (1995) asserting this point writes:

> Mao Zedong should perhaps be given the credit for enabling the Somali language to be written at so early a date, rather than Siad Barre, but nevertheless it remains the greatest achievement of the latter's regime.[98]

Ghalib's assertion carries some weight because at the time the SRC was talking about its 'cultural revolution', which seemed as a copycat of the Chinese Cultural Revolution. Certainly, for some time the military regime with its 'scientific socialism' in mind had been imitating socialist ideas of Mao Zedong, Kim Il Sung and L. Brezhnev.[99]

After that crucial decision, the SRC embarked on what was the biggest socio-political programme in the Republic's history: eradication of illiteracy within two years in a country with a population of around 4 million. Within three months of its first campaign in urban and settled areas, after drafting in 8,000 teachers, the SRC claimed that hundreds of thousands of people could read and write in Somali.[100] It then extended the second campaign, the most impressive one, to rural communities. And with a budget of US$10 million, by July 1974, the SRC dispatched 20,000 teachers and students[101] to the countryside to teach nomads not only how to write and read in their own language, but also educate them about basic hygiene and animal husbandry. At that time, with limited resources in one of the ten poorest countries in the world with less than US$80 per capita of gross domestic product[102] the SRC had not only to implement the literacy campaign, but had to resettle hundreds of thousands of destitute nomads, victims of the 1970s droughts. Yet, it handled both programmes competently. Thanks to the impressive campaign, by the late 1970s literacy rate jumped from 5 per cent to nearly 60 per cent, as the SRC introduced adult education programmes to consolidate the progress.[103]

Transformation of formal education curriculum from primary to secondary schools, in which huge materials were translated from foreign language sources to Somali, was another impressive and successful story. The SRC created a new way of learning for an illiterate society. Consequently, according to figures presented by Nelson (1982) school numbers and enrolment increased sharply. By 1979 primary classes increased from pre-SRC figure of 1,052 to 6,856. Enrolment in primary and secondary schools rose from 35,306 and 3,133 students to 263,751 and 18,416 students, respectively.[104] Female student enrolment in primary education improved considerably from a depressing figure of 7,937 in 1969 to 95,200, and from 358 to 4,373 female students in secondary school. The number of primary education teachers employed increased from 1,186 in 1969 to 8,141, of which 25 per cent were female.[105] Thousands of students enrolled in the Somali National University in a country that relied heavily on foreign countries for its higher education needs.

This was a great step forward for an illiterate society. Commenting on the positive impact of the impressive literacy campaign on the Somali society, Laitin and Samatar (1987) observed that the campaign encouraged egalitarianism and equal opportunity as nationals were able to write in a common language with equal chance to compete in employment and social opportunities.[106] It would increase citizens' ability to participate in the political process, for instance, even nomads would be able to give their opinions and views in written Somali to help create an equal society. It would make state bureaucracy more accessible and open to serve the citizen rather than having foreign language-based elites that saw themselves above citizens. They also observed that priority was given to rural development, which erased some of the inequalities that existed in Somali society prior to the SRC.

In addition to education programmes, the SRC, embodied in General Siyad Barre who was at the time described as having assumed the status of a 'prophet', autocrat and tyrant,[107] was impatient with conditions in the Republic and was determined to go ahead with social reform policies to create fairer society. By 1975, the SRC had enacted the family act, a gender equality law, a brave and daring step in a conservative Muslim nation like Somalia. The law, combined with the SRC's gender equality efforts, paved the way for women's participation in the Republic's political, economic and social life. Women became part of the workforce and maternity leave and equal pay for women became part of the Somali labour code.[108] Women became more visible in public positions, as more girls went to educational institutions.[109]

The rise of armed rebel movements

Let us now put aside the historical account of the evolution of the dictatorship, its early achievements and its victims, and return to political developments and the rise of opposition groups since the 1978 attempted military coup.

By 1975 General Siyad Barre, a man whose little knowledge of socialism was for political expedience,[110] had already lost his interest in the ideology. The disillusionment led to the detention of communist and socialist ideologues that the leader perceived as a threat to his personal rule.[111] After the disillusionment with socialist, the greater and pan-Somalism ideals were the regime's next enormous tasks. However, as mentioned earlier, the regime failed on this task as well because of the USSR's intervention in the region, which led to the Ogaden tragedy and the failed coup.

After the 1978 coup, the first wave of full-blown and structured opposition groups based outside the country as political parties were banned in the country had emerged. These opposition groups evolved from or joined early opposition groups formed in 1976, such as the Somali Democratic Action Front (SODAF) formed in Rome. Colonel Abdullahi Yusuf, the 1978 coup's ringleader joined this group and formed the Somali Salvation Democratic Front (SSDF) in Ethiopia, a country which was only too happy to accommodate any opposition group against the Somali regime. Ethiopia allowed them to operate from its territory and opened up a propaganda radio station, which was intended to incite wider opposition to the military regime. The SSDF became the most formidable group, and after formalizing its organizational structure and with the support of Libya and Ethiopia, it launched armed operations within Somalia against the regime, which they saw as working against the unity of the Somali people. The regime labelled the rebel groups as saboteurs and traitors who sold out to the enemy. The public just rallied around the regime's position. At the time and quite rightly it would have been national treason to ally with Ethiopia, the biggest enemy.

By now General Siyad Barre was manipulating and exploiting the divisive clan politics, arming one clan against the other, his henchmen punishing whole communities for the actions of a few individuals. Faced with full-blown insurgency, the regime imposed emergency laws in the Majeerteen regions of Mudug, Nugal and Bari, homelands of the opposition leaders, and continued with its repressive measures. These communities were the first to be subjected to extra-judicial killings, rape and scorched-earth policy to deprive the insurgency of a civilian base.[112] By the early 1980s, twenty-five students were arrested for sedition and association with the rebel groups: ten of them were sentenced to death.[113] Also, the security forces raped large number of women, as twenty commercial boats were confiscated as economic punishment to deny the community the benefits of long-term trade with the Arabian Peninsula.[114]

United States prolongs the dictatorship

While these opposition groups were being formed, the Republic was still under pressure from other internal and external problems. Although the Ogaden conflict had officially ended in 1978, WSLF rebels with the help of Somali regular units were still militarily active in the Ogaden region, and by May 1980, the WSLF claimed control of 60 per cent of the region.[115] The Republic was still under the mercy of unabating Ethiopian air force raids not only to flush out WSLF guerrilla forces, but also to destabilize and undermine the regime. Furthermore, with the help of Ethiopia, the Somali opposition groups were carrying out sabotages and bombings inside Somalia.[116]

Disillusioned with the socialism ideology, having lost the pan-Somalism cause, dumped by the Soviets and now faced with new security challenges, General Siyad Barre and his regime sought refuge in and re-ignited the Cold War superpower rivalry game because of some new global geopolitical events. Unlike last time, the Somali regime had new cards to play and good reasons to ask the United States for military and other assistance.

First, the now more powerful and Russian-supported Ethiopian forces were carrying out airstrikes inside Somalia. Indeed, the Carter administration noticed the shift of power balance in the region and was concerned about Ethiopia's threat to Somalia's national security and the presence of the USSR and its allies in the Horn and the Red Sea.[117] Second, the administration re-discovered the strategic importance of the Republic after the USSR's invasion of Afghanistan, and the Iranian revolution which led to the Iranian hostage crisis. Third, the regime, embodied in President Siyad Barre, was now born again capitalist and friend of the West,[118] having made some economic and political reforms. Fourth, the enormous refugee problem caused by the Ogaden conflict was something that the United States and the world in general could not ignore. The regime could use it as a bargaining chip for humanitarian aid.

Unlike before, the Somali regime had a listening ear in Washington; the Carter administration was now in search of air and naval military basis in the Red Sea to counteract against USSR's strategic interest.[119] The same Carter administration, which had been denying arms to Somalia in the first phase of the conflict, was now happy to turn a blind eye to its policies in the region, and was ready to provide weapons to the same Somali regime. United States's broader strategic and national security interests had superseded the administration's earlier policies.[120]

The Somali government was more than happy to exploit the new situation especially the Republic's newly found strategic importance. During negotiations between United States and Somalia, the regime demanded heavy weaponry: tanks, artillery, airplanes and other economic aid worth US$2 billion, much more than what the Carter administration was offering, which was US$100 million.[121] President Siyad Barre and his government even went as far as demanding the Carter administration to recognize Somalia's irredentist claims over the Ogaden region, and to provide arms for its liberation as part of any deal.[122]

After lengthy negotiations, the Somali and US governments signed economic and military aid agreement worth US$103.3 million in August 1980 for the next two years,[123] allowing US forces to use the Berbera port in the Red Sea in northern regions as a naval base and other military facilities in Somalia.

Because of the renewed superpower rivalry, the Republic again found itself embroiled in the Cold War politics and became one of the largest recipients of the United States's military/security assistance in sub-Saharan Africa. In the next seven years, the Somali government would receive more than US$500 million in economic and military aid from the US administrations.[124]

This is how President Carter justified his administration's change of heart in the Horn of Africa:

> The sale of US-origin defense articles and services to Somalia would strengthen a number of United States security interests in the region. Somalia is strategically situated in the Horn of Africa at the entrance of the Bab-el-Mandeb Straits, which is a major access route to petroleum supplies for Western Europe and Israel . . . Somalia desires assistance from Western nations. It is in the interest of the United

States, with the cooperation of our European allies and Arab friends, to help Somalia improve its ability to defend itself.[125]

Paradoxically, all these strategic and political realities existed when the administration was denying arms to Somalia during the first phase of the Ogaden war. However, the newly found strategic importance of the Republic overtook the administration's consideration of human rights abuses and other concerns. And by now, the successful military campaign of the USSR–Cuban in the conflict had forced the United States to establish rapid intervention forces in the Red Sea and the Indian Ocean.[126]

When President Ronald Reagan came to power, his administration went ahead with the Carter administration's process of re-arming Somalia, and accelerated it under his administration's confrontational policy against the USSR, propelling the United States towards a 'Second Cold War' engagement with the USSR.[127]

As part of the Cold War game strategy, President Siyad Barre even threatened to defect to the USSR and sought support from the USSR because he felt he could not co-exist with non-totalitarian Western governments.[128] According to Ghalib (1995) General Siyad Barre secretly offered to cancel the US military cooperation agreement, as he requested the USSR to reconcile him with the Ethiopian leader, Mengistu. However, to his disappointment, the Soviets rebuffed him after attaching strong conditions, such as relinquishing territorial claims in Ethiopia and acknowledgement of his past mistakes prior to any reconciliation efforts.[129] Ghalib's story does hold water as confirmed by new revelations by the Wikileaks cables that indicate the regime had approached Soviets to normalize relations and to help mediate between the Ethiopian and Somali regimes.[130]

By entering these agreements with the regime, Carter and Reagan administrations prolonged the life span of entrenched dictatorship because as will be explained later on, the regime would use resources provided by the United States for internal political oppression.

Rampant corruption and virulent clanism

President Siyad Barre had been warning against dangers of corruption, tribalism and nepotism almost in all his public speeches and once said:

> We will abolish bribery, nepotism and tribalism. Tribalism was the only way in which foreigners got their chance of dividing our people. We will close all roads used by colonialists to enter our country and into our affairs.[131]

However, as the dictatorship entrenched, he abandoned the rhetoric and was accused of using clan politics to consolidate his power base as early as the 1970s. He used a power cell mainly from his own clan Mareehaan, his mother's clan Ogaden and Dhulbahante: all sub-clans of the Daarood clan, to rule other major clan families, such as Hawiye, Isaaq and Rahanweyn. The power cell became known as the MOD, M stands for Mareehaan (president's clan), O for Ogaden (president's mother's clan) and D for Dhulbahante (his son-in-law's clan.[132] Although Majeerteen is a sub-clan of Daarood, General Siyad Barre was paranoid about Majeerteen conspiracy against him because of their dominance in politics during the civil government, and therefore they were not part of this power unit.

As mentioned earlier, by 1977, the president appointed his cousin, Abdurahman Jama Barre as foreign minister, a not so competent civil servant,[133] sacking Omar Arte Ghalib, a successful career diplomat just when the Republic needed a competent diplomat to promote the Ogaden cause. This was followed by the appointment of even more close relatives to sensitive military, security and political positions. He appointed his son Shire Mohamed Siyad and his son-in-law Abdinasir Haaji Haashi as heads of army brigades in Mogadishu.[134]

After introducing a state of emergency in October 1980, and reviving the SRC, the disbanded military council to 'correct mistakes made and energise the revolution', General Siyad Barre demoted senior government ministers like General Mohamed Ali Samatar, loyal and veteran defence minister only to be replaced by Omar Haji Mohamed, a fellow Mareehaan, hence confirming clan as a factor in contemporary Somali politics.[135] Although General Samatar was head of the newly revived SRC's defence committee, as the country was under state of emergency, power rested with the ministry of defence controlled by the president who had held ultimate authority in the country. And therefore appointing close kinsmen was a way of consolidating his power base.[136] Indeed, by the 1980s, when the 'disease of clanism' as Laitin and Samatar described it was destroying the body politic, locating key and sensitive economic and political government posts to the president's clansmen and wider Daaroods clans became the norm.[137] By taking these measures, President Siyad Barre who, for some time, had been evolving from being a 'prophet', 'prince' to an 'autocrat', finally became a 'tyrant' and 'dictator'.[138]

Although in fairness, ministers from other clans were included in his government and had held higher positions, this was just a divide and rule tactic, using some ministers from weaker clans as a token. This is how Lewis (2002b) described General Siyad Barre's Machiavellian attitude towards power machination and clan politics:

> President Siyad, who had the skills of a practical Machiavelli and the mind of a political computer, was particularly adept at selecting token figures from obscure, minority segment of major clan groups who were flattered to serve him and present themselves as clan representatives.[139]

Alongside the clan-based political power, control of the national economy, which was already centralized except the livestock, became national obsession for the higher rank of the government.[140] The president was accused of enhancing his relatives' and cronies' economic interest. A classic example of this economic favouritism was the rise of Abdi Hoosh enterprise, a fellow Mareehaan, once a government driver when General Siyad Barre came to power. Taking advantage of US$300–400 million contributed by the wealthy Arab Gulf states for the Ogaden war efforts, Hoosh, among others, was at once made a successful businessman,[141] probably overtaking the two Uunlaay brothers and Jirdeh Hussein, who were some of the wealthiest people in the country.

On some occasions, government ministers were sacked for opposing proposals to grant Abdi Hoosh fuel import licence, and after their expulsion, Hoosh was granted permanent franchise for fuel import, which lasted until General Siyad Barre's removal from power in 1991.[142] After his senior wife had fallen out with Hoosh, General Siyad Barre even tried to enhance his close family's business interests.[143] According to Ghalib (1995), a fellow citizen by the name of Mohamed Sudi Aflaw was executed in 1984 because he knew too much about the involvement of the president's senior wife in elephant poaching and smuggling business.[144]

This is how General Aideed, the man who would chase General Siyad Barre out of Mogadishu, described the rampant corruption at the time:

> Corruption became so rampant that if one wanted to secure the release of his or her relative, who had been arrested or detained illegally, he had to pay a heavy bribe ... The Custom Police and Civil officers of the Custom Department, most of who were close relatives and tribesmen of Siad Barre, built their luxury villas and amassed huge fortunes for themselves and several future generations by depositing their ill-gotten wealth in foreign banks.[145]

This unfair economic favouritism had forced ordinary business people to leave the country because they could not compete in this environment. Those daring merchants who decided to compete with the new elite had to use their fellow clansmen's connections to survive in centralized socialist economy.[146]

Control of an Italian development aid package worth US$1 billion in 1984–7, earmarked for developmental projects, including construction of Garowe-Boosaaso road, Boosaaso seaport, fisheries and other agricultural projects[147] was another example that showed regime's determination to enhance its economic position. To control this huge money, Abdirahman Jama Barre, foreign minister and General Siyad Barre's cousin, removed the department of cooperation from the ministry of planning, normally responsible for the coordination of international aid and merged the department into his foreign ministry. According to Ali Khalif Galaydh, former minister, normal government procedural accounting and regulatory frameworks were ignored in the management of the aid package and the project was placed in the hands of the foreign minister's cronies who were not even government employees. To make his point, Galaydh (1990) writes: 'blatant private appropriation of public resources made the state a *cosa nostra* for the Barre family.'[148] Certainly, corruption in the Italian aid money, involving former Italian prime minister, Pettino Craxi and senior Somali leaders, was a well-known fact at the time and is documented.[149]

Corruption and abuse of public office by senior government officials became rampant during the last decade of the regime's life[150] as it ditched its transparency and anti-graft policy, known as *Xisaab xil ma leh* introduced in the 1970s to make bureaucracy more accountable and punish corrupt government officials. Under the abandoned anti-graft policy, embezzlement of 100,000 Somali Shillings was punishable by death.[151] However, the penalty was not meted out on the higher officials that were making the country bankrupt[152] and seemed to be above the law.

Under this rampant corruption, ministers and their cronies pocketed 40 per cent of government tenders and contracts awarded to private companies, UN agencies and non-governmental organizations.[153] Business people bribed officials to avoid financial and monetary regulations. For instance, they would declare imported commercial goods as personal effects to evade taxation, under the *Franco valuta* system, a policy that allowed traders and overseas workers to use some of their foreign currencies to import goods into the country, hence impinging on the nation's wealth creation.[154] As corruption went viral, ordinary citizens had to bribe civil servants to secure basic things, such as scholarships, passports, government jobs, import and export licences, or even for a medical check-up abroad due to the country's inadequate health facilities.

The rise of Somali National Movement (SNM) and civil war in the north

It was under such prevailing socio-economic and political ills that riots broke out in Hargeisa, the second capital city in the north-west region of the Republic in 1982. The riots were led by students who were angry about the detention of a group of professionals by the security force. The group, calling themselves 'Uffo' or hurricane[155] were teachers, doctors and other professionals who were unhappy with the regime's neglect of social services in the region. They then organized themselves to improve the poor and appalling conditions of hospitals by using resources raised through the self-help scheme, a nationwide voluntary scheme in which citizens would contribute money and other resources towards developmental projects. They also raised concerns about misuse of public funds and corruption by the authorities in the region as they educated the public about these issues. However, government officials perceived the group as a challenge and threat to their authority, and immediately detained members of the group.[156]

The regime suppressed student-led riots, which were a turning point because this was the first time that the public expressed its unhappiness with the regime's handling of the country's affairs and this would intensify opposition to the regime.[157] The uprising was different from previous challenges that the regime had faced. It was not by some ambitious military officers staging a coup or disgruntled religious men against liberal family laws as the case was in the 1970s. But this time it was the public expressing its discontent with the regime's failures in the north-west region. The province is mainly inhabited by the Isaaq clan which, for some time, had been airing grievances over unfair economic and social policies, political oppression, rampant corruption and mismanagement of public funds by President Siyad Barre's regime.[158]

It was around that time when some Isaaq clansmen in the diaspora who had been unhappy with the regime's failures in the region formed a rebel group. Although it is unclear whether the idea was hatched in a London public house or in some houses in Saudi Arabia, a new opposition group called the SNM was officially launched at

Connaught Hall in London on 6 April 1981 after some Gulf and London-based groups had merged.[159] By the time of the riots, the group's leaflets clandestinely appeared in the region. The SNM was the second major armed rebel group formed after SSDF to oppose the regime.

After it had constituted its organizational structure and coinciding with the unrest in Hargeisa, by 1982, the SNM moved its operational headquarters to Dire Dawa in Ethiopia, a country that was already a base for the SSDF. Right away, Isaaq military officers in the north-west province who had been protecting Isaaq civilians against Ogaden refugees armed by the regime to suppress Isaaqs, deserted the Somali National Army (SNA) and joined the SNM. According to Lewis (1994a), this was the beginning of the civil war in the north between Isaaq-dominated SNM and what he described as Siyad's Daarood regime, which would last until the overthrow of the general in 1991.[160]

By now, life was not getting any easier for the regime either, as by the summer of 1982, strong force of 15,000 loyal to the SSDF[161] and supported by Ethiopian forces took part in a major military offensive against the regime. SSDF forces occupied some territories inside Somalia, including Goldogob town in the Mudug region, although some analysts suggested that the Somali regime allowed that to happen as a ploy to get military aid from the United States. Indeed, it was the Somali army, supported by the US forces, which repulsed the offensive.[162]

President Siyad Barre: Democrat or dictator?

Before proceeding with the unrest in the north, let us look back at other political developments at regional and international levels and also President Siyad Barre's character as a democrat or dictator. Having signed military and economic aid agreements with the United States, President Siyad Barre was now the darling of the West. The Republic was very much in receipt of and dependent on humanitarian and other aid from the West and other international agencies in what was dubbed the 'aid avalanche'.[163] President Siyad Barre initiated some political reforms intended to enhance his credentials as democrat to the West, and to outsmart his critics. A constitution was adopted and a new people's assembly (parliament), dominated by members of the Somali Socialist Revolutionary Party (SSRP), the only party, was elected by the electorate in December 1979. To coincide with his visit to the United States, the president lifted state of emergency as he disbanded the revived military council. Under pressure from the United States, he released former prime minister Muhammad Ibrahim Haji Egal and other long-term political detainees who had been in prison since 1969.[164]

President Siyad Barre visited the United States in 1982 and met President Ronald Reagan and discussed bilateral relations. By then General Siyad Barre was born again capitalist, having abandoned his socialist ideology, which his government made Somalis to believe as the guiding principle to eradicate imperialism, poverty, disease and ignorance. The regime's socialism and revolutionary rhetoric lost its momentum and many Somalis perceived General Siyad Barre's pragmatism in his ideology as a survival tool for his personal rule.[165]

The political reforms mentioned earlier proved to be cosmetic surgery for the president's visit to the United States. Upon return, General Siyad Barre detained seven high-ranking government ministers, accusing them of treason and other conspiracies. Some of them were people he had perceived as a threat to his personal rule; some ministers knew too much. Others he had suspected of agitating the unrest in the north-west region, such as Vice President Ismail Ali Abokar and Omar Arte Ghalib, former foreign minister, both of them Isaaq clansmen.[166] According to Ghalib (1995) at the time of the arrests, the president perceived Isaaq elites in Mogadishu as agitators behind the unrest in the north, and he construed this as Isaaq plots to secede the region from the Republic and to unite with Djibouti.[167]

The president's behaviour destroyed any hope of real political reforms. In sum, he had failed to honour the political reforms that were initiated in 1976 from the creation of the socialist party to the parliament. Laitin and Samatar (1987) explain the president's failure to support his people's democratic aspiration as despotism rather than cynicism.[168] Also his later behaviour would prove his determination to cling to power at any cost.

In May 1986, just when his popularity was low and year earlier he had considered leaving the country and politics on health grounds[169] the struggling president was struck by personal tragedy. He nearly died in fatal car incident on a road between Afgoye town and Mogadishu. He was immediately airlifted to Saudi Arabia for treatment because of the country's inadequate health care system. Indeed, the system was so shambolic that higher government officials and cadres were sent abroad for medical treatment and their expenses approved by the president.[170] Ordinary citizens had to bribe civil servants to secure medical treatment abroad.

While in Saudi Arabia recuperating, power struggle over succession in case of his death broke out within the ruling elite. On the one hand, his senior wife, Khadija, was grooming her son Major Maslah Mohamed Siyad for the top job while others opposed this, preferring other heavyweight politicians within the ruling Mareehaan family, such as General Mohamed Hashi Gani and Abdirahman Jama Barre, a fellow Mareehaan.[171] Outside the inner Mareehaan circle, groups loyal to his two vice presidents, General Hussein Kulmiye Afrah and Brigadier General Mohamed Ali Samatar were jostling for presidency[172] in accordance with the constitution, which stated that power will be transferred to the vice president.[173]

On his return home, unravelling web of conspiracies, General Siyad Barre sided up with his senior wife who was described as behind his political decisions, such as the appointment and promotion of officers.[174] He immediately reshuffled his cabinet and promoted his son, Maslah, as army chief of staff, presumably confirming him as heir to the throne.[175] By now, General Siyad Barre's manipulation and exploitation of virulent segmentary politics, unleashed by the USSR-induced Ogaden defeat, reduced the proud Republic to what Lewis (2002b) portrayed as 'a family or clan dynasty'.[176] Even the wider MOD Daarood power cell, which the president had used to protect his power base, finally collapsed[177] as the Mareehaan clan became more isolated.[178]

There again was a president this time not under the drama of a military coup, but bad omen and fate had offered him an opportunity to show humility and relinquish power. Regrettably, he decided to hold onto power may be because as explained by Laitin and

Samatar (1987): 'Plagued by internal opposition, by lack of reliable foreign patron, and by the threat of an Ethiopian-backed invasion, Siyad Barre's chief preoccupation since 1978 seems to have been to hang on to power at whatever cost.'[179] Or perhaps the old man was not entirely in control after his inner circle had hijacked power since the incident and wanted him to carry on as normal for its own advantage.[180] This was another missed opportunity for political reforms and a 'way out' for the beleaguered president, but he chose to hang on, leading the way for entrenched dictatorship with its devastating bloody outcome.

Returning to the civil war in the north, as unrest spread and the SNM intensified its military operations in the region, including an attack on the Mandera prison near Berbera city, in which it had released political detainees, the Somali government had already declared state of emergency in the region in 1982 to counteract what it described as traitors, tribalists and saboteurs who were a threat to national security. A range of state control measures from confiscation of properties and detention without trial and other draconian measures were imposed.[181] The government erected a mobile military court in trouble areas, and a regional security council with powers of passing death sentences, and lengthy sentences, and could make mass arrests. In cities such as Hargeisa, government security forces operated Tabeleh system, a neighbourhood watchdog system intended to spy on neighbours, as the military installed roadblocks to crack down on SNM rebels' movements.[182]

To its critics the Somali government conducted mass-arbitrary arrests, extra-judicial killings and unfair economic practices against Isaaqs. It also excluded them from sensitive government positions, such as the military in which Isaaqs made up one-third of military officers in the north.[183] Certainly, by appointing General Mohamed Hashi Gaani, a fellow Mareehaan and General Mohamed Hersi 'Morgan', his son-in-law as military commanders in the north, General Siyad Barre revealed that he only trusted his relatives in his campaign to destroy what he perceived as a secessionist movement determined to dismember the Republic.[184] To his critics General Siyad Barre intended these measures to exterminate Isaaqs, people he disliked because of their role in defeating the legendary national hero, Sayyid Mohamed Abdulla Hassan during his struggle against the British colonial powers.[185] The president, who was related to Sayyid from his mother's side who was from the Ogaden clan, saw himself as his embodiment.[186]

To his supporters, mainly through the state media, these measures were necessary in order to protect and defend national security and stability against traitors who had sided up with the enemy, Ethiopia. State media broadcasted non-stop campaigns vilifying what is described as secessionists.

By December 1984, forty-three men were massacred in Burao town in the north, accused of association with the SNM.[187] The horrible story of two young virgin girls raped by soldiers who had used their bayonets to smash the girls' virginity[188] was brutal exercise of using rape as a weapon to destroy SNM dissidents and to punish their civilian sympathizers.[189] When Isaaq elders complained to General Siyad Barre about human rights abuses and other unfair social and economic policies, General Siyad Barre demanded they first dismantle the SNM.[190] These atrocities were the beginning of what Africa Watch described as 'a government at war with its people'.[191]

At the regional level, after the official end of the Ogaden war, the Somali and Ethiopian regimes desperately needed to eliminate rebel groups against them, which were a threat to their political survival. They also needed to find solutions to the Ogaden refugee problem, which had been causing some insecurity in the region. The Ethiopian regime was keen to making peace with Somalia so that it could redeploy its forces to fight in the Eritrean war,[192] a conflict it was losing.

After series of negotiations that had started in 1986 in Djibouti, they finally signed the peace treaty in April 1988, normalizing the two countries' diplomatic relations and ending their support of each other's rebel groups in their countries. The Somali regime also renounced the claim over the Ogaden region. At that historical juncture, the power balance in the region changed, although for the worse for the Republic. This is because Somali rebel groups would be 'homeless' after the closure of their bases in Ethiopia and would either have to dissolve or move inside Somalia.[193] Indeed, the Ethiopian regime dismantled the SSDF, killing or detaining its leaders. The SNM was more vigilant and moved its forces to the north inside Somalia.[194]

The peace agreement or what Lewis (1994a) dubbed 'the price of peace with Ethiopia'[195] was one of the main factors that had precipitated the war in the north-west. Indeed, the agreement, seen as 'cynical attempt' by two repressive regimes to buy time, was a turning point as it was imminent that the SNM would have to leave its base in Ethiopia and return to Somalia to fight a war.[196]

Around this time, as a gesture of reconciliation, President Siyad Barre visited the north playing the clan card, setting one clan against the other. For example, to get non-Isaaq clans such as Warsangelis, Dhulbahantes and Gadabursi set upon clan militias against the SNM mainly supported by Isaaqs.[197] In a meeting with him, Isaaq elders told General Siyad Barre that his government's unfair economic and social policies in the region had increased support for the SNM. The president rejected their accusations for good reason because he knew the SNM would be dismantled and ejected from Ethiopia.[198] During his visit a public rally in Hargeisa meant to discredit the SNM descended into riots after stones were thrown at General Siyad Barre. His bodyguards opened fire, killing some rioters.

On 27 May 1988, the SNM, which had already carried out thirty raids against government forces and was now 'homeless', attacked and captured Burao town. Shocked by the popular support of the SNM as thousands of Isaaqs joined it,[199] government forces responded by bombarding the town with heavy artillery to flush out the rebels. A seventeen-year-old girl, who survived the onslaught, articulated the ferocity of the fighting:

> Shelling with long-range weapons started on Sunday. It hit a neighbour house, the Abdirahman family of seven people. Six of them died instantaneously. The only survivor was a little girl who had been sent to fetch sugar. The mother had just had a baby. They were after civilians. Their scouts would direct them to those areas where civilians were concentrated and then that spot would be shelled . . . .
> Our side was particularly targeted as it was one of the areas the SNM entered when they first came into town. When the bombing started, the sight of the dying, the wounded and the collapse of houses was too much to bear.[200]

Another survivor, giving an interview to the Africa Watch, a human rights organization, also described the nastiness of the fighting and government forces brutality: 'If they had made any distinction between SNM fighters and civilians, there wouldn't have been so many casualties and there wouldn't have been so much suffering. What they wanted, to put it simply, was to wipe us out.'[201]

On 31 May 1988, intensifying its military operation, the SNM attacked Hargeisa. In what was two days of heavy fighting, the security forces under the command of General Mohamed Siad Hersi 'Morgan', General Siyad Barre's son-in-law,[202] unleashed its full force, committing indescribable atrocities, including mass looting, indiscriminate bombardment, confiscation of properties and mass rape.[203] As it is too terrifying to repeat what happened, it would be enough to quote a resident's description of the fear that Hargeisa residents had to endure. This is what he had to say:

> As soon as I heard the attack on Hargeisa at 2:15 a.m., I jumped out of bed. I prayed for our safety and our success. When the military could not defeat the SNM, they turned on us. The soldiers were tense and nervous. They were shooting wildly, firing at everything. They jumped at the slightest sound. As soon as a door creaked, they would shoot, afraid there was an SNM fighter inside.[204]

The fighting reached its climax when, having failed to dislodge SNM fighters and faced with popular uprising, government forces launched air strikes against rebels positions in Hargeisa and Burao. Sadly, this was the first time that a Somali government had ever used its air force against its own people[205] in what was one of the Republic's darkest days. The Somali government was even accused of using white South African pilots to bomb Hargeisa and Burao[206] after Somali pilots refused to carry out the missions. By this act, it would appear that a secret plan to exterminate Isaaqs, which was detailed in a confidential report by General Mohamed Hersi Morgan,[207] was being put in practice.

Abdi Mohamed Hassan was one of those pilots who refused to bomb Hargeisa on 13 July 1988. After disobeying his orders, he flew his fighter jet to Djibouti where he sought political asylum. Mohamed who lives in Europe returned to Hargeisa the city he had refused to bomb in 2008 after twenty years where he received a hero's welcome. In a recent interview, this is what he had to say about his historical decision: 'The instruction was to bomb Hargeisa city using Russian made Fab 500kg bombs. But I had already made up my mind never to drop the bombs. As a soldier, I swore to protect my people. There was no way I could hurt my own countrymen.'[208]

By now, the conflict had degenerated into a full-blown civil war in which the two sides were determined to wipe each other out. As main cities remained in ruins, the SNM retreated into the countryside while government forces controlled urban areas. The north became a no man's land and a lawless territory where General Siyad Barre was arming non-Isaaq clans, such as the Ogadens, to fight Isaaqs,[209] where SNM fighters were waging war against Daarood and Gadabursi clans, committing atrocities and human rights abuses against civilian, including women and children.[210]

Although the airstrikes and the despicable atrocities committed were wrong, in hindsight, to those supporting the Somali government believed the government was doing what some governments would have done when faced with insurgents and secessionists, threatening their authority, national security and territorial integrity. As argued by Dool (1998) there were many examples in history where governments brutally suppressed insurgents.[211] For example, the massacre of Chinese students and demonstrators by the security forces at the Tiananmen Square, and the bombardment of an entire city to rubble by the late Syrian president Assad to dislodge Muslim brotherhoods, are some of the many examples, including the brutal suppression of Libyans, Syrians and other Arab citizens demanding democratic reforms by their long-term dictatorial and authoritarian regimes during the Arab spring in 2011–12.

Also, as will be shown, during the civil war in the northern regions in the early 1990s after the SNM had split into factions, Mohamed Ibrahim Egal, president of Somaliland, the breakaway region, which would declare independence from the rest of Somalia after the fall of the military regime, would even bombard his rival rebel positions. So, if former president Siyad Barre's regime had bombarded Isaaq cities so did President Mohamed Egal, an Isaaq himself, who would use state machinery to crash his Isaaq opponents.[212] As argued by Dool (1998), the evidence shows no matter how weak or powerful, democratic or dictatorship, governments do not sit idle when rebel groups threaten national security and stability. Ideally, the Somali government should have listened to the people's legitimate concerns and their rejection of political oppression and dictatorship and should have resolved the crisis through dialogue. But atrocities committed by the regime were heinous crimes against humanity.

During the conflict that lasted until General Siyad Barre's removal from power, both parties committed atrocities and war crimes.[213] The human cost was very high, and from May 1988 to 1989, up to 60,000 Somalis were killed directly or indirectly as a result of the conflict, as 500,000 people fled the country.[214] However, a US State Department report estimated the death toll around 5,000.[215]

The high civilian deaths could have been minimized had the SNM avoided deploying thousands of its fighters in cities.[216] Indeed, as argued by Dool (1998),[217] SNM's decision to take the fight to the regime in dwelling areas was a disastrous military action because it rendered towns and villages as battlefields between government forces sworn to annihilate what they saw as secessionists and traitors, threatening national security and stability,[218] and SNM fighters who were determined to remove dictatorship.[219]

The rise of United Somali Congress (USC) and troubles in the south

As main cities in the north lay in ruins, by 1989 opposition to the regime spread across the country, particularly in south-central regions. In what was described as 'opposition proliferation'[220] major clans, such as the powerful Hawiye clan family[1] formed their own armed rebel groups. Although it is debatable whether the Hawiye who had most of the good things that the state could offer, including the capital city, should or should

---

[1]   Hawiye is the one of the major clan families alongside the Daaroods, Dir and Rahanweyn.

not have formed an armed front,[221] it is, however, undeniable that some Hawiye circles had been unhappy with the dominance of President Siyad Barre's Daarood clan over the Republic's power for thirty years.[222] Certainly, out of the 567 ministerial and other senior posts created in the Republic since 1960–90, Daaroods happily controlled 216 followed by Hawiyes 125 and Isaaqs 102, and Rahanweyn with only 31 posts.[223]

Encouraged by an Isaaq underground movement in Mogadishu,[224] some Hawiye leaders, such as Ali Mohamed Wardhiigley, Dr Ismail Jumale Osoble, Ali Mahdi and General Mohamed Afrah Aideed unhappy with the regime's repressive measures against their clansmen, formed the USC in 1989. The USC's military wing, led by General Mohamed Farah Aideed was based in Ethiopia.

The rise of the USC led to more civil unrest and repressive measures by the regime in Mogadishu, which was largely safe haven for the regime. Certainly, eighteen months prior to the fall of the regime, Mogadishu was a lawless place where looting and extortion by government forces were endemic. The city was under the grip of long days of electricity blackouts, as state institutions, which had been failing for some time, were collapsing. Indeed, people stopped depositing money in banks because the regime had been hoarding money in military garrisons in order to fund the war in the north, including bribing some sections of the community to support his regime.[225]

As part of wider military and war strategies, the regime intensified forced conscription that was introduced earlier[226] to force young men to fight an unpopular war in the north as ordinary military units deserted the national army. The conscription, known as *qafaal* or *raaf*, was an awful experience for thousands of young men. Having lived in Mogadishu, the author can vividly recall how the security forces would put young men onto military trucks, and after a few days of 'training', they would ship them off to the front line in the north to die in a cause they did not believe in, killing their brothers. The public was very much against the *raaf*. A recent revelation by the Wikileaks confirmed that the regime, desperate for army recruits, sent press-gangs around Mogadishu to recruit by force.[227]

The year 1989 would prove annus horribilis for Hawiye clans after the regime unleashed its forces to take on what it saw as traitors and enemy collaborators. If yesterday the regime was persecuting Majeerteen and Isaaq clans, today the guns targeted Hawiye insurgency, which was closer to the regime's power base. The Somali historian Said Samatar described atrocities committed by the regime against the Hawiye clan in 1989:

> From the town of Belet Wayne in the middle valley of the Shabeelle river to Buula-Burte, a Hawaadle (Hawiye) town, to Jowhar and in the capital Mogadishu, the clan was subjected to ruthless and violent assault. . . . it is generally agreed that government atrocities on the Hawiye occurred on a scale and frequency that well matches those against the Majeerteen and Isaaq.[228]

While the newly formed USC was claiming military victories against the regime's forces in south-central regions, a lone gunman murdered Monsignor Salvatore Colombo, a long-term serving Roman Catholic Bishop, in Mogadishu on 9 July 1989. The regime blamed religious clerics for the bishop's murder[229] while others suggested that General Siyad Barre's security forces were behind it in order to implicate religious clerics as a strategy to attract the West.[230] The government immediately detained scores of clerics, as it offered ransom to any information leading to the killer.

For the first time in decades, on 14 July 1989 riots, which some sources blamed on Islamic fundamentalists and clerics, probably led by Sheikh Mahammed Mo'allin Hassan, a well-known cleric, who was detained by the regime few times, broke out in Mogadishu, a city that was becoming a lawless place.

The first fateful events in Mogadishu took place in the afternoon of 14 July 1989 at Sheikh Ali Suufi mosque at Casa Popolare quarter in Hodan district.[2] That afternoon, the Imam of the mosque, Sheikh Abdirashid Sheikh Ali Suufi, had given a sermon critical of the regime. The atmosphere was tense, as the brutal presidential bodyguards surrounded the building. After saying their prayers, people walked out of the mosque, and some started shouting *Allahu Akbar* (God is great), walking down the road just outside the mosque. The event degenerated into riots when stones were thrown at the security forces with which they responded with heavy machine gunfire. The riots spread across the city, but were broken up by the security forces, killing civilians. Subsequently, the regime imposed curfew on the capital.

In a city where suspicions and mistrust, plotters and agitators were everywhere, on 17 July 1989, the security forces murdered about forty-six Mogadishu residents from the Isaaq clan in a cold-blooded plot at Jasira beach at the outskirt of Mogadishu.[231] Ghalib (1995) claimed that President Siyad Barre was implicated in the massacre.[232] Indeed, Colonel Ibrahim Ali Barre (Canjeex), a fellow Mareehaan who was in charge of one of the army brigades in Mogadishu at the time, corroborated this line of the story. In a recent interview, after denying his involvement in the massacre and the murder of Isaaqs as a reprisal for the killing of Adan Magan, a Mareehaan Colonel during the previous Mogadishu riots, he mentioned that General Maslax, president's son, in association with commanders of air and naval forces, were behind the operation.[233] By these riots, another armed front opened in Mogadishu, the homeland of the powerful Hawiye clan with its deadly consequences to come.

Manifesto group: Missed opportunity

In its final months, the regime's behaviour was erratic and unpredictable. One day, it would detain political opponents and sentence them to death only to release them again as a gesture of reconciliation, but then only to detain other dissidents. The release of the seven high-ranking ministers detained in 1988 only to detain other opponents was classic example.[234] It was during these uncertain times that more than 100 prominent intellectuals, elders, spiritual leaders and politicians across clan and ideological spectrum, organized themselves and petitioned General Siyad Barre for political reforms. On 15 May 1990, they signed a comprehensive political document

---

[2]   The author was among the worshippers at the mosque when the riots broke out.

dubbed the 'Somali Manifesto', detailing his government's failures in socio-economic and political affairs, highlighting the widespread atrocities, lawlessness and insecurity in the country. Aden Abdulla Osman, the first democratically elected president and the only African who had stayed in his country after losing an election in the 1960s, was among the signatories. They proposed President Siyad Barre to resign, demanding an end to the civil war and other political reforms.[235]

Despite the suggestion that the president might have engineered the Manifesto group to outmanoeuvre his critics[236] and the rejection of the document by an Isaaq underground movement in Mogadishu,[237] most Somalis would agree the move was indeed a genuine attempt for a peaceful transition of power from General Siyad Barre. The group was representative of a broader Somali political spectrum, and its members were respected by the wider Somali community.

Sadly, General Siyad Barre and his regime rounded up and detained members of the group, dismissing them as remnants of the corrupt and tribalist civilian government, which his regime had overthrown in 1969. After their release due to foreign pressure, the group again called on the president and the armed rebel groups (SNM, SSDF, USC, etc.) to attend peace talks, such as the one in Cairo in December 1990 sponsored by the Egyptian and Italian governments. However, the talks collapsed because opposition fronts particularly General Aideed's USC, and Colonel Omar Jess, leader of the Somali Patriotic Movement (SPM) opposed them. The final blow to these talks came when the SNM rejected the talks while General Siyad Barre was still in power.[238]

In December 1990, the Somali government declared a state of emergency. On the political side, on 25 December 1990, the president announced free elections, and appointed a committee to draft a new constitution and interim prime ministers. In January 1991, members of the Manifesto group and another group called Sulux – mainly composed of government ministers sought a ceasefire from General Mohamed Farah Aideed, chairman of the USC whose forces were advancing onto Mogadishu, informing him that the president would relinquish power and he had appointed a new government consisting of seventy-five Manifesto members and twenty-five members appointed by the president. However, General Aideed, the man who was once General Siyad Barre's long-term political detainee, rebuffed the offer, insisting that General Siyad Barre would be killed, captured or forced to flee.[239]

Shortcoming of the opposition groups

At this point of events, it would only be fair to highlight some of the armed rebel groups' shortcomings to show that President Siyad Barre's government was not the main and the only culprit for the failure. First, choosing Ethiopia as their base was one of the rebel groups' biggest political blunders. The Somali government cleverly exploited this, discrediting them as traitors in bed with the enemy.[240] The public just rallied behind the regime's official description of the rebel groups because it would have been political suicide to ally with Ethiopia, the enemy. Thus by their misguided choice, the opposition groups failed to obtain wider public support. The choice had also hindered their cohesion and unity, which the Ethiopian regime had cleverly exploited by dividing them up as much as it liked. A classic example of the Ethiopian manipulation was when Colonel Mengistu's regime claimed that some Somali towns, Balamballe and Galdogob, captured by the SSDF were Ethiopian territories, which angered some SSDF leaders and created more division among them.[241] Indeed, Colonel Abdullahi Yusuf, leader of the SSDF, was detained by the Ethiopian regime after he had opposed the claim.[242] Certainly, Ethiopia had overall control over their destiny by either accommodating or expelling them as and when it wanted.

Despite having individual charters and political programmes, they failed to articulate unified and coherent vision of political programme post-Siyad Barre. For example, it was unclear whether the SNM, one of the well-organized fronts, favoured a unitary or federal state. It did not also make clear of any power-sharing arrangements with non-Isaaq minority clans in the north once the SNM came to power. Compagnon (1990a) observing the opposition groups' lack of united political vision quite rightly wrote:

> There is no obvious consensus between opposition forces on the future of Somalia, no common proposal for a political solution including all Somalis in the event that Mahammad Siyaad relinquishes voluntarily the power or manages to flee secretly. Nevertheless, many argue that an agreement ought to be urgently set up to prevent an extension of the civil war . . . . No evidence has been produced yet to indicate that the competing fronts are ready to share power tomorrow.[243]

Indeed, although they had been boasting of forming a transitional government, it was doubtful whether they could have come up with alternative political vision and programme had the president died in the fatal car accident in 1986 or left voluntarily. This is because they did not have answers to some practical arrangements required for real political reforms. Their eventual disintegration into tribal fiefdoms after the collapse of the central government in 1991 proves the point. Compagnon (1990a) again asks some hard-nosed questions that they failed or avoided answering:

> Who would be allowed to participate in the planned general elections? How to implement such a delicate process in a country completely disorganized? How would they prevent a rigged ballot at a time there is no credible data about potential voters? Would they recognise or ban political groupings based on clans? What would be the guarantees given to individuals who are not affiliated to the winner's clan-family?[244]

Undoubtedly, failure to answer these difficult questions is still haunting Somali politicians' souls almost thirty years after the collapse of the central government as warring factions and clans continue to fight over territory and resources.

Furthermore, the rebel groups were deeply divided among themselves along ideological and particularly clan lines that they even did not have a unifying umbrella organization,[245] and hated each other as much as they hated President Siyad Barre and his regime.[246] Despite several conferences to unite them under the auspices of prominent political leaders, such as Abdirazak Haji Hussein, former prime minister and Ahmed Mohamed 'Silanyo', chairman of the SNM, and despite creating alliances between themselves, using the word 'Somali' as a common denominator, these groups essentially remained fragmented and tribal in nature. In addition to their internal division, some leaders even wanted to divide millions of Somalis into clan-based villages and towns. Unquestionably, clan identity guaranteed you membership in these groups no matter of qualification, education or character, which led to some ignorant characters insisting to be Somalia's foreign representatives.[247]

Another crucial point was their dream that democracy and prosperity would prevail once the regime perished without first putting forward coherent and pragmatic political agenda. That wishful thinking was to avoid the difficult questions and real tasks that laid ahead. Compagnon eloquently commented on their naivety:

> These serious weaknesses are partly due to the naïve belief that the demise of General Barre's rule will automatically usher in a buoyant economy and democratic politics. This is compounded by an inability to envisage a coherent theory of mobilization and renewal.[248]

More crucially, the opposition groups failed to engage in a reconciliation process by taking advantage of peace initiatives organized by friendly countries and the regime's goodwill gesture. For example, the SNM refused to participate in the Cairo talks in December 1990 as long as General Siyad Barre was in power.[249] The majority of the rebel groups believed in the barrel of the gun to remove the dictatorship. Only some elements within the SSDF accepted various amnesties offered by President Siyad Barre. Undoubtedly and using the power of hindsight, engaging in serious political dialogue with the regime was again a missed opportunity that could have saved the Republic from the mayhem to come.

Therefore, as much as one could blame President Siyad Barre and his government for the Somali tragedy, armed fronts failed too to save the country from looming disaster and therefore must share the blame. Indeed, they were the other side of the same coin and copied the same policies of political intolerance and clan chauvinism, seeking salvation through violence[250] as their post-Siyad Barre behaviour confirmed. These rebel groups were a bunch of small minded, clannish and disillusioned characters whose concept of opposition was based on wandering in foreign and enemy capitals as a sign of their dissent.[251] Other characteristics of these opposition groups were that some of their leaders were disgruntled ministers who joined the rebel groups to show their unhappiness for losing their ministerial jobs during reshuffles, hence their motives were based on narrow parochial interests. Indeed, in a conversation with former US ambassador to Somalia, Peter Bridges, who raised the issue of political prisoners with General Siyad Barre, the late president, revealed the unprincipled character of the opposition leaders when he said:

> But, one of the leaders of these principled people is a man who served as a minister of the Somali government for over a dozen years, until I decided that he should be

moved to another post that lacked the ministerial titles but paid the same salary. At that point, this man declared that everything that we were doing was wrong, and he went to Addis Ababa to join our enemies.[252]

General Siyad Barre was, therefore, adamant not to be sympathetic with such disgruntled officials, and not let them bring down his government, saying: 'I could not be sympathetic toward men trying to bring down by violence the government to which I was accredited.'[253]

The outside world supported the Somali dictator even when his forces were committing atrocities against the Somali people because the international community could not believe in disorganized opposition groups led by visionless characters.[254] Mohamed Ibrahim W. Hadrawi, a famous Somali poet, summed the character and failure of the rebel groups when he said:

> All the Somali armed movements reflected the failures of the previous thirty years of Somali politics. For thirty years, mismanagement and injustice meant that a negative hatred was brewing. All those negative elements affected the struggles and the liberation movements. That is why they were all based on clan, hatred and revenge, with no plans, no visions, programmes or strategies.[255]

End of the Cold War: The world abandons Somalia

It was not only Somalis who had failed Somalia, but the international community failed too. Indeed, the international community's attitude towards Somalia in the late 1980s was one of apathy to say the least for the following reasons.

The Republic was not high priority on the world agenda because of other bloody upheavals and huge strategic changes in the Cold War order. Mikhail Gorbachev, leader of the USSR, was vigorously implementing his economic and political reforms known as *perestroika* and *glasnost*, respectively since he came to power in 1985.[256] The West was rejoicing in the changes, and President Ronald Reagan had been negotiating with Gorbachev on nuclear disarmament for some time. The giant socialist block was crumbling sometimes in bloodshed and chaotic scenes. By November 1989, thousands of cheering crowds had ripped apart the Berlin wall – the 'iron curtain', which had divided the German people for decades. The Romanian and Bulgarian regimes collapsed and the dictator, Nicolae Ceauşescu was executed on 25 December 1989. The USSR was falling apart too, some republics seceding from their old political master. This was the end of the socialist block and the Cold War.

Therefore, Somalia, which was already sliding towards anarchy like other third world nations, was a drop in that sea of huge political turmoil and could hardly attract much attention. While the international community made political and financial arrangements for European socialist states to ensure smooth transfer from the Cold War to post-Cold War era, adequate resources were not allocated to help third world countries during this painful period,[257] although end of the Cold War had helped resolved some African conflicts, such as the Ethiopian–Eritrean conflict when Eritrea became independent.[258]

Once they lost their strategic importance, third world countries like Somalia were left to fend for themselves just when they were experiencing some social and economic difficulties.[259] Therefore, the collapse of some third world countries was inevitable once the Cold War power structure that supported them had broken down particularly after the collapse of the socialist block. In fact, Somalia is a classic example of state disintegration as a direct result of the end of the Cold War and the beginning of the New World Order. This is how Patman (2010) explained:

> How the end of the Cold War affected the Somali state seems fairly clear: without superpower support, what was highly incoherent, corrupt and fragmented state could no longer withstand the centrifugal pressures that were being brought to bear upon it, particularly due to clan rivalries, a lack of respect and trust in the state, and ongoing border tensions.[260]

Except for some very isolated mediation initiatives by Italy and Egypt, there were hardly any significant attempts to encourage reconciliation. Even the Italian efforts were far from being genuine and satisfactory. The Italian prime minister Pettino Craxi's socialist government, which was the only Western government supporting the regime in its last days,[261] did not pressurize the regime hard enough to force to relinquish power. Italian politicians wanted to keep the regime alive so that they could steal millions of dollars from the Italian aid package worth millions of dollars through corruption networks that involved some senior Italian and Somali establishments.[262] Ironically, the Italian government failed to use aid as a carrot to pressurize the regime enough to introduce much needed political reforms.

In addition to that, armed fronts were suspicious of the Italian socialist government's reconciliation initiatives because of its long history of supporting the Somali regime. Indeed, Somalia was the largest receiver of Italian aid since 1978 and the two socialist governments signed a military aid agreement on October 1982.[263]

Even the United States, which had military base in Somalia, was not paying enough attention to the unfolding civil war in the country. Even though US administrations had conducted an investigation into the regime's atrocities in its military campaign in the north and published its findings, it did not publically criticize the regime hard enough in early phase of the civil war. To American administrations, the regime was the devil they knew and they were not prepared to risk regime change that could threaten their national interest.[264]

Rather than withdrawing their support, US administrations, having built in Mogadishu the largest and most expensive embassy compound in sub-Sahara Africa, regarded the military aid to the regime as critical 'to help Somalia retain its political and territorial integrity' and continued it well into 1990.[265] US governments saw the military aid to the regime as a means of protecting Somalia against Ethiopia and its socialist allies until they realized that the situation in Somalia degenerated into civil war. Friction within the State Department, and the Pentagon, which preferred continued support for strategic reasons, had hindered any reconciliation objectives and suspension of military aid.[266]

By supporting the regime in its unpopular and dying days, US administrations prolonged the life span of a regime with a dreadful human rights record only to commit further atrocities. This is how Paul Henze, a national security adviser in the Carter administration, who was never a fan of Somalia, lamenting on the fateful change of the US policy and its consequences, explained: by embracing Somalia in 1980, the United States helped prolong an odious regime which has killed – proportionately – as many of its citizens as Mengistu's regime has and has forced even larger numbers – proportionately – to flee.[267]

Undeniably, US administrations' support in the late 1980s when the regime was using American weapons against civilians was wrong. Most Somalis would agree with this, knowing the subsequent atrocities committed in the country, such as the civil war in the north. Unfortunately, the United States supported the regime for its strategic reasons as it needed to keep its military bases, but was not attentive and responsive to political and social problems that were engulfing the country, particularly the civil war in the north.[268]

However, the international community was in dilemma of whether or not to support the failing totalitarian regime. If it had withdrawn aid, social services and other public and private sectors might have collapsed hence hurting ordinary citizens, and the possibility of the regime becoming even more repressive. At the time, the country's socio-economic institutions heavily depended on what was dubbed the 'aid avalanche',[269] a country that had been reliant on foreign aid since the 1960s.[270] In fact, there were hardly any private or public institutions or sectors, which did not directly or indirectly rely on foreign aid or as Omar (1992) explained: 'the entire country had been reduced to a sort of "refugee camp" which mainly relied upon foreign food aid meant to help the Ogaden refugees.'[271] The culture of dependence was so bad that even supply of food was in the hands of international donors, as the country's economic and social institutions were gradually failing.

Using aid as a carrot to encourage the regime to undertake political reforms was another reason used for continuing foreign aid, which was run by international aid agencies with their vested interests to keep the industry functioning to justify their existence and monthly salaries.[272] In hindsight, although suspending aid completely would have probably worsened the situation as it could have hurt ordinary people, concerted diplomatic efforts with the curtailment of military aid might have forced General Siyad Barre to step down hence preventing the looming chaos and bloodshed.[273]

Equally, the United Nations failed in preventing the looming tragedy through preventative conflict resolution, early mediation and diplomacy. First, it ignored the grave human rights abuses in the north during the civil war. In fact, while the country was in a terrible need of UN leadership and guidance, the organization evacuated its staff from the north on security and safety grounds as early as 1988.[274] Second, during the Manifesto group, it ignored serious warnings coming from its field office in Mogadishu when the regime was detaining members of the Manifesto group. Drysdale (1994) commenting on the UN's failure wrote: 'Competing political interests in Somalia were by now running out of control. International guidance was needed urgently. The

UN, by failing to offer guidance, evidently misjudged the gravity of the situation. It left the destiny of Somalia in the hands of Sicas',[275] the Italian ambassador to Somalia who was frantically trying to mediate between the warring factions.

Regrettably, just before the collapse of the regime and as the fighting was engulfing Mogadishu, the international community evacuated its staff and embassies except a few non-governmental organizations, such as SOS, Medicine sans Frontier and International Red Cross, abandoning the Republic to collapse and disintegrate into fiefdoms.

In conclusion, the Cold War and its aftermath had a negative impact on the Republic on two occasions. First, Soviets had armed Somalis heavily only to spectacularly let them down during the Ogaden war and subsequent defeat, which led to the collapse of the state. Second, the Americans, in pursuit of their global strategic objectives, unwittingly or deliberately extended the life span of the collapsing dictatorship, turning a blind eye on full-fledged genocide and repression in the north. Unlike Ethiopia where the United States had helped peaceful transition of power from Colonel Mengistu's regime to the Ethiopian People's Revolutionary Democratic Front (EPRDF) in 1991,[276] the world abandoned Somalia once it has lost its strategic importance.

'Father of the Nation' is evicted from his villa!

General Siyad Barre, who was once quoted saying the following, was loyal to his character and did not relinquish power without fight:

> I, Mohamed Siyaad Barre, am singularly responsible for the transformation of Somalia and Mogadishu from a bush country and scruffy hamlet into a modern state and commodious city, respectfully. Consequently, I will not allow anyone to destroy me or run me out of here; and if they try, I will take the whole country with me.[277]

> When I came to Mogadishu . . . there was one road built by the Italians. If you try to force me to stand down, I will leave the city as I found it. I came to power with a gun; only the gun can make me go.[278]

In its last weeks and days and as USC forces increased their activities, the regime's security forces escalated the situation by raiding and looting stores owned by Hawiye businessmen in Mogadishu.[279] Challenged by Hawiye militias, the security forces immediately deployed a tank from the famous 77-army division on Mogadishu's outskirts. By now, the situation had degenerated into fully blown urban warfare as police and military units deserted the regime to join USC forces. Having lost ground forces, the regime indiscriminately shelled Mogadishu, a city of 2 million residents,[280] with heavy artillery and ground-to-ground missiles. This indiscriminate shelling caused civilian casualties and destruction of some parts of the city. As a desperate move, General Siyad Barre was even accused to have paid over half a million US dollars to hire pilots to fly Hawker Hunter fighter jets[281] perhaps to bomb the city to rubble just as his forces had done to Hargeisa and Burao in the north. He was also accused of even mobilizing militia from his Daarood clan in desperate clan ploy to get Daaroods fight Hawiyes in their homeland.[282] By now, a full-blown civil war between Hawiye and Daarood clans was spiralling out of control, or as Ghalib (1995), regretting of what happened, explained:

> Regrettably, this nevertheless triggered off another phase in the civil war and led to eventual Daarood-Hawiye ethnic retribution of serious dimensions and far reaching consequences, long after the aged dictator, Siad Barre, had to be bundled into an armoured car and hastily evacuated to the temporary safety of his clan homeland.[283]

From 29 December 1990, Mogadishu was in chaos and general uprisings after its residents armed themselves to dismantle the dictatorship. It was a city of fear and terror where the regime's troops indiscriminately shelled civilian populated areas to dislodge USC fighters. A city where both fighting forces committed atrocities, including government soldiers raping, killing, cutting up women's breasts and then lining their dead bodies on the streets as a show-off.[284] A city where, because of availability of plenty of dead human corpse, stray dogs, domesticated cats and chicken become wild beasts, scavenging and feeding on human flesh, where dogs attacked and bit people.[285]

On 26 January 1991, President Siyad Barre found himself holed up in Villa Somalia, the presidential palace with the minister of defence, General Mohamed Hersi Morgan, his loyal son-in-law, the man who stood up for him after his top generals had deserted him with their bags full of dollars and gold bars.[286] Finally, after collecting money and gold that he plundered from the central bank in a tank,[287] the dictator was disgracefully evicted from the Villa he had lived in for twenty years on 27 January 1991.

Paradoxically and to his humiliation, the old man, who was once praised metaphorically as the 'father of the nation' and described as 'Demigod'[288] was chased away from Mogadishu by forces loyal to General Mohamed Aideed, who waslong-term political detainee, the man he had exiled many times to destroy him. Mogadishu residents' popular uprising also ensured the old man's time was over. With his eviction from the Villa came the end of brutal dictatorship that had terrorized citizens and divided the Republic into fiefdoms.

If President Siyad Barre came to power to eliminate tribalism and nepotism to create a united and fairer society, to fight corruption and improve economic situation for millions of Somalis through the 'scientific socialism' ideology, he badly failed on all these counts. He abandoned the Republic to a situation worse than when he ascended to power twenty-one years before as the country was still economically underdeveloped and socially divided along clan lines more or less when his regime took power in 1969. Indeed, General Siyad Barre left the once-proud Republic as no more than a family dynasty controlled by his Mareehaan clan. Indeed, cities such as Hargeisa and Burao were left in ruins after forces of his regime had air-bombed them.

However and regrettably, the metaphorical father remains Somalis' 'real' father as his bad legacies still linger and his offsprings learn from them as they grow. A Somali proverb says: *Waxaad I baday waxaa iiga daran waxaad I bartay*, translated what you have made me go through (oppression, persecution) is less harmful than what I have learned from you, such as belief in the barrel of the gun.[289] When he came to power there were about 3.6 million Somalis and by 1990 this number had doubled to 6.596 million. Three million Somali citizens, half of them in their forties, either were born or grew up with and lived most of their lives under his dictatorship. This symbolical father–son relationship is most evident in the behaviour of today's factional leaders, warlords and politicians who use similar mindset, including the use of perverted clanism and brute force as means to power as described in the Ugly Face of the Civil War in Chapter 4.

However, to be fair to the late General Siyad Barre, his supporters argue that the former president was an honourable and good statesman who led his country to excellent socio-economic and political developments, some of them radical such as the writing of the Somali language. And he therefore deserves a golden page in Somali history as a hero.[290]

Equally important is that it was not only to blame General Siyad Barre and his regime, but armed rebel groups were guilty by using and manipulating divisive clan politics. They believed in violence to achieve political ends and not in peace settlement. They were also a bunch of small-minded, visionless bigots, power hunger and traitors who were in bed with Mengistu's Ethiopia, a historical enemy. Indeed, their behaviour after the collapse of the central government is much worse than the military dictatorship as the country is deeply divided along clan lines and is facing secession.

The ugly face of the civil war

'Clan cleansing' in Mogadishu

As the Republic continued to succumb to the long-term impact of the Ogaden defeat, it degenerated into anarchy after the central government had collapsed. Below are some of the major events, turning points, missed opportunities, mistakes, failures, action or non-action by Somali and foreign actors, which shaped the conflict.

After the ejection of General Siyad Barre and the collapse of the central government, the general situation in the country was one of anarchy and chaos. The proud Republic descended into clan fiefdoms where clan vendetta, including stoning an individual to death for belonging to the wrong clan, became the norm.[1] The SNM seized control of Isaaq territories in north-west regions having ejected the regime's remnant forces, and was persecuting non-Isaaq clans, which resisted its domination.[2] The SSDF took control of Majeerteen territories in north-east regions, setting up a regional administration with the help of clan elders. The USC asserted its authority over Hawiye territories from central regions to the south. The deposed president and his Daarood/Mareehaan clansmen retreated to their homeland – Gedo and lower Juba regions. Different armed fronts occupied Rahanweyn clans' regions of Bay, Bakool and lower Shabelle with no one having overall control over them.

In the first three months, the situation in Mogadishu was murderous and chaotic. Triggered by the deposed dictator's last clan card manoeuvre, unfortunately, USC leadership failed to recognize the divisive clan-trap left behind by the deposed regime[3] in a country already divided along clan lines.[4] In what started as hunting down of supporters of the dictator from Mareehaan and Daarood communities[5] had degenerated into what was dubbed 'clan cleansing'.[6] General Mohamed Farah Aideed's USC militiamen targeted Daaroods and killed hundreds of them, raping women and looting their properties[7] as USC militia attacked other Daarood towns in Mudug, Gedo and Juba regions. To summarize, it was clan and personal vendetta politics in which Hawiye militiamen were mobilized by clannish hatred against Daaroods who were seen as oppressors of Hawiye.[8] On the other hand, Daaroods were equally mobilized by hatred of Hawiye. Indeed, a video recorded during the height of the civil war, shows General Morgan, the deposed dictator's son-in-law explicitly urging Daaroods to fight Hawiye.[9]

USC leadership failed to demobilize and control its fighters, which had converged in Mogadishu for the last showdown with the regime. Much of the bloodshed, lawlessness and anarchy in Mogadishu could have been prevented had the leadership demobilized and reined in the armed militias.[10] That failure of leadership turned Mogadishu residents' popular uprising against the regime into a witch-hunt and persecution of Daaroods and non-Hawiye clans.[11]

General Siyad Barre ruled the city for twenty-one years, but USC leadership destroyed some parts of the city within twenty-one days ten times more than what General Siyad Barre had done to it. Indeed, Ali Geedi Shadoor, one of the USC founders was quoted lamenting that had he known the situation would end up like this he would not have supported the USC.[12] The following statement by Dr Abdishakur Jowhar, a Somali scholar, is more than enough to describe the ugliness of the unfolding post-Siyad Barre clan violence:

> The first genocide unfolded in its ruthless streets in 1991 right after the fall of the Siyad Barre regime. In that year Hawiye militia burned, raped and killed any person of Darood origin regardless of age, regardless of gender and regardless of their role in the defunct regime. It was enough to be Darood to be massacred in Mogadishu's first days of infamy. . . . This first genocide has become the driving force and the central reason for the intractable failure of the Somali state.[13]

Here is a poet's description of the ugliness of clan violence:

> Every enclosed space they turned into a grave.
> On how many bodies, dead since yesterday or the day before, did flies throng!
> As we staggered on, we were no longer able to move our legs from exhaustion!
> Our lips crusted over, none of their shine remaining.
> How did exhaustion show itself on Dahaabo and Faduumo!
> How they mounted sweet-smelling girls and married women!
> How many hijab-wearing girls had their belts torn from their waists?
> How were women pursued into mosques they deemed safe!
> Three generations of women raped on the same mat.
> Time and again they stabbed virgin girls who had not yet been deflowered.[14]

The clan vendetta was one of the biggest political mistakes post-Siyad Barre because as articulated by Jowhar (2007a) it stirred up bad blood leading to an intractable civil war.

Ali Mahdi as interim president and the fallout

Just as the 'clan cleansing' was being carried out, Ali Mahdi, an Abgaal, a sub-clan of Hawiye and General Mohamed Farah Aideed from Habargedir, another Hawiye sub-clan had fallen out overpower sharing within the USC. The root cause of their political fallout goes back to the formation of the organization in the late 1980s. Ali Mahdi, a wealthy hotelier and USC's financier[15] rejected an offer of a position as USC's interior minister made by the general in their meeting in Ethiopia, in which case Ali

Mahdi flew to Roma, where he strengthened his USC faction which was resentful of General Aideed's entrance into politics.[16] This had already resulted in USC split into a Mogadishu-Roma faction led by the hotelier and Mustahil-Ethiopia military wing led by the general.

After just two days of the dictator's fall, without first consulting with other factional leaders and establishing law and order in Mogadishu[17] the Mogadishu-based USC faction nominated Ali Mahdi as interim president on 29 January 1991, who then nominated Omar Arte Ghalib, an Isaaq clansman as his prime minister. Omar Arte formed what must have been one of the world's biggest governments of eighty ministers with eighty deputy ministers and eighty permanent secretaries in a country where competition over position of president became an elite obsession.[18] Supported mainly by the middle class of Mogadishu, the Manifesto group and some remnants of the regime, Ali Mahdi's faction saw the action as an alternative post-Siyad political transition strategy compared with the militaristic and radical approach adopted by the armed factions. The action antagonized armed groups, such as the SNM, the SPM, an Ogaden affiliated faction who felt that they had been cheated of their success and decisive role in defeating the regime, and many people saw Ali Mahdi faction's manoeuvre as a dishonest action by politicians.[19]

The action was particularly upsetting and disturbing to General Aideed, the man who believed that he had played a significant role in organizing and unifying the opposition fronts that dismantled the dictatorship, starting from the day he had published his manifesto, the New United Somali Democratic Organisation (NUSDO) in 1988, in which he detailed his vision for Somalia.[20] From there on he set out a plan of action to liberate Somalia from the dictatorship starting with his resignation from his position as Somalia's ambassador to India in 1989. He then moved to Ethiopia where he was welcomed by the Ethiopian government in Addis Ababa. He continued his journey to Mustahil in Ethiopia where he met with leaders of the existing opposition groups, the SNM, SPM and the USC, and managed to unite them. He was also elected as chairman of the USC-Mustahil wing.[21] Under the umbrella of a newly formed Somali Liberation Army (SLA), mainly forces loyal to his USC faction, he finally ejected the dictator from Somalia with the help of other rebel groups such as SPM, Somali Democratic Movement (SDM), a Rahanweyn faction and Southern Somalia National Movement (SSNM), a Dir-Biyamaal faction.

General Aideed believed that Ali Mahdi's USC-Manifesto faction was a group created by the fallen dictator,[22] and its decision to nominate Ali Mahdi was illegitimate because it was no more than a continuation of Siyad Barre's regime. He also believed that his USC faction, under the SLA umbrella, was the real fighting force that had toppled the regime.[23]

The hasty nomination of Ali Mahdi was the second gravest political blunder post-Siyad Barre, which exacerbated a gloomy political situation.[24] At that historical moment, the Republic was at the eve of some huge socio-political changes after the dictatorship had been removed. Unfortunately, the unilateral action by one of many competing armed factions destroyed any hope of real political reforms. Faction leaders, including Hawiye and non-Hawiye clans, rejected the antagonistic move. Indeed, the decision to nominate Ali Mahdi as president was one of the reasons behind SNM's hasty decision of declaring north-west regions of Somalia an independent country because people in the north were angered by the unilateral decision, as confirmed by Ahmed Mohamed Silanyo, who was the SNM's chairperson.[25] In hindsight, Ali Mahdi's faction should have allowed a cooling off period post-Siyad Barre for political dialogue and reconciliation before forming any government.

Deposed dictator fights back

In another development, after his eviction from Mogadishu, unlike another dictator, Mengistu H. Mariam of Ethiopia who went into exile in Zambia because of diplomatic efforts by the United States,[26] General Siyad Barre chose to fight to the bitter-end even though the United Arab Emirates had offered him political asylum.[27] In his mind, the fallen dictator believed he was a saviour and man of peace who was determined to fight off what he had described as 'hooligans', vandalizing and destroying the country he had built.[28] He immediately retreated to Gedo and Juba regions where he organized Mareehaan and Daarood militia under a new group called the Somali National Front (SNF).

Feeling threatened by the deposed dictator's new offensive, USC factions halted their initial internal conflict and political disagreement. Under General Aideed's command, USC militiamen and other forces fought the deposed dictator's forces in a series of clashes in towns and cities, such as Afgoye, Wanle Weyn, Kismayo, Jamaame, Doollo, El Waq, Garbaharrey and Buulo Xaawo. These battles were mainly Hawiye versus Daarood conflicts in which the deposed dictator's Daarood fighters were being chased away by USC and other factions. During this conflict, warring sides committed horrific atrocities, which included cutting off people's tongues, arms and legs and then left them to die. Children and old men thrown into oil drums full of boiling oil, water and salt; women gang-raped, and their vaginas bayoneted and their stomachs left cut open; even pregnant women had their stomachs slit open.[29] In addition, farmlands and food stores were destroyed.

In several counteroffensives against USC, General Siyad Barre's forces reached within 30 kilometres of Mogadishu and were in control of some regions like Gedo and Bay, committing atrocities against non-Daarood clans, such as Hawiye and Rahanweyn clans.[30] It took fifteen months before the dictator was finally expelled from the country. Indeed, despite armed front's role in his final defeat, it was his political fallout with his Daarood generals that finally forced him to flee the country.[31] The dictator and his Mareehaan faction wanted to regain power while other Daarood forces wanted to respond to the atrocities committed by USC forces against their kin in Mogadishu and this created division within the Daaroods,[32] which led to their defeat by the USC.

Finally, the dictator's Mareehaan forces deserted him when he insisted to fight on to the end. However, he took revenge on them by disarming them, and then fleeing to Kenya.[33] General Siyad Barre sought asylum in Kenya in January 1992, and ended his reign as 'the first regional warlord of the 1990s'.[34] He stayed in luxury hotels in Kenya, enjoying steaks, wines and spaghetti at the cost of US$1,800 a day while Somalis were starving in Somalia.[35] The dictator died in Nigeria of natural causes as a political refugee on 2 January 1995.

In the power of hindsight, Mengistu's wise decision to leave Ethiopia quietly just when the EPRDF fighters were encroaching Addis Ababa in their final push to oust his regime, saved Ethiopia from total anarchy and outright civil war. Unfortunately, the dictator's decision to fight on contributed to more anarchy, chaos, mayhem and bloodshed, which would lead to mass starvation.

Djibouti reconciliation conference

At the height of the conflict and while the dictator was being chased away from the country, President Hassan Guuleed Abtidoon of the Republic of Djibouti, supported by Italy, Egypt and other regional states, organized reconciliation conferences in June and July 1991. Armed groups such as the USC, SSDF, SPM, SDM, Somali Democratic Alliance (SDA) and SNF agreed to some political solutions, which included reintroduction of the 1969 constitution and its constitutional arrangements. A parliament of 123 members appointed Ali Mahdi as interim president for two years, who would nominate the prime minister from the Isaaq clan.

However, implementation of the agreements failed because of the intractability of the conflict in which factions had different agendas. For instance, Daarood politicians and factions were unhappy about the failure of the conference to discuss atrocities committed by USC militia in Mogadishu.[36] They also did not have faith in Ali Mahdi's government led by Omar Arte, from the Isaaq clan. Because they saw Omar Arte as less likely to persuade the SNM to abandon its secession decision compared with other reputable Isaaq figures, such as Mohamed Ibrahim Haji Egal, former prime minister of Somalia[37] who attended the Djibouti conference.

Furthermore, confirmation of Ali Mahdi as president by the conference in Djibouti was poor political judgement because it alienated General Aideed who had already rejected Ali Mahdi's presidency. Aideed boycotted the Djibouti conferences as long as Ali Mahdi was still claiming to be president. He also held other parallel conferences in Mogadishu in which he was elected chairman of the USC. He finally rejected Ali Mahdi's government which was appointed in September 1991 on the basis that Ali Mahdi had not consulted the USC as agreed in another meeting in August 1991, which confirmed General Aideed as USC chairman and Ali Mahdi as interim president in which case both leaders recognized each other's position.[38]

Also, SNM leadership boycotted Djibouti conferences because it had already declared the north-west region independent from Somalia, and the leadership was mainly associated with General Aideed's faction, in which Abdirahman Tuur, SNM chairman, was to be prime minister in a power sharing between the two factions.

In addition to that, lack of international leadership and guidance on mediation and conflict resolution contributed to the failure of Djibouti conferences. As argued by Sahnoun (1994), a UN diplomat, leadership in conflict resolution by the international community could have helped conference organizers to assert greater pressures on warring factions.[39] Unfortunately, Somalia was not high on the world agenda because of other major political events like the first Gulf war. Indeed, the international community ignored Somalia throughout 1991 and 1992 except for a few non-governmental organizations that were involved in humanitarian efforts. USC faction leaders were left to settle their disagreements and differences through the barrel of the gun.

Mogadishu wars: Mooryaans, looting fuel the conflict

After the failure of Djibouti initiatives, the political disagreement gap between the two USC factions widened, their positions becoming irreconcilable. Ali Mahdi, an ambitious successful hotelier and once a civilian politician, believed he was the legitimate president blessed by the Djibouti conference and agreed by most factions. On the other hand, General Aideed, a power-thirsty military man, believed he was the rightful heir to the presidency because his forces had removed the dictator from power. Indeed, he was the most powerful man and became de-facto president at that historical moment.[40] He also perceived Manifesto/Ali Mahd's USC faction as fat cats who had enriched themselves in the dictator's era[41] and described their 'self-appointed government' as nothing more than continuation of the dictator's rule indirectly.[42] The two men, therefore, did not only have conflicting personal ambitions, but different ethos: an authoritarian general against a merchant bourgeoisie.[43]

At clan politics mentality level, although there was no traditional clan animosity between Habargedirs and Abgals, on one hand, the USC/Habargedir faction saw themselves as liberators of lands occupied by the fallen dictator's forces and therefore claimed the presidency.[44] They also saw Abgaals as inferior who cannot lead Somalia, and therefore Habargedirs were determined to show their superiority as a warrior caste and natural leaders.[45] On the other hand, Abgaals believed that Mogadishu was their traditional homeland[46] and were adamant not to hear nonsense from General Aideed and his Habargedir clansmen who hail from central regions of Mudug and Galgaduud.

Immediately and after having ejected the dictator, the two men pursued their hunger for power forcefully and ruthlessly, although General Aideed would prove more confrontational, belligerent and ruthless.[47] The two factions dug in their trenches as another wave of vicious cycle of sectarian violence was unleashed on Mogadishu streets after Ali Mahdi refused an Italian delegation to visit General Aideed because Ali Mahdi believed he was the legitimate president. Subsequently, General Aideed's forces shelled the airport just before the landing of the Italian delegation forcing the aircraft to return. Ali Mahdi retaliated by shelling Aideed's house.[48] The Italian delegation was sent by the Italian government to mediate between the two leaders.[49]

This was the beginning of Mogadishu wars, which would last until around March 1992 in which Mogadishu residents would be subjected to indiscriminate shelling fired by militiamen not trained in the art of shooting at a target.[50] Or as George Alagiah, a British journalist put it: 'So indiscriminate was the targeting that the people of Mogadishu referred to the shells as 'to whom it may concern'!'[51] as a tragic comedy to ease the pain.

The two Hawiye sub-clans led by their factions, who probably had never fought in a traditional clan conflict, took clan warfare to a much destructive level in pursuit of personal leadership ambitions, financial benefits and spoils of the state's public offices.[52] The killing machinery included anti-aircraft guns, mortars, rocket-propelled guns (RPGs) and what became known as 'technicals'[53] which were looted pickup Toyota vehicles mounted with heavy machine guns manufactured in garages in Mogadishu run by some characters, such as Osman 'Atto',[54] General Aideed's war financier. The 'technicals' or Mad Max, driven by gangs and militiamen crazed on drugs were effective killing machines that, unlike tanks, could easily manoeuvre in Mogadishu's narrow streets. As many as 14,000 people were killed and 27,000 wounded during this conflict.[55]

This brutal war was void of any traditional norms, such as not harming the innocent, the weak, and respecting and burying the dead. Indeed, defenceless and minority clans, such as Reer Hamars were subjected to atrocities by the fighting factions. The abduction of a sixteen-year-old girl from a non-combatant minority clan in Hamar Weyn district in Mogadishu at gunpoint by militiamen in front of her parents for a ransom was classic example of wide phenomenon of atrocities. The gang eventually left the family's home, taking the daughter at gunpoint after having pulled out her father's golden teeth with mechanics pliers to take it as war booty.[56] That was the last time the father had seen his daughter. The family's six-year-old son also died within a few days.[57]

As law and order broke down, looting became one of the biggest problems in Mogadishu, fuelling the fighting because anyone with an AK47 gun could use their weapon to make living by looting[58] in a city of millions of inhabitants and the seat of the nation's wealth, and 8,000 tons of food up to loot.[59] Armed youth gangs dubbed 'mooryaans'[60] and their non-satiable hunger for a big loot to feed their drug addiction drove much of the looting and the killing. The 'mooryaans' were urban street children who had lived in Mogadishu streets prior to the civil war after they were forced to leave their homelands when the deposed regime was clamping down on armed rebels in central regions in late 1980.[61] They were influenced by General Siyad Barre's bodyguards who used their famous Toyota pick-ups mounted with heavy machine guns to terrorize people and loot. These street children-cum-gangs were mainly from the Habargedir clan.[62] Alongside the more organized clan militiamen, used by factional leaders, the mooryaans, high on drugs to cope with the war's trauma, looted, raped and killed. They became uncontrollable by their closest relatives.[63]

Although factional leaders and warlords could inspire militiamen, including the mooryaans to fight, they were unable to control them and impose law and order in the areas they controlled.[64] They also condoned looting in order to maintain their political authority.[65] Far from curbing looting some of the warlords institutionalized greed and pursued unscrupulous business transactions, such as handling robbed and stolen goods and arms business.[66]

Furthermore, clan elders and traditional leaders were unable to assert their political authority because of the breakdown of traditional social order and customary laws and Islam (*Xeer and Islam*) and subsequent murderous politics, which are the heart of the Somali catastrophe.[67] This is particularly important given the divisive nature of lineage structure with its contested political leadership in peace and war times as anthropologists, such as Lewis would argue.

Lyons and Samatar (1995) describing scale of the looting in a city where thousands of armed militiamen roamed in search of food and loot wrote:

> In the course of fighting, looting became all encompassing-not only were homes looted of their furnishings but also their door frames, wiring, pipes, and structure steel. Nearly all public infrastructure, from bridges to power and water lines, was blown up or dug out.[68]

In addition to the mooryaans and militia factions, a war economy and war profiteering run by factional leaders and other businessmen instigated much of the violence and anarchy in major cities across southern Somalia, such as Mogadishu.[69] Tons of *Qat*, an stimulant drug used by Somalis worth US$100 million annually circulated in Mogadishu to finance warlords' war machine and militiamen's drug addiction.[70] Certainly, factional leaders and war entrepreneurs used the conflict to enhance their economic interests through looting, control of economic sources (air and sea ports) and exploitation of foreign aid.[71] The banana war over control of lucrative banana business in the lower Shabelle region in the later years of the conflict was classic war economy case in point.[72] Frankly, economic interest motivated the conflict in Mogadishu and many other parts in the country as much as the clan conflict.

Availability of weapons also inflamed much of the conflict not only in Mogadishu but throughout the country. Vast amount of small and heavy weapons, worth millions of dollars provided mainly by superpowers, were seized by clans and factions, or even individuals. At the collapse of Siyad Barre's regime, over 100,000 weapons inherited from the Cold War were in circulation in the country.[73] For example, SNM and other factions simply seized the nation's military hardware, as General Siyad Barre's regime was being dismantled. In the post-regime collapse, warlords converted garages as arms production factories and smuggled arms from neighbouring countries, particularly Ethiopia, which was also teaming with weapons after the collapse of the Mengistu's military regime. Arms became what was described the 'most useful currency' in the country, as people traded in arms in Mogadishu's arms markets.[74]

Mogadishu, the capital and centre of the nation's wealth, was a 'fatal attraction' and factor that motivated Hawiye factions to fight for every inch of this huge city.[75] As the conflict went on, this beautiful metropolitan city, once a home for millions of Somalis regardless of their clan affiliation, was effectively divided into two zones with a green line in the middle. The Ali Mahdi's Abgaal faction, although in their city and more numerous than General Aideed's Habargedir clan, controlled only the north because the Habargedir faction who controlled the south zone had superior firepower.

Mogadishu became a lawless and 'insane city' where militiamen armed with deadly weapons fought running street battles; where dead bodies were left to rot as no one dared to bury them.[76] A city where gunmen dictated who got treatment in hospitals; where patients smuggled guns for their own protection and only hospitals became the safest place.[77] The once beautiful metropolitan city was in ruins and remained a war zone and ghost town throughout the conflict.

Famine and foreign power intervention

Other regions or cities did not escape the engulfing violence. Daarood factions, such as the SPM led by Colonel Omar Jees of the Ogaden clan and the SNF led by General Mohamed Hersi Morgan of the Majeerteen clan fought over control of Kismayo, an important port city in the deep south of the country. Towns in the north-west regions became scenes of heavy fighting, as SNM fought other non-Isaaq clan militiamen in order to assert its authority.[78] SSDF militia dug their trenches in cities in north-east and central regions, such as Galkayo to defend General Aideed's USC militiamen who attempted to subjugate this city, traditionally contested by Hawiye and Daarood clans, to their authority.[79]

More serious lower Shabelle, Bay and Bakool regions in south-western Somalia inhabited mainly by the Rahanweyn clans became the most contested territories. Daarood and Hawiye factions fought over control of these fertile farming lands, normally the country's breadbasket while the dictator and his militia were being chased away.[80] The factions occupied farmlands once they had 'liberated' from the dictator and his militiamen who had also committed a 'scorched earth' policy as they fled.[81]

Although Rahanweyn clans did have rebel groups, such as the SDM, they could not defend their communities because they were militarily weak and were divided among themselves, some fighting alongside Daarood or Hawiye factions. Indeed, elders from Bay region pleaded with General Aideed, the powerful warlord who was seen at the time as one of the 'liberators' or mujahideen to help them liberate their lands from the dictator and his forces who were committing atrocities in the region.[82]

Destruction of inter-riverine farmlands by the dictator's militiamen[83] and other factions, disruption of food supplies from Mogadishu and Kismayo ports and looting of food aid convoys caused massive famine in the south-western regions. Thousands of people were starving to death. At the early stage of the famine in December 1991, food was available at ports, but widespread looting was hampering its delivery by the few international charity organizations, such as the International Commission of Red Cross (ICRC). They were even forced to hire thousands of gunmen to protect food convoys from looters, paying them as much as US$50,000 a month to 'protect' their operations and the Mogadishu seaport where food aid was delivered at.[84] Some factional leaders condoned looting to maintain their authority.[85] As starvation spread and food convoys could not reach their destinations due to insecurity, the ICRC created chains of food kitchens to feed people in Mogadishu and other regions as a desperate act. Top American officials were impressed by ICRC's great humanitarian work that they nominated the organization for the Nobel Peace Prize.[86]

At the height of the famine, the international community was absent from Somalia because it was fighting other wars and conflicts in Bosnia, the Gulf war. It was also busy to contain disintegration of the USSR. The United States, the only superpower, was reluctant to get involved in the Somali conflict because it perceived it as a humanitarian issue which did not directly threaten its national security and interest.[87] A handful of non-governmental organizations, such as the ICRC, were the only agencies, leading much needed humanitarian assistance operations.

After a high-profile campaign by the media and the ICRC, highlighting widespread looting, lawlessness and insecurity, which were causing mass starvation, the United Nations Security Council (UNSC) adopted resolution no. 733 in January 1992, which called for ceasefire, urgent humanitarian assistance and imposed arms embargo on Somalia. This led to a UN-facilitated ceasefire agreement between the Mogadishu factions in February and March 1992. The ceasefire was the first important action by the UN and provided political dialogue and a breathing space for Mogadishu's residents who had been subjected to indiscriminate shelling since 1991.

However, the UN failed to seize the new momentum as it hesitated about what to do next. First, there were some diplomatic hiccups, which undermined UN neutrality. Concentrating on Mogadishu factions in a factionalized country had marginalized other factional leaders.[88] For example, assuming Ali Mahdi as president during the UN special envoy's visit, Mr James Jonah in Mogadishu had alienated General Aideed thus complicating the murky situation.

In May 1992, in what was a positive move, the UN secretary general, Boutros Boutros Ghali appointed Mohamed Sahnoun, a competent UN official as his special representative to lead and coordinate the United Nations Operation in Somalia (UNOSOM-I), which was established by resolution no. 751 adopted in April 1992. The aim of the mission was to monitor the ceasefire and support humanitarian assistance with the deployment of fifty unarmed UN officials as peace monitors followed by 500 security forces to protect food convoys.[89]

Politically, Sahnoun was a man who believed earlier preventative and mediation work by the international community in the 1980s could have prevented much of the Somali tragedy.[90] Nonetheless, the task ahead was gigantic and was not going to be easier because of some logistical and UN bureaucratic nightmare. Logistically, there was no well-organized UN structure on the ground for months, hence Sahnoun had to share office and support with other aid organizations, as he sometimes had to beg UN headquarters for support, but nothing was coming through.[91]

The negative impact of UN bureaucracy on relief and reconciliation efforts disgusted the diplomat. For example, while the ICRC could deliver 53,900 metric tons of food between February and June 1992 and operated 400 soup kitchens, feeding 600,000 people in Mogadishu, the World Food Programme (WFP) could only deliver 18,857 metric tons of its 68,388 food supplies.[92] As bureaucracy went mad, a Russian plane marked with the UN logo transported arms and money to Ali Mahdi just when Sahnoun was establishing and gaining the trust and confidence of General Aideed and his rival hence undermining UN neutrality, and creating unnecessary tension.[93] Sahnoun was determined to fight the UN red tape, though it would cost him his job.

When he took up the office, 300,000 people had already starved to death; 500,000 were in refugee camps and 3,000 mainly children and women were dying daily, and 70 per cent of the country's livestock was lost and farmlands destroyed.[94] Within a short period, thanks to his diplomatic skills, incidents of robbery of food convoys decreased, as starvation went down from 1,700 to 300 a day.[95] Through his successful fundraising appeals, the international community increased funds for humanitarian assistance. More importantly, he brokered a ceasefire between the factions, and even convinced Ali Mahdi to relinquish his presidential claims, an important political step given the hostility between the factions.[96] He even made General Aideed, the most powerful warlord, who opposed deployment of UN peacekeepers, accept the deployment of 500 Pakistani troops to protect humanitarian aid deliveries. Thanks again to his political manoeuvres SNM and SSDF were agreeable to the deployment of UN troops in their regions. Also, SNM in the breakaway region did not rule out discussions on future settlement regarding the region.

However, Sahnoun was criticized for concentrating mainly on General Aideed, the more belligerent warlord who was an obstacle to international community's work, and was refusing the deployment of UN security forces to protect food aid convoys while people were starving to death in areas under his control.[97] With the power of the hindsight and taking into account General Aideed's later behaviour, Sahnoun should have opposed him at this early stage as preferred by the UN secretary general, Boutros Boutros Ghali.

Unfortunately, the much-loved Sahnoun who won the respect of Somalis and the international community resigned in October 1992 after political fallout with his boss, Boutros Boutros Ghali who was unhappy with Sahnoun's criticism of UN bureaucracy.[98] The secretary general wanted to deploy more troops to protect the humanitarian operation, which was opposed by General Aideed, while the diplomat felt he could achieve that through negotiations. Also, there was jealousy within UN secretariat of Sahnoun's success on the ground.[99]

By November 1992, the secretary general appointed new special representative, Ismat Kittani to replace Sahnoun. This man was very much not like Sahnoun. He was an ageing man with poor health, a man described as incompetent, pompous with few diplomatic skills, who lacked intellectual curiosity with no vision or sincerity.[100] Politically, Ismat Kittani, an Iraqi Kurd, agreed with his boss's doctrine of making the UN a peace-enforcer organization in the post-Cold War era so that the international community could intervene in any country regardless of national sovereignty when abuses of human rights and genocide required.[101] In other words, he believed in stick rather than in carrot politics, which was opposite of Sahnoun. He thought that by using force they could just destroy warlords and their militiamen who had been obstacle to humanitarian efforts.

Mr Kittani's diplomatic skills were put to the test. He had fallen out with General Aideed's faction over the deployment of UN troops at the Mogadishu airport. General Aideed's faction, already unhappy with the announcement by the secretary general of the deployment of further 3,000 UN troops, as authorized by resolution no. 775, shelled Mogadishu airport when 500 Pakistani UN troops seized the airport in collaboration with Hawaadle faction, another neutral Hawiye sub-clan, which was controlling the airport. General Aideed's faction interpreted seizure of the airport and the announcement of the deployment of more troops as UN imposing trusteeship on Somalia, in which Kittani would be its governor.[102] In a meeting with General Aideed, Kittani failed to resolve the airport issue. Hence by this diplomatic failure, he had undone Sahnoun's good diplomatic work in trying to persuade the general to accept more troops. The reality of the situation was that UN leadership was determined to follow a forceful policy to destroy those who were obstacles to its humanitarian work.[103]

Kittani's disastrous meeting with Abdirahman Tuur, leader and president of the breakaway region (Somaliland) over proposal to deploy Egyptian troops in the region, was another example of his poor diplomatic skills. Kittani threatened to cancel food aid to the region unless Tuur signed the proposal even though the Somali leader needed more time to discuss this with his government.[104] Furthermore, Kittani's refusal to meet with General Mohamed Abshir, leader of the SSDF, was clear evidence of his disrespect of Somali leaders,[105] the very people he was supposed to help. Certainly, by threatening to cancel food aid at the height of starvation was the last thing needed in a broken country like Somalia.

Therefore, the sacking of a competent diplomat only to be replaced with an inefficient envoy was another UN blunder.[106] This action made much of Sahnoun's good work, including his painstaking efforts to repair UN reputation in Somalia, worthless and made any political solutions temporarily impossible during this critical time.[107] According to Maio (2009) apart from Sahnoun, the UN mission would lack the guidance of a trusted, high ranking and skilled negotiator throughout its operation in Somalia.[108]

With the power of hindsight, had the UN supported Sahnoun's efforts much of the following UN debacle could have been avoided, and many human lives could have been saved. Unfortunately, UN leadership did not allow Sahnoun to get involved deeply in Somali culture and politics to enable Somalis resolve their conflict. Instead the leadership perceived US military power as the easier option or as Stevenson (1995) explained: 'the United Nations was both too grandiose and too callow to let Sahnoun get deeply involved into Somali politics and culture. It was easier to arm the United States with a Security Council resolution and let it pave a highway for the United Nations, as it had done in the Persian Gulf.'[109] In other words, use American fire power to destroy warlords, as the US forces had done to Saddam when they ejected him from Kuwait.

Once he had his man, Kittani, on the ground, the secretary general took up the Somali case with the UN Security Council, which seemed uninterested in the country at a time when the world was more concerned about genocides in former Yugoslavia and the reunification of the two Germans. He had already made critical speech to the Council on 22 July 1992 in which he angrily warned of double standard in world politics, stating that while the world was fighting a rich man's war in Yugoslavia, it was not lifting a finger to save Somalia from self-destruction and disintegration.[110]

On 3 December 1992, the Security Council adopted resolution no. 794, authorizing member states to intervene in Somalia countrywide and use any necessary means to safeguard passage of humanitarian assistance to the starving population. Under what became known as the United Nations Task Force (UNITAF), the United States offered to lead a multinational force of 37,000 strong of which 28,000 were Americans and 9,000 from twenty countries to be deployed to secure safe passage for the delivery of food aid, and to pave the way for normal peacekeeping forces. This mission was for a six-month period, and the Security Council authorized the use of force under Chapter VII of the UN charter, which was established to deter aggression against other states. Authorization of military action under the chapter was used few times before Somalia, as it was also the first time in history that the UN authorized member states to use force not under UN command, for humanitarian reasons and in internal conflicts.[111]

Once again, the Republic found itself as an experimental ground for the world leaders' vision for a new post-Cold War order and its untested waters, where the UN and other troops would be used as peace-enforcers and nation builders.

From the beginning, there was tension among US and UN policy makers over the mission, which would impact on the operation, making Somalia torn apart by US-appointed political leaders and UN ambassadors with conflicting interests.[112] UN leadership envisaged a more comprehensive nation-building mission, including disarmament, institution building and reconciliation using foreign military power.[113] However, because of the Vietnam syndrome, US leadership saw the mission as a limited military and humanitarian intervention meant to crash looters, warlords and their militia, and open roads for food convoys.[114] In addition, President Bush (senior) did not have much time left in office to prepare for an overall plan for Somalia, as he did not want to leave foreign engagement mission to the next administration to worry about.[115] President Bush's speech on 4 December 1992, outlining his troops' mission, said it all:

Once we have created that secure environment, we will withdraw our troops, handing the security mission back to a regular UN peacekeeping force. Our mission has a limited objective: To open the supply routes, to get the food moving, and to prepare the way for a UN peacekeeping force to keep it moving. This operation is not open-ended. We will not stay one day longer than is absolutely necessary.[116]

Fresh from victory in the first Gulf war in which his troops had repelled Saddam Hussein's forces from Kuwait, President Bush declared the beginning of the UNITAF mission popularly known as 'Operation Restore Hope' to end what was world's largest famine at the time. He announced marines would be deployed in Somalia doing 'God's work' in a mission they 'cannot fail'.[117] Robert Oakley, former US ambassador to Somalia, would lead the mission in conjunction with the UN special representative, Kittani, and Lieutenant General Robert Johnston of the United States as commander of the force as Americans had the largest troops.

On 9 December 1992, heavily armed US marines arrived in Mogadishu, giving the impression of being soldiers sent in to fight third world war rather than as aid workers or 'salvation army troops' supposed to save starving children and women. They kicked in doors as though gunmen and looters were lurking everywhere.[118]

At this initial stage, most Somalis welcomed the mission. From December 1992, much of the 37,000 troops and their convoys were gradually deployed in towns and centres across south-central regions without much resistance thanks to Oakley's diplomatic skills.[119] Furthermore, the two Mogadishu warlords' public handshake and their agreement on ceasefire and disarmament just few days after the start of the mission, made possible by Robert Oakley diplomatic skills, was seen by UN leadership as success story[120] given Hawiye factions' conflict, which was serious obstacle to peace and reconciliation. However, other analysts saw the handshake as a stage-managed 'quick fix' operation by Oakley[121] who needed the cooperation of the two warlords to avoid American casualties.

At this point in time, the two warlords embraced the mission for different reasons, and also as they realized the military intervention was irreversible and had UN backing.[122] For Ali Mahdi, who was always supportive of outside military intervention because he was less armed than General Aideed, perceived international troops would legitimize his presidential claim. For Aideed who had been resisting deployment of peacekeeping forces, welcomed the mission because he had realized that he could not oppose the mission militarily.[123]

Nevertheless, there were some problems with the Oakley's approach. For many Somalis, his approval of the warlords was an error of judgement because it had legitimized the authority of two men who had blood on their hands, who should have been disarmed as most Somalis expected.[124] Meeting Mogadishu warlords only and ignoring other warlords was unhelpful move that exposed UN/US bias in the conflict. While dismissing other warlords, such as General Mohamed Hersi 'Morgan' as war criminals, the ambassador accepted Mogadishu warlords despite atrocities committed by them in Mogadishu.

The US-led forces, under Oakley's leadership, did undertake some initial disarmament, but gradually abandoned it after few high profile disarmament operations in Mogadishu. Unfortunately, the decision to abandon the disarmament was for realpolitik. To Oakley, this was humanitarian mission with limited time-scale, and if he was to avoid US casualties, initial disarmament with the cooperation of warlords was the way to open roads for food convoys.[125] The ambassador knew well how hard it would be to disarm fearless Somalis when he remarked:

> If you think the National Rifle Association has a fixation regarding weapons, it is nothing compared to the Somalis. It is part of their manhood. And they learn how to use them. Like the Chechens, if there is nobody else to fight they fight among themselves. But if there is a foreigner who comes in, everybody is perfectly happy to fight him and fight even harder because he's from the outside.[126]

And he also realized how just to disarm Mogadishu alone, 45,000 troops would be required hence disarming the whole country was impossible.[127] This is how Oakley expressed his anxiety about the disarmament: 'We can't disarm New York or Washington; how could we disarm Mogadishu.'[128] This was to the disappointment of the UN secretary general who wanted UNITAF to stabilize the country and create environment for normal peacekeeping forces.

UN and US leadership's anxiety over disarmament revealed earlier tension of their policy makers over the UNITAF mission, in which UN leadership wanted forceful disarmament of the warlords. They had different interpretation of the terms of the Security Council's mandate, the United States interpreting it just as a humanitarian mission while UN leadership interpreted it as bigger mission with disarmament element included.[129] Indeed, at this early stage, the US leadership avoided getting involved politically in Somalia by not punishing or disarming warlords and factional leaders, such as Colonel Omar Jees and General Mohamed Hersi 'Morgan' who had been fighting over control of Kismayo city and had been committing atrocities there.[130] Somalis were also disappointed by the abandonment of the disarmament as articulated by an observer: 'Overwhelmed by guns, we cried out for the help of a greater force. Without disarmament, the Americans have missed the whole point. Unless they are going to disarm nationwide, they might as well pack their bags and go home.'[131]

Although Ambassador Oakley had succeeded in deploying UNITAF troops smoothly without much trouble and the mass starvation had decreased, however, by not disarming the warlords completely, he surrendered Somalia to the warlords, as the following events will demonstrate, and indeed Mogadishu streets would become again as dangerous as they were before UNITAF intervention.[132] Robert Oakley left Somalia in May 1993, having handed the responsibility of the UNITAF mission, which cost the United States up to US$750 million, to a subsequent larger UN operation, dubbed the United Nations Operation in Somalia (UNOSOM-II).[133]

General Aideed factor and the manhunt debacle

As the UNITAF mission was going to end in May 1993, the UN secretary general took up the Somali issue again with the Security Council in order to extend the UN mission in Somalia from humanitarian to more comprehensive one. The Security Council had already adopted resolution no. 814 in March 1993, which authorized the second phase. This mission was much different from any previous mission because for the first time in history the UN could use force to disarm and enforce peace and build national institutions.[134] Member states could 'occupy' and use military force in another member state not in the state of war, but because of humanitarian reasons regardless of its national sovereignty as allowed under the Chapter VII of the UN's Charter. In other words, this was a nation-building mission. By May 1993, 17,000 out of the envisaged 28,000 troops[135] were deployed in Somalia under the leadership of Admiral Jonathan Howe, as the new UN special representative to Somalia. A Turkish Lieutenant General, Cevik Bir became the mission's military commander, supported by Lt General Montgomery, the commander of the US forces as his deputy.

Now equipped with tougher resolution, UNOSOM-II leadership pursued disarmament and nation-building work vigorously. Once established in Mogadishu, on 5 June 1993 Pakistani troops were sent to inspect some of General Aideed's communication and weapons stores, including Radio Mogadishu, which he was using as propaganda outlet against the mission, accusing the UN of 'imperialist designs' and 'colonization'.[136]

The action was politically motivated and was intended to undermine General Aideed's authority and disrupt his operations. Indeed, the UNOSOM leadership wanted to destroy Aideed[137] who was seen as the main obstacle to the mission and was obstructing UN efforts to establish police and judicial institutions. Admiral Howe and his UNOSOM team saw the inspection as part of their mandate to disarm and had already notified General Aideed of their action.[138] For General Aideed's faction, they rejected the inspection and saw it as declaration of war.[139]

On their return from the inspection, armed militiamen ambushed the Pakistani troops' convoy, and in series of fighting, twenty-four of them were murdered, and other fifty-six soldiers injured for the first time in the UN mission in Somalia.[140] The inspection operation was misjudged, ill-planned and executed, and the Pakistani troops were sent without adequate military equipment to what was war situation.[141] The higher UNOSOM-US leadership knew the operation would lead to war, but failed to pass on sensitive information to the Pakistani contingent. For example, inspecting General Aideed's radio Mogadishu would mean war,[142] hence Pakistanis were sent there without adequate military hardware to allow them to prepare for any eventuality. The Pakistani troops were massacred because they were unprepared for a pre-planned and coordinated enemy action. However, according to Admiral Jonathan Howe and his team, they did not anticipate or expect trouble as they had already informed the general about the inspection visit. To them, the ambush was a well-orchestrated action by General Aideed who wanted to force UNOSOM troops out of Somalia because he saw them as a threat to his power.[143]

The international community saw the massacre outrageous which should not be left unpunished. UNOSOM leadership was in no doubt that General Aideed was responsible for the murder of the Pakistani troops.[144] Aideed denied any involvement in the incident and indicated he would abide by the finding of an independent enquiry, but UNOSOM leadership did not believe him.[145] In later enquiries, one found that the General Aideed's faction was responsible for the massacre, while another concluded that his faction had orchestrated the violence, but was not premeditated.[146]

By this brutal murder of the Pakistani troops, bad blood between UNOSOM leadership and Aideed's faction had been stirred up, and the search for a culprit and revenge for the UN troops' blood were unstoppable.[147] The massacre ended the beginning of peaceful UN mission, as it aborted any hope of implementing some of the state-building, reconciliation agreements that were achieved at UN-sponsored reconciliation conferences held in Addis Ababa in March 1993.

Immediately, the Security Council issued resolution no. 837 on 6 June 1993, authorizing all necessary measures to arrest those responsible for the massacre as this was direct challenge to its authority,[148] and also to disarm the city and to destroy General Aideed's radio station, his propaganda machine.[149] Madeline Albright, the US secretary of state, nicknamed 'Madam War' for her belief in military muscle to achieve political ends, was behind the resolution.[150]

Equipped with the resolution and after discussion with the UN/US leadership in New York, the UNOSOM leader, Admiral Howe, a retired US submarine commander and once adviser to President George Bush, put a bounty of US$25,000 on the General's head as by then the UNOSOM team was convinced that Aideed was very much waging war against UNOSOM as Admiral Howe put it: 'he really was a menace to safety and he really ought to come off the streets, he ought to be detained. He needed to (go) through a legal process.'[151]

About 80,000 'wanted man' posters were air-dropped on Mogadishu. The general was branded a terrorist, thug and wanted man for murder, making him one of America's most wanted 'evil' men, the likes of Colonel Qaddafi, N. Ortega, Saddam Hussein and Slobodan Milosevic.[152] The Clinton administration wanted to destroy General Aideed because he saw him as an obstacle to be removed.[153]

However, General Aideed, who resembled Sayyid Mohamed Abdulle Hassan, the nineteenth-century Somali legendary freedom fighter who took on the British colonial power, in terms of arrogance and stubbornness,[154] would prove them wrong, as he went underground into hiding. And as a mocking gesture and defiance, his faction placed a bounty of US$1 million on Admiral Howe's head.[155] From the beginning, he adopted the right psychological calculation. If killed, he would be a martyr to his supporters because he died defending his country against what he described as neocolonialist and imperialist invaders. If he survived, he would be a third-world strongman who had opposed a superpower determined to impose a new world order.[156]

In the state of war, Admiral Howe and his command and control machinery retreated into a bunker at the UNOSOM's headquarters inside the former US embassy's compound in Mogadishu. This was an 80-acre site, which cost US$160 million to build, a luxurious city within Mogadishu, another city which lacked adequate basic services, such as electricity and water.[157]

From 5 June 1993 to March 1994, Mogadishu became a war zone. The admiral, who was dubbed the 'self-appointed UN Sheriff' of Mogadishu, was hunting down General Aideed who was described as a villain and an outlaw.[158] The two sides fought in a series of military campaigns, ranging from disarmament operations to full-scale daylight airstrikes by the UNOSOM against the other side.

On 12 July 1993, fifty elders of General Aideed's Habargedir clan met in a house, discussing how to bring about peace between the fighting parties. According to their intelligence sources, in a city full of spy networks,[159] the admiral and his team believed the renegade general would attend the meeting. US Cobra helicopter gunships were ordered to attack the house. In what was a seventeen-minute operation, they fired sixteen anti-tank missiles into the house, reducing the building to rubble. They killed more than seventy people, including clan elders.[160] The elusive general, who had been hiding in disguise, did not attend the meeting which was a challenge to his authority and hence escaped from death.

To Admiral Howe and his UNOSOM team, the house was a legitimate military target in which plotters and terrorists, including General Abdi Awale 'Qeybdiid', General Aideed's interior minister, were planning their next attack against UNOSOM troops thus challenging Security Council resolutions.[161] To them, UNOSOM forces had to use force to destroy the headquarters of General Aideed's command and control.

To Somalis/Habargedirs, the event was a public meeting organized by mediators who had already been in contact with UNOSOM leadership in their search for peaceful conclusion of the conflict.[162] To them, the air strike was unprovoked action, which led to cold-blooded murder and turned Operation Restore Hope into a new war, thus destroying any hope of salvaging UNOSOM operation. The following statement by a survivor of the attack sums up the response of many Somalis:

> Americans did this action themselves. They always talked about human rights and democracy, so this really surprised me. I could not believe the US could do that. They (the Americans) lied, you know? They came to Somalia for relief – Operation Restore Hope – but they changed it to another thing, a war which had never been seen before.[163]

To Peterson (2000), a journalist who covered the event, the killing of Habargedir elders was a massacre and revenge for the UN Pakistani troops' blood. Indeed, a US diplomat,

Robert Gosende, confirmed the revenge theory when he said: 'What happens when twenty four militiamen are killed by a rival clan? Of course, they retaliate and take revenge. Not to do so – it's the same for the UN – would be political suicide.'[164]

The operation, dubbed 'bloody Monday', was a disastrous act in which no one should have died had the Americans had the right intelligence information. In his view, Peterson believes the operation ignored guidelines of the Geneva Convention on war, and American soldiers who executed the operation got away with murder. And they would have been found guilty of war crimes had they been tried in an international court of law.[165] Even though General Aideed's faction used civilians, especially women and children as a human shield,[166] the use of force in this occasion was not proportional, and a lower level of force could have been used.[167] Even an internal UNOSOM report questioned the legality of the attack because there was no warning given to the residents of the house prior to the attack[168] and no firing from the building against UN security forces. UNOSOM leadership had even tried to cover up the massacre by preventing journalists from reporting it as a cold-blooded murder. This is how Peterson (2000) described the attack:

> We were steered away from calling the Bloody Monday attack a massacre or a slaughter, but it was difficult not to reach the conclusion that this was murder on a grand scale. It was a war crime, pure and simple. Though witnesses were plenty, the perpetrators made no apologies.[169]

Indeed, while the massacre of the Pakistani troops was fully reported in the chronological events in *The United Nations and Somalia – 1992–1996*, the UN secretary general's book on the UNOSOM operation, the Monday incident, which was a turning point in the UN operation, was only briefly mentioned.[170] One can only speculate why such a critical event was not fully reported in the secretary general book perhaps to hide UN embarrassment and failure.

Black Hawk Down and the end of UNOSOM

The botched operation was a turning point for the UN's mission, and only became part of a list of atrocities committed by Italian, Belgian and Canadian soldiers, which included drowning men, women and children into the river, torturing men to death and roasting a boy over flaming brazier.[171] Another massacre was on 9 September 1993 when a US Cobra helicopter fired missiles and killed 100 people, mainly women and children who were watching gunmen who had ambushed UNOSOM engineers cleaning barricades in Mogadishu. Bodies of the murdered women and children were left scattered on streets. The Americans tried to cover up by claiming that the women and children were combatants.[172] Nevertheless, in fairness and according to Admiral Howe it was always difficult to avoid civilian casualties when insurgents and snipers fired mortars and other weapons at UNOSOM forces from civilian populated areas.[173]

From then on, many Somalis turned against the unpopular UNOSOM mission, which was already spending 90 per cent of its budget on military and not on relief operations.[174] Shortly afterwards, immense anger towards the UNOSOM forces particularly the Americans was displayed on streets of Mogadishu. On 25 September 1993, Somali militiamen shot down an American black hawk helicopter, killing three American soldiers. A dancing crowd of Somalis decapitated the body of one soldier, stuffed in a food pack with the label 'Gift from the US' to be sold.[175] This provoked some more brutal and heavy-handed military strikes by the Americans.

By October 1993, the blood feud reached its climax when US forces, using helicopter gunships, launched a series of military campaigns to destroy General Aideed's command and control centres. One of these military strikes was on 3 October 1993 when the Americans raided Olympic Hotel in Mogadishu to detain Aideed and his top aides. While detaining their targets, heavy firefight broke out and the general's militiamen shot down two more US helicopters, killing eighteen Americans and one UN-Malaysian soldier and injuring seventy-five others. Also, an American soldier by the name of Michael Durant was captured by the Somalis, while an angry mob dragged the dead American soldier's body in the streets. On the Somali side, the death toll was estimated between 300 and 1,000 people.[176] Peterson (2000), who covered the fighting, captured the Somali anger and ferocity of the battle:

> Of the 18 who died during America's most significant fire fight loss since the Vietnam War, there were still five unaccounted for, their desecrated bodies paraded through the streets by jubilant Somalis. . . . But some strips of flesh would remain here and there, with scraps of uniforms and dog tags, all coveted by the gunmen as trophies or held to remind them that the revenge target must always be American.[177]

Pictures of the mutilated American soldiers' bodies were instantaneously broadcasted by satellite onto TV screens across the world. By now it was clear who was winning the conflict, which had been turned into a manhunt project by the belligerence and stubbornness of the general and UNOSOM/US leadership's policy and diplomatic failure with its determination to destroy him by force. The scruffy militia of the man they had demonized as a terrorist had shown their fighting spirit. They shot down American helicopters to dancing jubilant crowds. General Aideed's gunmen paraded the mutilated American soldiers' bodies as trophies and as expression of their anger for the massacre of their clan elders. It is tempting to equate the Mogadishu battles to those of the legendary Somali hero Sayyid Mohamed Abdille Hassan when his forces had presented him with the severed parts of the British commander Corfield, killed in the battle of Dul Madoobe, former British Somaliland, in 1913, similar to what general's militiamen were doing.

From here on, American soldiers' morale was low and their attitude cynical and vindictive. According to Peterson (2000), they were not agents of a humanitarian mission anymore, but saw the conflict through a three-dimensional video game in which their guns were joysticks targeted at Somalis, and would shoot at anything that moved.[178] Shortly afterwards, American soldiers expressed their anger when they massacred fourteen Somalis, including children who were later found in possession of pistol toys.[179] The UN leadership was unhappy with the United States' military operation which was unilateral outside the UNOSOM's operation structure, which could undermine the mission's integrity.[180]

During the conflict, Mogadishu became a lawless place again full of fear where General Aideed's Habargedir clansmen were threatening to storm and ransack the fortified UNOSOM headquarters with 17,000 Habargedir militiamen.[181] The UNOSOM forces supposed to restore law and order in the city found themselves in a sea of hostility and barricaded themselves in the UNOSOM's compound. Even the fortified compound was not safe as soldiers died of explosions, probably planted by Habargedir men working for UNOSOM. Indeed, the office of Admiral Howe was sprayed with shrapnel several times, and he was so anxious that he had his hair cut in a bunker and had to keep a plastic bottle to urinate in at night.[182]

The public humiliation of the American soldiers on TV screens shocked and angered the American public, as the *New York Times* explained: 'Americans were told that their soldiers were being sent to work in a soup kitchen and they were understandably shocked to find them in house-to-house combat.'[183] Even President Clinton himself was surprised by the operation, and in newly released documents he admitted that he was not aware of the operation. He blamed military commanders in the field for the operation which happened while diplomatic progress was being made.[184]

The American casualties were a turning point for the Americans and for the whole UNOSOM mission. By now the Clinton administration's strategy was to persuade the Congress to give him few months to round up the mission and get out of Somalia to avoid the general impression that the downing of the American helicopters had forced his administration to 'cut and run'.[185] In a televised speech, President Bill Clinton was forced to announce the withdrawal of the American forces by early 1994. On the political front, having realized the manhunt project had failed, he dispatched Ambassador Robert Oakley back to Mogadishu to help release the American hostage, and to find a political solution to the conflict.

The Clinton administration's policy was by now on 'cut and run' basis just when the going got tougher, and when UN leadership hoped Americans would stay put to accomplish the peace-enforcement and nation-building project as authorized by the Security Council.[186] The administration's defeatists and 'cut and run' policy was obvious from President Clinton's speech when he said: 'It is not our job to rebuild Somalia, or even create a political process that can allow Somalia's clans to live and work in peace; the Somalis must do that for themselves.'[187]

Unfortunately, although his administration had been bragging about using US military muscle to support the UN as a peace-enforcer organization, using Somalia as an example, the small US casualties were enough to convince Clinton administration to abandon Somalia, and to disregard the rhetoric policy of state-building, which was outlined by M. Albright, secretary of state when she said: 'Feeding starving people to establishing security in the region . . . we will embark on an unprecedented enterprise aimed at nothing less than restoration of an entire country as a proud, functioning and viable member of the community of nations. . . . We will vigorously support it.'[188]

The fighting in Mogadishu disrupted much of UNOSOM's political and reconciliation efforts, and although some achievements in humanitarian and relief work were made,[189] the whole mission really degenerated into one manhunt project confined in Mogadishu at that moment in time.

On 17 November 1993, the Security Council suspended the arrest warrant of General Aideed by resolution no. 886. This was for realpolitik, which reflected Clinton administration's unilateral decision to withdraw its forces from Somalia. Immediately, Ambassador Robert Oakley, the man who should have tamed and disarmed Mogadishu warlords under the previous UNITAF mission, was in Mogadishu. He had not only to meet General Aideed, but had to admit that the manhunt, which had hijacked the UNOSOM's nation-building project, was a mistake.[190] In fact, President Clinton admitted the manhunt project or the vendetta, which his administration was behind 'never should have been allowed to supplant the political process'.[191]

Incredibly as it may sound, after few months in hiding during which he had edited his biography, the Lion of Africa,[192] General Aideed came out having shown that one of the largest military interventions had failed to capture him or destroy his command and control structure. The belligerent warlord dubbed the 'perfect beast or heartless warlord'[193] who had been real obstacle to the UNOSOM, which could have saved Somalia, was now declared as an important 'clan leader' instrumental to any political solution; his status raised to a folk-hero status and a third world underdog fighting a superpower.[194]

Although the United States-led UNOSOM mission embodied in Admiral Howe had the fire power, it lost the war because the arrest warrant and manhunt had to be called off.[195] General Aideed was the man who could claim victory as Lewis (2002b) explained: 'Aideed had had, as the saying goes, a good war: the same could not be said for Admiral Howe, who was evidently quite on an American ship at sea in Somalia.'[196]

To make the mission look worth the effort, Robert Oakley persuaded General Aideed to attend a UN-sponsored political reconciliation conference in December 1993 in Addis Ababa, which failed to produce any real political settlement.[197] Incredibly, the Americans had to airlift Aideed in one of the American helicopters which was used to hunt him down after he had refused to go on a UN plane to attend the meeting.[198] The airlifting of Aideed by an American aircraft accompanied by Robert Oakley created political debate and disquiet among the American public and the Congress, although President Clinton supported Robert Oakley's decision, explaining it as facilitating the proposed conference in Addis Ababa.[199]

In Washington, as a face-saving exercise, Clinton administration was busy spinning the events that had led to America's biggest military disaster since Vietnam, which destroyed the euphoria and optimism created by the first Gulf war victory. The administration blamed Iran, Sudan and Libya as behind Aideed's war machinery.[200] Ironically, the administration even blamed the UN for dragging the United States into the conflict, suggesting that the UN had created the green line that divided Mogadishu, even though the UN had limited control over the UNOSOM mission, led and dominated by the Americans.[201]

Finally, after fifteen months, the Americans, having dominated UNOSOM, withdrew from Somalia on 3 March 1994; other European countries left around that time. The biggest superpower left in a hurry but quietly to avoid more casualties, as a Somali observer remarked: 'It looks like the Americans are slipping out quietly.

It's a strange way for a superpower to act.'[202] As Peterson (2000) put it: 'Despite its altruistic hype of the New World Order, Washington had decided to turn the lights out on Somalia because, and who wanted to stay alone in that dark room?'[203] Indeed, despite its altruistic and ambitious mission, history will remember UNOSOM as one Mogadishu-based manhunt project with disastrous outcome.

After withdrawal of the Americans, the remaining UNOSOM forces mainly from third world countries were left with the impossible task of peacekeeping after the UN had downgraded the mission from peace-enforcement to peacekeeping as per resolution no. 897 on 4 February 1994. This was in a country where insecurity and lawlessness in some regions remained the same as pre-UNOSOM intervention. They left Somalia quietly in March 1995 evacuated by American marines under the 'Operation Quick Withdraw'.

However, their departure was not easy. The UNOSOM mission had to pay millions of dollars to Somalis as 'salaries' or for 'services' in what was really not more than extortion money paid to secure safe departure of the remaining UNOSOM forces.[204] Put it differently, the payment was similar to the extortion money paid by passengers and aid workers to armed militia when departing or embarking at Somalia's sea and ports prior to the UNOSOM mission. Had they not bought their way out, there may well have been casualties triggered by angry Somali mobs, militiamen and looters. The withdrawal was so shambolic and troops' morale so low that in the final weeks and days they spent their time shopping at the UNOSOM compound, a place described as a replica of America with its shopping malls, tennis courts, a modern sewage system.[205] Lewis (2002b), explaining the shambolic withdrawal and its aftermath, articulated:

> The final UN exodus, in March 1995, was marked in Mogadishu by extensive looting. The great, unwieldy UN fortress, with its elaborated constructed shopping mall and other comforts for expatriate UN personnel, including a state-of-art sewage system, all built with money from the Somalia aid budget, was besieged by Somali scavengers who swarmed like vultures round the compound gates . . . the very foundation of the US$ 160 million UN headquarters had disappeared. This represented a kind of literal 'dust-to-dust' as the international operations that had proudly heralded the 'new world order' were finally buried in Somalia.[206]

Instead of giving to the Somali people, UNOSOM forces destroyed furniture, vehicles, and other valuable stuff because of mistrust and lack of communication between them; the withdrawal was like a defeated army withdrawing from a chaotic war zone.[207]

The UNOSOM spent substantial portion of its US$1.5 billion budget on military, shopping and construction of the UNOSOM compound, which Somalis nicknamed 'camp of murderers' as it was where military operations were initiated from. However, it spent only US$100 million on humanitarian and development projects,[208] and although huge number of lives had been saved from mass starvation, the real legacy of the UN intervention could be summarized as follows.

At the time of the American troops' withdrawal there were 28 mobile clinics, which treated 5,000 Somalis; 50 dirty tents; 1,000 cots; 600 miles of rehabilitated roads.[209] This was drop in the ocean if compared with the huge loss of life and material destruction caused by the conflict. This included the death of 2,000–13,000 Somalis, two-thirds of them women and children[210] compared to 136 UN peacekeepers.[211] Furthermore, there was no real political reconciliation or nation-building except the very few failed political reconciliation attempts. Indeed, after the withdrawal because of power vacuum, factional leaders immediately resorted to violence, as each one of them wanted to get the upper hand post-UNOSOM era. The ruthless warmonger General Aideed led his forces, invading and conquering other clan territories, destroying what was left of Somalia. Mogadishu and other regions became war zones as a new type of warlords, including Muuse Sudi Yalahow, Osman Ato, and Mohamed Qanyare Afrah, had emerged and fought over power.

By cutting and running in 1995, the international community abandoned Somalia just as it did in 1991 when the country was sliding into anarchy like irresponsible parents, abandoning their children when they most need them, or as a Somali professor explained: 'we feel bitter towards the UN because it acted like an irresponsible parent who walks out of the house when his children are turning knives against each other.'[212]

Nevertheless, the UN and the international community, although admitting mission failure, believed they had made some progress in what was an unprecedented and unpredictable mission. For UNOSOM leadership, it was Somali leaders, like General Aideed who had failed to save their country from perpetual violence for obstructing and sabotaging the ambitious UN mission, which was one of the first humanitarian and nation-building of its kind in post-Cold War era with its altruistic motives meant to save their country. Here is Boutros Boutros Ghali, former UN secretary general's verdict on the UNOSOM mission:

> When the United Nations resolved to help bring peace and end the widespread human suffering in Somalia, the Organisation was well aware that it was setting out into unchartered waters . . . . Under such circumstances, the United Nations can take considerable satisfaction in having curbed the rampant violence and saved countless thousands of lives. At the same time, however, it is equally clear that UNOSOM I and its successors did not manage . . . the goal of achieving political reconciliation.[213]

Certainly, failure of the Somali leadership was obvious and abundant ranging from lack of vision, narrow-mindedness, personal greed and parochial interests and the politics of clan and personal vendetta. Dool (1998) explains some of the root causes of the civil war: 'In Somalia, civil war was based on neither on ideology nor theology. The nation was in the process of being seized and terrorized by opportunistic and greedy warlords whose primary motivation was to enrich themselves.'[214]

This was clearly true in the case of General Aideed who had demonstrated by his behaviour all the bad qualities of leadership from stubbornness, belligerence, arrogance, confrontational and heartlessness, a man, according to Dool (1998), is one of the leaders who had destroyed Somalia.[215] Certainly, General Aideed factor is there for everyone to see. Undeniably, he played a crucial role in removing the dictatorship, but showed the same qualities of dictatorship, militarism and authoritarianism. His behaviour demonstrated that he believed he was the de-facto president of Somalia having defeated General Siyad Barre, his enemy number one who had attempted to destroy him many times. With his stubbornness and belligerence and warmongering, he defied anyone who attempted to make him realize his tyranny. He was one of the main obstacles in implementing political agreements reached by Somali factions in reconciliation conferences in Djibouti in 1991 and Addis Ababa in 1993.[216] He failed Somalia for obstructing the UN mission which could have helped Somalia get back on its feet.

However, in fairness to history, to General Aideed and his supporters and those who knew him, he was exceptionally honest, principled, charismatic, devout Muslim and nationalist leader.[217] He was the military man and guerrilla leader who worked very hard to liberate his country from the dictatorship that he finally dismantled. He had a vision to save Somalia from dictatorship, which he detailed in his personal manifesto, NUSDO.[218] However, after defeating General Siyad Barre he was betrayed by his fellow USC-Manifesto faction's unilateral decision to appoint Ali Mahdi as president. To General Aideed, to accept this decision would have meant agreeing to the continuation of dictatorship because the USC-Manifesto faction was created by General Siyad Barre.[219]

With regard to his confrontation with the US-UNOSOM, he maintained he had welcomed the mission believing it was purely for humanitarian reasons, but UN/US leadership changed it to political one hence interfering in his country's internal affairs and this was wrong.[220] To him it was US-UNOSOM leadership that obstructed implementation of the reconciliation and peace agreements reached by Somali leaders in Addis Ababa in May 1993 by attacking the headquarters and radio station of his alliance, the Somali National Alliance (SNA) in June 1993.

In relation to the death of the Pakistani forces, he felt that this was an unfortunate incident, in which US-UNOSOM leadership wrongly accused him of being responsible for it, although there was no concrete evidence to prove this.[221] His supporters felt that General Aideed was unfairly treated and demonized by US-UNOSOM, calling him names, such as 'warlord' while many other factional leaders, such as Ali Mahdi, General Mohamed Hersi Morgan, General Mohamed Aden Gabiyow, Colonel Omar Jees, leaders of the breakaway region 'Somaliland', who even dismembered the country, were pampered, tolerated and protected by US-UNOSOM.[222] Furthermore, in terms of disarming Somali factions, his supporters believed that he was singled out by the US-UNOSOM leadership that wanted to destroy him while other factions were allowed to keep their military arsenal, and this was unfair. This is how Ruhela (1994) explained:

> In a country like Somalia, by tradition everyone keeps some weapon, at least a knife, or a dagger, and now a rifle. Since this is so, how can anyone except that a leader of the stature of Aidid would be able to live for even a single second if he is completely disarmed and no protection to him is possible? . . . how can Aided who has the responsibility of defending his supporters and helpers in Somalia agree to become a monk?[223]

With regard to the arrest warrant against him, to General Aideed and his sympathizers, US-UNOSOM led by Admiral Howe were all foreign powers who had no right under the UN Charter and international diplomacy to detain a national hero like General Aideed, a man they described as someone 'with a blameless moral character and exemplary nationalism, who has devoted all his life for the service of the Somali people . . . fighting for the unity, freedom and democracy of the country'[224] His supporters believed God was with their leader who they described as a devout Muslim, and God would help him to rebel the US-UNOSOM aggression and its new form of colonialism and apartheid in Somalia. They also believed, if anything, his life was not in the hands of US-UNOSOM, but with the Almighty God who had saved him on other occasions.[225]

Critique of the UNOSOM mission

In conclusion, although UNOSOM mission was ambitious with all good intensions, it had, however, failed Somalis for the following reasons.

From the start, the intervention was too late as by then hundreds of thousands of people, who could have been saved by early intervention in 1991, had starved to death. As Somalia was not a priority in post-Cold War era, dominated by the collapse of the USSR and subsequent Balkan and Gulf wars, it was only after Boutros Boutros Ghali's critical speech at the Security Council on 22 July 1992 that the international community paid attention to the mass starvation in Somalia.

The removal of Sahnoun, UN's envoy to Somalia, at a critical moment in the conflict when he was really making a difference on the ground in terms of political reconciliation only to be replaced by not so competent and less effective envoy was probably the biggest mistake. Had the UN leadership allowed Sahnoun to continue with his good work, the need for larger missions and the subsequent manhunt debacle could have been avoided by his diplomatic skills, and UNOSOM could have been a successful story. Unfortunately, UN leadership did not allow the Algerian diplomat to get too much involved in Somalia because it assumed American military power, backed by UN resolutions, could easily destroy warlords and their militia just like Americans did in the first Gulf war after rebelling Saddam's forces from Kuwait. The ambassador was therefore removed because he was an obstacle to UN leadership's determination to intervene and pacify Somalia by force under the peace-enforcement and nation-building vision that was pursued by the UN leadership. Because of the failure of the UNOSOM mission, that vision seems to have been buried in Somalia. In another word, the UN/US leadership's vision and ambition of a 'new world order' post-Cold War era were buried in Mogadishu after UNOSOM had failed to rebuild a functioning Somali state.

The tension within US/UN policy makers' assumptions and expectations of the mission complicated the situation. For the Americans, from day one the mission was a humanitarian intervention with limited objective and time-scale, while the UN wanted a long-term comprehensive mission of peace-enforcement and nation-building, using American military power under the Security Council authority. That tension became clearer when the United States 'cut and ran' after the going got tougher, failing to pursue complete disarmament, which is what the UN had hoped for. With the power of the hindsight, rather than 'cut and ran' the United States should have stayed longer to finish the job of peace-enforcement and nation-building, particularly during Clinton administration, which had been bragging about the 'new world order' and wanted to use Somalia as an example of peace-enforcement. This is how Prof. Ahmed Samatar, a Somali scholar, describing the UNOSOM debacle, put it:

> For those Somalis who expected UNOSOM to disarm the warring factions, the inordinate focus on General Aideed and subsequent lack of resolve to punish him for his vainglorious and violent ways, together with the announcement of the date of the withdrawal of U.S troops, amounted to defeat. Many were resigning themselves to a return of violent anarchy and starvation.[226]

Emphasis on the militaristic nature of the mission and the deployment of large military force based on wrong analysis and assumptions were a mistake.[227] For example, UN leadership assumed the famine was a countrywide phenomenon that required larger military intervention to destroy warlords and their militiamen who had been obstacle to humanitarian efforts. It was assumed that military power would create security and stability; however, this marginalized much needed political reconciliation and conflict resolution.[228] In reality, the famine was mainly in isolated pockets in south and south-west regions, where farmlands were destroyed by the warring factions. In many regions of the country, there was relative peace and security and no mass starvation.

As the operation went, the militaristic nature of the mission overtook political reconciliation efforts and the attention of the US policy makers was to watch out for American casualties.[229] Both Bush and Clinton administrations did not have an overall diplomatic strategy for the Somali mission.[230] The overwhelming military presence did not result in improved security, and probably because of its militaristic nature UNOSOM-II degenerated into a military operation in which Admiral Howe was its leader, opposed by a belligerent warlord thus leading to the unwise manhunt and vendetta disaster in Mogadishu.

The manhunt debacle was the second biggest political blunder. The whole UNOSOM-II mission was reduced to one big project of controlling Mogadishu while other stable northern regions were neglected or did not get enough attention. Had US-UNOSOM leaders treated General Aideed as one of many obstacles and tried to destroy him through politics and diplomacy rather military power, the mission could have reached its potential as the biggest project of nation-building post-Cold War era. For example, Somalis should have been involved in the decision-making process of the mission just before it had degenerated into manhunt project. Even though Somalis wanted to be part of the decision-making process, they were excluded throughout the conflict. In other words, the mission became top-down level process in which US-UNOSOM leadership dictated terms of engagement. In fact, US-UNOSOM troops and personnel did not interact much with local Somalis who they stereotyped as lazy drug addicts, cowards and disorganized militiamen.[231]

The international community, including regional organizations, such as the African Union, the Islamic Conference Organisation, and the Arab League, which also failed to help Somalis, should have engaged Somalis in more political dialogue and reconciliation work. Comparing the behaviour of the international community in Somalia with other conflicts, such as the Balkans, it is clear that the international community acted differently in each case. The Somali mission was allowed to fail because of lack of long-term and comprehensive political commitment and plan. The death of a few UN and American soldiers was enough to precipitate end of the mission. On the other hand, in the Balkan conflict a long-term political commitment, backed by US/NATO military power, was pursued until the conflict ended. Indeed, the international community stayed in the Balkan even after the end of hostilities. The real point was no country was prepared to politically commit itself to a poor, Black and Muslim country like Somalia with no or little known natural resources. Somalia that lost its geopolitical strategic importance once the Cold War was over.

With the power of the hindsight, given the bloodshed and perpetual violence, which followed after UNOSOM's departure, the UN should have stayed put in Somalia, and after destroying warlords, should have placed the country under UN trusteeship exactly as they did to Kosovo, where UN trusteeship helped people of Kosovo in restoring law and order and their ambition for self-determination. It is however doubtful whether Somalis would have accepted UN trusteeship given their mistrust and dislike of foreign power intervention.

The rise of Somaliland and Puntland

As the humiliated Republic continued to struggle with the long-term effects of the Ogaden debacle and the failure of UNOSOM, it went into an ugly phase of balkanization and disintegration into clan fiefdoms.

The historical narratives in the previous chapter concentrated mainly on the events that shaped the conflict in south-central and south-west regions of the country, starting from the removal of the dictator from power, clan cleansing in Mogadishu, the fallout of Ali Mahdi and General Aideed over power sharing and the mass starvation that led to the UN intervention.

This chapter will analyse actions taken by different Somali stakeholders as a coping mechanism or as an instrument in asserting new socio-political rights, paying particular attention to the rise of new political entities, such as Somaliland and Puntland out of the ashes of the civil war. The chapter will describe how factionalism and virulent clan segmentation within the new entities resulted in inter-communal violence while these entities were being created. It will also analyse different reconciliation initiatives, particularly those sponsored by the international community and why they failed to resolve the Somali conflict compared with other successful locally driven reconciliation initiatives.

Somaliland: The hasty decision to secede

Immediately after the collapse of the central government in 1991, the SNM, which was by now the most powerful organization, took control of the north-west region. By January 1991, its fighters, estimated between 3,000 and 4,000 personnel,[1] seized major cities, such as Burao, Hargeisa and Berbera. Along its way to conquer, SNM launched serious military attacks against non-Isaaq clans, such as Gadabursi, Isse, Ogadens and Harti Daarood clans,[2] which the SNM perceived as sympathizers of the fallen regime. For example, SNM fighters attacked Warsangelis at Hadaftimo, Dhulbahante at Aynabo and the Gadabursi at Dilla town, all contested clan borders and areas. In February 1991, they clashed with the United Somali Front (USF), an Isse clan militia which had attempted to annex the historic city of Zeila to Djibouti.

In what was Isaaq victory over the deposed regime through their 'people's war',[3] SNM's military actions destroyed towns such as Dilla, west of Hargeisa. Its fighters would have even destroyed Borama, Gadabursi's main city, had Colonel Abdirahman

Aw Ali, from Gadabursi clan, not intervened to mediate the conflict.[4] These conflicts were clan revenge in which SNM fighters persecuted non-Isaaq clans, committing atrocities,[5] and forcing thousands of them out of their homes exactly as the military regime had done to Isaaqs in 1988. They also conducted summary trials and executions against former government officials for alleged 'war crimes'.[6] In other instances, SNM did not force its authority over the Sool region inhabited by Dhulbahantes because of mediation efforts by Garaad Abdiqani Garaad Jama, a clan elder from Dhulbahante, who had good relationship with the movement, and because of other traditional mediation methods.[7]

With the power of the hindsight, the clan elder's mediation efforts prevented further clan vendetta and score-settling given the traditional clan rivalry particularly the animosity between clans created by the fallen regime's divisive clan politics. The conflict, which forced about 125,000 people mainly non-Isaaqs out of their homes, seeking refuge in Ethiopia, ended after clan elders of Warsangeli, Dhulbahante and Isaaq had reached ceasefire in Berbera in February 1991.[8]

On the ground, SNM inherited a devastated region with 70–80 per cent of buildings in Hargeisa and Burao destroyed, where mass graves were common, and only a few relief organizations worked. Moreover, 500,000 people, mainly Isaaqs, were still rotting in refugee camps in Ethiopia having fled there in 1988 during the civil war, as their houses in major towns lay in ruin and became ghost places.[9]

Before analysing security and political developments in the region since 1991, let us briefly describe this region of Somalia. The province is composed of 20 per cent of Somalia's landmass, roughly the size of England and Wales, and its topography ranges from semi-arid (*Guban*) plains and (*Ogo*) plateau. It hosts the highest point, the *Shimber Berris* (2,000 metres), which is part of *Gollis* mountain ranges, stretching from Ethiopian highlands to a coastal line of 850 kilometres rich in minerals.[10] Various clans such as Isaaq, Warsangeli, Dhulbahante, Gadabursi, Isse, Tumaals, Midgaans and Yibirs known as Gabooye live in the region.

The region was once British protectorate in the nineteenth century. And after its independence on 26 June 1960, it joined the Italian Somali colony in formal union, which formed the first Somali Republic on 1 July 1960. Before the collapse of the central government in 1991, Hargeisa was the second capital of the Republic, and the region was divided into regional administrations: Nugal, Sanaag, Togdheer, Waqooyi Galbeed and Awdal. The population was estimated at 3 million in 1997,[11] and people are mainly nomads except few living in urban environments.

As events moved on, in May 1991, a conference called the Grand Conference of the Northern Peoples, attended by clan elders from across clan spectrum, was held in Burao in order to consolidate previous reconciliation efforts, and to set up a provisional governance structure. However, SNM fighters and crowds of Isaaqs mainly refugees who returned from Hartisheikh refugee camps in Ethiopia angered by the USC's unilateral decision to nominate Ali Mahdi as president, hijacked the conference and demanded declaration of independence for the region. This is because they heard that SNM leaders were in peace talks with the USC and other factions to form post-Siyad Barre national government.[12] The demand for independence was a surprise to the SNM leaders because at the time they were still in favour of Somali unity with decentralized state structure.[13] Indeed, just a few months before the conference, Ahmed Silanyo, one of SNM's chairmen who became president of Somaliland, drafted a proposal of power sharing with the USC.[14]

Besieged by SNM fighters, on 18 May 1991, SNM leadership reluctantly declared the region as the independent state of Somaliland Republic within the borders of the former British Somaliland protectorate. They based their decision that the region was once a sovereign state and had voluntarily withdrawn from the union with Somalia in 1960, which had failed and led to the atrocities in the region in the 1980s during the military regime.[15,16]

Proceedings and decisions taken at the Burao conference are fiercely contested. Some participants were unsure of whether what was created was an independent state.[17] Non-Isaaq clan delegates felt they were coerced to accept the independence decision in an emotionally charged conference in Isaaq territory hijacked by gun-trotting SNM fighters, intimidating participants.[18] Indeed, some Isaaq and Harti clan leaders retracted from their support of the declaration of independence.[19] However, others while pointing out the emotional circumstances under which the decision was taken, and the confusion surrounding the rights or wrongs of the decision, argue that the unilateral decision reflected the wishes of the overwhelming majority of the people in the north.[20]

Although Burao conference ended hostilities between Isaaq and non-Isaaq clans, and created an administration for two years, the disputed independence decision, however, did complicate the political process, which still haunts the region. Harti Daarood clans (Warsangeli and Dhulbahante) saw the conference as no more than an Isaaq-SNM military wing's secession project, imposing its will on them.[21] Furthermore, any hope of the spirit of Somali unity under SNM was shattered when a government dominated by Isaaqs was formed, and SNM became the governance structure. Indeed, its chairman Abdirahman Tuur became president of the new entity hence, marginalizing other clans in terms of political representation. The appearance of a memo allegedly issued by SNM, visioning strategies to ensure Isaaq dominance of the new entity did make matters worse.[22]

Factors that precipitated the decision to secede included emergence of an Isaaq political community based on shared history of victimhood and oppression because of the atrocities committed by the fallen regime; their feeling of marginalization since the union, and the existence of secessionist wing within SNM. Furthermore, the hasty manner in which Ali Mahdi was installed as president immediately after the dictatorship had been removed was another factor.[23] Indeed, SNM was not secessionist movement, and the secession decision was reaction to the USC's unilateral decision.[24] However, in recent Wikileaks cables indicated SNM had secession ambition. This was revealed by Abdulkadir Mohamed Aden Zope, leader of the Somali Democratic Movement (SDM), a Rahanweyn clan opposition group, who was planning to persuade SNM to attend the Cairo meeting in December 1990 to reconcile the fallen regime and the armed rebels.[25,26]

At that particular moment in the broken Republic's history, the country was on the eve of some huge challenges and changes after the dictatorship had been removed. Regrettably, USC's hasty unilateral decision and SNM's decision to secede destroyed any hope of positive political reforms, such as reconstituting unitary or federal state peacefully. The rights and wrongs, and the legal aspects of SNM's decision, whether it was to reclaim the 'lost sovereignty' or as an 'act of secession' still remains hotly contested issues in Somali politics.[27] However, many Somalis saw SNM's decision as betrayal of its original principles, which were to remove dictatorship, and not to divide the country. This is how Lyons and Samatar (1995) put it: 'The SNM actions contributed to the dissolution of Somalia as a nation state, the destruction of pan-Somalism, and the acceleration of the balkanization of northeast Africa.'[28]

With the power of hindsight, had USC and SNM waited for general consultation and reconciliation with other stakeholders much of the bloodshed in the south and north-west, and subsequent SNM's unilateral decision could have been prevented. These unilateral and hasty decisions were again turning points and missed opportunities in resolving the Somali conflict.

However, events in 1992 in the breakaway region (Somaliland) showed that the new political entity was not immune from political instability and insecurity that were ravaging the broken Republic. Exposing the ugly face of divisive lineage politics, competing Isaaq sub-clans settled their political disagreements over public resources and territory through the barrel of the gun, although one would have thought they would settle their differences peacefully having formed a new political identity based on shared experience of suffering.

From January to March 1992, fighting broke out in Burao and Berbera towns. In Burao, *Habar Jeclo* and *Habar Yonis* clans fought each other when forces loyal to Abdulrahman Tuur (*Habar Yonis*), Somaliland's first president, attempted to seize weapons. In March fighting in Berbera erupted between *Isse Muse* (Berbera being their traditional territory) and *Habar Jeclo* clan on one side against *Sa'ad Muse* and *Habar Yonis* clans when Tuur's government's attempted to place Berbera seaport in the public domain after it had fallen into private hands.[29]

These clashes, as much as they were about Abdirhman Tuur's administration asserting its authority, revealed political tension within Isaaq clans over the breakaway decision, some supporting it, while others objecting it. Real SNM fighters and their supporters, dubbed the *Maano-gaaho*, named after a street in Ethiopia where SNM had its base, supported the decision. But those who did not directly take part in the struggle against the military regime were unsure about it.[30] It also revealed the ugly face of the divisive clan system with its unstable foundations which divides Somalis into ungovernable small units as the anthropologists would argue. Besides that, personal ambition and leadership rivalry among political elites over resources were there for everyone to see.

The fighting in Burao revealed historical political leadership conflict within SNM, which divided the movement into Ahmed Silanyo from *Habar Jeclo* and one of its chairmen and Abdirahman Tuur, a *Habar Yonis*.[31] The conflicts which killed 1,000 people shattered Burao's reconciliation efforts, and threatened the existence of the Somaliland project because non-Isaaq clans and factional leaders in the region looked further down the south for reconciliation and unity with other Somali factions, such as the USC.[32]

The mini-civil war ended after reconciliation initiatives, such as a conference in Sheikh town in 1992. Attended by clan elders from Isaaq, Dhulbahante and Gadabursi, except Warsangelis, the Sheikh conference was a turning point for the reconciliation process. When Isaaqs failed to end their inter-clan conflict, Gadabursi clan elders helped them resolve it.[33] Consequently, the 'Guurti', an Isaaq clan elders' governance body that was created during SNM struggle, was expanded to include non-Isaaq clans in recognition of their reconciliation efforts, hence emergence of a wider system of clan governance. More importantly, the conference reaffirmed status of Berbera seaport as public asset.[34] This was to prevent public assets being misappropriated by factions leading to more bloodshed, as the case was in the south where warlords and clans fought over the control of sea and airports.

The Borama conference

The reconciliation initiatives in the region continued with meetings held at village, district and regional levels, discussing clan relationships, coexistence, safety, security and militia de-mobilization. The Borama conference, from 24 January to May 1993, was one of those defining events in the breakaway region's future political life. Attended by some 2,000 people, it adopted peace charter (*Xeer*), stipulating a framework of peaceful clan coexistence, security and state formation measures.[35] More importantly, it was constitutional conference, which transferred power from the militaristic SNM leadership to a civilian regime. A transitional national charter, which confirmed the sovereignty and independence of the new entity, was produced, and a governance structure approved. A bicameral legislature, composing of a clan elders' assembly or *Guurti* and the people's representative or *Wakillo*, was formulated, while a council of ministers, a central bank and regional governors approved. In this new structure, *Guurti* is the highest authority in the country to oversee the representative and executive bodies. Seats of the two houses were allocated to clans proportionally. However, no seats were allocated to women for cultural sensitivity reasons.

In that conference, majority of clan elders who gathered at Borama elected Mohamed Ibrahim Egal as president of the new entity. Egal was a veteran politician, and once prime minister of the Republic of Somalia. Despite concerns over his failures during his premiership in the 1960s, his relationship with General Siyad Barre, and his attendance of the 1991 reconciliation conferences in Djibouti, he was elected president because he was seen as a neutral and unifying figure that could unite Isaaqs. Moreover, it was hoped that his previous status as an African statesman would attract international recognition for the breakaway region.[36] Colonel Abdirahman Aw Ali, from the Gadabursi clan, was elected vice president, while speaker of the lower house went to the Harti Daarood clans.

Astonishingly, Egal, the same man, once prime minister of the Republic, the man who had participated in 1991 Djibouti reconciliation conferences which rejected SNM's secession decision, was sworn in as president of what most Somalis perceived as a secessionist region. Egal's acceptance of the new role exposed Isaaq elites' shifting loyalty over the new entity triggered by their ambivalent and mixed emotions towards the independence decision.

To some analysts, Borama conference was the foundation of the new entity, and an excellent example of modern Somali politicians working with traditional clan elders on conflict resolution, something that had not worked in the south.[37] To them, this low-cost marathon conference, which lasted for about five months with not much assistance from the international community, deserves recognition as a successful grassroots-based political reconciliation initiative.

However, to the opponents of the independence decision or secession, the conference was not a grassroots reconciliation process, but a fabricated venue to reconcile Isaaq political elites after the civil war fallout so they could divide government positions among themselves.[38] In fact, the conference did not resolve all problems because representatives of the Harti Daarood clans felt badly treated over power-sharing after the Gadabursi clan had taken the position of vice president. Furthermore, some politicians from other Isaaq sub-clans, such as Habar Yonis and Idagale, were unhappy with their share of parliamentary seats.[39] With the benefit of hindsight, given the prevailing clan animosity and general lawlessness in the country's post-Siyad Barre era, the conference deserves good record in Somalia's political history books for resolving what was irreconcilable political impasse in which not only clans in the region were deeply divided but even Isaaqs themselves were at each other's throats.

After forming a government, the Egal regime embarked on disarmament programmes, dismantling roadblocks, demobilizing SNM fighters and cracking down on bandits, which were obstacles to previous Abdirahman Tuur's administration and contributed to his downfall. In what was series of disarmament efforts at different social levels, by 1994, 5,000 militiamen were demobilized at a ceremony in the Hargeisa stadium.[40] Although these disarmament activities did not cover Harti Daarood clans' regions of Sool and Sanaag where there were thousands of armed militia, these efforts were success stories given the limited resources and lack of external assistance, particularly from the UNOSOM, which failed to assist the breakaway region.

Major civil war in the north

Regrettably, just when the situation was improving, another wave of sectarian violence over control of resources and territory erupted again in 1994 just after 18 months of the Egal presidency. Militiamen loyal to Idagale and Habar Yonis clans and forces loyal to the Egal regime fought in Hargeisa, the capital city, after the regime had attempted to seize Hargeisa airport, which was in Idagale's traditional territory. This angered Idagale who had been making money from the facility by imposing fees on other clans, such as Habar Awal who supported Egal.

At lineage mentality level, the opposing clans, such as Habar Yonis who had grievance over the distribution of parliamentary seats at the Borama conference, felt that the government was dominated by President Egal's Habar Awal clan.[41] The conflict spread to Burao, and the historical town of Zeila when the regime attempted to extend its authority, dismantling roadblocks, seizing Zeila port. This resulted in regime forces clashing with non-Isaaq militiamen from the Isse and Gadabursi supported by Djibouti. Moreover, the opposing clans were unhappy with the regime's fiscal policy (devaluation and evaluation of a new Somaliland shilling), which they perceived as means of enriching the regime and its supporters thus giving the conflict an economic dimension.[42] Actually, at the time the new Somaliland shilling was not accepted in Burao, a stronghold for the clans that opposed the regime. The old Somali shilling was still in circulation there.

The conflict had another political dimension over the decision to break away from the rest of Somalia because the opposing forces, including former president Abdirahman Tuur, from Habar Yonis and General Jama Mohamed Ghalib, from Idagale, opposed the breakaway decision. Having lost his presidential ambitions to Egal, Tuur was now against the secession project, and had been in contact with USC leaders, reiterating his support for Somali unity. On the opposite side, Egal the same former prime minister of the Republic was now defending the new entity. Certainly, the pro-independence camp portrayed the conflict as one between supporters of the independence 'Somaliland nationalists' and the 'unionist/federalist' who favoured union with the south.[43] This again revealed Isaaq elites' personal ambition and their political bickering.

More importantly, other 'external' factors influenced the violence, especially the conflict in the south. Having 'won' his war with UNOSOM, General Aideed was now the most powerful man in the south, his militiamen invading and conquering other clans' lands. He formed a government, offering the position of vice president to Abdirahman Tuur to fulfil a power-sharing agreement between SNM and his USC-Mustahil faction in the late 1980s. The new development in the south, particularly General Aideed's 'victory' over UNOSOM, strengthened unionists/federalists' position in which case Egal administration used this to undermine and weaken unionists' position in the breakaway region.[44]

The human cost of the civil war, the worst of its kind since 1988, was high. It claimed 4,000 lives in Burao alone, forcing 180,000 people to flee to Ethiopia.[45] Regrettably, Egal government, supposedly elected by the people of the north through their clan elders, waged war against his own people, and bombarded towns and cities to dislodge what it perceived as rebels. One cannot help but to compare this action with the deposed dictator's actions in the region. General Siyad Barre, although accused of dictatorship and tribalism, was, nonetheless, a leader elected by his people. Indeed, despite being a one-party state and accusation of vote rigging, the 1986 national election, 99.9 per cent of the electorate had voted for him.[46] In fairness, General Siyad Barre's position would have been more legitimate than President Egal's position because Somali citizens had formally and directly elected President Siyad while Egal was only selected by clan elders allegedly representing clans.

Despite different scales of violence and casualties, if the deposed regime was accused of killing thousands of Isaaqs so was President Egal's regime, an indigenous Isaaq government, which killed thousands of people too, and bombarded rebel positions in towns just like the military regime had done.[47] Although, the deposed General Siyad Barre's regime was accused of genocide against one particular people, the regime was a legitimate government recognized by the international community, and was at war with what it had perceived as secessionist and subversive groups that were threatening the sovereignty and territorial integrity of the Republic. The regime acted as many governments in similar situations would have acted.[48] Certainly, in political history there were many examples of governments, no matter how democratic, autocratic, dictatorship, weak or strong, which used extreme violence when faced with insurgents, secessionists and rebels, although that does not justify it.

No one can deny the vital role that Isaaqs played in Somali unity as they were among the first people who joined the union after the British colony in the north became independent. However, in fairness to history, although it was precipitated by Isaaqs' feeling of victimhood and their grievance and the hasty decision to nominate Ali Mahdi as president, SNM decision to secede seems to have vindicated the late president Siyad's perception of the 1980s' SNM as a secessionist group adamant to dismantle the Republic. Had he been alive today, General Siyad Barre would have been the first among millions of Somalis who would say: 'I told you so, Isaaqs wanted secession.'

Hargeisa conference heralds new dawn

During the civil strife, Egal government and the Guurti were divided among themselves and failed to end the war.[49] This showed the fragility and inability of the new entity's higher institutions to act in civil war situations whereby ultimate authority was contested. Indeed, the war raged for about two years once again threatening the very foundation of Somaliland. It only ended in 1996 after various reconciliation efforts by Isaaq diaspora communities from the region. These peace initiatives reached their climax in October 1996 when a large delegation, including some 300 delegates attended national conference in Hargeisa. After adopting an interim national constitution, Egal was re-elected president for further five years, aided by Colonel Dahir Riyaale Kaahin, from the Gadabursi clan, as his vice president. The conference resolved Isaaq conflicts, by allocating more parliamentary seats to disgruntled sub-clans, as it also helped to integrate Gadabursi and Isse sub-clans of the Dir clan family in the Somaliland project.

In this new power-sharing arrangement, Gadabursis again secured the position of vice president. This, however, alienated Harti Daarood clans which felt marginalized for the second time when the position of vice president went to Gadabursi. Indeed, Garaad Abdiqani Garaad Jama, an important Dhulbahante clan elder, withdrew his support from the Somaliland project over his disagreement with Egal on power sharing after President Egal rejected Garaad's list of government minister portfolio.[50] This was confirmed by Suldaan Maxamed Cabdulqaadir, a senior Isaaq clan elder. He mentioned that Egal rejected Garaad Abdiqani's list of government for the Dhulbahante, and that their political disagreement even reached to the point where Egal asked Garaad Abdiqani to mark Dhulbahante territory in Somaliland and he would surrender it to him.[51]

From Hargeisa congress, the breakaway region enjoyed relative peace and stability compared to the turmoil in the south. For the first time since the fall of the military regime, national constitution was accepted on national referendum on 31 May 2001, which also included accepting the declaration of independence. However, the referendum was boycotted in Harti Daarood clans' regions which constitute 40 per cent of Somaliland's territory.[52] The referendum, marred by irregularities, was also rejected in some parts of the Awdal region of the Gadabursi clan.[53] This revealed that all clans in the former British colony did not whole-heartedly support the 'secession initiative' or the restoration of the 'lost sovereignty' as pro and anti-secessionist groups would describe the situation. In addition, the Transitional National Government (TNG) in Mogadishu, which was formed through other reconciliation efforts in Djibouti to represent the whole country, condemned the referendum as illegal.

If anything, the 2001 referendum remains as a base for the Isaaq clans' majority decision for independence[54] and their attempt to incorporate other clans into the new political body. After establishing a multi-party system in which political parties contested, the entity held three general elections and elected three presidents, Dahir Rayaale Kaahin, from Gadabursi, Ahmed M/ Silanyo, former chairman of SNM and Musa Biixi, both are Isaaqs.

Nonetheless, opponents of the secession saw these elections as no more than an Isaaq project determined to impose its will on other clans.[55] Some observers described Somaliland's democratic claims as 'pseudo-democracy' dominated by Isaaq clans.[56] And although there is peace and stability in the region, there were/are underlying communal tension within Isaaq clans and Isaaq versus non-Isaaq clans.[57] It has also been desperately seeking international recognition, but so far no country has offered recognition. Indeed, the international community recognizes Somaliland as part and parcel of the Federal Republic of Somalia.

Final remarks

In conclusion, although it had its share of violence and sufferings, at the height of the civil war the breakaway region was relatively safer and secure than the south and did not disintegrate into fighting fiefdoms for the following reasons.

Having won the war against the deposed regime, the SNM, unlike the numerous factions in the south, was the most powerful political organization which quickly asserted its authority over the region. Its decision to seek peace with non-Isaaq clans from position of strength may have saved the region from total anarchy and lawlessness.[58] This is important if compared to the mayhem caused by the USC and other factions attempting to conquer other clans' lands by force. Isaaq as the dominant clan was another factor that might have helped reduce tensions and violence in contrast to the south where three major clan families, Hawiye, Daarood and Rahanweyn with their multiple sub-clans, fought over resources and power.

However, it must be stated that at the height of the civil war non-Isaaq clans, such as Harti and Gadabursi clan militias resisted SNM adventure into their traditional territories, and some serious conflicts and bloodshed were prevented through traditional mediation initiatives: customary laws (*Xeer*) at different social levels. For example, Burao, Sheikh and Borama conferences, and some initiatives instigated by individual leaders, such as Garaad Abdiqani Garaad Jama of Dhulbahante and Colonel Abdirahman Aw Ali prevented SNM fighters from destroying Borama and the Sool region. These reconciliation efforts were locally driven initiatives with emphasis on a bottom-up approach unlike other foreign power led reconciliation initiatives in the south with their top-down approach, which led to one faction dominating the political process in the south,[59] as will be described in this chapter later.

Despite some serious conflicts over control of public assets, poor economic resources in the region reduced the role for warmongers to wage economic wars, as the case was in the south where war-profiteers fought over huge economic resources from farmlands to sea and port facilities.[60] Certainly, the huge international aid worth hundreds of millions of dollars, which encouraged war economy and looting in the south, was absent from the north, hence less temptation for clan militiamen to fight on for resources.

Although a big share of the aid money should have been allocated to facilitate reconciliation and institution building efforts in the breakaway region, with the power of hindsight, the lack of avalanche of foreign aid was a blessing in disguise because it lessened the prospect for war economy: looting.

The role of Isaaq business community and diaspora in providing funds for demobilization and disarmament and other advice was another crucial factor. For example, diaspora community helped to end the 1994 conflict after the Egal regime had failed to do so. Also, the role of regional powers, such as Ethiopia, had helped pressurize feuding Isaaq clans to reconcile rather than fight.[61]

The secession decision might have helped northern regions to protect themselves from the perpetual violence in the south. Perhaps it was the best way to cope with the sweeping civil war that reduced the proud Republic to no more than fighting clan fiefdoms. Nevertheless, the breakaway region is far away from being harmonious political entity and is far from securing international recognition.

Harti Darood clans in Sool, Sanaag and Ceyn regions rejected the raison d'etre and legality of Somaliland.[62] And despite divisions within Harti leadership over the Somaliland project, they created various resistance movements and states, such as Maakhir and Khatumo states to defend Harti regions. Since 2011, clan conflict between Isaaq and Dhulbahante militiamen has been raging in the Harti regions.

Leaders of Puntland, an autonomous state in the north-east regions of Somalia, which supports the Harti clans, and Somaliland had been exchanging strong words, accusing each other of massacre of civilians.[63] At one point, leaders of Somaliland were accused of using white South African 'mercenaries' to eradicate anti-secessionist natives of the SSC regions.[64] This sounds similar to the allegation that the deposed military regime used white South African mercenaries during the 1980s civil war in the north. The conflict between Somaliland and Puntland over the Harti regions is still ongoing.[65]

Furthermore, although the Gadabursi clan accepted Somaliland, creation of resistance movements, such as an Awdal state in the Awdal region, indicated that some sections of the Gadabursi clan are unhappy with the Somaliland project, particularly the lack of fair political participation.[66]

The international community, particularly the African Union, has so far not recognized Somaliland as independent state, and this is unlikely to come soon given sensitivity of the infamous issue of inherited colonial borders, which still haunts the African continent, and produces border conflicts. In other words, the international community said 'yes' to Somaliland as part of a federal state of Somalia but 'no' to as an independent state.

Birth of Puntland state of Somalia

Let us now examine the political and security developments in the north-east region of the Republic (Puntland) since 1991.

Once known as 'Majertynia' land because of the dominant Majeerteen Daarood clans and ancient Majeerteen sultanates, by 1991, the SSDF rebel group supported by Majeerteens was the most powerful authority and easily seized the region, establishing an administration in collaboration with clan elders. Despite factional political disagreements within SSDF leadership, Colonel Abdullahi Yusuf versus General Mohamed Abshir, unlike Isaaq and Hawiye clans, there were no major conflicts within Majeerteen clans, except a few conflicts with 'outsiders', such as SSDF clashing with Al-Ittihad Al-Islami (AIAI), an Islamic fundamentalist organization, which it defeated in 1991. More notably was the conflict with USC forces in the Mudug region in central Somalia where SSDF defeated General Aideed's Habargedir militiamen who attempted to conquer the region: traditionally a region contested by Habargedirs and Majeerteens.[67]

Except these isolated conflicts, the region escaped much of the clan-related violence at this early stage of the civil war because of reconciliation efforts by modern politicians and traditional clan leaders 'issimo' working together.[68] The 'issimo' filled in the power vacuum that followed the collapse of state institutions, taking responsibility for administering customary laws (*xeer*) to resolving clan conflict.[69] By 1990, there were twenty such 'issimo' compared to eight in 1900 because each clan had installed its 'isin' to cope with the civil war, seeking social recognition and political participation.[70] Nevertheless, the role of the 'issimo' was ambiguous and some of them became warmongers, inflaming situations.[71]

More significantly, unlike central, south and south-western regions of Somalia with its different major clan families, such as Hawiye, Rahanweyn and Daarood, dominance of Majeerteen and other related Daarood clans as the only unchallenged clans helped prevent serious hostilities in the region which remained relatively peaceful during the height of the civil war.[72] Even the war economy with its devastating consequences in other regions was abated through income sharing arrangements. For example, by 1996, income from a seaport in Boosaaso city was allocated to Puntland regions and stakeholders as following: 12 per cent and 10 per cent to Mudug and Nugal regions, respectively, 50 per cent to Bari region and 28 per cent to the SSDF.[73]

Although the SSDF had been in control since 1991, it failed to establish an effective governance structure due to leadership failure, lack of political vision and secure resources of public revenue.[74] The region moved towards structured governance form in May 1998 after a Majeerteen wide conference was held in Garowe city in which traditional clan elders and modern politicians of Majeerteen participated. Harti clans (Dhulbahante and Warsangeli) in Sanaag and Sool regions, which are contested by Somaliland and Puntland, also participated in the conference. Consequently, Puntland[75] State of Somalia, composing of Nugal, Bari, a part of Mudug, Sanaag, Sool and Ceyn regions was declared as an autonomous regional state within a future Somalia federal structure.

The regional state occupies landmass of 212,510 square kilometres, roughly one-third of Somalia with a population estimated at 2.4 million of which 65 per cent are nomads.[76] Located at the eastern portion of Somalia, the state is sandwiched between the Gulf of Aden in the north, the Indian Ocean in the south-east, Ethiopia in the south-west, Somali central regions in the south-east and Somaliland or the north-west regions in the west.[77] State institutions such as new charter and regional parliament, composed of sixty-six members, were created. A judiciary structure, based on the Somali Republic's 1960s legal framework, was established.[78] Clan elders elected Colonel Abdullahi Yusuf, one of the prominent leaders of the 1978 coup against General Siyad Barre's regime and the SSDF, as president for four years. Unlike Somaliland, Warsangeli and Dhulbahante delegates accepted Puntland on consensus, although some intimidation by SSDF leaders was reported.[79]

SSDF leaders, particularly Colonel Yusuf was behind the Puntland initiative, which was envisaged along the lines of the 1990s' United Nations' 'building block' formula, which was meant to empower autonomous clan-based entities to prevent one particular clan dominating any future state. Under the UN formula, the Hawiye would have formed their regional state composed of Benaadir, Hiiraan, Mudug, Galgaduud regions; Isaaqs had already formed their state; Rahanweyn clans would have formed a regional state composed of Bay and Bakool regions, and Puntland state for the Harti/Daarood clans.[80] SSDF leadership imagined creation of Puntland as a blueprint for a future federal structure, which they perceived as a solution for disintegrating the country.[81]

However, the idea of federalism for Somalia, although was practically introduced by the creation of Puntland, was not something new. In fact, leaders of the Rahanweyn clans with their Hisbiya Digil and Mirifle or the Hizbia Dustur Mustquil Somalia (HDMS) political party had campaigned for federalism as early as the 1950s to protect their communities' interest against the dominant Daarood and Hawiye clans.[82]

The idea of an autonomous region in SSDF-controlled areas existed as early as the 1990s but was not vigorously pursued because of factional disagreements within Majeerteen elites over a federal or unitary state model.[83] However, by 1998 significant political developments forced SSDF leaders to follow their deferred dream. The powerful Isaaq clans were not only vigorously pursuing international recognition for Somaliland, but were also forcefully claiming Harti regions as part of their new entity for historical reasons.[84] SSDF leadership could not sit idle, watching their kin's territories taken over by force by Isaaqs. In addition, they could not accept the idea of an internationally recognized secessionist enclave as their neighbour because this would undermine Majeerteens' claim over Harti regions in a future federal structure arrangement for the whole of Somalia.[85] Therefore, setting up an autonomous state was a counterbalancing act against the Somaliland project. Equally, delegates of Dhulbahante and Warsangeli clans, feeling vulnerable in Isaaq-dominated Somaliland, accepted the initiative in order to enhance their interests in a wider Daarood alliance.[86]

On the other hand, the powerful Hawiye factions, while slaughtering each other in Mogadishu, were consolidating their power. After General Aideed's death in 1995 in fighting in Mogadishu, his son, Hussein Mohamed Aideed, former American marine, was appointed leader of the general's faction. Taking his father's position, Hussein led a Habargedir dominated faction invaded and conquered Rahanweyn clans' regions. This was at a time when SSDF leaders were feeling disappointed with the failure of other reconciliation conferences in which they had been participating with Hawiye and other factions since 1991 to form national government. After the failure of holding a national reconciliation conference inside the Majeerteen region as agreed by armed factions at a previous conference in Sodere in Ethiopia, SSDF leadership did not feel investing any more resources in these initiatives, which were top-down process dominated by warlords and foreign powers. It also gave SSDF leaders the momentum to push for the creation of their regional state.[87]

One of the reasons for the failure of the Sodere meeting was because General Aideed's faction, led by his son, boycotted it as this would have meant their faction's militia withdrawing from Rahanweyn territories and facing Rahanweyn leaders at the conference table.[88] Furthermore, by 1998, Rahanweyns were establishing their own autonomous regional state, and therefore for SSDF leadership it was logical to create an autonomous region in a disintegrating country.

More crucially, establishing an autonomous state was seen as a way out of the vicious cycle of instability and insecurity in southern and south-western regions of Hawiye and Rahanweyn clans.[89] Also, ordinary people were behind the idea having realized that a formal government structure was required to restore law and order. This is how an observer described the desperate need for a government: 'The government is like a "qawsar" (a caretaker hired to look after someone else's livestock). If he does a good job, he is paid well and retained. If he does poorly, he can be fired and a better one found to replace him.'[90]

Furthermore, Islamic extremist organizations, such as the AIAI, which the SSDF had defeated in the early 1990s, were on the rise again. SSDF leadership, anxious about these groups filling in a power vacuum in the region, saw converting their organization to a government structure essential to offset the rise of extremism.[91]

Even though the new state was a success story of the 'building block' scheme and a blueprint for a future federal structure,[92] and some achievements had been made in the first few years, events in 2001 proved that it was not immune from political instability and insecurity, as its architects hoped. Having served his presidential term, Colonel Abdullahi Yusuf refused to step down on 30 June 2001. He pushed a motion through the regional parliament to extend his term, which was passed by some clan elders. However, several traditional leaders and other opposition groups challenged the legality of the move. Yusuf Haji Nur, chief justice minister, declared the extension unconstitutional. Clan elders appointed him as a caretaker president to prepare for elections in November 2001. This resulted in a series of armed clashes between the opposing forces, which lasted well into late 2001.

By November 2001, another congress was held in Garowe, the regional state's capital city in which clan elders elected Colonel Jama Ali Jama, another rival of the colonel as president. Colonel Abdullahi rejected this, claiming that Islamic extremists had hijacked the conference.[93] This stand-off plunged Puntland into political instability and divided it up into pro-Jama Ali Jama camp (mainly Bari region) and pro-Abdullahi Yusuf (Mudug, Nugal, Sool and Sanaag regions). The conflict was a power struggle between the two colonels over the leadership of Majeerteen clans. Abdullahi Yusuf, from Omar Mohamoud, a sub-clan of Majeerteen, believed that he had a 'divine right' to rule Majeerteens since the formation of the SSDF in the 1980s, and would use force to maintain his position. This was opposed by Jama Ali Jama of Osman Mohamoud, another traditional rival sub-clan.[94]

The war on terror was another factor that influenced the conflict, both sides exploiting it for their advantage.[95] AIAI, an Islamic extremist organization, and the TNG formed out of foreign-led reconciliation conferences, were pushing Jama Ali Jama for power, while Ethiopia, having fought AIAI extremists, supported Colonel Abdullahi Yusuf's war machine.[96]

Colonel Abdullahi Yusuf declared himself president after his forces defeated his opponents in what was a series of military operations that killed 400 people.[97] The pro-Abdullahi Yusuf camp 'won' the conflict because the public and important traditional clan leaders were against the pro-Islamist and TNG camps, which they perceived as a threat to their newly found identity as Puntlanders.[98] The pro-Jama Ali Jama's faction was not seen as strong and credible. The power struggle staged by Colonel Abdullahi Yusuf ended the consensus-based indigenous political system, replacing it with dictatorship and autocracy led by the same man who had initiated the 1978 coup against the military dictatorship, hence becoming an authoritarian man not known for his democratic credentials.[99] Indeed, during his leadership, extra-judicial killings, political assassinations, atrocities, human rights abuses and bad governance were all too common in the region.[100] Colonel Abdullahi vacated his position to pursue his higher ambition of becoming president to all Somalis, which he achieved in 2004 through another political process.

Since its creation, Puntland did not follow Somaliland's footsteps in declaring independence. Instead, as enshrined in its constitution, it became an autonomous state within a future federal structure. This shows the importance that Majeerteen clans attach to wider Somali identity within greater Somalia. Some analysts interpret this as a reflection of their efforts in promoting wider Daarood interest in broad Somali context because a united Somalia would encompass Daarood clans in the south (Gedo and Juba regions), north-east (Puntland) and in north-west (Sool, Sanaag and Ceyn regions) in any future political settlement.[101] Daarood clans had dominated Somali politics since independence compared with Hawiye, Isaaq and Rahanweyn,[102] and indeed may wish to continue their dominance through wider Daarood interests in any new power-sharing federal structure for Somalia.

Nonetheless, there may well be some overzealous groups that would support outright independence for Puntland state, an idea that would kill the ideals of pan-Somalism. For example, some supporters of Colonel Abdullahi Yusuf during the 2001–2003 conflict with Jama Ali Jama, declared an independent state within Puntland.[103]

Other groups appeared in 2008–2009 when Colonel Abdullahi Yuusuf was being forced to step down as president of the Transitional Federal Government (TFG) by Hawiye representatives.[104] This TFG was borne out of another reconciliation process in Kenya.

Unhappy with the maltreatment of their man by Hawiye elites, they designed a new flag and national anthem for Puntland, perhaps pushing for eventual independence to reclaim their region's old glorious days as the old Majeerteen kingdoms. Indeed, Puntland's suspension of its ties with the TFG on a few occasions was interpreted as secession from the rest of Somalia.[105] However, it is very unlikely that Majeerteen clans would go for independence unless and until future events (such as recognition of Somaliland as an independent state) precipitate it.

Not surprising, Somaliland leadership did not welcome the rise of Puntland because this would jeopardize its case for international recognition, which is based on historical colonial borders that encompasses the Harti regions of Sool, Ceyn and Sanaag claimed by both Puntland and Somaliland, a thorny and explosive issue. As part of a smear campaign, the Somaliland regime described Puntland entity as no more than 'Majertenia' clan land, a term that Majeerteens would find offensive old clannish term, referring to their old Majertenia sultanates.[106] Border skirmishes between the two entities continued since the formation of Puntland.

Within lineage politics, Isaaqs know that Majeerteens would not tolerate attacks or intimidation against their Harti cousins who are normally reliant on them for protection.[107] In an interview by the BBC Somali section with President Abdurahman Faroole of Puntland with regard to conflict in Kalshaale area in the Sool region between Somaliland militias and those opposing it, he warned Somaliland authorities that Puntland will not tolerate any aggression and will defend Sool region.[108] It is likely that majority of the Harti clans would prefer to be part of a united Somalia rather than in Somaliland in which they would be a minority.

Despite difficulties in demarcating borders in a war-torn society, and the problem of creating a Puntland state identity solely based on an exclusive Majeerteen identity or otherwise,[109] Puntland state has so far remained as one political unit, and has held five presidential elections since 1998. Nevertheless, the emergence of resistance movements and mini-states in the Sool, Ceyn and Sanaag regions, such as Maakhir and Khatumo states that challenge both Somaliland and Puntland claims, and Puntland's border dispute with Somaliland, and Galmudug another regional state are some of the factors that threaten the existence of Puntland as a stable political unit.

More importantly, the lack of open democracy (direct election) and lack of economic revival, Islamic extremism, conflict over resources, such as exploration of oil which caused conflicts in the state and the piracy problem remain some of the factors that challenge Puntland. In addition, non-Majeerteen Harti clan leadership's ambivalence over whether to join Somaliland or Puntland is another significant factor that threatens the existence of both entities. Indeed, Harti factions are divided over this issue; defections and betrayals by political elites are rife, as mini-states and resistance movements appear or disappear. Some of these elites held or hold senior government positions in both Somaliland and Puntland.

Rahanweyns and their struggle for survival

The less aggressive and peaceful Rahanweyn clans[110] and other non-ethnic Somalis, such as Benaadirs, Bravanese, Bantu/Jareer and Bajuns suffered most during the early years of the civil war as their fertile regions, the breadbasket of Somalia, became battlefields for Hawiye and Daarood militiamen and warlords.[111]

The Rahanweyn (Reewin) clan family, which is a federation of clans, is subdivided into Digil and Mirifle clans. Unlike the nomad/pastoralists Hawiye, Daarood and Dir clans, they are mainly agro-pastoralists and speak *Af-Maay Maay* (Mai) a distinctive language that is equal to the *Maxaa Tiri,* spoken by Daaroods, Hawiye and Isaaq. Indeed, until the 1960s *Af-Maay Maay* (Mai) was an official language in the official Radio Mogadishu alongside the 'Maxaa Tiri' until the first post-independence Somali government stopped it for language consistency.[112] They mainly inhabit riverine regions situated between Shebelle river in the north, Juba river in the south; Ethiopia borders in the west. Non-Somali ethnic groups also inhabit the region's coastal strip bordering Juba and Shabelle valleys and the southern islands of the Indian Ocean. Besides their other languages, they speak Af-Maay Maay as a lingua franca.[113]

Rahanweyns and other minority non-ethnic Somalis make up one-third of the Somali population.[114] In the pre-military regime era, Rahanweyn and non-ethnic Somalis regions were part of regional administrations of Benaadir, upper Juba, lower Juba and Hiiraan regions.[115] Except Hiiraan, the military regime subdivided Rahanweyn regions into smaller administrative regions for political reasons to create regions for favoured Daaroods clans, such as Gedo region for President Siyad Barre's Mareehaan clan hence Rahanweyns losing out in this administrative process.[116]

Ecologically, Rahanweyn land is fertile, and the only two permanent rivers in the country cut through it. It can sustain different methods of production, including agro-pastoralism. It has always been a contested region ripe for land grabbing. Indeed, different power brokers from the Italian fascist regime to successive Somali governments used state machinery to seize these lands from their owners, while others, such as warlords, used brute force during the civil war.[117] Certainly, introduction of land reform laws and policies particularly during the military regime, accompanied by forced displacement of indigenous clans, and resettlement of non-indigenous clans in the region, forced indigenous communities out of their lands.[118]

In political history, prior to and during the Italian colonization, some communities in Rahanweyn regions particularly Jareers and Bantus, suffered most from forced labour and slavery. Ownership of slaves by dominant Somali clans was a shameful feature in Somalia's history.[119] Indeed, combating slavery in the Italian Somali colony was a contributory factor in imposing full Italian colony, although colonial administrations condoned and were implicated in it.[120]

Leaders of Rahanweyn communities played significant roles in anti-slavery movements during the struggle for independence. However, their history and their social status are often marginalized compared to the dominant Daarood, Hawiye and Dir clans. A one-sided and distorted version of Somali history written by biased scholars who viewed Rahanweyn communities as an inferior race because of traditional oral narratives based on mythology had contributed to this view.[121]

During civilian government era (1950–69), Rahanweyn communities had their own political organizations, such as Hisbiya Digil & Mirifle (HDMS) being the main party. However, they were politically marginalized throughout modern Somali history by dominant Daarood, Hawiye and Dir clans. To counterbalance dominant clans' position, Rahanweyns campaigned for a federal structure to enhance their interests, but federalism was never adopted in the early days of the Republic. Although Rahanweyns had held the position of the speaker of the parliament during the civilian government era, they hardly held premiership or presidency positions. Even during the military regime with its fair and equal society rhetoric based on socialism, Rahanweyns were not well represented in the Supreme Revolutionary Council (SRC), the highest political body. Certainly, out of the 567 ministerial and other senior posts created in the Republic since 1960–90, Rahanweyn politicians held only 31 posts while Daaroods happily controlled 216 followed by Hawiyes 125 and Isaaq 102.[122]

During the rebellion against General Siyad Barre's regime, there were some Rahanweyn rebel groups, such as the SDM. However, they were not strong militarily and their political elite did not have access to the state military arsenal like the high-ranking military leaders of other Hawiye, Daarood and Isaaq factions who looted state arsenal. Rahanweyn elites did not also have an economic power base and a diaspora community to support their movements, factors that helped other factions. They were also divided among themselves, supporting different rebel groups. For example, the SDM had to ally itself with USC's different factions to eject remnants of President Siyad Barre's forces from their lands. Indeed, clan elders from these regions asked General Aideed to help them 'liberate' their land from forces loyal to President Siyad Barre, which were committing atrocities in the region.[123] As it turned out, General Aideed's USC faction betrayed them politically when its militiamen occupied Rahanweyn regions under the pretext that they had 'liberated' them from the fallen regime.[124]

Therefore, at the collapse of the military dictatorship, Rahanweyn clans and non-Somali ethnic groups found themselves defenceless and trapped between marauding Hawiye and Daarood factions in what became known as the 'triangle of death' in which Baidoa, the capital city of the Bay region, became the city of death. They suffered most when up to 500,000 people starved to death because of the destruction of farmlands and properties and confiscation of farms by the warring factions.[125] And also because of what was described 'genocidal policy' under which Hawiye and Daarood factions were determined to exterminate Rahanweyns.[126] If you compare Rahanweyn's experience with any other clans' experience, it becomes obvious that they were not only marginalized throughout Somali history, but also suffered more than any other clan during the civil war as hundreds of thousands of people died because of the conflict and other war-related causes.

As early as 1993, because of the war and communal suffering, some kind of Rahanweyn political community based on shared history and experience of political marginalization and victimhood throughout modern Somali history, had emerged.[127] By March 1993, SDM organized reconciliation conference to unify Rahanweyn clans, which was held in Bonkain in the Bay region. Participants of the conference elected a council of clan chiefs, and a supreme body of traditional clan elders. The following resolution adopted in the conference explains some of the political realities under which the conference was held:

> In the light of the current political realities of Somalia, where parts of the country have declared secession, and others are talking about the possibility of federation or regional autonomy, the future reconciliation process should accommodate all these views and put them into perspective . . . . Somalia should focus on efforts to reconstitute itself by working on its grim reality, forgetting about the past myths which led to the current humiliating political conditions . . . . The international community should support Somalis in putting their nation back together in whatever form of government they choose: a unified state, a confederation or federated states, or even several independent states.[128]

By 1994, while UNOSOM was still in the country, Rahanweyns had established their own district and regional administrations and Baidoa was no longer the city of starvation.[129] That was followed by another pan-Rahanweyn congress held in Baidoa in early 1995 to unify the inter-riverine communities, and to enable them demand for regional autonomy. Participants of the conference envisaged four autonomous regional states for a future Somali state. A riverine state in the south-west for the Rahanweyn people; a Somaliland state in the north for Isaaqs; a central state for the Hawiye, and a cape state in the north-east region (Puntland) for the Daaroods.[130]

The riverine state vision was ambitious and comprised six administrative regions of Bay, Bakool, middle Juba, lower Shabelle, Gedo and lower Juba. Under this proposal, Rahanweyn clans were considered as the rightful majority of these regions, which are also inhabited by Daaroods and Hawiyes.[131] At the conference, which lasted until May 1995, new political entity called the Riverine State, with Baidoa as its capital and seat of government, was created. Two councils, a supreme administrative council, headed by Dr Hassan Sheikh Ibrahim 'Hassey', a lawyer and a supreme house of clan elders with Haji Mukhtar Malaaq Hassan as its chairman were elected. Abdulqadir Zope, a veteran Rahanweyn politician, was elected head of the entity.

However, some huge obstacles and challenges made it doubtful whether the envisaged riverine state would be viable and sustainable. First, Rahanweyn lands were still occupied by Daarood and Hawiye factions. Second, massive displacement of people had disrupted the region's socio-political and economic activities. Third, the future of Daarood, Hawiye and other minority clans' enclaves in the new entity was an issue which would have been an obstacle to the unification of Rahanweyns under one regional state.[132]

Furthermore and more importantly, the new entity was a direct challenge and threat to some political forces.[133] Certainly, General Aideed whose forces were already occupying some parts of the region, the man who had 'liberated' the region from the forces of General Siyad Barre, was not going to allow it to materialize unchallenged. In addition, the future of minority clans in the region was not clear-cut.[134]

Regrettably, the new entity proved to be no more than a passing night's dream that could not be realized in cut-throat culture of Somali politics. General Aideed's faction by now had 'won' its war with UNOSOM forces, forcing them to elevate him from a warmonger and warlord character to a national leader, essential to political reconciliation.[135] By 1995, General Aideed formed a government he called 'Salballar' (the inclusive) supported by fifteen armed factions, and by September his militiamen, which were perceived as the new scourge post-Siyad Barre regime era,[136] invaded and captured Baidoa. By this military adventure, General Aideed's faction aborted an embryonic regional state, killing and detaining its senior members, forcing others to flee to neighbouring countries.[137]

Rahanweyn elites were divided on General Aideed's action, some supporting it. But those opposing it were not going to tolerate constant acts of aggression by different factions. For years, they saw their lands occupied, changing hands between Daarood and Hawiye factions, and now a ruthless warlord smothered their new political body.[138] Straight away, on 13 October 1995, a group of young officers and intellectuals formed a resistance movement called Rahanweyn Resistance Army (RRA) at Jhaffey, west of Baidoa, to liberate the regions from what they saw as invaders, and to mobilize Rahanweyn clans.[139] Colonel Hassan Mohamed Nur 'Shaatigaduud', a former intelligence officer in the military regime, was elected chair, leading an executive committee. Rahanweyn communities were mobilized, and even young girls, traditionally supposed to stay at home to look after families, joined RRA militia, refusing to marry until they had liberated their country.[140]

From October 1995, RRA launched series of military campaign against General Aideed's invading Habargedir militiamen.[141] The liberation struggle did not end until RRA gradually captured Rahanweyn regions, and by 6 June 1999, it seized Baidoa, the capital city liberating it from the general's faction now led by his son, Hussein Aideed, who took the leadership after his father's death. This was a deserved victory for Rahanweyns. Jubilant RRA armed men danced traditional folklore in war victory ceremonies, celebrating their victory over Habargedir militiamen.[142]

Rahanweyn communities finally established the south-western state of Somalia (SWSS) on 1 April 2002 on the same geographical composition as the aborted riverine state, hence asserting their political autonomy from dominant Daarood and Hawiye factions. To them, they finally realized their long-held dream for an autonomous regional state under a federal structure, which their ancestors had campaigned for as early as the 1950s. Colonel Hassan Shaatigaduud, RRA's chairman, was elected president. They created state paraphernalia, such as a flag and anthem. However, Rahanweyns did not secede from Somalia but remained as part of wider federal structure.

The rise of RRA and subsequent declaration of the SWSS were a landmark for community's victory over dominant factions, hailing from as far away places as the central regions. By declaring their own state and army, Rahanweyn communities asserted themselves as a formidable political entity in Somalia, a country already divided into clan-based entities. In a way, that historical action was a coping mechanism with the impending civil war just like Isaaqs and Majeerteens had done by creating their own regional states.

On the other hand, their shared communal suffering had united them as never before, seeing themselves as a distinctive community with shared history of political oppression. They felt that only regional autonomy would enhance their political, economic and social security in Somalia.[143] Nevertheless, as the region is the breadbasket of the entire country, Rahanweyns will have to continue facing threat of exploitation and domination by others in the future.[144]

However, and regrettably, as Somaliland and Puntland, the new SWSS was marred by inter-factional fighting. Factional leaders such as Sheikh Aden Madoobe, Muhammad Ibrahim Haabsade and Colonel Hassan Mohamed Nur, 'Shaatigaduud', fought each other over political control and leadership of the new entity, joining the endless list of Somali warlords and warmongers. As early as 2000 until 2005, Baidoa, the capital city, was a battlefield between these warmongers, changing hands between them, until the regional state was disbanded in February 2006 after the warring factions had joined the Transitional Federal Government of Somalia (TFG), formed out of another reconciliation conference in Kenya. Baidoa became the seat of the TFG, the first federal government since independence hence fulfilling Rahanweyns' long-held deferred dream of a federal structure for Somalia.

The SWSS was re-established again in 2009 and became an official member state of the Federal Government of Somalia. It comprises three regions: lower Shabelle, Bay and Bakool regions; its capital city is Baraawe, but Baidoa as its interim capital city. It had held few indirect elections where clan elders elected parliament, and presidents such Mohamed H. Abdinur, Shariif Hassan and Abdiasis Laftagare.

Alongside the formation of Rahanweyn state, in a factionalized country, it was not surprising other regional states mushroomed. The short-lived first Jubaland state of Somalia, comprising of Gedo, lower and middle Juba regions was one of them. These historical regions once called Jubaland were ruled by the Sultans of Oman and Zanzibar, the British and finally by the Italians until independence. The region is 87,000 square kilometres and its main cities are Kismayo, Baardheere and Buulo Xaawo. The total population was estimated around 1.3 million inhabitants in 2005.[145]

During the military regime, the region experienced massive resettlement programme to help resettle victims of the 1974–5 droughts in central and north regions as thousands of Daarood clans were brought in the region traditionally inhabited by a mixture of Daarood, Hawiye, Dir, Rahanweyn and non-ethnic Somalis, such as Bajuns and Bantus.[146] The region, particularly Kismayo in the lower Juba, had been a contested area by warring Daarood and Hawiye factions throughout the civil war, from General Aideed's faction chasing away remnants of the deposed military regime, and occupying it and then challenged by other Daarood factions, and finally Daarood factions fighting over its control.

The Somali National Front (SNF), led by General Mohamed Hersi Morgan, from the Majeerteen clan and the deposed president's son-in-law, was one of these factions. As UNOSOM forces were battling with General Aideed's forces in Mogadishu, SNF captured Kismayo in December 1995, and by 1998, it asserted its authority over the region and declared it the autonomous Jubaland state of Somalia with Kismayo as its capital city. This was a Majeerteen faction initiative to chase away other Daarood factions, such as Colonel Omar Jees who was leading SPM, an Ogaden affiliated faction. General Morgan, who was able to control the city during much of the 1990s by stirring up conflict between Daarood sub-clans of Majeerteen, Ogaden and Mareehaan, became head of the entity on 3 September 1998. During his leadership, some atrocities and human rights abuses were committed in the region.[147]

Ironically, the SNF faction declared their new entity just when Rahanweyns had envisaged these regions as part of their unsuccessful riverine regional state, which included the lower Juba region. This showed how bad factionalism and land grabbing was, and how each faction would just declare a new entity. Morgan's SNF administration lasted until 11 June 1999 when it was brought down by another political alliance called Juba Valley Alliance (JVA), composed of mixture of Daarood and Hawiye factions. The JVA formed a new administration that lasted until 2006 when the ICU, an Islamic movement dismantled it.

Jubaland state was re-established again in 2011 under the name Azania led by Professor Gandhi, and finally became an official member of the Federal Government of Somalia in 2013. A parliament was set up by clan elders, and Ahmed I. Madoobe was elected as president.

Finally, in what was dubbed the 'Mushrooming Cabbie Statelets',[148] a mixture of Somali diaspora and their clansmen in Somalia continued to form regional states. These regional states included Khatumo state, Maakhir state in the Sanaag region for Warsangelis, Hiiraan state for different Hawiye clans, Xeeb and Hanman for Suleybaan, a sub-clan of Habargedir, and Waax and Waadi for Abgaals, and Udubland in the lower Shabelle, lower Juba and middle Juba were all political initiatives taken by stakeholders determined to redress injustices and grievances or to reclaim political rights and empower their constituencies.

At one point, there were roughly up to twenty such regional states, some of them on paper only. Abdirazak H. Hussein, former prime minister (1964–7) warned that proliferation of these mini-states would lead to the disintegration of Somalia into tribal fiefdoms where every 200,000 people would constitute their own tribal land as the case was before the colonial imposition. Indeed, he predicted that there will be fifty states in a country with an estimated population of 8–10 million.[149] This is a danger to Somali unity and nationalism.

Currently there are five regional states: Galmudug state, Puntland state, Hirshabelle state, Jubaland state and south-western state of Somalia, which form part of the current federal structure under a draft national constitution to be ratified. Somaliland does not consider itself as part of this federal structure, but the international community recognizes it as a member of the existing structure of the Federal Republic of Somalia.

Top-down reconciliation conferences: The wrong medicine

In parallel with clan-based regional state-building efforts, there were other reconciliation initiatives aimed at reconstituting a central national government. The process, which started in 1991 in Djibouti, was mainly led by regional and international actors, and was aimed at reconciling armed factions, which had been ripping the country apart since 1991. Whereas local reconciliation efforts, such as those in Somaliland and Puntland, were effective low-cost initiatives that enjoyed wider community participation, the internationally supported ones were top-down processes dominated by armed factions, which dictated the outcome. Lack of real ownership of the process by Somalis and agendas driven by foreign stakeholders adamant to concocting a Somali central government in a pressurized time-framework were the predominant characteristics of these conferences.[150] As of 2010, there were around seventeen such conferences held inside and outside the country.[151] Furthermore, the process concentrated on state building rather than peace building, which are two different issues.[152] This approach resulted in more bloodshed and conflict as Somali political stakeholders fought over the domination of any proposed state structure.

In addition to the Djibouti conference in 1991, the Addis Ababa conference in 1993 was one of such hurried up process, which could have saved Somalis from another fifteen years of vicious warfare, had sponsors of the conference handled it differently. First, led by the UN, conference sponsors wrongly assumed that armed factional leaders were representatives of the people of a war-torn society where representation and legitimate authority were bitterly contested.[153] Indeed, while self-appointed leaders enjoyed the comfort of luxury hotels, the nitty-gritty business of resolving daily clan conflict at village, district and regional levels were left to traditional leaders who were marginalized from the process. This was at the height of the civil war in which society was disintegrating into fiefdoms, and powerful clans, factions and warlords easily manipulated fearful and weaker communities. Second, a pressurized time frame of a few weeks with foreign-led agenda was allocated to the conference to force factional leaders to come up with a comprehensive political roadmap of nation-building.[154] In fact, while factional leaders were discussing huge issues of state building, Boutros Boutross. Ghali, the UN secretary general, was threatening to put Somalia under UN trusteeship unless they came up with a political deal at the conference.[155] The fact of the matter was UN leadership was hurrying up the process because they wanted a political agreement to coincide with the authorization and deployment of the UNOSOM-II in Somalia to replace the earlier UNITAF mission. In other words, to say to the world, here is an agreement reached by Somalis to be supported by the UNOSOM. The time factor destroyed any hope of real reconciliation, considering the importance of allocating plenty of time to Somali traditional conflict resolution process, which could last for months.

The timing of the Addis Ababa conference was a critical factor in shaping the atmosphere of the talks. It was held not so long after the massacre of Daaroods in Mogadishu, and just when Hawiye factions were slaughtering each other in the city. Emotions were running high and animosity within Somalis was deep as shown by an incident when a drunken Daarood man privately confessed to a journalist that they (Daaroods) were not interested in reconciliation, and that after killing Hawiye leaders, they will form their own independent state. Here are the drunken man's own words: 'You journalists are just like the Hawiye. You have no respect for the Daarood. I say we kill (the chairman of his own faction), kill (the president), and start our own independent country. We will call it the Land of Punt.'[156]

Such emotions and strong words were not surprising in light of what had happened. Therefore, one could conclude that Somalis were not yet ready to reconcile between themselves in the early 1990s because wounds had not healed. The drunken man's words revealed that although some factions were at the negotiation table, they had their own thoughts and agendas, which included setting up their own regional states.

Indeed, one is left to wonder whether such heartfelt strong emotions stirred secessionist movements and bloodshed in which Isaaqs declared their own independent state and Daarood had inaugurated their semi-autonomous state, Puntland state of Somalia.

After discussing the issue of decentralization versus centralization, participants of the conference described as 'not more than Somalis living high on the UN expenses,'[157] agreed to establish a transitional national council (TNC) to be elected by the country's eighteen regions through a process of grassroots involvement, to prepare the country for an elected government. The country's sovereignty was to be deposited with the TNC temporarily during a two-year transitional period.[158] The agreement also called for the disarmament and demobilization of armed militia. Nevertheless, the conference, with its limited resources and the quick-fix mentality adopted by UN organizers failed to produce detailed plans of nation and institutional building, necessary to implement the agreement.[159]

Domination of factional leaders and warlords of the conference, despite their bad human rights records, was seen as legitimizing their power.[160] In addition, the conference created more animosity among factional leaders who had sensed that the UN was going to create a recognized national government, hence increasing political rivalry and wrangling. It also failed to address the thorny issue of the breakaway region (Somaliland) whose delegation had left the conference before any agreement was reached[161] probably angered by the depository of sovereignty in the TNC as Somaliland had already declared independence from Somalia.

The UN team was also divided on the conference and its outcome. While Lansana Kouyate, UN deputy special representative supported the agreement, his colleague, Leonard Kapungu, head of UNOSOM's political division, and Robert Gosende, American envoy to Somalia, were unhappy about a conference dominated by unsavoury factional leaders who could use national sovereignty to sabotage important UN decisions on humanitarian and other wise.[162] The UN was already establishing regional and district councils, supporting those stable regions. Therefore, some UN/US leadership favoured political developments at regional level, but not at national level,[163] which is what Addis Ababa agreement proposed, at a time when the UN mission was the highest authority in the country with no national government to negotiate with. Indeed, Secretary General Boutros Boutros Ghali was determined to convert his organization to a peace enforcing body and was already threatening to place the country under UN trusteeship unless Somali factions reached a political agreement. In fact, the Security Council immediately adopted resolution no. 814 in March 1993, which authorized UNOSOM-II, which effectively made the UN the highest authority in Somalia.

The main outcome of the conference was the production of an 'agreement' document signed by unscrupulous 'leaders' with no intention of implementing them because of their parochial interests. They had even exploited flaws in the process in order to undermine it, claiming that it was 'forced on' them by external forces, adding clauses to the document to give them control over the selection of members of the TNC, which was meant to be a grassroots level process.[164]

These sleazy characters who were described as 'spoilers' of peace[165] used any excuse to disrupt peace initiatives. General Mohamed Hersi Morgan's attack of Kismayo, controlled by the General Aideed's faction, which led Aideed's faction leaving the negotiation table, was an example of tactics that peace spoilers and war entrepreneurs had been using throughout the conflict for political and economic reasons. General Aideed's opposition to the formation of district and regional councils as agreed in the Addis Ababa conference,[166] his opposition to holding a reconciliation conference in Mogadishu to resolve the Hawiye conflict were painful examples of his ruthlessness. Certainly, while Ali Mahdi's faction was cooperative and less belligerent, General Aideed's stubbornness and his opposition to reconciliation efforts, which he perceived as a challenge to his authority, hampered the reconciliation process. He was not interested in reconciliation because his faction was controlling much of southern regions.[167]

Although it is simplistic to argue one person destroyed Somalia, however, General Aideed and General Siyad Barre are the main characters who led their country to self-destruction.[168] Indeed, as described in the previous chapter, General Aideed was belligerent throughout the conflict, refusing to allow UN peacekeeping forces to protect food convoys while thousands of people were starving in areas under his control.[169]

Regrettably, any hope of implementing the Addis Ababa agreement was destroyed by the massacre of the Pakistani troops by General Aideed's faction, which led to the manhunt debacle in Mogadishu. With the power of hindsight, had the ambitious UNOSOM and the Addis Ababa agreements worked harmoniously much of the later bloodshed and chaos could have been prevented. This was a missed opportunity.

Djibouti conference: Cornerstone of the peace process

A Somali reconciliation conference held in the Republic of Djibouti in 2000 was different from earlier conferences and would become a cornerstone for the reconciliation process. The conference was the brainchild of President Ismail Omar Geelle of Djibouti, building on his predecessor, President Hassan Guuleed Abtidoon's previous peace initiative. In a speech to the UN Assembly General in September 1999, President Geelle attacked Somali warlords and factional leaders, describing them as power-hungry individuals who failed their country, and who should be punished for their crimes. He wanted warlords marginalized by not holding further conferences dominated by them. His vision was a new reconciliation process led by what he called 'Somali civil society' facilitated and supported by the international community. The following quote from his speech highlights the president's vision for Somalia:

> I'm loath to support yet another conference held uniquely for the warlords who have lost the confidence of their people. It is time the Somali civil society, including intellectuals, artists and mothers, take the responsibility. The Somali people have matured politically during these years of suffering and know what it lacks economic prosperity, social progress, democratic governance, liberty and peace. In line with the wishes of the Somali people.[170]

The Djibouti government based its strategy for holding the conference on three principles. First, it would facilitate the peace process. Second, it was up to Somalis to decide their destiny, and third the international community should back the outcome of the process.[171]

The government immediately undertook diplomatic missions across the Horn of Africa, seeking support for its initiative from regional states. On 26 November 1999, heads of the Intergovernmental Agency on Development (IGAD), a regional development body for Kenya, Ethiopia, Somalia, Sudan, Djibouti and Eritrea, endorsed the Djibouti initiative unanimously. The international community also endorsed it. In addition to that, a Djibouti government commission, designed to seek support for the initiative from the Somali people, travelled across Somalia.

Most Somali stakeholders generally welcomed the commission, except Somaliland. The breakaway region, led by Egal, the same man who had participated in the 1991 Djibouti reconciliation conference, was relatively stable with functioning institutions compared to the chaos in the south. The Egal regime was vigorously pursuing international recognition, the only missing goal. Therefore, it would have been politically difficult for the leadership to endorse a conference, designed to revive a unitary Somali state,[172] which would undermine Somaliland's efforts for recognition. By now, Somaliland politicians had already categorized the Somali conflict into two: the stable, peaceful and democratic north (Somaliland) against the unstable, chaotic and murderous politics of the south, meaning the rest of Somalia. Indeed, some politicians were accused of hate-mongering and stirring up the conflict in the south as a strategy to keep it in chaos, hoping that the world would recognize Somaliland as a reward for its achievements.[173] In their political calculation, southerners who, in their political dictionary, meant all of Somalis except Somaliland should first resolve their problems before the breakaway region could start negotiation with them for a future Somali state.[174]

Under such political uncertainties, Egal regime, feeling threatened by the Djibouti initiative, introduced emergency laws, detaining people from the region for participating in the conference.[175] However, there were some pro-Djibouti conference voices, such as a demonstration in Borama in the Awdal region, and the attendance of prominent clan elders and leaders from the region in the conference. Boycotting the conference led to the deterioration of relationship and closure of borders between the breakaway region and Djibouti.[176]

Other stakeholders that opposed the conference included a new brand of Mogadishu warlords and other factional leaders, such as Osman Atto, (Habargedir), Muuse Sudi Yalahow (Abgaal) and Hussein Aideed, General Aideed's son. Some of these new warlords, dubbed 'scrap merchants of Mogadishu' were entrepreneurs who made money by selling scrap metal salvaged from the ruins of the costly UNOSOM compound,[177] after looters and scavengers had reduced it to rubble. They were engaged in a power struggle inside and outside Mogadishu, as different factions of Daarood and other clans contested over the lower Juba region. They rejected the conference, which they saw as a challenge to their authority.[178]

In 2000, the Djibouti government held the conference in Arte, a city located in south-eastern Djibouti. By erecting huge tents, President Ismail O. Geelle, being a Somali himself, was probably honouring the traditional Somali way of conflict resolution *Gogol fidis* to make his guests feel at home. A dedicated TV channel to broadcast conference deliberations to Somalis and to raise its profile was opened. In early 2000, about 3,000 Somalis gathered at Arte for a conference not held in traditionally hostile countries like Ethiopia or Kenya, but in a brotherly neighbour country headed by Somali brother and peacemaker, with Somalis' best interests at his heart. The conference was described as 'Djibouti Peace Promoter in Somalia'.[179] And unlike previous conferences, time was not a constraint, indeed, it lasted eight months from March until October 2000.

In series of formal and informal meetings from preliminary to in-depth ones, a wide range of stakeholders from clan elders, religious leaders, business community, intellectuals to women's groups, had discussed competing interests and different political agendas and philosophies. Representation and legitimacy in a war-torn society where different actors claimed legitimacy without any real authority to verify, state building (whether a federal or unitary structure) and a formula for power sharing, were among many big issues that were discussed in those meetings.[180] Unlike the previous warlord dominated conferences, it was clear that representation would be based on unarmed and civic organizations to marginalize factional leaders.

Using clan as a base for state building was a contentious issue. Some stakeholders argued that the formula is the only way of state building in a war-torn tribal society. However, others argued that clan is a social formation and not political, and with its narrow-minded clannish agenda it cannot therefore provide checks and balances for democracy and cannot be the base for a democratic nation-state.[181]

The clan-based formula group 'won' the argument because of the political realities on the ground where clan-based political entities were the norm and not the exception. The conference adopted what became known '4.5 formula' under which the four major family clans Hawiye, Dir, Daarood and Rahanweyn would share power equally, hence 4 stands for the big four, while minority clans (non-ethnic Somalis and other minority clans) would get half of the main clans' share hence the (0.5).

At the early stage of the conference, traditional clan elders had concluded their meetings in June 2000, nominating 180 delegates from Somali clans in accordance with the 4.5 formula to participate in the political phase of the conference. This was followed by a political phase to nominate members of a new transitional national parliament. At this point, participants had to set up an arbitration committee to resolve political disagreements because of underlining mistrust and lack of confidence among participants, which were not resolved in previous meetings.[182] Indeed, with hindsight it would appear that most of the previous reconciliation conferences were based on political power sharing rather than a social reconciliation process along the lines of the South African Truth and Reconciliation Commission. Previous reconciliation conferences were held while armed militiamen were occupying other clans' territories.

Finally, a strong 245-member Transitional National Assembly (TNA) was inaugurated on 13 August 2000 for the first time since the collapse of the central government in 1991. After a hugely contested presidential campaign with twenty-nine candidates vying for the post[183] in a country where obsession with the highest office became national pastime, the TNA elected Abdulqassin Salad Hassan, from Habargedir clan of Hawiye, as president for a three-year transitional period. The international community endorsed the outcome of the conference, and the UN secretary general described it as a landmark in Somali history, welcoming the broken Republic back as member of the international community. Regional heads of states and diplomatic missions in Djibouti participated in and blessed the presidential inauguration on 27 August 2000.

Compared to the previous initiatives, Djibouti reconciliation process was the most inclusive and genuine initiative. For the first time, it marginalized factional leaders and warlords and empowered other emerging power brokers mainly from civil society and non-armed constituents. This was a big achievement, which ended the vicious cycle of a warlord driven process, and supported new stakeholders, including women constituents. It also empowered the Somali people by engaging them in the process through a dedicated TV channel thus making them feel they had a stake in the process. Although it had not dealt exhaustively with social reconciliation along the lines of the South Africa's Truth and Reconciliation commission, it had however contributed to building trust and confidence among stakeholders.[184] In addition, it had produced the first Somali national government, which was recognized and supported by the international community. Indeed, the humiliated Republic was allowed to reclaim its seat at the UN and other international bodies officially for the first time since 1991.

Nevertheless, the Arte process failed to engage other important stakeholders, such as Somaliland and Puntland. Djibouti leadership's interest in united Somalia under a unitary state structure might have alienated the two autonomous entities, while Ethiopia's preference of a weaker federal structure and its suspicion of Islamist involvement in the process and in the TNG might have contributed to the failure of the process.[185]

Although Puntland supported the process initially, its delegation withdrew from it at later stage over disagreements on a formula for power sharing in which Puntland preferred regional-based power sharing, although some clan elders and other leaders from the region stayed in the conference after the withdrawal of the Puntland delegation.[186] With the power of hindsight, it is clear that Somaliland and Puntland were not prepared to sacrifice their self-determination and regional autonomy by supporting the creation of a national central government for a unitary state again run by warlords or Hawiye elites in Mogadishu. This showed the importance of the issue of unitary state versus federal structure which was not comprehensively discussed in the Djibouti conference and how this would affect the outcome of the conference. The lack of support by Puntland and Somaliland would prove disastrous during implementation of the conference's outcome. Regimes in Hargeisa and Garowe would do everything in their capacity to sabotage it. Although the Arte process quite rightly marginalized Mogadishu warlords, this would also prove to be an obstacle to the implementation of its agreements because these factional leaders would oppose the TNG and would ensure that it was no more than a Mogadishu-based entity as will be described soon.

Also, the conference failed to analyse the rise of Islamic fundamentalist movements in Somalia at the time outside the clan box analysis.[187] Islamic fundamentalist organizations, such as the Al-Ittihad Al-Islami were active in Somalia since the beginning of the civil war, and its leaders, such as Sheikh Hassan Dahir Aweys were influencing powerful stakeholders in Mogadishu and in the Arte process. Therefore the Arte process failed to deal with this as a separate issue (an emerging force), which required more attention considering how this would play critical role in the Arte aftermath and immediately after the 9/11 terrorist attacks on the World Trade Centre. Indeed, as will be shown later, Ethiopia would use the rise of Islamic extremists as a pretext to intervene in Somalia's affairs immediately after the end of the Arte process, hence sabotaging implementation of the Arte agreements.

Another important agreement reached in the Arte conference was to make Baidoa city in Rahanweyn regions as a temporary seat (capital) of the TNG because of insecurity in Mogadishu and until such time when the city's social status as a respected capital city was restored, particularly considering the city's bloody history post-1991. By locating the TNG to Baidoa would have been a symbolic gesture, which might have encouraged the RRA or Rahanweyn factions to support the outcome of the Arte process, especially if the TNG had addressed the occupation of the Rahanweyn regions by other factions.[188]

However, the issue of stabilizing Mogadishu and reconciling Hawiye factions by using President Abdiqaasim Salad Hassan of the Habargedir clan, one of the main protagonists of the Mogadishu conflicts, and after he was welcomed by 100,000 of people when he visited the city in August 2000[189] convinced TNG leadership to relocate to Mogadishu. By not locating TNG to Baidoa was another missed opportunity at that point in time because this might have alienated Rahanweyns, who might have perceived TNG as a Mogadishu-based Hawiye-dominated government.

Having nominated Ali Khalif Galaydh, a Dhulbahante of Daarood clan, as prime minister on 8 October 2000, which then formed a TNG, the new administration relocated to Mogadishu and embarked on building state institutions from judiciary, law enforcement and other institutions. Initially, it won over some Mogadishu warlords, and dispatched delegations to some parts of the country to resolve conflicts.[190] Nevertheless, the TNG immediately faced overwhelming challenges posed by those disgruntled warlords, factional leaders and other business people who viewed it as a threat to their interests.[191] Furthermore, Daarood and Rahanweyn factions in favour of the 'block-building' or federal structure approach convened a meeting in 2001 in Elberde near the Somali-Ethiopian border. They formed the National Restoration Council (NRC), a political body to oppose what they saw as a Hawiye-dominated TNG in Mogadishu.

On the other hand, Puntland and Somaliland, which had been enjoying benefits of regional autonomy, were not prepared to accommodate a centralized unitary state allegedly controlled by President Geelle[192] and they plotted against the TNG. The position of Somaliland and Puntland towards the TNG revealed the unresolved issue of federal structure versus unitary state, which the Arte conference failed to resolve. Indeed, it was around that time when Rahanweyn leaders were planning their regional state, which they would realize in 2002. With the power of hindsight, the Arte initiative should have resolved the unitary versus federal structure given the fact that one of the main reasons for the collapse of the central government in 1991 was rebellion against centralized state.

Ethiopia undermines the Arte peace process

More crucially, the lack of real support for the Arte initiative by some regional states would contribute to the downfall of the TNG. Ethiopia, although its prime minister, Meles Zenawi, had publicly blessed the TNG would prove to be one of the main obstacles to it. And he would contribute to its collapse because of Ethiopia's national security concerns, including its fear of Islamic extremism and its policy of not supporting strong united Somali but a weaker federal structure that it could control.[193]

Ironically, the same Ethiopian prime minister who had blessed the TNG at Arte quickly interfered in Somalia's internal affairs by accusing the TNG of having links with Islamic extremists. This is not surprising because Ethiopia had been meddling in Somali affairs by playing Somali factions against each other, as it had been obstructing peace initiatives.[194] He immediately encouraged even those warlords who had attended the Arte conference to oppose the TNG, inviting them along with the NRC group for a conference in Awassa in Ethiopia in March 2001.[195] Sixteen factional leaders or 'situational spoilers' as described by an scholar[196] attended that meeting, creating another political group called the Somali Reconciliation and Restoration Council (SRRC) to oppose the TNG.

The fact of the matter was that Ethiopia, a historic and hostile enemy of Somalia with history of manipulating Somali stakeholders, opposed the TNG. This is because the TNG was a centralized national unity government to unite all Somalis as preferred by the Djibouti government which was against a regional-based federal structure preferred by Ethiopia. The TNG's political position that it stands for all Somalis including, Puntland and Somaliland, might have exacerbated Ethiopia's fear of Somali nationalism and unity.[197] This shows how regional neighbouring countries had been shaping the Somali conflict – Djibouti preferring centralized national unity government opposed by Ethiopia.

Under the new SRRC umbrella and supported by Ethiopia, in a series of clashes with TNG forces, militiamen loyal to Mogadishu warlords and other factional leaders ensured that the TNG and its weak institutions were no more than political entity isolated in a few quarters in Mogadishu. The TNG, marred by accusation of corruption and association with Al-Qaeda linked Islamic extremists and terrorists[198] was unable to extend its authority over Mogadishu, let alone the whole country. The momentum and huge goodwill generated at the Arte peace conference was lost when the TNG could not carry the public with it because of corruption, incompetence, bickering, foreign interference and the powerful stakeholders: Puntland, Somaliland and other factional leaders that plotted against it. This practically killed the Arte process, and throughout 2001–2 insecurity and lawlessness in the country had increased.

Although with its weak institutions it resolved some local conflicts in some regions and enabled the broken Republic to claim its legitimate seat at the UN and other international bodies, the TNG will be remembered as a non-warmongering government, which is a good thing if compared to what was to come. With the power of hindsight, the TNG could have paved the way for real reconciliation and state building considering the popularity of the Arte peace conference, but it was aborted by some formidable stakeholders. This was the best chance since 1991 and another missed opportunity.[199]

It was under this atmosphere of renewed hostilities that the TNG's term in office was coming to an end in 2003. Blessed by heads of the IGAD states, President Daniel A. Moi of Kenya organized another reconciliation conference in Kenya in 2002 to broker ceasefire between the SRRC and TNG, and to initiate further negotiations on another transitional charter to replace the one adopted in Djibouti.

The Kenyan process, known as 'Mbagathi reconciliation process' was intended to focus on deeper conflict issues (e.g. justice and reconciliation) rather than the usual power sharing. Nevertheless, regional and international actors' conflicting positions and interests[200] overshadowed this. Ethiopia, which dominated the process,[201] supported SRRC's 'building block' federal structure approach, whereas Arab countries and Djibouti sided with Arte/TNG group's unitary state slogan. More importantly, the usual inter-factional quarrels and squabbles among Somalis without coherent ideological or political positions resulted in competing and shifting alliances in the conference.[202] Consequently, the usual power sharing, state building and 'quick-fix' approach hijacked the conference hence marginalizing other important issues of representation, security and stabilization, and transitional justice to address war crimes.[203]

Even Kenya, the host country, with its retiring President Arap Moi, who wanted to use finding solution to the Somali conflict as his last achievement to enhance his status as an African statesman, was accused of allying with Ethiopia. Indeed, the Kenyan leader confirmed that the two countries could not be entrusted with Somali reconciliation because of their fear of Somali nationalism and greater Somalia ideology.[204] In addition to the African Union and IGAD's squabble over the Somali issue, Arab countries, particularly Egypt had their own interests. They were supportive of centralized, stronger and united Somalia with an Arab identity as a regional counterbalance against Ethiopia's influence in the region[205] in which Ethiopia controls the Nile river, which feeds millions of Egyptians.

The Kenyan process was the longest (from 2002–4) and the costliest peace process since the Arte conference as millions of dollars donated by the international community were spent. Different stakeholders were deeply divided on many thorny issues, such as the contentious issues of political representation and legitimacy, criteria for power sharing, selection of members of a new parliament, and the issue of federalism versus unitary state. The Arab/Djibouti/TNG group supported federalism at a later stage of transition, while the pro-Ethiopia SRRC group wanted federalism as a base for any new political agreement. The TNG insisted Mogadishu to be the capital city, whereas the SRRC supported an alternative interim capital city.[206]

Among other issues discussed at the conference was the status of the 'Af-Maay Maay' language spoken by Rahanweyns as an official and equal language to the 'Maxaa Tiri' language. This was a sensitive issue that Rahanweyn leaders had to fight for its realization.[207] 'Af-Maay Maay' was finally recognized as an equal official Somali language, which was victory for the Rahanweyns as confirmed by Dr Mukhtar, a Rahanweyn intellectual.[208] Furthermore, Arabic as second language was hotly debated, the TNG advocating for it, whereas the SRRC opposing it. At one point the delegation of the Arab League of which Somalia is member, withdrew from the conference over the controversy of adopting Arabic or not.[209] In the end, Arabic was adopted as second language. This again revealed some primordial and historical tension over Somalis' identity as Arabs first or Africans second or vice versa, and how Somali elites are still struggling to come to terms with this identity issue.

On the issue of power sharing, adoption of the 4.5 formula again proved that clan is an influential factor in contemporary Somali politics. A strong 275-member TNA or parliament selected by traditional clan elders was established. By embracing a transitional national charter as an outline for a federal structure, the pro-Ethiopian SRRC won the political battle over the formula for state building.

Under the power-sharing arrangement, the president would come from Daarood to replace the Hawiye president, and the prime minister to come from Hawiye. The speaker of parliament would be from Rahanweyn. After ruthless political wrangling and alleged corruption by stakeholders facilitated or dictated by IGAD states, particularly Ethiopia, according to different opinions,[210] Colonel Abdullahi Yusuf Ahmed, a long-term Ethiopian ally and former president of Puntland was elected president of the TFG on 10 October 2004. Over 70 per cent of the lawmakers elected him as president out of twenty-six presidential candidates. Sharif Hassan from Rahanweyn was elected speaker of the new parliament.

Colonel Abdullahi Yusuf, an unpredictable and authoritarian warlord[211] quickly took the following actions that would remain controversial throughout his government. First, with his style of confrontational and authoritarian leadership[212] he appointed Ali Mohammed Geedi, an Abgaal of the Hawiye clan as prime minister in accordance with the clan power-sharing arrangement. This was in violation of the Transitional National Charter, which stipulated the premiership should come from the parliament. The president's excuse was that Mohamed Dheere, a lawmaker from the same clan, had swapped his seat with Mr Geedi, who was not a member of the parliament. The appointment of the prime minister was rejected by the parliament, although it later approved on 23 December 2004.

The new prime minister nominated eighty-two strong member cabinet dominated by the SRRC wing and factional leaders, in which the Ethiopian government was accused of dictating the outcome of the selection process.[213] Indeed, a video was leaked in which an Ethiopian diplomat was reportedly dictating the selection of the new cabinet to the president and his prime minister in a meeting.[214] This warlord dominated government with Ethiopia's hand behind it did not impress the Somali people. And President Abdullahi Yusuf's style of confrontational and authoritarian leadership[215] would ensure that he fell out with all of his prime ministers.

Second, with his belief in using force to pacify and stabilize Somalia, he immediately requested deployment of strong 20,000 African peacekeepers without first securing approval by the parliament or the cabinet in disregard with the Transitional Federal Charter.[216] By this action, Colonel Abdullahi Yusuf, a military man who made no secret of his preference of using Ethiopian forces to stabilize the country, particularly Mogadishu,[217] had fired the first shot of a political disagreement between groups who were pro- or anti-intervention by foreign troops. This was a controversial and divisive issue that would dominate the political landscape for years to come. Indeed, in March

2005, a parliament session held in Nairobi to debate a motion to allow the deployment of peacekeepers from neighbouring states in Somalia as endorsed by IGAD heads of state, collapsed, resulting in lawmakers fighting with chairs to settle their political differences. Some lawmakers interpreted president's request for foreign troops as an invitation of an Ethiopian invasion.[218] This caused split within the parliament and the government into two wings: a pro-foreign troops' wing led by Colonel Yusuf and another group against it led by Sharif Hassan Sheikh Adan, speaker of the parliament. The issue of foreign troops still remains controversial as pro- and anti-factions are still fighting in Somalia, including Al-Shabaab, an extremist Islamist group.

After political wrangling over the seat of the government, the president's group relocated to Jowhar town in the middle Shebelle region near Mogadishu in June 2005 on the basis that the capital city was not safe and secure. After reconciliation efforts by President Ali Abdalla Salah of Yemen between the president and the speaker, the government relocated to Baidoa town in the Bay region in early 2006. For the first time in history, a government based on a federal design was installed on Somali soil. This was good news for Rahanweyn factions as their long-held dream of federalism seemed to have been realized. Public demonstrations were held in Baidoa to support the TFG, in which the speaker of parliament from Rahanweyn, addressed the public. The TFG started building state institutions and infrastructure from scratch.

One of the most important outcomes of the Mbagathi process was it dealt with the contentious issue of state building: federalism versus unitary systems, which was not given enough attention during the Arte process and was left unresolved. By embracing a national charter based on a federal formula, the Kenyan process accepted and endorsed the real politics on the ground in which powerful autonomous regional states were asserting their authorities, undermining any centralized national government. The process confirmed that real power was not in Mogadishu, but in regional state capitals from Hargeisa to Boosaaso and Baidoa.

With the power of hindsight, before the Kenyan process which produced proposal for a federal structure, although an scholar argued that the structure and what it meant had not been thoroughly thought about,[219] the earlier foreign-led reconciliation process from 1991 with its emphasis on imposing a unitary central government was the wrong medicine to cure a misdiagnosed illness, which required some form of decentralized state structure. Indeed, the desire for a decentralized state structure was there to be seen when regional-based states and administrations mushroomed across Somalia, providing some form of local governance amid anarchy because of the failure of these top-down process.[220]

However, the Kenyan conference failed to reconcile warring clans along the lines of the South African Truth and Reconciliation process. Indeed, immediately after the election of President Abdullahi Yusuf, some Daarood and Hawiye factions clashed in Eastleigh in Nairobi, revealing that old hostilities and wounds had not been healed.

Unfortunately, interference by regional actors, particularly Ethiopia and Kenya, domination of warlords of the process and marginalization of non-armed civil society groups and Colonel Abdullahi Yusuf's first two actions, particularly inviting foreign troops, would prove disastrous, contributing to the failure of the Mbagathi process as will be discussed in the next chapter.

The war on terror prolongs the conflict

Political Islam in Somalia: Al-Ittihad Al-Islami

As the broken Republic continued to suffer from the ills of a colonially divided nation, stresses of the USSR-induced Ogaden defeat and failure of the 1990s foreign power military intervention (UNOSOM), it found itself again torn apart by the cut-throat global politics of America's war on terror. Below are some of the major events, turning points, missed opportunities, actions and non-actions by Somali and foreign actors, which have resulted in the current situation.

Traditionally, Somalis are Sunni Muslims and follow the Shafiya doctrine, one of the four Islamic schools of jurisprudence. Since they converted to Islam, Somalis followed and practised Sufism, the more mystical and spiritual side of Islam. Historically, Sufism once dominated the Muslim world, and Somalis had and still have various Sufi orders, such as Al-Qadiriyah, Al-Salihiya, Al-Ahmediya and Al-Rufaiya under which they practise spiritual ritual dances and meditation, and sing holy chants.

However, by the 1960s, some Somali intellectuals were inspired by the rise of Muslim Brotherhoods founded by Hassan Al-Bana in 1929 to liberate Egypt from British rule, and to establish a global Islamic state. They formed Wahdat Al-Shabaab al-Islami and Jamat Al-ahli al-Islami and other organizations, which were very different from the mainstream Sufism because they were part of wider political, missionary and jihadism Islam in the Muslim world.[1]

After the military regime seized power in 1969, political Islamic groups went underground, their leaders fleeing to the Gulf countries because it was too dangerous to come out during the Republic's Marxist-inspired socialism era with the military leadership's rhetoric on gender equality. One only needs to remember the fate of those Saudi-Wahhabi-supported religious Somali clerics who questioned the 1975 gender equality law issued by the military regime to equalize men and women.[2] Indeed, other movements in the mid-1970s, such as the Al-Islah founded in 1978, ceased to exist because of the regime's repressive measures. Meanwhile, traditional Sufi orders continued to flourish with their popular mystical practices without much interruption because they were not interested in politics thus filling people's spiritual needs with their traditional mystic practices.

Political Islamic movements found their voice again in the 1980s. Young graduates from universities in the Middle East like Saudi Arabia with its generous scholarships to thousands of Somalis[3] founded AIAI (Unity of Islam) in the early 1980s. This was a merger of two groups: Mogadishu-based Al Jama'a Al-Islamiya (1982) and Wahhabiya-inspired Wahadat Al-Shabaab al-Islamiya in the north-west region (1984). They were influenced by militant jihadist messages of Egyptian clerics, such as Sayyid Qutb and Saudi clerics of the Wahhabiya branch.[4] These young men, across clan lines, were determined to use Islam as a unifying force to liberate Somalia from rampant corruption and virulent tribalism[5] that were ripping the country apart in what was the Republic's lowest point with armed rebels threatening the military regime's rule. They were quite active although under the watchful eyes of the regime's security forces. They were even accused of being behind the 1989 Mogadishu riots in which the Bishop of the Italian Roman Catholic Church in Mogadishu, Monsignor Salvatore Colombo, was killed.[6]

By 1991, as warring factions and clans were tearing the country apart, the AIAI re-emerged again and asserted its political presence to fill the power vacuum left by the collapse of the central government. In its conference in June 1991, the AIAI finalized its political and military wings under the leadership of Sheikh Ali Warsame and Hassan Dahir Aweys, respectively. Throughout the 1990s, the AIAI vigorously pursued to dominate economic and political power, siding one political faction against the other to achieve its jihadist objective. The organization plotted assassinations of Western workers and its opponents.[7] It captured cities and towns, such as Kismayo in the lower Juba region, and Luuq in 1991 where it imposed Islamic Sharia law to restore law and order. This experiment was aborted in 1996 when Ethiopia, suspicious of the AIAI links with the Ogaden liberation movements, supported other Somali secular forces to dismantle the group's infrastructure.[8] Furthermore, the defeat of the AIAI by the SSDF forces in the north-east regions was another classic example, which showed the organization's attempt to seize strategic cities, such as Boosaaso on the Red Sea in Puntland.

Even during the UNOSOM era, political Islamic groups played a role in undermining the ambitious mission, and rejected the operation.[9] Well before General Aideed's conflict with the UNOSOM, Islamic radical organizations and states, such as Sudan and Iran under the zeal of their Islamic revolutionary ideologies were determined to use Somalia as a base to spread their ideology in the region. Their intelligence agents founded and supported covert and overt Somali groups, such as a pro-Sudan Somali Islamic Union Party and a pro-Iranian Somali Revolutionary Guard trained to execute the two countries' objectives under the wider context of regional geopolitical rivalry, West versus Islam.[10] Their secret forces had helped General Aideed's propaganda and war machine, and were behind the massacre of the UN Pakistani troops and the shooting down of the US military helicopters,[11] which were turning points in the conflict.

Osama Bin Laden's Al-Qaeda structure was not absent from Somalia. He visited Somalia during the UNOSOM era, and Aiman Zahrawi, his deputy, took part in the fighting. Bin Laden had actually boasted about his organization's role in defeating the United States in Somalia.[12] In fact, President Clinton in need of face-saving action and justification for the US-UNOSOM debacle claimed that Iran, Sudan and Libya had supported General Aideed's war machine.[13]

Since its defeat in the early 1990s, the AIAI changed its strategy of alienating clan and secular forces to that of infiltrating them to achieve its objective of Islamization of Somali masses, as they adopted strategy of deep Islamization through education and charity work.[14] It established strong economic power base through informal financial networks, taking advantage of Muslim charity markets, such as Saudi Arabia's multi-billion petrol-dollar market, which the country and its Wahhabiya charitable organizations had been spending on Islamic evangelism.[15] Al-Barakaat, a Somali money transfer company, which was later banned by the United States for its links with terrorist network organizations, was one of these informal financial institutions that the AIAI had links with.[16]

The rise and fall of the Islamic Courts Union (ICU)

Well before the Djibouti reconciliation process in 2000, as part of the growing political Islam in Somalia, another power broker had emerged in the south, particularly Mogadishu. After the failure of previous peace initiatives to end Hawiye factional conflicts and after Mogadishu warlords had failed to establish a regional administration in Mogadishu, some Islamic courts were established in the city to fill the power vacuum. Supported by businesspeople, these were clan-based courts set up to restore law and order by using Islamic Sharia, and they sprung up during the civil war across Somalia. Its founders had links with the AIAI.[17] The courts became known as ICU and by 2000, they established a body called Sharia Implementation Council to unify and coordinate its members. They became formidable power brokers, supporting some stakeholders in the Arte conference, infiltrating the TNG, which was formed in Djibouti. The ICU grew in strength and organizational structure while the TNG was in power struggle against other factions, such as the SRRC.

This was followed by the 9/11 terrorist attack in 2001 on New York and President George Bush's 'war on terror', which changed post-Cold War world politics. It was under this huge political development that the TNG, which was formed in Djibouti, was accused of association with Islamic extremism, particularly the AIAI with its members in the ICU. In a campaign led by the media, Ethiopia and anti-TNG Somali factions, the TNG was described as a Trojan horse for the AIAI allegedly with links to Al-Qaeda.[18]

By 2002, Mogadishu and southern Somalia were full of rumours of the existence of foreign fighters, extremists and training camps, particularly in Ras Kamboni, a remote sea enclave in the lower Juba region.[19] Although never proved, it was alleged that Al-Qaeda had training camps. The Bush administration came close to attacking Somalia, although it later found out that the TNG was no more than a divided group unable to control few roadblocks in Mogadishu.[20]

By 2004, while the final stages of the IGAD led Mbagathi reconciliation process in Kenya were being finalized, the ICU established a consultative council (*Majlis Shura*),[21] headed by Sheikh Hassan Dahir Aweys, an AIAI leader who fought in the AIAI war with the SSDF in the 1990s. Sheikh Hassan, who was on the United States' list of terrorists with alleged links to Al-Qaeda, became ICU's spiritual leader;[22] Sheikh Sharif Sheikh Ahmed was selected as its executive leader. Having grown in power and structure, it focussed its attention on Mogadishu in order to remove warlords who had been controlling it since 1991. Mogadishu warlords, Muuse Sudi Yalahow, Bashir Raage, Mohamed Qanyare Afrah, Omar Finish, Abdi Awale Qeybdiid and Mohamed Habeeb Dheere of Jowhar town, formed the Alliance for the Restoration of Peace and Counter-Terrorism (ARPCT), a United States-backed counter-terrorism body to oppose ICU's growing power and influence.[23]

From March 2006, Mogadishu, a place of death since 1991, again witnessed another wave of deadly violence waged by the ICU and ARPCT. Hundreds of people lost their lives in a series of fighting. Finally, by June 2006, the ICU defeated the notorious Mogadishu warlords. For more than a decade and for the first time since 1991, the ICU achieved something that other Somali factions could not. It put the divided city under one single authority. This was a huge achievement and relief for Mogadishu residents who had been under the mercy of much hated and ruthless warlords who had been terrorizing the city for fifteen years.

For the first time, the ICU re-opened Mogadishu's international airport under one single authority. With its victory in Mogadishu, the ICU established itself as one of the most powerful political bodies in Somalia alongside the Transitional Federal Government (TFG), which was formed in Kenya. Its power and influence reached most regions apart from Somaliland and Puntland, and Bay and Bakool regions, which were under TFG control.

Generally, most Somalis in the south, particularly Mogadishu residents welcomed the rise of the ICU in the hope that this would put the city under one single authority, and would end fifteen years of anarchy.[24] With its rise to power, its supporters heralded new era for Somalia, a popular revolution, which will unify all Somalis through Islamic Sharia to save them from self-destruction that they had been inflicting on themselves for a long time. It was seen as a period that Islamic principles and Sharia will be used as unifying forces to restore law and order. Indeed, from June 2006 lawlessness and insecurity reduced across much of the southern Somalia.[25] Unfortunately, the respite of peace for the ordinary Somalis was to be proven false hope as events to come would show.

The ICU attempt to overrun TFG, Puntland and Somaliland

Having defeated Mogadishu warlords, the ICU took on the TFG, which was marred by inter-factional fighting and squabbles, accusing it of being a puppet of Ethiopia, Somalia's historical enemy. By using the African Union's decision to send in peacekeeping troops requested by the TFG, the ICU mobilized the public by appealing to Somalis' nationalist emotions to defend their country against foreign aggression particularly Ethiopians, whose forces were already in Somalia, supporting the TFG.[26] The ICU demanded withdrawal of the Ethiopian forces and invited Islamic jihadists to join holy war to install an Islamic state in the Horn of Africa. Osama Bin Laden, after warning nations not to send troops to Somalia, declared his support for the ICU, and urged Somalis to establish an Islamic state when he said: 'You have no other means for salvation unless you commit to Islam, put your hands in the hands of the Islamic Courts to build an Islamic state in Somalia.'[27]

The broken Republic, once humiliated by the USSR in the Ogaden conflict during the Cold War and let down by the UNOSOM in the 1990s, was again caught in the cut-throat politics of the war on terror, and a regional proxy war in Somalia waged by Ethiopia and Eritrea to settle their border dispute: Ethiopia supporting the TFG, and Eritrea backing the ICU. The TFG had already branded the ICU as a terrorist organization and appealed to the international community to send in foreign troops to dismantle terrorist networks.[28] The stage was set for another round of bloody confrontation and escalation of violence. From July 2006 until September 2006, the ICU seized major strategic towns, such as Kismayo, Beledweyn, Hararardhere and Burhakabo, a town few miles away from the TFG's headquarters at Baidoa, hence threatening the very existence of the government. The Ethiopian government sent in Ethiopian soldiers to save the TFG, which was cornered by the powerful ICU.

Having consolidated its power in the south and having cornered the TFG at Baidoa, the ICU took on Puntland and Somaliland. By November 2006, fighting between Puntland forces and the ICU militia in Galkayo city broke out over the establishment of Islamic courts in the Mudug region. The ICU infiltrated Somaliland after Sheikh Ali Warsame, one of the AlAI's founders who lived in the region and brother-in-law of the ICU's spiritual leader, Sheikh Hassan Dahir Aweys, had met with the ICU leadership in Mogadishu.[29] In its campaign to destabilize Somaliland, the ICU used a video footage in which Somaliland's security forces allegedly tortured a Muslim cleric. It urged people to demand implementation of Islamic Sharia in the region, as it threatened to dispatch thirty suicide bombers to eliminate Somaliland leaders who it described as infidels.[30] Consequently, several public rallies took place in Hargeisa and Burao, as some constituents embraced the ICU's Islamization project in Somalia. This was a serious threat to the region's security posed by the ICU and its supporters who were determined to use Islam as a rallying card in a conservative society where Islam and tribalism trigger strong emotions. In fact, Somaliland leaders were forced to publicly announce that they would implement Sharia, and were at the edge of establishing Islamic courts in Somaliland.[31]

As a monster jumping out of its cage, ICU's spiritual leader, Sheikh Hassan Dahir Aweys, even talked up the issue of Greater Somalia, and vowed to liberate Somalis in Kenya and Ethiopia when he said: 'We will leave no stone unturned to integrate our Somali brothers in Kenya and Ethiopia and restore their freedom to live with their ancestors in Somalia.'[32]

Khartoum talks: Missed opportunity

As the conflict was unfolding, the Sudanese government initiated new peace talks to mediate between the ICU and TFG. The talks, supported by the Arab League, took place in an environment where both sides were reluctant to talk to each other because of the hostile political environment. On a wider regional and international political context, Ethiopia and the United States were unhappy with the rise of the ICU under the leadership of Sheikh Hassan Dahir Aweys, already on the United States' terrorist list. The two countries perceived the ICU as a terrorist organization, sheltering foreign jihadi fighters, including those behind the bombing of the embassies of the United States in East Africa. Ethiopia had its own security concerns over the ICU's pan-Somalism rhetoric and for sheltering anti-Ethiopian insurgents, such as Ogaden and Oromo liberation movements.[33] Therefore, to them to support the TFG to offset the growing influence of Islamists was the logical conclusion of the unfolding conflict. On the other hand, the ICU accused the United States and its allies of Islam-phobia. Ethiopia's interference in Somalia's affairs attracted sympathizers from the Arab and Islamic countries, such as Djibouti, Saudi Arabia, Libya, Syria and Iran.[34]

At a regional level, having fallen out over a border war between the countries in the 1990s, Ethiopia and Eritrea were executing proxy war in which Ethiopia supported the TFG while Eritrea assisted the ICU. Effectively, the internationalization of the Somali conflict rendered the broken Republic an experimental ground for the execution of the global war on terror with its competing and conflicting agendas and actors.

More importantly, historical animosity and mistrust between lead characters of the conflict were fuelling the crises. President Abdullahi Yusuf and Colonel-cum-cleric Sheikh Hassan Dahir Aweys were old enemies who had already fought against each other in the north-east region (Puntland) in which Colonel Abdullahi's SSDF militia defeated Sheikh Aweys's AIAI forces in the early 1990s.[35] The two men's political and ideological positions as an Islamist and secularist have never been reconciled. Colonel Abdullahi Yusuf made clear of his opposition to political Islam and extremism,[36] as his earlier actions proved that. On the other hand, Sheikh Hassan D. Aweys was adamant to install an Islamic state, which he saw as a solution to Somalia's problems.[37]

In addition to their ideological differences, at clan level politics, Sheikh Aweys is Ayre, a sub-clan of Habargedir of Hawiye, while Colonel Abdullahi Yusuf is Omar Mohamud, a sub-clan of Majeerteen Daarood, hence giving the conflict the ruthless clan vendetta politics. Indeed, some Daarood constituents perceived the ICU as an instrument for Hawiye domination, while many Hawiye factions saw Colonel Yusuf as Daarood president determined to avenge for the massacre of Daaroods in Mogadishu in the early 1990s.[38]

The Khartoum peace initiative initially achieved some progress, for example, both sides recognized each other, agreed to set up a united national army, and to hold further talks on power sharing. However, the initiative stalled because of AU/IGAD leaders went ahead with their plan to deploy African troops in Somalia. This was a turning point that angered the ICU, which then went on to intensify its military action against the TFG.[39] An assassination attempt on President Abdullahi Yusuf's life on 18 September 2006 in what was the first suicide car bombing in Somalia executed by the ICU's military wing[40]contributed to end the talks. Eight people, including the president's brother, were killed in the incident. This escalated the violence and hostility between the parties.

US collusion in the Ethiopian invasion of Somalia

In November 2006, while the stand-off between the two parties remained unresolved, a UN group, which was monitoring arms embargo imposed on Somalia in 1992, submitted a report to the Security Council. The report named and shamed states that had been arming both parties in violation of the embargo; it particularly highlighted Ethiopia and Eritrea's deep involvement in arming both sides.[41] The group recommended tighter arms embargo, including the use of air and sea blockage, and imposing financial sanctions against violators. It also warned against the deployment of foreign troops and alerted that a violent confrontation of factions would lead to a protracted and wider civil war.[42]

Despite such an explicit report warning of the dangers of a looming war, following a request by the AU/IGAD, the US ambassador, John Bolton, masterminded a UN resolution to lift the arms embargo so that 8,000 African peacekeepers could be deployed in Somalia to support the TFG.[43] On 6 December 2006 and just less than a month after the report, the Security Council adopted resolution no. 1725, which partially lifted the embargo, and allowed the deployment of peacekeepers to protect TFG institutions. The resolution excluded regional states: Ethiopia, Kenya, Eritrea and Djibouti from providing troops. Some analysts interpreted the resolution as escalation of already gloomy and complicated situation, and a prelude to war instigated by the United States.[44] Indeed, it was unbelievable to lift the arms embargo just after the UN report had already warned against it, and when IGAD states were deeply divided over the conflict.

The United States-backed resolution had some similarities with the events leading up to the UN resolution prior to the Iraq invasion by the United States and its allies in 2001. In the Somali case, just less than a month a UN report had warned of the severity of the situation and recommended tightened arms embargo. Few months prior to the resolution, the TFG and ICU were engaged in peace talks in Khartoum, and, therefore, with some encouragement there was a room for further peace talks just as more time and further negotiations with Saddam Hussein's regime could have averted the war. The ICU had even signed a communiqué in Djibouti with IGAD under which it had condemned terrorism, vowed to respect neighbouring countries' territorial integrity, and not to host anti-Ethiopia insurgency groups.[45]

Nevertheless, although the international community led by the UN special representative to Somalia, Francois L. Fall, had initiated some mediation efforts to reconcile the parties, the United States-backed resolution had in effect destroyed any hope of that ever happening. By allowing the deployment of foreign forces, it had in effect signalled the beginning of war given ICU's strong objection to any foreign troops and in light of the monitoring group's report. Although the new resolution excluded frontline states, it had tacitly encouraged Ethiopia to continue its intervention in Somalia. As they say, actions speak louder than words because Ethiopian forces were already deeply involved in Somalia, supporting the TFG, which angered ICU leadership who called for jihad.[46]

The reality of the situation was that a few months earlier the United States had formed alliance with Ethiopia to invade Somalia to dismantle the Islamist structure.[47] In fact, a watered down earlier UN resolution, backed by the United States, would have been a cover up to allow Ethiopia to intervene in Somalia directly.[48] Therefore, the resolution was just a cover up for the US/Ethiopia decision to invade the broken Republic. Somalia, destroyed by murderous civil war, found itself in the frontline of the war on terror, which was ripping the country apart.

With the power of hindsight, more negotiations could have saved Somalia from what was to come. Had the Somali sides put their difference aside, continued with the Khartoum talks and then formed a national unity government, and had members of the UN Security Council not endorsed the United States-backed resolution, which paved the way for the Ethiopian invasion, southern Somalia would probably have emerged from the protracted civil war in 2006. Certainly, Khartoum initiative was another missed opportunity among the list of the many missed opportunities. In sum, dynamics of the war on terror had contributed to prolonging the Somali conflict.

Not surprisingly, the resolution sparked mass protests in Mogadishu organized by the ICU, calling Somalis to jihad to defend their faith and country. By December 2006, as clouds of war had been gathering over Somalia's blue skies for some time, the country faced not the usual clan conflict, but another kind of war, in which President George W. Bush (junior) divided the world into 'Either you are with us, or you are with the terrorists. From this day forward, any nation that continues to harbor or support terrorism will be regarded by the United States as a hostile regime.'[49]

ICU leaders demanded withdrawal of Ethiopian forces within seven days and by 24 December declared jihad, calling on Muslims to join a holy war.[50] On the other hand, Ethiopia had already declared war on the ICU after its parliament had authorized its prime minister Meles Zenawi on 30 November 2006 to take all necessary actions to defend Ethiopia's national sovereignty.[51] Ethiopian forces were already defending TFG positions across southern Somalia.

In a series of fighting at Baidoa, Beledweyn, Kismayo, Bandiiradley, Jilib and Ras Kamboni, ICU militia attempted to destroy TFG forces. The 'war of miscalculation' as Dr Abdishakur Jowhar (2006b) described it reached its climax when Ethiopian fighter jets bombed Mogadishu's international airport and other ICU strongholds. As the war escalated, Islamist forces abandoned their positions and simply melted away in crowds without much resistance.[52] Their last stronghold was in Ras Kamboni in the lower Juba region, where AC-130 American gunships bombarded Islamist positions in Afmadow and Ras Kamboni in pursuit of Al-Qaeda suspects and cells.[53] ICU's Islamist forces, mainly composed of lightly armed youth and ragtag militia, crumbled in front of 50,000 heavily armed Ethiopian troops supported by tanks, helicopters and jet fighters.[54] This is how Dr Abdishakur Jowhar articulated the disparity of the firepower and bitterness of the fighting:

> The youth were gallant beyond belief; they threw themselves with gusto into the battle. They mowed down wave after wave of Ethiopian army. . . . They fought on in spite of the shortages of food, fuel and reinforcement. But the Ethiopians kept coming. They came on foot, with tanks, with armored personnel carriers, with heavy equipment and heavier mighty flying machines. The Somali youth stood their ground, volunteered, advanced and martyred. Volunteered, advanced with *Takbiir*[55] on their lips and martyred.[56]

Within four weeks of the UN resolution 1725, Ethiopian forces occupied southern Somalia. From the sequence of events, including US airstrikes, it is clear that Ethiopia with the approval of the Bush administration invaded Somalia in what was a proxy war on behalf of the United States.[57] Indeed, although US officials publicly claimed to have warned Ethiopia not to invade Somalia, Wikileaks cables revealed that the former US under secretary of state for Africa Jendayi Frazer, a close associate of the former US secretary of state Condoleezza Rice, had pressurized or 'twisted' Ethiopia's arms to invade Somalia.[58]

Commenting on the real power politic behind the invasion, this is how Dr Abdi I. Samatar, a Somali scholar, explained:

> While most analysts knew that America was implicated in the invasion, it was the use of American airpower against villages in Southern Somalia in early January 2007 that confirmed how deeply the US was involved. About 73 nomadic individuals and their livestock were killed by the air raid and no one openly condemned this aggression, including the AU. More recently, it has been discovered that American, British, and hired mercenaries supported the Ethiopian invasion.[59]

To some Somali constituents, the invasion aborted a revolutionary movement, which could have saved Somalis from the curse of clanism, although to its opponents, it was no more than a movement of clan demagogy harbouring foreign jihadist to install religious dictatorship.[60] The movement, which restored law and order during its six months reign by using draconian Islamic Sharia, made some strategic mistakes in what was a 'war of miscalculation'.

First, before consolidating a solid governance structure, ICU leaders provoked the TFG, thinking that by using its thousands of militiamen it could just abort the weak government. However, the TFG protected itself by affiliating with formidable allies, such as United States and Ethiopia.[61] Second, the more radical and young elements within the ICU known as 'Al-Shabaab' had hijacked the movement, causing more divisions and increased militant rhetoric against Ethiopia/TFG, which then led Ethiopia putting more pressure on the movement before the movement was ready. The division within the movement was serious and attacking TFG/Ethiopia was a pressure-releasing valve in order to accommodate the young radicals who had hijacked the movement.[62] This means that had the ICU not attacked TFG/Ethiopia, it would have crumbled within on its weight because of inter-fighting and leadership conflict.

Divided Republic

The broken Republic, once defeated by USSR/Ethiopia in the Ogaden war, was again humiliated by Ethiopia supported by the United States, another superpower in pursuit of its national security interests. The Ethiopian military adventure surprised many Somalis who felt humiliated by the experience. For the first time in history, Ethiopian forces erected an Ethiopian flag on the broken Republic's capital city by force. Some analysts interpreted the invasion as part of Ethiopia's determination to annex Somalia to its multi-ethnic empire.[63] Furthermore, it had not only dismantled popular local revolutionary movement,[64] but it installed unpopular government dominated by some characters who were seen as warlords and traitors. Indeed, escorted by Ethiopian forces, Colonel Abdullahi Yusuf, the first man who had led Ethiopian forces into Somali soil in 1978 to fight General Siyad Barre's government, a treacherous act at the time, entered Mogadishu on 8 January 2007 on Ethiopian tanks. Just few days before, Ethiopian helicopters had flown the prime minister, Ali Mohamed Geedi, another man with suspected Ethiopian connections, to Mogadishu.[65] With the power of hindsight, had he been alive today President Siyad Barre would have quickly reminded his supporters of his views that Colonel Abdullahi Yusuf was one of power-hungry characters who would do anything for their long-term presidential dreams.

The invasion deeply divided the international community and Somalis. Some UN member states demanded immediate withdrawal of Ethiopian forces from Somalia because Ethiopia's action was illegal and against international laws, particularly resolution no. 1725, which excluded neighbouring countries from sending troops to Somalia. Although the invasion was clearly in breach of the resolution, United States and its allies in the Security Council were reluctant to call on Ethiopia to withdraw its forces.

To the supporters of the invasion, mainly factions of some sub-clans of President Abdullahi Yusuf's Majeerteen Daarood and some Abgaal factions[66] it was time of celebration and jubilation as their version of the history of power struggle and clan warfare in Somalia had been vindicated.[67] To them, their man, President Abdullahi Yusuf, supported by United States/Ethiopia, was in power, and it was their turn to run the country as Hawiye had their time during the previous Transitional National Government (TNG). To them, Ethiopian military adventure was not invasion, but an act of salvation by Ethiopia to dismantle warlordism and radical Islamism, and the action was approved by the TFG, a legitimate Somali government borne out of the Kenyan process determined to restore law and order.[68] These constituencies set up their own organizations and their own media outlets in support of the new power structure.

To the opponents of the invasion, it was time of national humiliation and disgrace to see a historical enemy erecting its flag on Somali soil. It was time of lamentation, sorrow and reflection on the deep divisions among Somalis, which allowed their enemy to occupy their country. To them to allow Ethiopia to dismantle the ICU, a genuine national movement, only to be replaced by a puppet, ineffective and warlord dominated government, was treason and national tragedy.[69] To clan-minded constituencies, this was a government led by a Daarood president[70] in uncertain times with painful things to come given the past hostilities between Hawiyes and Daaroods.

To the Bush administration, it was job well done by Ethiopia[71] for dismantling a Taliban style terrorist organization with Al-Qaeda links,[72] which could have instigated religious and nationalist wars in the Horn. To Ethiopia, with its fear of Somali nationalism and irredentism, installing a government led by their long-term collaborator was the best outcome of the adventure.[73] Knowing his poor country could not sustain war efforts on a long-term basis, Ethiopian prime minister Meles Zenawi, after boasting of his quick and sweeping victory over the ICU, said his troops would not stay in Somalia more than what is necessary.[74] Nevertheless, his political calculation of the military adventure was to be proven wrong by the events to come.

To the global Islamists and jihadists, the invasion was a Zionist-Crusaders' conspiracy to convert Somalis to Christianity and destroy their national and Muslim identities. Hence, to them it was religious duty to liberate Somalia from Ethiopian colonialism.[75] Immediately, out of the ashes of the defunct-ICU, a variety of Islamist groups, such the Popular Resistance Movement in the Land of the Two Migrations, Unity and Struggle, the Young Mujahideen Movement in Somalia and Al-Shabaab, had emerged and flourished.[76]

Puntland supported the invasion, and was a power base for the TFG, which was now led by Colonel Abdullahi Yusuf, its previous leader, propping it up financially and militarily.[77] Somaliland with its usual hostility towards any government formed in the south viewed the TFG/Ethiopian adventure with hostility and reiterated its unilateral independence.[78] The invasion re-ignited animosity between Puntland and Somaliland, which started since Colonel Abdullahi Yusuf was elected president of the TFG in 2004. Their militias fought over the disputed regions of Sanaag and Sool from April 2007. In the context of clan politics and dynamics of the creation of regional states, Isaaq-dominated Somaliland was not prepared to allow Daarood-dominated Puntland supporting Abdullahi Yusuf's government undermine its quest for independence.[79] On the other hand, Puntland and TFG were adamant to defend Sool region from what they described as a secessionist enclave.[80]

To secular nationalists and intellectuals across clan spectrum inside and outside the country, they opposed the invasion and established their own political and media organizations. Indeed, as far away as Europe and United States, they stepped up their campaign against the occupation, expressing their anger through poems, songs and literature.[81]

To ordinary Somalis, it was national humiliation as their historical enemy, Ethiopia, had occupied their national capital city. They took to the streets as far away as Minneapolis in United States, condemning the occupation.[82] Poets and artists wrote and composed nationalistic songs and waved the blue coloured national flag.

Clan vendetta dimension of the conflict

It was under such deeply divided Somalia that Colonel Abdullahi Yusuf and his prime minister descended on Mogadishu on Ethiopian tanks and helicopters. It was particularly nerve-racking event for the president to come to Mogadishu, considering atrocities committed by Hawiyes against his Daarood kinsmen. After short-lived jubilation by some Somali constituents who welcomed TFG/Ethiopian victory, hard reality set in, as insecurity and lawlessness in Mogadishu increased. The TFG, using Ethiopian firepower, started to assert its authority, and pursued its disarmament programme. But some Mogadishu residents did not welcome this and staged demonstrations. Within a week of the occupation, resurgence movements of Islamists, secular nationalists to clan-minded groups with different motivations and objectives[83] started their struggle against the occupation. Immediately, insurgents killed Ethiopian soldiers, assassinated government officials, as they bombed government positions, including Villa Somalia, the presidential palace.

By the end of March 2007, the conflict intensified when TFG/Ethiopia forces tried to disarm armed groups by force in a city where ICU fighters had simply disappeared and hid their weapons or handed them over to their clans. When insurgents refused to hand in weapons and in response to insurgency fire, TFG/Ethiopian forces used heavy artillery and tanks, and indiscriminately shelled civilian populated areas, causing the death of hundreds of civilians and injury of thousands of people.[84] An estimated 340,000 civilians were displaced from the city[85] the largest displacement the city had ever experienced.[86] The shelling reduced some Mogadishu quarters to rubble. TFG leadership including, the president, his prime minister and his interior minister Mohamed Sheik Mohamoud Guuleed 'Gacmadhere', made no secret that their forces would shell civilian populated areas in pursuit of the insurgency, which they described as terrorists. Asked if his forces would bombard civilian areas, President Abdullahi Yusuf said they would if they were fired upon regardless of who resides there.[87]

Other TFG officials who were actively involved in these military operations during the shelling, included General Abdi Awale Qeydiid, commander of the police, Mohamed Omar Habeeb 'Dheere', mayor of Mogadishu and Mohamed Warsame Darwish, head of a security agency. On the Ethiopian side, General Gabre Heard, Prime Minister Meles Zenawi's military commander in Mogadishu, was the man leading the Ethiopian forces which were indiscriminately shelling Mogadishu and committing atrocities and war crimes against civil population.[88] By late April 2007, the TFG claimed victory over insurgents in Mogadishu.

To put the new conflict into perspective, the TFG backed by Ethiopia had won the war and was adamant to disarm insurgents by force to do its job as legitimate government born out of the Kenyan reconciliation process. In other words, TFG/Ethiopians were 'winners', dictating the rules of the game to the insurgency. They would just label all insurgents as Al-Qaeda-linked terrorists to be dealt with.[89]

Although the conflict had multiple actors with different objectives from America's war on terror, global radical Islamists, Ethiopia's fear of Somali nationalism, a proxy war by Eritrea and Ethiopia, the TFG/Ethiopian military adventure re-ignited the 1991 inter- and intra-clan conflict.[90]

In Mogadishu, to clan-minded Hawiye constituencies, they simply saw the disarmament as an attack by Daarood president using Ethiopian forces to disarm them by force, which they perceived unfair as other rival clans would still be keeping their weapons. To them, the TFG was a Daarood-dominated institution led by President Abdullahi Yusuf who was determined to avenge for the massacre of Daaroods in the 1990s. Indeed, a leading figure of Mogadishu's civil society voiced his concern about the revenge dimension of the conflict when he said: 'This is a government bent on revenge against the Hawiye.'[91] As a contribution to TFG forces, Colonel Yusuf had already recruited thousands of militiamen from his Majeerteen clan, as he had given sensitive security and intelligence positions to his close associates.[92] He was on the throne at the famous Villa Somalia where General Siyad Barre, Daarood president, was forced out by Hawiye-dominated USC. He was adamant to rein in what he described as 'certain genealogical groups (that) oppose his sectarian and clanistic agenda' to be dealt with.[93]

Although his prime minister was Hawiye, some Hawiye constituents saw this not as real power sharing because the prime minister lacked experience and higher status to represent them, and was associated with Ethiopia.[94] In addition, the prime minister himself was an Abgaal, and therefore some Habargedir constituencies might have worried that he might use his position to settle old scores in relation to the Abgaal and Habargedir's conflict in Mogadishu in the early 1990s between Ali Mahdi and General Aideed. Indeed, the prime minister and his vice defence minister Salad Jeelle, both Abgaals, were caught in a rant in a meeting in which they had vowed to dislodge Habargedirs from Mogadishu.[95]

Clan-minded Hawiye constituencies formed their own resistance organizations, such as Hawiye Elders Council (HEC), its leaders included Ahmed Diriye who was detained by TFG/Ethiopian forces, and Hawiye Action Group (HAG). To them, they had to defend themselves against invading Daarood militia from Puntland, as articulated by Abdullahi Sheikh Hassan, one of the founders of the HEC: 'This is a clan war. The Hawiye [clan of most Mogadishu residents] are defending themselves against an invading Puntland [President Abdullahi Yusuf's home region] militia.'[96]

Some analysts perceived the emptying of certain quarters of Mogadishu as genocide against particular clans. The TFG/Ethiopian leadership, Prime Minister Meles Zenawi, President Abdullahi Yusuf and his prime minister saw members of Ayr, a sub-clan of the Habargedir as the backbone of the insurgency, and therefore a culprit and enemy to be 'cleansed' out of Mogadishu.[97] It was at this time when thousands of civilians, mainly Habargedirs fled Mogadishu, seeking refuge in their traditional homeland as far away as Mudug in central regions, a homeland for Habargedirs. In addition, at the time the Ayr sub-clan was perceived as harbouring Al-Qaeda terrorist cells in Mogadishu, as revealed by Wikileaks cables.[98] Therefore, the scene was set for a mixture of clan revenge and pursuit of terrorist cells. Certainly, vindictive clan politics had been one of the main factors throughout the civil war.[99] Here is how Dr Jowhar, a Somali analyst, described the new clan cleansing in Mogadishu in what was a multi-dimensional war:

> Mogadishu, the capital of Somalia, is a city living a clandestine nightmare that even Dante could not imagine. But on this day, nothing could conceal the truth as told by dead bodies piling up on its streets. Every freshly killed body, every dead body thrown into the impromptu mass graves; every one of these belongs to only one Somali tribe and no other. Over 1000 bodies of civilians have been found so far; and every last one of them belong to the same tribe - the Hawiye. The dead do not lie. And this is the story they tell; the story of the curse of tribal cleansing yet again; the story of yet another reenactment of the first phase of the Tutsi genocide.[100]

Professor Abdi I. Samatar, another Somali scholar, not only explained President Abdullahi Yusuf's appetite for revenge against Hawiyes, but also the inter-Hawiye conflict in which the Prime Minister Geedi and his deputy defence minister Salad Jeelle, both Abgaals, called on their clan to assist Ethiopians to evict Habargedirs from Mogadishu:

> The Ethiopian occupations and the TFG and its militia are tantamount to supporting the murderous Interahamwe of Rwanda, the Hutu radicals which perpetrated Rwanda's genocide. One of the features of the Rwandan Hutu radicals

was the categorical demonization of moderate Hutus and all Tutsis. This is exactly the language used by the TFG and prime minister. Mr. Yusuf has often repeated that certain genealogical groups oppose his sectarian and clanistic agenda. . . . In one instance, he refers to taking revenge in such a way that some of the victims of the 1991/2 killing fields becoming today's killers. . . . In addition to Mr. Yusuf's call for revenge, the TFG's prime minister and the deputy minister of defense have subsequently convened a meeting in which they called on 'their clan' to assist the Ethiopian troops in cleansing the city of the opposition genealogical groups.[101]

The clan vendetta dimension of the conflict was bad as Togane a Somali-Canadian poet articulated in one of his polemic poems:

Ina Yay (President Abdullahi Yusuf) is a Daarood Demean and there is nothing uglier than a Daarood who is demean; who is dummpkofp: Abdullah Yusuf has nothing going for him: he only understands QABIIL IYO QORIGA MADOW: Tribalism: the most insidious sort of racism and her attendant naked black gun just like his buddy Aidiid!

Hirab: (Somali) The collective clannish name for the Abgaal and the Habarg Gidir; the Cain and the Abel of Somali suicidal politics; the Habar Gidir are Cain and my Abgaal are Abel.[102]

The war between ICU and TFG, Ethiopia's military adventure, the multi-faceted insurgency and the clan vendetta dimension of the conflict, bungled all under the disguise of the war on terror, practically killed all the goodwill and optimism generated in the Mbagathi reconciliation process in Kenya, which created the TFG.

Birth of resistance movements

If the United States-backed Ethiopian military adventure was meant to enable the TFG stabilize the country and dismantle radical Islam infrastructure, it failed on both counts.

From the moment of the occupation, Somalia, particularly Mogadishu became war zone where multi-faceted insurgence movements fought ruthless TFG/Ethiopian forces in an Afghanistan–Iraq insurgency style. Somali suicide bombers, a new phenomenon in Somali culture, attacked and destroyed TFG/Ethiopian military convoys, as roadside bombs maimed and killed Ethiopian soldiers whose mutilated bodies were dragged in Mogadishu streets exactly as General Aideed's militiamen had done to American marines in Mogadishu in 1993. The quick victory by the Ethiopian forces turned into nightmare, and it was not that long before Ethiopian leadership realized the strength of Somalis' opposition and anger at the invasion, which indeed radicalized Somalis.

Straight away, ICU leaders and some members of the Transitional Federal Parliament (TFP), who opposed the invasion, led by the parliament speaker, Sharif Hassan Sheikh Aden, fled to neighbouring countries, having refused to participate in a reconciliation conference organized by the TFG in Mogadishu. By September 2007, they established a base in Asmara, the capital city of Eritrea, a country only too happy to accommodate any anti-Ethiopian groups in pursuit of its proxy war with Ethiopia. They formed Alliance for the Re-Liberation of Somalia (ARS) in September 2007. The group, a mixture of parliamentarians and diaspora, but dominated by Islamists, formed a 191 central committee and elected Sheikh Sharif Sheikh Ahmed, former ICU executive chairman, as its leader.

The ARS in Asmara became a focal and pilgrimage point for those against the Ethiopian occupation and the TFG. From there on, different personalities and groups conducted and led resistance campaigns as ARS's spokesman, Zakaria Mahamud Abdi explained: 'The alliance is undertaking every effort to get rid of Ethiopia. We plan to spread the resistance in Mogadishu, and we have already sent people inside Somalia. This is our job.'[103]

Inside the country, alongside secularist and clan-minded insurgency groups, an Islamist insurgency movement spearheaded by Al-Shabaab (youth in Arabic) took on Ethiopian/TFG forces. The group, mainly dominated by Somali Islamists with links to Al-Qaeda, was ICU's military and militant youth wing.[104] Its leaders include Aden Hashi Ayro, who would be killed by an American missile on 1 May 2008 in Dhuusa Mareeb, Mukhtar Robow ('Abu Mansur'), Ahmad Abdi Godane (Abu Zuber) who would be killed by American strike in 2014; Ibrahim Haji Jama ('al-Afghani'); Sheik Hassan Dahir Aweys; Sheik Ali Dheere; Ahmed Diriye (Abu Zubeyr); Sheikh Hassan Abdullah Hirsi al-Turki and Sheikh Fuad Shangole.[105]

The group had one thing in common, they were militant and hardliner jihadists inspired by global militant Islam and *Al-Qaeda*, and some of them were fighters in Afghanistan. Their fighters, known for their masked faces, although taking heavy casualties, fought TFG/Ethiopian forces on a hit and run basis, using roadside bombs, mortar attacks and suicide bombers on nearly daily basis. They certainly introduced suicide bombings to Somalia, and as early as April 2007, suicide bombers, such as Abdul-Aziz Dawood Abdul-Qader and Adam Salad Adam[106] drove trucks laden with explosives into Ethiopian army bases in Mogadishu. This was followed by many more suicide bombings of over ten incidents throughout the occupation and its aftermath.

Under their strict interpretation of the *Islamic Sharia* (Islamic law) they introduced harsh and draconian laws in the areas they controlled. They cut throats of those they suspected as traitors, infidels and spies and posted executions on the open social media. As it consolidated its power in south, the group invited global Islamist and jihadist groups to congregate at Somalia to liberate Somalia from the Crusaders. Here is how Sheikh Mukhtar Robow (Abu Mansur) articulated their fighters' objectives:

> We assure our Muslim brothers and beloved companions who march alongside us on the path of *jihad*, that God has granted the people of Somalia many bounties that many other people in other places do not have. . . . The doors of encampment, fighting, and martyrdom are wide open. Your Somali brothers are engaged in one of the bloody decisive battles against the Crusaders.[107]

The invasion re-invigorated fully fledged radical Islamist movement, proud of its ideological links with Al-Qaeda with the blessing of Osama Bin Laden, which would last well after Ethiopian forces' withdrawal from Somalia.[108] This was exactly the opposite of what the United States-backed Ethiopian invasion was supposed to achieve. The real outcome of the military adventure was, therefore, the radicalization of many Somalis who could not tolerate Ethiopian occupation. Out of the ashes of the defunct-ICU rose the Al-Shabaab movement and other nationalist movements, such as the ARS.

As events moved on, the ARS in Asmara split into factions. One group, led by Sheikh Sharif Sheikh Ahmed, accepted peace talks and negotiations offered by the TFG under the leadership of Prime Minister Nur Hassan Hussein ('Nur Adde'). This faction was based in Djibouti. The other group, led by Sheikh Hassan Dahir Aweys, rejected talks with the TFG and remained in Asmara.

By June 2008, the TFG and the ARS-Djibouti faction started peace talks under the auspices of the UN special representative of the Secretary General (SRSG) Ahmedou Ould Abdallah. Both sides agreed to three months ceasefire, withdrawal of Ethiopian troops within 120 days, and deployment of peacekeepers. The Asmara-based faction and Al-Shabaab rejected any negotiation with the TFG and urged the insurgency to fight Ethiopian forces.[109] By this action, the original Asmara-based resistance movement, the focal point for the resistance, had lost its momentum. Sheikh Hassan Dahir Aweys and Sheikh Sharif, ICU's old friends, became bitter enemies with accusation and counter-accusation of betrayal.

The ARS's split, caused by one group accepting peace initiative and another rejecting it, is typical of Somali factionalism with its multi-dimensional clan, religion, foreign interests and resource factors behind it, and its usual devastating consequences as Prof. Menkhaus argues. Indeed, the division was not an isolated phenomenon within the ARS, but the TFG, which was already factionalized since Colonel Abdullahi Yusuf's election as president, was also divided. Indeed, from October 2007, President Abdullahi Yusuf was in political confrontation with his prime minister Ali Geedi over constitutional arrangements, particularly the time-scale in which the government was supposed to prepare a federal constitution to be approved by the Somali people.[110] The prime minister, the same man he had handpicked for the job, was forced to resign. The president's woes did not end there, and by December 2008, he had another political disagreement with his new prime minister Nur Hassan Adde who he appointed to replace Geedi. The president, sticking with his tough stand against resistance groups,[111] was determined to remove Nur Hassan Adde, who was in favour of negotiation with the opposition groups.[112]

The power struggle was played out openly when the president sacked Nur Hassan Adde and appointed new prime minister Mohamed Guuleed 'Gamadhere', only to be rejected by the parliament. Supporters of the two men exchanged accusations and counter-accusations of treason, abuse of power and incompetence.[113] The most important slogan was Prime Minister Nur Adde's portrayal of the president as an obstacle to peace,[114] which moved the international community against the president[115] who was forced to resign in December 2008.

His supporters would remember him as the man who brought a Somali government to Villa Somalia for the first time since the removal of General Siyad Barre from power, and they would blame Hawiye politicians for his downfall.[116] They would remember him as the man who attempted to impose law and order on Hawiye clans whose factional fighting had been major phenomenon which prolonged the Somali conflict. On the other hand, his opponents will remember him as a dictator, confrontational and a man who had led Ethiopian forces to occupy Somalia only to use them as a mechanism for clan revenge as mentioned earlier.

During this inter-factional squabble between the TFG and ARS, the Ethiopian government had by then announced its attention of withdrawing its troops from Somalia. Reasons behind Ethiopia's decision included relentless military campaign by the insurgency, and the Djibouti-based ARS and TFG agreement, which stipulated a timetable for the withdrawal. And equally important factor was Ethiopia's inability to sustain war efforts due to lack of resources. Indeed, the Ethiopian prime minister's original political plan was to withdraw his troops within a few weeks from the invasion in 2006, and to hand the process of peacekeeping and stabilization to international peacekeepers.[117] However, to his frustration, his plan was proven wrong because the occupation lasted two long years. Ethiopian forces withdrew from the broken Republic in January 2009 just one month after Colonel Abdullahi Yusuf was forced to resign. It seems though Ethiopia and its man Colonel Abdullahi Yusuf and his government were destined to leave together.

In this conflict, which lasted two years, some 20,000 Somalis were killed, and 2 million people were displaced.[118] Both sides committed human rights abuses, genocide and war crime.[119]

The Ethiopian invasion practically killed all the goodwill generated in the reconciliation process in Kenya. Although there was a need for peacekeeping forces to support TFG's programme of disarmament and stabilization, by allowing Ethiopia to take the lead was a huge political misjudgement given the historical animosity between the two countries. To the objective analysts and most Somalis, a mixture of neutral forces led by Islamic, Arab and other countries would have been ideal and would probably have encountered lesser hostility and anger. Failure of the Khartoum peace initiative, aborted by the UN Security Council resolution 1725, also destroyed any hope of the two sides forming a national unity government.

Although the TFG organized some reconciliation conferences inside Somalia, it had lost its credibility and momentum generated at the Kenyan peace process after Colonel Abdullahi Yusuf and his constituency called on the deployment of foreign troops immediately after his election. This is because from the onset the decision divided his government and Somalis into pro and anti-foreign troop's factions. Also, President Yusuf's confrontational leadership style ensured that his government was deeply divided all the way through his resignation. Indeed, Colonel Abdullahi Yusuf had fallen out with all his prime ministers from Ali Mohamed Geedi to the friendly Nur Hassan Adde.

Equally, the blame goes to ICU's intransigency and its militant and provocative stands against the TFG and its disregard of the outcome of the reconciliation process in Kenya, which was meant to reconcile Somalis. Certainly, by opposing the TFG, ICU's action could only be described as 'situational spoilers': factions or groups that would do anything to disrupt peace initiatives or state building for different economic, political or clan reasons.[120]

In summary, the United States-backed Ethiopian military adventure will be remembered for the occupation of Somalia, which re-ignited inter-clan vendetta, causing atrocities, mass human rights violation and the death and displacement of thousands of people. The TFG will not be remembered as a government of national reconciliation that brought peace and stability, but as a warmongering government, which for the first time in history allowed Ethiopia to erect its flag on the nation's capital by force. The occupation will also be remembered for radicalizing Somalis who found themselves trapped in the power-politics of the war on terror. It goes without saying that powerful external forces, particularly America's war on terror and its dynamics, which instigated Ethiopian invasion as clearly shown earlier, played a critical role in prolonging the conflict.

Religious wars and the rise of Al-Shabaab

After the fall of Colonel Abdullahi Yusuf, under the auspices of the UN and Djibouti government, another reconciliation process in Djibouti resulted in power sharing between the ARS-Djibouti wing and the TFG. An additional 275 members from the ARS were added onto the existing 275 TFP, which was born out of the reconciliation process in Kenya. This made the parliament one of the largest parliaments in Somali history. Aden Madoobe, from the Rahanweyn clan family, who was acting president since the downfall of President Abdullahi Yusuf was elected speaker of the parliament. Sheikh Sharif Sheikh Ahmed, from Abgaal of the Hawiye clan family and once chief executive of the ICU, was elected president to replace the Daarood president Colonel Yusuf. He then appointed Omar Abdirashid Ali Sharmarke from the Daarood clan and the son of a former president, as his new prime minister. The transitional period was extended by further two years.

President Sheik Sharif and his government relocated from Baydhabo to Mogadishu in February 2009. However, his regime's honeymoon in power was cut short after Sheikh Hassan Dahir Awes, leader of the ARS-Asmara wing, returned to Mogadishu in April 2009. Having rejected the power sharing between the ARS-Djibouti and the TFG, he immediately assumed leadership of another organization called Hizbul Islam (Islamic Party), which was formed in February 2009 by the ARS-Asmara, and other Islamist factions, such as Jabhat al-Islamiya, Mu'askar Ras Kamboni and Mu'askar Anole.[121]

Hizbul Islam rejected President Sharif's offer of power sharing and peace talks, accusing him of collusion with the enemy[122] for accepting peacekeepers, known as the African Mission of Somalia (AMISOM), which is the African Union's peacekeeping force in Somalia to support Somalia's federal governments. The mission replaced an earlier Peace Support Mission in Somalia (IGASOM), which was a military training mission provided by the IGAD states to support President Abdullahi Yusuf's government. AMISOM was authorized by the UN Security Council's resolution no. 1744 adopted in 2007. It has strong peacekeeping force of about 22,126 provided by Ethiopia, Uganda, Djibouti, Kenya, Sierra Leon, Burundi, Ghana and Nigeria. And it has been supporting Somali federal governments to dislodge the Al-Shabaab movement and to restore peace and stability in the country.[123]

Under Sheik Hassan Dahir's leadership, Xizbul Islam faction in collaboration with the powerful Al-Shabaab launched a series of serious military operations against the new TFG and the AMISOM. This violent conflict, which claimed hundreds of lives, was mainly between ICU's old friends. The post-ICU Islamist movements borne out of the Ethiopian invasion had split into factions, hence old friends, accusing each other of betrayal leading to acrimony and bad feeling. After the withdrawal of the Ethiopian forces, their main enemy, the Islamist movement and other resistance forces failed to seize the opportunity to unite and join ranks with their friend, President Sharif who was leading government dominated by Islamists. This was another missed opportunity, which could have saved the country at least Mogadishu from the mayhem and destruction that were to come.

The post-Ethiopian insurgency wanted to eject AMISOM peacekeepers. Al-Shabaab considered the TFG as un-Islamic and apostate government[124] that should be aborted so that they could install an Islamic state in Somalia. Indeed, Al-Shabaab had been implementing Sharia laws under which they stoned women adulterers to death and amputated the hands of thieves.

However, in fairness to history, Somali leaders could not be solely blamed for the deep division because the internationalization of the conflict not only re-ignited clan conflict, but it also has divided them along ideological and religious lines. Somalis have probably never been divided along religious lines as they are today with their different Islamic groups and denominations.[125]

The continuing violence in south-central and south-western Somalia post-Ethiopian invasion could be described as religious wars because Al-Qaeda and Wahhabi-inspired Al-Shabaab vilified their opponents as heretics and vowed to spread Islamic Sharia throughout the world. They desecrated Sufi shrines and their mosques[126] and had been persecuting Sufi saints and scholars.[127] Sufi movements, under the banner of Ahlu-Sunna Wal-Jama, were forced to defend their traditional Sufi orders and fought the Al-Shabaab[128] in what they described as religious wars as articulated by Sheik Omar Mohamed Farah, a Sufi leader: 'Clan wars, political wars, we were always careful to stay out of those. But this time, it was religious.'[129]

In conclusion, with the power of hindsight the classic Somali civil war of warlordism, factionalism and clan warfare should and could have ended in 2000 after the Arte-Djibouti reconciliation process that created the first TNG. However, regional dynamics of the war on terror, which started after Ethiopia accused the TNG of links with Al-Qaeda in 2001, prolonged the Somali conflict, giving it a religious dimension.

Although it is impossible to point out one factor as the main cause of Somalia's protracted conflicts, the prognosis of the post-2001 conflict could mainly be analysed through the lenses of America's war on terror. Indeed, years after the end of the Ethiopian occupation, which was triggered by the war on terror, United States airstrikes alongside AMISOM and the Somali National Army (SNA) continue their military operations against the Al-Shabaab movement. In pursuit of their war on terror, Americans are currently deeply involved in the conflict since President Donald Trump expanded the operation. The United States has been receiving casualties from the ongoing war, and indeed American soldiers were killed by Al-Shabaab's military raids, including an attack on Manda Bay airfield in Kenya in January 2020 in which they damaged aircrafts.[130]

Although Al-Shabaab was ejected from main cities and towns, it controls the countryside and has shown its resilience and adaptability to changing situations. Indeed, the movement has been fighting guerrilla warfare since 2006 against all Somali federal governments and AMISOM. And it has intensified its military operations through its non-ending suicide bombing missions, the deadliest was its attack on KM-4 in Mogadishu in 2017 in which over 500 people were killed,[131] and on ex-control near Mogadishu in which they killed over seventy people in 2020. It has also shown its long reach ability by attacking and executing military operations and suicide bombing missions in neighbouring countries such as Kenya, including Al-Shabaab's daring attack on Manda Bay airfield in Kenya in which they killed an American soldier.

Furthermore, as part of the war on terror, Kenya and Ethiopia have been violating Somalia's territorial integrity regularly, as their forces enter and leave Somalia as and when they want. The Kenyan invasion of Somalia in October 2011 to dismantle Al-Shabaab was classic example of how the first United States-backed Ethiopian invasion failed to destroy terrorism in Somalia. Although Kenya and Ethiopia are officially part of the AMISOM, they are in Somalia to protect their national interests, for example Kenya adamant to destroy Al-Shabaab, which it failed to achieve. Indeed, Al-Shabaab continues to launch military operations inside Kenya on regular basis.

The latest diplomatic crisis in the Gulf is another classic example of the impact of the war on terror on Somalia. Saudi Arabia and its allies cut diplomatic ties with Qatar not because of economic row, but mainly on terrorism grounds. The wealthy Gulf club 'family', once the most stable unit within the fractured Arab world, is now facing existential crisis. Poor Somalia was again forced to take sides, although it chose to remain neutral in the Gulf conflict. Gulf countries have been interfering in Somalia's internal affairs by funding Somali stakeholders and politicians to protect their national interests. For example the United Arab Emirates reportedly entered an agreement with Somaliland to secure the use of Barbara seaport facility as a military base. This is perhaps to support the war efforts of the Saudi-led coalition in Yemen. This has been a destabilizing factor in Somalia as Somali stakeholders, for example regional federal states such as Somaliland, have been playing one Arab country against the other in pursuit of their political and economic interest.

Turkey, another regional power, is deeply involved in Somalia and built a large embassy in Mogadishu. Turkey's action was mainly motivated by humanitarian reasons. However, by building a large embassy and a military base and by investing millions of dollars on some huge developmental infrastructure, Turkey may have sensed the importance of this strategically located country in the Horn of Africa for its future political, economic and military interest.

And the irony of the situation is that current Gulf diplomatic row and Turkey's involvement are embedded in America's war on terror after Qatar had been accused by Saudi Arabia and its allies of supporting terrorism. So Somalia has not only been ground for executing regional dynamics of the war on terror from Ethiopia's invasion to present realities of AMISOM/United States and Somali government on one side and Al-Shabaab on the other side. But it also found itself as a victim of the Gulf states' fallouts caused by the global war on terror.

Positive news amid the ruins

The human and material cost of the Somali civil war through its different stages from 1988 up to present day is immeasurable. Major cities, such as Hargeisa, Mogadishu, Baidoa, Garowe and Kismayo, had experienced destruction and some of them laid in ruins at one point in time. Up to 1 million people were killed[1] directly or indirectly by a mixture of governments massacring their own people, clan factional fighting or invading foreign armies. Millions of people were displaced inside and outside Somalia as refugees and asylum seekers. Writers, artists, academics and politicians have struggled to describe the national tragedy.

Diplomats and writers, such as Omar (1992) simply put it 'The Road to Zero'. However, Aden Abdulle Osman, former and the first democratically elected Somali president, was the man who captured and articulated the public mood. Asked to compare the 1960 Somalia with post-1990 Somalia, the former president made it clear that they were incomparable and said: 'Somalia of 1960 was united country. Today there is not even a single document archived. Somalia went backwards by 100 years. . . . Those fighting factions have killed, maimed or displaced the people they want to rule. Even animals and plants (country's natural resources) have been destroyed.'[2]

Despite the obvious gloomy picture and unhelpful intervention by foreign military powers, Somalis have, however, shown remarkable resilience in the face of unimaginable obstacles and have revealed their character as masters of survival in their unforgiving and harsh environment. With difficulties and limited resources, Somalis have made some remarkable achievements in some sectors, and, indeed, some Somalis have come out and are coming out of the tragedy stronger and much better than ever. Somalia remains on the lowest ranks of the United Nations' Human Development index, and is often described as a failed state,[3] however, in comparison with developing countries in Africa, Somalia's developmental trends seem similar to those stable neighbouring countries with central governments, and Somalis in general have performed better in some sectors as is analysed in this chapter.[1]

---

[1] Statistics, numbers and figures in this chapter are mainly extracted from the early years of the civil war (1990 – 2010). This is meant to show how socio-economics have performed despite the challenges at the time.

Emerging federal structure

Politically, if the main reason for the civil war from 1988 was rebellion against centralized state structure and dictatorship, in which Villa Somalia, the presidential palace, was the main powerhouse dominated by some elites, then Somalis dismantled the repressive structure successfully. Despite threat of secession, what Somalis have right now is strong and assertive regional states or administrations, which are exercising some kind of self-rule. In general, Somalis are today autonomous and independent of a formal centralized government structure since independence. Today political power is based in cities of Hargeisa, Garowe, Baidoa, Dhuusa Mareeb, Kismayo and Jowhar and not in Villa Somalia. Indeed, rather than govern the whole country most of the internationally recognized successive Mogadishu-based national governments have been reduced to no more than some factions trying to control Mogadishu surrounded by rebels, such as Al-Shabaab.

However, it is really sad it took thirty to forty years and a lot of suffering before those cities could taste regional autonomy and assert their freedom from Mogadishu's central governments. Also, one wonders whether some of these regional states with secession tendency, such as Somaliland, are really seeking total independence, or are merely craving for, and expressing their desire for greater freedom and self-autonomy, which they were denied by previous governments, particularly the dictatorship in which the famous Villa Somalia was the power house.

In addition, if the civil strife from 1988 was because of clan conflict in which certain clans felt marginalized and oppressed by other clans, today Mareehaan or Daarood government officers do not rule Hargeisa or Baidoa, which are now run by local leadership. In summary, what Somalis have now is an emerging weaker federal structure embodied in the Transitional Federal Constitution, which could be utilized as a proposal for looser federal structure. Current regional states may be a way towards achieving a negotiated structure that will hopefully lead to the rebirth of stronger and more decentralized Somali state. However, as mentioned earlier, veteran politicians, such as the late Abdirazak H. Hussein, former prime minister, warned that proliferation of mini-states could lead to the balkanization of the country.[4]

Despite uncertainty surrounding future development of a federal or decentralized state structure, the Somali situation is more or less similar to neighbouring countries, such as Ethiopia with its inherent secessionist and liberation movements that threaten the cohesion of this diverse and huge country. Indeed, recent conflict in Tigray region between Tigray rebels and the Ethiopian federal army is a powerful evidence of how this country could disintegrate into ethnic-based fiefdoms. In addition to this, one only needs to reflect on the political unrest in 2007 in Kenya in which the country was brought to the edge of civil war during the disputed presidential elections.

Economy without treasury survives

Despite the chaos, Somalis within their regional states and administrations have shown resilience and ingenuity in maintaining informal economy, which have survived and in some cases thrived throughout the conflict. Some economists have described the post-1990 Somalia as a laboratory to test 'purest capitalism' at work where an un-regulated free market economy has overtaken the public sector due to lack of government intervention.[5] This informal economy, although precarious, is not qualitatively different from other countries with weaker and failing economic and political institutions where people lose money they deposed in banks due to failing institutions.[6] What has happened in effect is that an efficient private sector has overtaken the collapsed, corrupt and failing state economic institutions. Indeed, some economic sectors, such as telecommunications have performed much better than the pre-war era as described later.

Although the centralized Somali treasury with its bureaucracy such as the central bank collapsed in 1991, Somali citizens have maintained faith in their currency, the Somali shilling. Indeed, the shilling has been in circulation as a transaction method in the country throughout the civil war. The symbolic value of the picture of the Somali Central Bank or a modern government factory on one side of the Somali shilling note, which represented the state, disappeared with the collapse of the central government in 1991. However, the value of the picture of livestock on the other side of the shilling note, which represent civic or public aspirations, has survived and sustained the Somali currency to function without centralized treasury.[7] In other words, the private ownership of livestock has given the shilling its value, taking the role of the state in regulating the monetary system – demand and supply. This is how a scholar put it: 'In the Somali economy the public or civic dimension of money is the power behind the "currency without a treasury".'[8]

Indeed, to the millions of Somali citizens, the survival of the Somali shilling as a transaction method throughout the civil war is a symbol of continuity of the Somali economy in the face of permanent challenges and turmoil. And in a way the survival story is a good indicator of social and economic welfare despite the chaos and mayhem.[9]

Although the shilling was banned in some regions in Somaliland, which printed its own currency, this was for political reasons and not for the weakness of the Somali currency. Indeed, the shilling was used in other regions in Somaliland at some point. Certainly, the shilling was used as a valuable transaction currency in the Somali regions in Kenya, Ethiopia as well as Djibouti hence uniting Somali traders in these countries.[10]

Unbelievable as it may sound, despite the lack of a central bank during the civil war to regulate financial and monetary sectors, the Somali shilling survived as a transaction means, and only lost a fraction of its pre-civil war value.[11] While the value of the Somali shilling declined more than 98 per cent in the1980s, it lost only a fraction of its value in the 1990s at the height of the civil war.[12] Its exchange rate with major currencies, the shilling showed remarkable stability and resilience compared with neighbouring countries with stable and functioning central governments. For example, in 1995 the Somali shilling lost 26 per cent of its value compared with 36 per cent loss of the Kenyan shilling and 27 per cent of the Ethiopian bir.[13]

The point here is that although the shilling is and has been under pressure since the collapse of the central government because of political instability and lack of centralized monetary and fiscal national authorities, the shilling has been resilient and remained a valuable financial transaction means. This is one survival story among many that had been happening throughout the civil war.

It is also quite impressive how the pastoral economy, although marginalized during the collapsed central government (only 6 per cent of its annual expenditure) allocated to rural economy,[14] defied all the odds. The rural economy remains marginalized, but the nomad with his camel had been the master of the Somali economy, and like many other Somalis, 'life goes on' amid the ruins, or as a scholar explained:

> In fact, in an era when affluent Western consumers bemoan high fuel costs and energy shortages, Somalis get on with their lives under far more trying circumstances, taking care of their families and herds, and trying to make the best of a situation for which most hold little responsibility.[15]

Throughout the civil war, while mayhem prevailed in major cities, nomads, sometimes caught in the crossfire between the fighting factions, continued with their struggle for survival in an unforgiving environment, moving their herds and families across territories in pursuit of ever elusive water and pasture. At one point, while only 38.5 per cent urban population was economically active, 59.3 per cent of the rural and nomad population were economically active[16] thus supplying meat not only to Somalis, but to the outside world, where 16 per cent of the meat consumed in Nairobi came from Somalia.[17] This helped boost the livestock trade, Somalia's traditional trade with the outside world, which by 1999 increased with 2.9 million head of animals exported to the world through Berbera and Boosaaso ports.[18]

Pastoralists had not only helped the livestock export business boom but also benefitted from it by receiving a good share of the revenue generated by the trade. For example, Somali herders received about 60–70 per cent of the revenue of the Kenya–Somali border trade worth over US$10 million.[19] Although the share was not as high as it would have been in normal circumstances (e.g. 1980s), without this border commerce, the nomad's share would have been much less.

Pastoralists' livelihood in terms of income and their purchasing power (i.e. one goat buys 45 kilograms of wheat etc.) and food security was not worse than it was during the central government. The overall food security in the country, which had been dependent on food aid pre-war, was not worse than Kenya and Ethiopia at some point as explained by a scholar:

> The discussion here suggests that pockets of severe food insecurity remain in the Somali borderlands, but local herders have generally fared as well as – if not better than – neighbouring pastoral populations. Even with the devastating drought of 1999–2000, the food situation in Somalia was not markedly different from other parts of the Horn of Africa including large parts of Ethiopia and northern Kenya where upwards of 10 million residents were in dire need of food assistance.[20]

Remittances by diaspora help trade

At one point, about 1.5 million Somalis in the diaspora transferred up to US$1 billion to Somalia to support their relatives and families,[21] making Somalia the fourth mainly remittance dependent country in the world.[22] In 2003, 40 per cent of Somali households depended on remittance in a country where overseas development aid was approximately US$272 million, and its exports totalled just US$55 million.[23] The money transfer industry contributed 25–50 per cent to the country's GDP in a country where 43 per cent of population live in extreme poverty and annual average per capita income is US$210.[24] This generosity offers much needed subsistence to relatives and acts as a lifeline[25] not only for immediate families, but also to the wider society as the money trickles down via domestic commerce to remote rural communities. The remittance helps much needed construction projects, small business, credit and loan schemes as it assists in creating job opportunities and income.[26]

This diaspora-led remittance was facilitated by a network of money transfer operators (MTO), which have their own regulatory body called the Somali Money Transfer Association.[27] Even though this informal sector faces future regulatory and structural challenges to integrate into the global financial system, and despite setbacks caused by the closure of some companies due to alleged links to terrorism financing, the sector has proven to be resilient. Indeed, it facilitates international money transfer to Somalia, a system more efficient and smoother than the pre-civil war system. For example, majority of money transfer (*xawaalad*) sent from Europe/United States takes one day to reach relatives in Somalia[28] if compared to the pre-war era where because of bureaucracy it was time consuming to transfer money via official banks.

Arguably, today Somalis have more access to financial services and institutions (although mainly informal) than during the collapsed regime when the few state-owned banks dominated the market. More formal and informal financial institutions have been created by regional states and private entrepreneurs in contrast with the centralized banking system during the military regime.

Furthermore, the informal Somali financial sector seems more efficient and reliable than those in other countries in Africa, such as Liberia where a customer lost US$50,000 in a government bank because of weak, corrupt and cumbersome bureaucratic banking system and where the official and unofficial is blurred.[29]

More importantly, the remittance sector played a significant role in the country's economic recovery. First, at some point 90 per cent of the country's main foreign exchange came from the sector. Second, the diaspora invested 80 per cent of start-up cost in small- and medium-scale enterprises.[30] It goes without saying that, besides diaspora's role in emergency, relief, developmental projects and peace building efforts,[31] this community participated in re-starting up small-scale industrial plants.[32] Third, the sector facilitates Somalia's international trade in which exports and imports reached record level of US$265 million and US$400 million, respectively, in 2004.[33]

In the inward investment sector, anarchy and lack of formal state institutions (e.g. treasury and judiciary) did not discourage global firms in investing or operating in Somalia throughout the conflict. African, Asian and European companies continued doing business in the country,[34] example of companies include, Total Oil Company, General Motors of Kenya and British Airways.[35] Australian and other oil exploration companies invested in exploring oil in Puntland state of Somalia. In fact, the Canadian oil and gas exploration company Africa Oil Corporation was involved in drilling an exploratory well in Dharoor in Puntland. The existence of Coca Cola Company in

Mogadishu at one point, one of the dangerous cities in the world, showed global firms' appetite for business adventure in dangerous places like Somalia and Afghanistan. The corruption story surrounding the British Soma Oil & Gas company's attempt to gain access to oil exploration in Somalia is a classic example of how far Somali and foreign elites and companies would go to do shoddy business in war-torn countries. Furthermore, current scramble by foreign companies such as DP world to invest hundreds of millions of US dollars in Somali seaports is another good example.

Vibrant telecommunications sector

Access to telecommunication services prior to the civil strife was very expensive and inaccessible to most Somalis. Indeed, there were only 17,000 fixed telephone lines in major cities.[36] The infrastructure was then destroyed during the conflict, where looters dug up telephone cables as well as electricity wires to be exported as a trade commodity to the outside world. However, since the collapse of the central government, thanks to the entrepreneurial spirit of Somalis led by the diaspora and revolution in information technology, a variety of private-owned operators have been providing competitive services to hundreds of thousands of landline users and mobile subscribers.[37] The sector grew and availability of telephone lines (tele-density) in the country was at some point higher than in many neighbouring countries.[38] Access to international telephone calls was probably the most affordable in Africa, and in 2005 a one-minute long distance phone call from Mogadishu or Hargeisa cost $0.50–0.80. The rate of one-minute international phone call from a small town or village in Somalia was cheaper than that in Addis Ababa, Nairobi and Khartoum.[39] Certainly, unlike the pre-civil war era, when telephone service concentrated in main cities, there are now telephone services in towns and villages. And people from neighbouring countries crossed the border to Somalia at some point in time to make cheaper phone calls, and as of 2010 mobile use in the country was higher.[40] Compared to neighbouring countries, Somalia is a leader in this sector, and Somalis' access to telephone mainlines has improved.[41] Although in need of regulatory and structural framework, the private sector driven industry provides much needed services that improve the lives of thousands in terms of job creation and income generation.

Thanks to their entrepreneurial spirit and lack of a strict regulatory framework, at some point in 1997, fourteen small private airline companies operated sixty-two small aircraft to connect Somalia to the outside world.[42] In mid-late 2000 there weresome small airline companies, such as Daalllo and Juba airlines providing flight services to neighbouring countries. These carriers had been a lifeline to Somalis' booming trade, as they had been delivering crucial humanitarian assistance. So if the now bankrupt and defunct Somali Airline – the national carrier – was the only carrier that dominated Somali skies for a very long time, by creating these companies Somalis have shown their entrepreneurial skills. Although small sized and in need of regulatory framework, improvement of safety standards and investment, these private carriers had been connecting Somalis to the outside world.

Media and freedom of expression

Unlike the pre-war era, particularly during the military government, which controlled the media sector and suppressed freedom of expression, the post-1990 Somalia has experienced growth in the media sector. If the collapsed military government's Radio Hargeisa and Mogadishu were the only radio stations in the whole country, by 2005 there were twenty-two radio stations in the country[43] led by radio stations such as Radio Shabelle, HornAfrik, Radio Galkayo and Radio Garowe. In a pre-war country with only one TV station, 200,000 television sets and 600,000 viewers, by 2005 there were seven TV channels serving the country with some viewers getting access to many channels by installing a satellite dish, which cost US$180–250.[44]

The collapsed central government had two newspapers *Xiddigta October* (October Star) and *Halgan* (struggle) which monopolized the printed media. However, the creation of up to fifty newspapers post-1991,[45] revealed Somalis' appetite for news, information and freedom of expression. As part of this growing media industry, by 2010 about 739 journalists operated in the country.[46] They created their own organizations and unions, such as the Somali National Union of Somali Journalists (NUSOJ), the Somaliland Journalist Association (SJA) and the Somali Journalists Club (SJC) to lobby for media protection laws and employments rights, something which was unthinkable during the military regime. Although, like many other sectors, it needs regulatory frameworks and investment, and although journalists are being killed or detained because of political violence and persecution,[47] the media industry is a sector that could serve democracy in the long run in a country which was heavily censored during the military regime.[48] More importantly, compared with the pre-civil war era when most forms of free expression were controlled by the state, Somalis enjoy more personal freedoms where they can use different kinds of social media to express their political opinions with little differentiations between administrations.[49]

Education

With an illiteracy rate of around 85–90 per cent, Somalia inherited poor formal secular education system from the colonial powers. By 1966–7 there were only 389 primary schools, 107 intermediate schools and 33 secondary schools with a total enrolment of 23,286, 5,595 and 1,455 students, respectively.[50] The education system improved during the revolutionary era with primary and secondary enrolment jumping up to 263,751 and 18,416 students, respectively, in 1979 because of the mass literacy campaign, compulsory enrolment, free education and investment in educational infrastructure.[51] In higher education, alongside vocational and technical training institutes, the Somali National University (SNU) was the only national university for the whole country.

The education system deteriorated during the 1980s because of the Ogaden war efforts. Just a few years prior to the civil war, the education system was bankrupt, and its institutions were supported financially by donor countries.[52] The primary and secondary enrolment dropped from 300,000 to 60,000 students only.[53] This was followed by civil strife, which destroyed the educational system and its infrastructure. Due to state failures in the 1980s and the civil strife in the 1990s, Somalis lost two young generations that are without education. Somalia lags behind most countries in primary education enrolment with net 20 per cent enrolment ratio and only 20 per cent adult literacy.[54]

However, throughout the civil war, Somalis created or restored educational institutions, which provide essential education services. For instance, primary education enrolment, although fluctuates between regional administrations, improved, and in 2003/4 enrolment increased to 300,000 students which is 19.9 per cent increase of 8.2 per cent just a few years prior to 1991.[55] Furthermore, although in need of further training and financing, at some point there were 11,344 primary school teachers[56] compared to the 1978–9 figure of 8,141.[57] Secondary school and tertiary education sectors had been growing. In 2003–4 secondary school enrolment in north-west regions (Somaliland) was 9,266[58] and in Puntland 2,868[59] which totalled 12,134 students. If figures from south central and south-western regions, unavailable due to the lack of statistics, were added to the figure, the overall secondary school enrolment would have been much higher than the 1978–9 figures of 18,416.[60]

Most impressively, led by the private sector and the diaspora, Somalis created new higher education institutions from scratch throughout the civil war era. The success story of residents of Borama city in the Awdal region in Somaliland, faced with 8,000 students in primary and secondary schools, transforming Amoud Higher School residential areas to university called Amoud University is worth mentioning.[61] So if the defunct SNU with its 13 faculties, 800 instructors and 7,500 students[62] was the only institution in monopoly of higher education during the central government, by 2011 there were about nine universities in the country,[63] including Hargeisa University, Puntland State University, Mogadishu University and East African University. Student population in these institutions seems to be growing and at one point an estimated 10,000 students studied in Somaliland alone.[64] If figures from the rest of the country, which were unavailable, were added to that, the figure would have been higher than the pre-war era.

Ownership, financing and management of these emerging educational institutions vary from public-community-charity to international development and private sectors. Despite the fact that some of them are underdeveloped and operate through varied and different curriculum and standards, although accessibility and affordability are limited due to insufficient public funding with regional governments spending on education only 1–5 per cent of government budget at one point in time,[65] these institutions provide much needed education services to Somalis. It is fair to conclude the higher education system is stronger than it was in the pre-war era when only one university served the whole country. This is very impressive midst the anarchy with no coordinated education strategy, compared with other neighbouring countries, such as Eritrea which has only one or two universities. Therefore, Somalis should be commended for the hard work and tireless efforts in the face of unimaginable obstacles.

From this analysis, it seems as though Somalis have performed well in some economic and human development indicators compared with pre-war situations. Indeed, whereas during the dictatorship, there were few choices under centralized economy Somalis took advantage of the lack of repressive government policies and used their ingenuity, resilience and intelligence to utilize economic opportunities to enhance their fellow citizens' welfare and development. While there was one thing for everything prior to the collapse of the central government, for example one Radio station, one airline company and one university dominated by the state, there are now more choices as shown earlier. Hargeisa and Boosaaso and other major cities are leading hubs and centres of business and human development without the need for approval and licensing from the Villa Somalia as the case was during the oppressive military government.

The provision of delivering public goods (hospitals, education, water, telecommunications) with slight differentiations and fluctuations between regional administrations is improving thanks to Somalis' entrepreneurial spirit. Although public goods have yet to reach all stakeholders, including rural communities, which were even neglected during pre-civil war era, the public service provision has been expanding, for example, to more schools and universities as mentioned earlier.

Conclusion

The broken Republic in a changing world

The negative impact of some huge global and regional political events from the Cold War to the present day on the initiation and perpetuation of the Somali civil war has been demonstrated in the previous chapters, the last event being the cut-throat politics of the war on terror, which has prolonged the Somali conflict and divided Somalis along religious lines. To conduct its global war on terror, the United States is deeply involved in Somalia and has been launching military operations, in particular airstrikes against Al-Shabaab.

At the regional level, Somalia has to live with hostile neighbours fearful of Somali nationalism for historical reasons. Ethiopia and Kenya have all shown their determination to use force as and when they want. They invaded Somalia in 2006 and 2011 in pursuit of their national interests in a realist world in which nation-states would always pursue their national interest. However, the international community should keep in mind the existing unbalanced power structure in the region in which Somalia, a poor and broke nation, found itself tormented and bullied by two powerful neighbours that are resolute to enhancing their national interests through the barrel of gun regardless of the outcome and human suffering or material cost.

The international community should be extremely wary of Ethiopia's and Kenya's manoeuvres or motives because of some primordial historical reasons. Indeed, supporting Kenya's and Ethiopia's interventions and war efforts in Somalia reminds us of those old days during the colonial era when and if a European colonial power invaded and annexed a Somali region, for instance the Somali region in Kenya, other colonial powers would have approved or opposed it for their imperial interests. Certainly, the new scenario in the region seems more likely the Somali nation in the nineteenth century when colonial powers were conquering and dividing it up among themselves. Somalis themselves are deeply divided along clan and religious lines and worse of all their division is being aggravated by the actions of foreign powers and neighbours.

The UN was one of the first organizations to have left Somalia while the military regime was destroying towns and cities during the first civil war in the north in the 1980s, hence failing to initiate early conflict prevention and resolution. During the second phase of the civil war in the 1990s, the UN failed to intervene earlier to save hundreds of thousands of people from starvation. When it did intervene, bureaucracy hampered smooth running of the humanitarian and relief effort. It was a power struggle within the organization that led to the sacking of some competent UN diplomats, such as Mohamed Sahnoun, who could have helped end the conflict earlier.

Since the withdrawal of the UNOSOM in the 1990s, the UN attitude towards Somalia was described as cynical, treating the country as a failed state which does not deserve UN support. Indeed, a case in point was that until recently the UN refused to relocate its staff to Somalia on the flimsy ground of lack of security. In the last twenty years it kept its office in Kenya, its staff operating from the comfort zones of some skyscrapers in Nairobi for most part of the civil war. The role of the UN special representatives for Somalia seemed to have been that of remote-controlling and micro-managing the Somali conflict from Nairobi, organizing conferences now and then to formulate unpopular and weak transitional Somali governments.

While the UN kept offices in Bagdad and Kabul, which are as dangerous as Mogadishu, if not worse, the UN failed to establish competent and comprehensive mission presence on the ground until 2012 when it opened an office in Mogadishu. During the early stages of the civil war in the 2000s, lack of UN presence on the ground had been undermining the political efforts of the transitional governments and had failed to instil confidence in government leaders and the general public as well. It had also been encouraging insurgency groups to undermine governments' efforts in peace building and reconciliation because they interpreted the lack of UN presence on the ground as lack of international recognition and support to Somali governments.

It seems though since the UNOSOM debacle, the international community, including the UN, grew wary of the Somali conflict, which they saw as a complex and intractable problem that was beyond their ability.

However, Turkey is one of the few countries that showed their real commitment to the Somali people when its then-prime minister Tayyip Ordugan visited Mogadishu in 2011. Quite recently, other states opened their diplomatic missions in Mogadishu, which is a positive move because it encourages the role of the international community in the reconciliation and state-building efforts. It also indicates the international community's focus and determination to help Somalia stand on its feet again.

In a post-Cold War world power structure where failed states need to be rebuilt, it is understandable that the international community might have a different approach in resolving problems depending on the availability of resources and the strength of political commitment by member states. For example, it seems the international community sees the Somali conflict as a regional one in which the African Union is supposed to take the lead, using the African peace keeping mission, AMISOM, to help Somali governments stabilize the country. To some extent, AMISOM has contributed to the stabilization of the country and the fight against Al-Shabaab. However, it is too early to assess the long-term impact of this foreign power intervention on the country's political stability, security and state building. It is a matter of wait and see.

Despite the failings and shortcomings of foreign power interventions, there is one positive element that has come out of the international community's approach to the Somali conflict. In a broken country that is being threatened with secession, so far no single member state has openly recognized the breakaway region of Somalia (Somaliland) as an independent state. This is a healthy outlook, which shows that UN member states are not prepared to stab another member state in the back in one of its most difficult times in its history. Therefore, protecting the sovereignty and territorial integrity of Somalia should prevail at all times. One way of helping Somalis come together is by encouraging Somali stakeholders to form some kind of decentralized governance structures under a federal or decentralized structure more or less like the existing regional administrations/states as envisioned by the current provisional federal constitution.

Considering how foreign power interventions have been unhelpful and destabilizing factors throughout Somalia's political history, the rule of thumb must be to prevent future foreign military interventions by engaging Somali stakeholders through diplomacy, political dialogue and peaceful means. And most important of all to discourage, name and shame, and if necessary punish regional powers, such as Ethiopia and Kenya, for intervening and invading Somalia.

Post-conflict economic development

The weak and failing pre-war public services and economic production sectors, namely health, education, employment, telecommunications, transport, electricity and water supply, had been destroyed during the civil war. Although this will depend on the prevailing political situation, current regional or central administrations or states should be encouraged to undertake the task of assessing economic sectors in their regions in order to find out (1) the ones that can be rescued and sustained; (2) those sectors that need investment; (3) if there are potential natural resources that can be explored and exploited and many more sectors. The assessment will help plan long-term economic developments. With their current debt relief efforts, the World Bank and the International Monetary Fund (IMF) are potential organizations that could assist in carrying out the assessment with the consent of Somali stakeholders.[1]

Meanwhile, while keeping this in mind as a long-term goal, there are some emerging economic sectors that have been initiated by a mixture of public and private entrepreneurs. Some of these are rudimentary and their productivity is limited due to lack of finance, investment and skilled labour. In the short term, all these emerging infrastructure segments should be strengthened and harnessed regardless of their location, ownership and investment. An example is the private-led telecommunications sector, which should be allowed to grow and self-regulate itself with less interference by regional states/administrations or create a regulatory body to oversee them.

As mentioned earlier, there is a mixture of public–private agencies and organizations that provide some kind of education, health and utility services (e.g. clinics, hospitals, schools, universities, water and electricity). These are again basic and access to them is limited due to issues around availability and affordability. Therefore, regional authorities should allow growth of these services, which should not be hampered by stringent regulatory frameworks. However, it is also important to support initiatives aimed at helping out the poor to get access to these services.

In these uncertain times when developed nations' debt and the impact of COVID-19 are threatening to plunge the whole world in a severe recession and economic collapse, it would be hard to imagine how a poor, black and Muslim country like Somalia could attract the attention of the global financial institutions.

However, the international community needs to find resources from somewhere to help war-ravaged poor countries like Somalia recover economically. Somalia has hardly been allocated any substantial money compared with Iraq and Afghanistan where the projected cost of the efforts of the war on terror plus the reconstruction of these nations on the US economy was estimated at US$2.4 trillion by 2017.[2]

The irony of the situation is that Iraq, Afghanistan and Somalia are all post-Cold War and post-9/11 conflicts, although with different magnitudes and scales. The war on terror has affected Somalia as much as it has affected Iraq and Afghanistan; therefore these conflicts need to be treated equally. This unbalanced financial commitment towards these conflicts again shows a double standard in the international community's dealings with failing or failed states. While only a few hundred millions of US dollars are being allocated to Somalia to help the reconciliation and stabilization efforts by the AMISOM mission and the Somali governments, billions of dollars are being spent yearly on Iraq and Afghanistan conflicts.

To resolve the Somali conflict and help the country stand on its feet again, a substantial amount of money is required to rebuild Somalia, and this should come from the burse of the IMF, World Bank and from member states. It is not being argued here that a Marshal Plan or a magic wand be found in these gloomy and uncertain economic circumstances to rebuild Somalia, but the world needs to find resources to help Somalia.

Islam and customary law (*Xeer*)

In civil-war-ravaged countries, the basic social fabric breaks down, which creates a vicious cycle of mistrust and hostility among the citizens. The reconciliation and healing process is long and sometimes treacherous and torturous. It may take years or even decades before the wound is healed and citizens decide to create new forms of socio-political contracts based on ancient cultures and customs or new ideologies.

Somalia is not different from this pattern. Therefore, Somalis may wish to create new forms of social contracts or harness existing cultural and moral codes to help them govern in a modern state structure. On the basic social contract, Somalis could use their customary law (*Xeer*) to govern their political, social and economic lives as they have been doing for many centuries. Islam has been an important guiding principle or ideology in their civic life as it has been a source of their laws for centuries. In addition to that, Somalis have been exposed to other forms of foreign cultures, particularly European ones, and have used them as instruments to manage their affairs in a modern world. Democracy with its multi-party system, free market economy and socialism are some of the examples that Somalis adopted.

Therefore, the challenge for Somalis is how to strike a balance between these different and sometimes conflicting and contradicting cultural systems and beliefs, which could be used for socio-political and economic development. Too rigid or extreme in the approach and application of any of them would lead to the risk of undermining others, thus missing out on their benefits or advantages.

The current debate about whether or not Somalia should be an Islamic state and the many emotive questions that this evokes is a classic example. Some extremist constituents would go as far as adopting a Somali Islamic state similar to that of Saudi Arabia, where the Islamic Sharia prevails and there is no space for secular legal constitutions. However, moderate constituents would go along the lines of Turkish or Malaysian models where Islam is still an important guiding tool, but not the only dominant force. This is because these two countries are secular states, which accommodate secular legal systems, modernity, and at the same time not only conserve traditional values but also keep up with scientific and technological developments.

Although, it will be up to the Somalis to decide, in line with modern Somali history, Somalia should be allowed to continue to be a secular state as the broken Republic has always been so prior to the current civil war. Somalis could use Islam, *Xeer* and other ideologies as a source of law. Indeed, Somalis have been using a mixture of Islamic Sharia, *Xeer* and European jurisprudences as sources of their laws since independence.

Somalism or clan identity

As mentioned earlier, the causes of the Somali conflict are multiple, and anyone who purports to single out one factor as the main cause would not be giving justice to this complex tragedy. However, from the sequence of events, it is clear that the Ogaden debacle, induced by the intervention of the former USSR stirred some of the factors that ultimately led to the collapse of the state.

From 1978, the ruling regime degenerated into entrenched dictatorship, which then manipulated the divisive lineage political system, leading to the first civil wars in the north-eastern and north-western regions in the 1980s and reducing the country to a family business. From 1991, chaos, anarchy, leadership failure, warlordism and factionalism, instigated by parochial interests, rendered popular uprisings against the dictatorship to no more than another vicious cycle of clan revenge politics. Somalis are today deeply divided along clan lines than any other time since independence.

Although some historians and anthropologists would say, 'I told you that Somalis would disintegrate into clan fiefdoms,' it is fallacy to blame the clan system per se as the main reason for the conflict without analysing other imposing factors, including the superpower intervention in the Ogaden war in 1977, which disturbed the equilibrium of Somalis' social order. Because of the trauma and stresses that the Ogaden debacle caused to their social order, it is understandable that Somalis disintegrated into clan fiefdoms exactly as other nation-states, such as ex-Yugoslavia and Iraq had fallen apart along ideological or ethnic lines once their social equilibrium was disrupted either by foreign intervention as the case in Iraq, or by the collapse of the socialist bloc system as the case was in ex-Yugoslavia.

At times of social upheavals when neighbours turn their guns on each other, people often seek safety and protection in the ideologies or social/communal systems that they can identify with and relate to. Somalis are not different from this human behaviour, and this is exactly what happened when Somalis returned to clan identity in the last twenty years or so. However, it must also be stated that Somalis had shown in the past they can rise above clan identity to that of common Somali citizenry. In Somali history there are some examples where Somalis lived side by side in harmony under a modern state regardless of their clan affiliations, beginning from the SYL struggle in the 1940s where there was strong pan-Somalism and Somali unity, to the era of the military regime where 'scientific socialism' – a foreign concept – helped to erase clan identities to some extent.

The author vividly remembers the time when one's neighbours in Mogadishu came from as faraway places as Zeila in the far north-west region to Ras Kamboni in the deep south and lived as Somalis, regardless of their regional or clan differences. The clan factor became poisonous after Somali leaders, traditional or modern, manipulated and used *clanism* for narrow self-interest, which led to the rise of the politics of inclusion and exclusion based on clan identity. This precipitated the rise of regional states, such as Somaliland and Puntland. However, inter-clan conflicts in these new entities proved that clan-based identity is unstable and fluid particularly in a virulent divisive clan system where an extended family of a few hundred people or less is sometimes the most stable and the only trusted social unity where people are guaranteed safety and protection. As all reconciliation conferences at regional or national levels have shown, clan has become a means of power sharing in contemporary Somali politics, and unfortunately it is threatening the concept of *Somalinimo*: belonging to a common Somali citizenship regardless of clan affiliation and differences.

Even if clan identity is used as a base for power sharing, as the case is under the 4.5 formula, the issue of clan territory borders remains controversial in a society where traditionally clans lived and mingled with each other in their search for pasture and water for their livestock, where demarcation of the clan territory and borders were not clear cut. Indeed, one of the most difficult tasks that colonial powers faced was how to contain Somali herdsmen in demarcated border lines so that they could be subjected to taxation and levy. This issue is important particularly in the light of the civil war where some powerful clan militias simply have occupied other clan lands. The vulnerability of clan territory and borders is most obvious in the contemporary clan-based regional states/administrations where different clan militias are fighting over the control of territories and resources, and no single clan is able to declare outright victory or dominance without being challenged by minority or weaker clans.

Somaliland where inter- and intra-clan conflicts have been threatening the creation and sustainability of an independent state is a classic example. Puntland, which is trying to extend its territorial claim over Sanaag, Sool and Ceyn regions, also claimed by Somaliland, is another good example which highlights the explosive nature of clan territory.

The issue of minority or weaker clans in territories dominated by stronger clans is a daunting task that cannot and should not be ignored. These minority clans and non-ethnic Somalis had been subjected to what can be described as 'ethnic cleansing'. Classic examples of these are the Arabs, Bantus, Bravanese and Reer Hamars whose traditional lands had been misappropriated or occupied by marauding powerful Hawiye and Daarood clans and some powerful Islamist militiamen. These minority clans need to be protected and their rights recognized in any political settlement.

Despite these difficulties and as no one can deny the clan factor in contemporary Somali politics, it is therefore common sense to use clan as a temporary mechanism to rebuild a broken nation. However, clan identity should not be an end in itself, and Somali intellectuals, leaders and politicians need to think 'out of the box'. For example, they should use other ideological and economic factors to create new communal identities where people, regardless of their clan identity, could seek welfare, safety and protection. For example, they should create commercial enterprises, labour unions, women's associations, political parties and socio-economic associations that could win over the hearts and minds of ordinary citizens and could discourage them from clan affiliation.

The issue of Somaliland

The emergence of strong regional states demonstrated Somali stakeholders' thirst for a decentralized state and their rejection of a centralized/unitary state. Although there is a danger of secession and disintegration of Somalia into clan-based fiefdoms, current regional administrations could be used as a model for a decentralized state or federal system along the lines of other modern state structures, such as Malaysia. This will have to be achieved through negotiations and political settlement and not by force in order to prevent more violence and bloodshed.

Reconstructing an acceptable state structure from scratch is a daunting task. Politically, there are many layers of overlapping governance structures from parliaments, local assemblies and local authorities at regional and national levels. Some forms of locally based constitutions and laws have sprung up. Supporting and harnessing these structures for future political settlement should be paramount, for example exploring ways of harmonizing the current federal parliament with other regional state parliaments such as Puntland and Somaliland. This will be the hardest task of all knowing how some clans in Somaliland are pursuing international recognition as an independent state while others are fiercely opposing it. Political consensus by the Somali people either through locally organized or internationally supported referendums on Somaliland is one of the ways out of this political impasse. If Somalis agree on re-union between Somaliland and the rest of Somalia, then existing parliaments could be amalgamated to create a bicameral institution: one for unelected clan elders and the other for elected members of parliaments, or the existing parliaments could be replaced by a directly elected new parliament. Once that political decision is reached, then practical arrangements to harmonize existing laws, constitutions, state machinery from judiciary to law enforcement agencies and military could be implemented.

However, if the result of the referendum is not clear cut, and those supporting secession go ahead with their project and some states recognize Somaliland as an independent entity, then there is a risk of dragging the Somali nation into a protracted civil war in which pro- and anti-camps would use military power to settle their political differences. Although the pro-secession camp argues that the region was once British colony and gained independence with internationally recognized borders, the fact of the matter is that Isaaq clans are only among other four major clans that reside in the north regions of Somalia. Indeed, Isaaqs mainly reside in about two regions out of the six or so regions in the former colony in which some non-Isaaq clans such as Dhulbahante had never accepted the British colonial administration as their ruler. The former British protectorate had never existed as a fully fledged independent nation-state for a long time. It immediately joined the former Italian colony in the south in union on 1 July 1960 just after five days of becoming independent and the union was accepted by the people in a general referendum.

The two former colonies were recognized by the international community as the independent Republic of Somalia with recognized territorial borders in accordance with article three of the African Union's charter. Therefore, recognition of Somaliland could be seen by other clans particularly the Harti Daarood clans as creating an Isaaq state, something that they are unlikely to accept.[3] It is also very unlikely that a high percentage of the population of the Federal Republic of Somalia would accept the creation of a clan-based independent and internationally recognized state in Somalia.

Restorative justice and accountability

Restorative justice in civil war situations is always a difficult task as each part in the conflict claims innocence; the Somali case is not different. From early civil wars in the 1980s to the current mayhem in Somalia, different actors perpetuated abuses against human rights, committed war crimes and genocide. The list of violators included government sponsored violence against particular clans, such as Isaaqs, Majeerteens and Hawiyes in the 1980s. The 1990s inter-clan violence instigated by warlords from Mogadishu to Hargeisa to Baidoa in which 'clan cleansing' against particular clans, such as Daaroods and other non-Hawiye clans in Mogadishu and other minority groups were good examples of the ugly face of the conflict. Atrocities committed by foreign powers in Somalia from the UNOSOM to the Ethiopian invasion and AMISOM are reminders of the negative impact that foreign intervention has had on the stability, safety and security of Somalia.

According to reports by human rights organizations, war crimes and other atrocities had been committed throughout the different stages of the conflict. Although this could be dealt with at different stages, and could take years if not decades, there is a need for the creation of local or international tribunals to investigate war crimes and other atrocities to bring those responsible to justice.

This is a sensitive issue because some of the perpetrators are still alive and some of them are involved in Somali politics and might use their power to prevent their trial in a court of law. The civil case in the United States against Brigadier General Mohamed Ali Samatar, former defence and prime minister, filed by some victims of the 1980s civil war seeking financial compensation for alleged torture, was a controversial issue that divided Somalis along pro- and anti-trial groups. The victims claimed the former minister was responsible for their torture and other crimes against humanity.[4] During the trial, victims and their supporters insisted the former minister, one of the few surviving senior government officials, should be tried in a court of law for these crimes.[5]

On the other hand, the anti-trial group argued that Brigadier General Samatar was a national hero who was a member of a legitimate and internationally recognized government. At the time of these alleged crimes, he was defending the Somali Republic against secessionists and traitors who, in collaboration with Ethiopia, were determined to dismember Somalia.[6] To them, singling out Mohamed Ali Samatar for prosecution was unfair, and reeks of clan revenge politics because other former senior government officials, for example, Ismail Ali Abokar, former vice president and Omar Arte Ghalib, former foreign minister, architectures of General Siyad Barre's personality cult, were not being pursued to face justice,[7] and some of these personalities may be still living in Somaliland as heroes.[8] They argued that the only difference is that Ismail Ali Abokar and Omar Arte Ghalib are from the powerful Isaaq clan while Mohamed Ali Samatar was from a minority clan of the Daarood clan.[9] Therefore, fairness requires all former senior government officials regardless of their clan affiliation should all be brought to justice to answer what they knew about what had happened, and then punish those found guilty.[10]

The civil case against General Samatar concluded in August 2012 after eight years of legal battle, and a US judge ordered the general, who died in 2016, to pay $21 million as financial compensation to seven people who sued him.[11] This might lead to more victims speaking out and taking legal actions against those they believed were behind their sufferings. This is particularly important in the post-1991 period in which various factions with different denominations from warlords to Islamists and clan-minded agents committed war and other heinous crimes.

At the international level, over the past few years there had been some talk about war crimes and genocide and the need for justice; however, so far very little has been done about this. Setting up criminal tribunals locally or internationally to punish violators is important if one has to break away from the culture of impunity in clan tradition in which criminals were/are protected by their clans, and how this could stir up revenge if the other clan attempted to punish the culprit.

Somali clans have traditional ways of settling homicide and other crimes through their legal customary system called *Xeer*; however, and unfortunately, sometimes criminals got away with murders due to clan protection.[12] Indeed, after the collapse of the central government, some senior government officials who might have committed atrocities sought clans protection and simply melted away, and this indicates that the tradition has yet to die out.

However, due to the seemingly non-ending nature of the conflict, and lack of a strong central government or international will to persecute violators, it might be unrealistic to bring all perpetuators to justice. Therefore, Somalis could adopt or follow suit of a restorative justice process that is similar to the South African Truth and Reconciliation process so that violators are made to face and accept their criminal acts and then seek forgiveness from the victims or their relatives.

Settling civil disputes or criminal offences through conflict resolution is a well-recognized Somali tradition under the *Xeer* legal system in which disputing parties either offer or accept financial compensation, or other means of redress, such as seeking forgiveness. As well as learning from other conflict resolutions, Somalis could use the *Xeer* system; indeed some conflicts in some regions, such as Somaliland and Puntland, had been resolved through this indigenous legal system.

Throughout the conflict, some communities suffered more than others in terms of confiscation of properties and occupation of their lands by other powerful clan militias. For example, the occupation of Rahanweyn lands and non-ethnic Somalis, such as the Bravanese and Bajuns by Hawiye and Daarood militias, were some of the examples where some powerful clan militia simply occupied lands, claiming to have 'liberated' from the dictatorship. Some of these occupied lands were 'liberated' by their indigenous clans, for example the ejection of the late general Aideed's faction from Bay and Bakool regions by the RRA. However, there might be cases where properties or territories are still with the occupiers and have not been returned to their rightful owners or landlords. Therefore a commission for civil justice should be established to investigate these issues, and then if necessary create specific courts outside any existing judiciary system.

Glossary

Abgaal is a sub-clan of the Hawiye clan family. The clan inhabits middle and lower Shabelle regions, parts of Mudug, Galgaduud regions, Mogadishu and its environs.

Abyssinian is the ancient name of Ethiopia.

Adal was one of the oldest Muslim emirates in the Horn of Africa. It gained prominence during the holy wars of Imam Ahmed ibn Ibrahim Al-Ghazi (Ahmed Gurey) against Abyssinian kingdoms.

Adan, Sharif Hassan Sheikh was former speaker of the Transitional Federal Parliament of Somalia. He is from the Rahanweyn clan family and rose to fame in 2004 during the reconciliation conference in Kenya after he led some parliamentarians who opposed former president Colonel Abdullahi Yusuf's plan for the deployment of African peacekeeping force in Somalia. He became president of the south-western state and resigned in 2018.

Adde, Nur Hassan Hussein was the prime minister of Somalia from November 2007 to February 2009. He was from the Abgaal clan. He played a leading role in the reconciliation efforts that led to the Djibouti peace accord between the ARS and the TFG. He died in London in April after catching the COVID-19 killer disease.

Afar (Danakil) people are one of the ethnic groups in the Horn from the Hamitic/Cushitic ethnic group. They inhabit Djibouti and Ethiopia.

Afweyne, Mohamed Abdi Hassan was a pirate leader from Harardheere, a coastal town in south central Somalia. He is from Saleeban, a sub-clan of Habargedir of the Hawiye clan family. He was detained in Belgium and convicted for his part in the hijack of Pompei, a Belgian vessel in 2009, which was released after a ransom was paid.

Ahmed, Abdullahi Yusuf was a colonel in the Somali National Army (SNA). He was from Omar Mohamud, a sub-clan of the Majeerteen clan. He rose to prominence as one of the ring-leaders of the 1978 coup d'état against the military regime and became one of the founders of the rebel group SSDF. He was one of the founders of the Puntland state of Somalia and became its first president. He then became president of Somalia from 2004 to 2008. He played a crucial role in the events leading up to the Ethiopian invasion and occupation of southern Somalia in 2006–7. He died in 2012.

Ahmed, Sheikh Sharif Sheikh was the president of Somalia from 2009 to 2012. He is from the Abgaal clan. He rose to prominence in early 2004 when he became one of the founders and leaders of the Islamic Courts Union (ICU). He became one of the founders of the ARS, which was established to oppose the Ethiopian invasion and occupation of Somalia.

AIAI – Al-Ittihad Al-Islami (Unity of Islam) was a political Islamic movement founded in the 1980s by Somalis who were inspired by the militant messages of an Egyptian cleric, Sayyid Qutb, to establish global Islamic state. Its offshoots included the ICU.

Aideed, Mohamed Farah was a general in the Somali National Army (SNA). He was one of the founders of the USC and led its forces to overthrow General Siyad Barre's regime in 1991. He was from Sa'ad, a sub-clan of Habargedir. He fought Ali Mahdi's Abgaal USC faction during Mogadishu wars in 1991–2 between Habargedir and Abgaal. In 1992, he was the target of the manhunt operation by the UNOSOM to capture and detain him for his role in the killing of Pakistani peacekeepers in Mogadishu. He died in August 1996 in Mogadishu in a fighting with other forces loyal to Ali Mahdi and Osman Atto.

Al-Shabaab is a terrorist organization, which is the offshoot of the ICU. It rose to prominence as a resistance movement during the Ethiopian invasion. It has links with Al-Qaeda and some of its leaders were/are on the USA's terrorism list. Since 2006, it has been waging war to overthrow Somali governments, and to eject foreign troops from Somalia.

AMISOM – The African Mission of Somalia is the African Union's peacekeeping force in Somalia to support Somalia's federal governments. AMISOM was authorized by the UN Security Council's resolution no. 1744 adopted in 2007. It has strong peacekeeping force of about 22,126, and it has been supporting the Somali federal governments to dislodge the Al-Shabaab movement and to stabilize the country.

ARPCT – Alliance for the Restoration of Peace and Counter-Terrorism was a United States-backed counter-terrorism body established in Mogadishu in 2006 by Somali factional leaders/warlords: Muuse Sudi Yalahow, Bashir Rage, Mohamed Qanyare Afrah, Omar Finish, Abdi Awale Qeybdiid and Mohamed Habeeb Dheere, to oppose the ICU.

ARS – Alliance for the Re-Liberation of Somalia was a resistance movement formed in September 2007 in Asmara in Eritrea to oppose the Ethiopian invasion and occupation of Somalia. Sheikh Sharif Sheikh Ahmed, former executive chairman of the ICU, was its leader. The movement split in two factions, one based in Djibouti and the other in Asmara, led by Sheikh Sharif Sheikh Ahmed and Sheikh Hassan Dahir Aweys, respectively.

Atto, Osman Hassan Ali was one of Mogadishu's factional leaders/warlords. He was once a close associate and the main financier of late General Mohamed Farah Aideed's USC faction. He died in Mogadishu.

AU – the African Union is a continental organization consisting of fifty-five African nations. It was founded in 2001 to replace the old Organization of the African Unity (OAU). Its main office is in Addis Ababa, Ethiopia.

Awdal is a region in the north-western regions of Somalia (present-day Somaliland). Gadabursi and Isse clans reside in the region.

Aweys, Sheikh Hassan Dahir, born in Dhusa Mareeb in 1935, was a former colonel in the Somali National Army (SNA). He became Sheikh – religious cleric, and was one of the founders of the Al-Ittihad Al-Islami, the ICU and the ARS. After the split of the ARS, he founded Hisbul Islam (Islamic Party) and opposed President Sheikh Sharif's TFG. He is on the United States' terrorism list. He is currently in house arrest by the Somali government after defecting from Al-Shabaab of which he was one of the leaders.

Ayr is a sub-clan of the Habargedir clan. The sub-clan mainly resides in the Galguduud region in central Somalia.

Ayro, Aden Hashi was a militant Islamist and one of the prominent leaders of Al-Shabaab. He was from Ayr, a sub-clan of the Habargedir clan. He was killed by American missile strikes on 1 May 2008 at Dhuusa Mareeb in the Galgaduud region.

Bantu is the name for a group of 300–600 ethnic groups scattered throughout Africa. Bantu groups live in Somalia as an oppressed minority group.

Barsana is a sub-clan of the Gaaljecel clan of Hawiye clan family. The clan resides in middle and lower Shabelle regions and is engaged in agro-pastoralism. The sub-clan was one of the first resistance movements which fought against the Italian fascist government in 1923–7 under the leadership of their spiritual and political leader Sheik Hassan Barsana who died in 1927 in prison.

Barsana, Sheikh Hassan was a cleric and spiritual leader of the Barsana clan. He was the first to lead an armed revolt in southern Somalia against the Italian fascist government after Mario de Veccho was appointed as the governor of Somalia in 1923. He led what was known as the 'Barsane Revolt' against Mario de Vecchi's decision to disarm his clan. He was later captured by the Italians and died in prison in 1927.

Boyah, Abdullahi Abshir was a fisherman-pirate-cum leader from Eyl, a town in Puntland. He is from Issa Mohamoud, a sub-clan of the Majeerteen Daarood clan.

Bravanese – or Barawaani in Somali is a non-ethnic Somali minority group in Somalia. The group mainly resides in Brava or Baraawa, a coastal town in the middle Shebelle region. The group speaks Bravanese, a distinctive dialect closer to Swahili.

Burton, Richard was a famous British explorer, cartographer and linguist who visited the Horn around 1845–55. He travelled extensively in the Somali nation, particularly towns such as Harar in the Ogaden region and Zeila in the north-west region of the Somali nation.

Cirro, Mohamed Sheikh Osman was one of the ring-leaders of the 1978 attempted military coup against General Siyad Barre's regime. He was sentenced to death by the National Security Court and was executed with seventeen other military officers and civilians in October 1978.

Corfield, Richard was a British political and police officer who served in the British Somaliland colony in the early twentieth century. He was the commanding officer of the Somaliland Camel Constabulary, a police force set up to police tribal hinterlands. He led his forces to hunt down Sayyid Mohamed Abdulle Hassan, leader of the Dervish movement that opposed British colonial rule. Richard was killed on 9 August 1913 after a fierce battle involving the Dervish and his forces in Dul Madoobe, about 25 miles south-east of Burao town in the present-day Somaliland.

Daarood – or Darod is one of the four major clan families alongside Hawiye, Dir and Rahanweyn clans. Daarood clans reside in Bari, Nugal, Sool, Sanaag and Ceyn regions, part of Mudug, lower Juba and Gedo regions. The clan also inhabits Ethiopia and Kenya.

Dafle, Ahmed Suleyman Abdalla was a member of the Supreme Revolutionary Council (SRC). He was a brigadier general in the Somali National Army (SNA). He was the head of the National Security Service (NSS), the military regime's intelligence and security body. He is the son-in-law of the late president Siyad Barre.

Dergue was a military committee, which overthrew Emperor Haile Selassie of Ethiopia from power on 12 September 1974. Colonel Mengistu Haile Mariame emerged as a strong man and became leader.

Dervish – pronounced 'Daraawiish' in Somali – was a term given to the followers of Sayyid Mohamed Abdulle Hassan, leader of the nineteenth-century resistance movement against British colonialism, to discourage them using their clan names.

Dheere, Mohamed Omar Habeeb was a warlord/factional leader. He established a regional administration in Jowhar town, capital of the middle Shebelle region. He was one of the founders of the ARPCT. His regional administration was dismantled by the ICU. He died in Mogadishu.

Dhulbahante is a sub-clan of Harti, a subdivision of the Daarood clan family, which includes Majeerteen, Dhulbahante and Warsangeli. The clan mainly resides in Sool and Ceyn regions of northern Somalia (Somaliland).

Digil is one of the main two subdivisions of Rahanweyn, the fourth clan family alongside Hawiye, Daarood and Dir clans. Its sub-clans consist of Dabarre, Jiddu, Garre, Tunni and Geledi.

Dir is one of the main four clan families alongside Daarood, Hawiye and Rahanweyn clans. The clan family can be subdivided into Isaaq, Gadabursi and Isse clans that mainly inhabit north-west regions of Somalia. They can also be found in Ethiopia and Djibouti. The Biyomaal clan which resides in the lower Shabelle region in southern Somalia belongs to Dir.

Diriye, Ahmed was one of Hawiye elders who rose to prominence during the Ethiopian invasion and was one of the founders of the Hawiye Elders Committee formed to defend Hawiye clans against what they perceived as aggression by a government led by the late Colonel Abdullahi Yuusuf, a Daarood president.

Diya-Paying group – is a group within Somalis' clan system, which is constituted by association of families related through patrilineal blood ties and matrimonial ties. The group, bound by a customary social contract (*Xeer*), acts as a political unit under which its members share responsibilities for political, security, defence and social contracts.

Gaaljecel is a clan of the Hawiye clan family. It is also said to be part of Saransoor, another clan association, which includes Dagoodiye, Massare and Isse. The Saransoor is said to be descendants of Samaale, one of the two main mythical ancestors of the Somali nation. The word 'Gaaljecel' is said to form using *Gaal* (camel) and *Jecel* (love), in other words 'camel lovers'. The clan speaks 'Maxaa Tiri' language and mainly resides in parts of the Hiiraan, middle and lower Shebelle and lower Juba regions.

Gabooye – also known as 'Midgaan', a derogatory term, is a caste-like group in Somalia. The group is seen as inferior by dominant clans who do not intermarry with it because of the group's engagement in professions like blacksmith and butchery, which nomadic clans traditionally consider inferior professions. The group can be subdivided into Tumaals and Yibirs (Yahar). It is scattered throughout the country and has been politically oppressed and marginalized throughout the Somali history.

Gadabursi – also known as Samaroon is a sub-clan of the Dir clan family. The clan mainly resides in the Awdal region in further north-west region of Somalia (Somaliland) and has borders with Djbiouti. It can also be found in Ethiopia and Djibouti.

Geedi, Ali Mohamed was the prime minister of Somalia from 2004 to 2007. He is from the Abgaal clan. He played a crucial role in the events leading up to the Ethiopian invasion of southern Somalia in 2006. He was dismissed from his job after political disagreement with President Abdullahi Yuusuf.

Geledi is a sub-clan of the Digil, a subdivision of the Rahanweyn clan family. The clan speaks 'Af-Maay Maay' and resides mainly in the lower Shebelle region (Afgooye town and its environs). One of the most well-known history of the sub-clan was Goobroon or Geledi kingdom and its sultans. Afgooye town, its capital, was well known for its *istunka*, traditional martial arts festival held during Somalis' new year (*dab-shidka*) or the 'fire-works'. During *Istunka*, which literally means 'beating or hitting each other', people engage in combat with sticks.

Godane, Ahmed Abdi – also known as Mukhtar Abdirahman 'Godane' was an Islamist militant/extremist and one of the leaders of the Al-Shabaab terrorist movement. He was from the Isaaq clan. He had links with Al-Qaeda and openly supported Osama Bin Laden's message of holy wars. He was killed by a US airstrike in 2004.

Greater Somalia – or pan-Somalism – is the concept of liberating and unifying all five Somali territories as one great Somali nation-state. The concept has been a political motto for liberation movements, such as the SYL, and has inspired Somali nationalism. It shaped the Somali Republic's relationship with its neighbours. During the colonial era, the British proposed Greater Somalia under the Belvin plan that would have placed the Somali nation under the British colonial administration leading to independence. This was rejected by other colonial powers, which perceived the British move as territorial expansionism.

Gurey, Ahmed ibn Ibrahim Al-Ghazi – was a fourteenth-century Muslim leader in the Horn of Africa who waged holy wars against Abyssinian kingdoms and conquered much of Abyssinia. He was known as 'Gran, Gurey' the left handed. His ethnicity is disputed but Somalis claim he was one of them. He was also related to Somali clans by marriage. During his rule, Somali clans, mainly Dir and Daaroods, fell under the control of his Adal emirate in present-day Awdal region in north-western regions of Somalia (Somaliland).

Guurti is an Isaaq clan elders' governance body created during the SNM's rebellion against the military regime. In the early 1990s, the Guurti was expanded to incorporate non-Isaaq clan elders in recognition of their reconciliation efforts during the civil wars within Isaaq clans. The Guurti is now the upper house of Somaliland's bicameral parliament alongside the house of the representatives 'Wakiillo'.

Habargedir is a clan of the Hawiye clan family. The clan mainly inhabits central regions: Galguduud and part of Mudug. It can be subdivided into Sa'ad, Suleyman, Ayr and Sarur.

Habar Jeclo is a sub-clan of the Isaaq clan. The clan can be divided into Mohamed Abokor, Ibrahim, Muse Abokor, Ahmad (Toljaalo).

Harti is one of the subdivisions of the Daarood clan family. The Harti subdivision includes Majeerteen, Dhulbante and Warsangeli clans. They reside in Bari, Nugal, Sanaag and Sool, and Ceyn regions. Some Harti clans can also be found in the lower Juba region of Somalia.

Hassan, Abdulqassin Salad was the president of Somalia from 2000 to 2004. He is from Ayr, a sub-clan of the Habargedir clan. He rose to prominence during the reconciliation conference in Djibouti in August 2000 where he was elected president of the Transitional National Government (TNG).

Hawaadle is a sub-clan of the Hawiye clan family. The clan mainly resides in the Hiiraan region in central Somalia.

Hawiye is one of the four clan families alongside Dir, Rahanweyn and Daarood clans. It is said to be a descendant of the Samaale, one of the two mythical ancestors of the Somali people. The clan speaks 'Maxaa Tiri' language and mainly resides in some parts of the Mudug region, Hiiraan, Galgaduud, middle Shebelle, Benadir, lower Shebelle and lower Juba. Its sub-clans include Abgaal, Gaaljecel, Habargedir, Hawaadle, Murusude and Baadicade.

HDMS – Hisbiya Digil & Mirifle or the Hizbia Dustur Mustquil Somalia was a political party formed by Rahanweyn leaders in the 1940s to promote and protect their communities' political interest. It campaigned for a federal state structure because its leaders were unhappy with the dominance of Daarood, Dir and Hawiye clans over the Republic's politics.

Heard, Gabre was the military commander of the Ethiopian forces during their occupation of southern Somalia in 2006 and 2007. He was heavily involved in the military operations carried out by the TFG/Ethiopian forces against the insurgency which led to indiscriminate shelling of civilian-populated areas in Mogadishu. He was later removed from his job by Prime Minister Meles Zenawi.

Heer – pronounced *Xeer* in Somali – is a traditional Somali customary law, which is adopted by clans or lineages in order to govern their socio-political and economic life.

Howe, Jonathan is a retired US navy commander. He was the UN's special representative for Somalia and led the UNOSOM-II. He held that position from 9 March 1993 until February 1994, seeing through the UNOSOM's critical period. His time in office was bogged down by the manhunt operation against General Aideed, which led to the killing of American soldiers in Mogadishu and subsequent withdrawal of US troops from Somalia.

ICU – Islamic Courts Union was a religious/political movement that operated in Somalia between 2000 and 2006 to impose law and order in Mogadishu using Islamic Sharia. It was a group of different courts supported mainly by Hawiye clans. In 2006, it defeated Mogadishu warlords who had been ruling the city since the 1990s. It controlled southern Somalia, but was dismantled by TFG/Ethiopian forces in 2006. Its prominent leaders included Sheikh Hassan Dahir Aweys and Sheikh Shariif Sheikh Ahmed, its executive chairman.

IGAD - Intergovernmental Agency on Development is a regional development body for Kenya, Ethiopia, Uganda, Somalia, Djibouti, Eritrea and Sudan. The body was set up in 1986 to coordinate regional efforts to deal with droughts and natural disasters.

Isaaq is one of the major clans which is part of the Dir clan family that also includes Gadabursi, Isse and Biyomaal. Isaaq clans mainly reside in Burao, Hargeisa, Berbera, Gabiley and Erigavo cities and towns in the north-west regions of Somalia (Somaliland). The clan can also be found in Djibouti, Kenya and Ethiopia.

Jeelle, Salad was the deputy defence minister during Colonel Abdullahi Yusuf's Transitional Federal Government. He is an Abgaal. He rose to fame during the conflict between the ICU and the TFG. He was heavily involved in conducting the TFG military operation against the ICU leading to the Ethiopian invasion of Somalia.

Jonah, James was the United Nations' special representative for Somalia in the early 1990s.

Kaahin, Dahir Rayaale was the third president of the breakaway region of Somalia (Somaliland). He was elected president on 14 April 2003 after the death of Mohamed Ibrahim Egal.

Maay – Af Maay or Af-Maay Maay is a distinctive Somali language spoken by the Rahanweyn communities of the south-western regions of Somalia. It is one of the East Cushitic branch of the Afro-Asiatic languages. Speakers of the language cannot communicate with speakers of the 'Maxaa Tiri', the other Somali language spoken by Dir, Hawiye and Daarood clans as Spanish speakers cannot communicate with French speakers.

Mahdi, Ali Mohamed was a factional leader/warlord who rose to prominence in 1991. He was one of the founders of the USC and claimed to be president of Somalia after the Mogadishu-based USC Manifesto faction selected him for the post. His Abgal USC faction fought General Aideed's USC Habargedur faction in the Mogadishu wars in the early 1990s. He is from Abgaal. Prior to the civil war, he was a petty politician and businessman/hotelier.

Majeerteen is a clan of the Daarood clan family. The clan is part of the Harti confederation – a subdivision of the Daarood. Majeerteen clans mainly reside in the north-eastern regions of Somalia (Bari, Nugal and some parts of the Mudug region); they can also be found in the lower Juba region in deep south. Majeerteen sub-clans include Osman Mohamud, Isse Mohamud and Omar Mohamud. Historically, Majeerteen clans were known for their Majeerteen sultanates/kingdoms.

Manifesto – was a political movement created in May 1990 by over 100 prominent intellectuals, elders, spiritual leaders and politicians across the clan and ideological spectrum. The group submitted Manifesto (a political document) to General Siyad Barre's government, demanding political reforms. But the initiative was aborted after its leaders were detained by the security forces.

Mareehaan is a clan of the Daarood clan family. Its sub-clans are Reer Dini, Reer Hassan and Eli Dheer. The clan resides in the Gedo, middle Juba, lower Juba regions and parts of the Galguduud and Mudug regions. President Siyad Barre was a Mareehaan of the Reer Diini lineage.

Maxaa Tiri is a distinctive Somali language spoken by Dir, Hawiye and Daarood clan families. It is one of the East Cushitic branch of the Afro-Asiatic languages. Speakers of the language cannot communicate with speakers of 'Af Maay Maay', the other Somali language spoken by Rahanweyn clans, similar to how Spanish speakers cannot communicate with French speakers.

Midgans – *see* Gabooye.

Mirifle is one of the main subdivisions of the Rahanweyn clan family. They speak Af-Maay Maay and mainly reside in the Bay, Bakool, Gedo regions and parts of the lower Shebelle and middle Juba regions. It can be divided into Sagaal, which includes Jilible and Hadame clans, and Sideed, which includes Harin, Eelay, Jiron, Leyasn clans.

MOD is an abbreviation for a clan-based power group said to have been created by the late General Siyad Barre to protect his political/personal rule against other clans. 'M' stands for Mareehaan, his clan; 'O' for Ogaden, his mother's clan; and 'D' for Dhulbante, the clan of his son-in-law, who was the head of the notorious NSS. All these clans are Daarood sub-clans.

Mohamed, Garaad Mohamud was a pirate leader from Eyl, a town in Puntland. He is from Issa Mohamoud, a sub-clan of the Majeerteen Daarood clan. He came to prominence during the hijack of the American ship Maersk Alabama in 2009, which ended after three pirates were killed by the American special forces the Navy SEALs.

Mooryaans was a term given to street children who had lived in Mogadishu streets prior to the civil war after they were forced to leave their homelands when the military regime was clamping down on armed rebels in the central regions in the late 1980s. The word Mooryaan was then used to describe USC factions militia, mainly from Hawiye clans in Mogadishu.

Morgan, Mohamed Hersi was a factional leader/warlord and military officer in the Somali National Army who rose to prominence during the military regime. He was once one of General Siyad Barre's bodyguards and his son-in-law. He was the military commander of the north-west regions and played a crucial role in the military regime's campaign against SNM fighters and its supporters in 1988. He was promoted as minister of defence and was one of the few men who stood up for the late General Siyad Barre when USC forces were driving him out of Mogadishu.

NFD – Northern Frontier District was an old name that the British colonial administration gave to the Somali region which was part of its colonial administration in East Africa, including Kenya. The region is mainly inhabited by Somalis. However, the British annexed it to Kenya arbitrarily even though its inhabitants voted for independence and unity with the Republic of Somalia in a referendum in 1963. The annexation led to the Somali government cutting its diplomatic ties with Britain. Somali nationalists believe the region is one of the missing Somali territories to be liberated and unified in one greater Somali nation-state.

NSS – National Security Service was the main security and intelligence gathering organization created by the military regime with the help of the KGB. The powerful internal security service was headed by General Ahmed Suleyman Abdulle Dafle, the late president Siyad Barre's son-in-law.

Oakley, Robert was an American diplomat and former US ambassador to Somalia. During the 1990s civil war, Oakley led multinational forces from twenty countries, known as UNITAF, deployed in Somalia to secure a safe passage for the delivery of food aid convoys to famine-affected areas. Robert Oakley left Somalia in May 1993, having handed the responsibility of the UNITAF mission to the subsequent larger UNOSOM-II operation. He was then sent back to Somalia by President Bill Clinton during the manhunt operation against General Aideed to negotiate the release of Michael Durant, an American hostage held by the General's faction.

OAU – Organizaton of the African Union was the political organization for African states, which was established on 25 May 1963 to promote solidarity and unity among African nations and to act as collective voice for the African continent. The organization was disbanded on 9 July 2002 and was replaced by the African Union (AU).

Ogaden is a clan of the Daarood clan family. Its sub-clans include Makabul, Mohamed Zubeir and Auliyahan. The clan mainly inhabits the Somali region in Ethiopia (the Ogaden region), in the lower Juba region in southern Somalia and in the Somali region in Kenya.

OLF – Ogaden Liberation Front was a resistance movement founded in 1963 in Hoyado near Wardheer in the Ogaden region to oppose Emperor Haile Selassie's attempts to legitimize occupation of the region. Its first leader was Garad Makhtal.

Oromo is one of the major ethnic groups in Ethiopia and constitutes 34.49 per cent of the population, making them the largest group. The group can also be found in northern Kenya and parts of Somalia. Its native language is Oromo, which is part of the Cushitic branch of the Afro-Asiatic language family.

Puntland is an autonomous regional state in Somalia. It was founded in 1998 by a constitutional conference attended by traditional clan leaders and politicians of the Daarood clans of Majeerteen, Warsangeli and Dhulbahante. Garowe is its capital city.

Qabiil is the Somali term for clan or tribe. The word is originally Arabic.

Qadiriya is one of the main Sufi orders *(tariiqa)* alongside Salihiya, Ahmadiya and Rufaciya orders. The order reached Somalia in the fifteenth century having spread from Iran/Iraq where its founder Sheikh Abdulqadir Al-Jeylani was born and buried. Its spiritual leaders in Somalia included Sheikh Aweys Al-Qadiri, buried in Biyooley town in the Bay region where his followers visit yearly to remember the anniversary of his death.

Qanyare, Mohamed Afrah was a factional leader/warlord and politician. He is from Murusade, a clan of the Hawiye clan family. He was one of the early members of the USC and was allied with Ali Mahdi's USC Abgaal faction. He was a founding member of the United States-backed ARPCT to fight the ICU.

Qat – also pronounced 'Jaad, Khat, Qaad' in Somali is a flowering plant that grows in East Africa and Yemen. It is member of the *Catha edulis* plant family and contains cathinone, an amphetamine line stimulant that may cause excitement and euphoria. The leaves of the plant are chewed by people in East Africa and Yemen as a recreational stimulant drug. It can cause health and social problems, for example users developing addiction, dependence and psychological problems.

Qeybdiid, Abdi Hasan Awale was a factional leader/warlord. He is from Sa'ad, a sub-clan of the Habargedir clan. He was one of the early founders of the USC and rose to prominence during the late General Aideed era and became his interior minister. During the UNOSOM era, Qeybdiid house was targeted by US gunship helicopters in their pursuit of the fugitive General Aideed. The attack caused the massacre of Habargedir elders. He was arrested by the US forces in 1993. He was also one of the founders of the ARPCT.

Raage, Bashir, was a Mogadishu factional leader/warlord who rose to prominence in 2005–6 during the conflict between the ARPCT and ICU. He was one of the founders of the ARPCT. He is from Abgaal.

Rahanweyn or Rewin, is one of the four major clan families alongside Daarood, Hawiye and Dir clans. It is said to be descendant of the Sab, one of the Somalis' mythical ancestors/ fathers. It has two major subdivisions: Digil and Mirifle, which in turn have sub-clans and lineages. Ulinke the Daarood and Hawiye clan families, the Rahanweyn clan family is said to be a confederation of clans which may include non-ethnic Somali groups and other co-opted clans. They mainly speak Af-Maay Maay and inhabit Bakool, Bay, lower Shebelle, Gedo, middle and lower Juba regions and Benadir. They are mainly sedentary farmers and their land can sustain pastoralism and some of their clans are pastoralists.

Reer Xamar – as the name 'Hamar' or *Xamar* in Somali (the popular name for Mogadishu) suggests are non-ethnic Somalis who mainly live in Mogadishu's old quarters of Shingani, Shibis and Xamar Weyn, etc. They are called Reer Hamar which literally means the 'people of Hamar'. They are mainly descendants of Arab, Persian and other non-ethnic Somali migrants who migrated to the Horn many centuries ago. They also form part of a wider community called the Benadir people who live in the coastal towns of Mogadishu, Marka and Barawa.

Rodd, Rennell was a British diplomat who conducted the 1897 Anglo-Ethiopian Treaty with Emperor Menelik II. Under this border treaty, the British arbitrarily returned the Haud area, an important grazing area for Somali clans and part of the Somaliland British Protectorate, to Ethiopia without the knowledge and consent of Somali clans in order to secure Emperor Menelik's neutrality in Britain's war against the Mahdist rebellion in Sudan that was under the British control.

Roobow, Sheikh Mukhtar was a rebel leader and militant Islamist/jihadist. He rose to prominence during the Ethiopian occupation of southern Somalia and became spokesman for the Al-Shabaab movement. Prior to Al-Shabaab, he was the deputy commander of the ICU. He is from Leysan, a sub-clan of the Rahanweyn clan family. He had links with Al-Qaeda. He defected from Al-Shabaab and surrendered to the Somali Federal Government in 2017.

Sahnoun, Mohamed was an Algerian diplomat who was the United Nations' special representative for Somalia from May 1992 to October 1992. He led the UNOSOM-I to monitor ceasefire between Mogadishu warlords. He resigned in October 1992 after political disagreement with Boutros Boutros Ghali, the UN secretary general.

SALF – the Somali-Abo Liberation Front was a guerrilla organization which was active in Bale, Sidamo and Arusi in the south and west of the Ogaden region where it conducted military operations during the 1977 Ogaden war. It was made up of non-Somali ethnic groups, such as Oromo and Arusi but had close links with the Western Somali Liberation Front (WSLF). It was controlled by the Somali military regime.

Salihiya is one of the main Sufi orders (tariiqa) in Somalia alongside Qadiriyah, Ahmadiya and Rufaciya. It originates from the Arabian peninsula and its founder Sheikh Mohamed Salah was located in Mecca in 'Hijas', present-day Saudi Arabia. Its prominent spiritual leaders in Somalia included Sayyid Mohamed Abdalla Hassan who founded the Dervish resistance movement. Also, Sayyid Mohamed Quuleed and Sheikh Hassan Barsane were prominent spiritual leaders in the middle Shebelle region.

Scientific socialism – or *Hantiwadaagga Cilmiga ku Dhisan* (in Somali) was a political ideology invented by the Supreme Revolutionary Council (SRC). It was the SRC's Somali version of socialism under which the nation's wealth belonged to the state and would be distributed equally using the principles of a united, just and fair society. The SRC used the ideology to discourage/eliminate social balkanization and to enhance economic development.

SDM – Somali Democratic Movement was a guerrilla movement created in 1989 in Dubai and Rome to oppose General Siyad Barre's government. It was affiliated to the Rahanweyn clan family. SDM leaders included Abdulqadir Mohamed Aden 'Zope', its founder; Colonel Mohamed Nur Aliyow, who was pro-General Aideed faction; and Abdi Muse Mayo, pro-Ali Mahdi faction.

Selassie, Haile – born as Tafari Makonnen – was the late emperor of Ethiopia from 1930 to 1974. He was the chairman of the OAU from 1963 to 1964. His monarchic regime was overthrown in 1974 by the military junta known as the 'Dergue' led by Mengistu Haile Mariam.

Shangole, Fuad Mohamed Qalaf is a militant/extremist Islamist who was the senior member of the ICU, particularly its militant military wing – Al-Shabaab. He rose to prominence in 2007–9 after becoming a senior member of Al-Shabaab.

Silanyo, Ahmed M. Mohamoud was president of the breakaway region of Somalia (Somaliland) from 2010 to 2017. He is from Habar Jeclo, a sub-clan of the Isaaq clan. Prior to 1990, he held ministerial positions during the late president Siyad Barre's government but later defected and joined the SNM rebel movement and became one of its leaders.

SNA – Somali National Alliance was a factional group established in 1992 after the collapse of the central government. It was a combination of General's Aideed's USC faction and other factions, such as Somali Patriotic Movement (Ogaden) and Southern Somali National Movement. Its leaders included General Mohamed Farah Aideed, Mohamed Nur Aliyow and Hussein Mohamed Aideed, General Aideed's son who became its leader after the General's death. It was mainly dominated by the Habargedir faction.

SNM – Somali National Movement was an Isaaq rebel movement created in 1982 in London to oppose the late president Siyad Barre's regime. Its leaders included Ahmed Mahammad Culaid, Ahmed Islamiil Abdi, Abdulqaadir Kosar Abdi, Ahmed M. Mahamoud Silanyo and Abdirahman Ahmed Ali Tuur. The SNM declared the north-west region of Somalia as an independent state on 18 May 1992 within the borders of the defunct British Somaliland Protectorate.

SODAF – Somali Democratic Action Front was one of the first opposition groups formed outside Somalia to oppose the late General Siyad Barre's government. It was formed in Rome in 1976.

Somali-Abo – *see* SALF

Somaliland is the breakaway region in Somalia. The SNM declared the region independent on 18 May 1992 within the borders of the defunct British Somaliland protectorate. Somaliland has been seeking international recognition, but so far no single state has formally recognized it. The international community recognizes it as part of the Federal Republic of Somalia.

Soomaali Galbeed is the Somali term for western Somalia or the Ogaden region. The term is preferred by Somali nationalists who emphasize the status of the region as part of the greater Somali nation. The term became popular during the 1977 Ogaden war.

SPM – Somali Patriotic Movement – was a rebel movement established in 1989 to oppose the military regime. It was affiliated to the Ogaden clan but also had Harti Daarood factions. Its main leaders were Colonel Bashir Bililiqo, Colonel Ahmed Omar Jees and General Aden Abdullahi 'Gabiyow'.

SRC – Supreme Revolutionary Council – was the highest political and military authority in Somalia that was created by the military junta, which overthrew the democratically elected civilian government of the late president Abdirashid Ali Sharmarke in 1969. The SRC originally composed of twenty-four military officers but that number was reduced after some officers were executed due to a power struggle within the junta. It was dissolved in 1976 after the formation of the Somali Revolutionary Socialist Party (SRSP).

SRSP – Somali Revolutionary Socialist Party was the only political party formed by the military government in 1976 to prepare the nation for civilian elections. It had a political bureau and a central committee. General Mohamed Siyad Barre was elected as its first secretary general.

SSDF – Somali Salvation Democratic Front, initially known as the Democratic Front for Salvation of Somalia (SODAF), was one of the first rebel groups founded in 1978 mainly by Majeerteen military officers to oppose President Siyad Barre's government. It was based in Ethiopia and mainly operated militarily in Mudug, Nugal and Bari regions. Colonel Abdullahi Yusuf, Dr Hassan Abshir Mire, General Mohamed Abshir Muse, Musse Islam and Mohamed Abshir Waldo were its main leaders.

SYL – Somali Youth League was the most influential nationalist movement and political party established in 1943. The SYL played a significant role in leading modern Somali liberation and anti-colonial movements and promoted the concept of Greater Somalia and Somali unity regardless of tribal affiliation. Founders of the SYL included Haji Dirie Hirsi, Mohamed Osoble Adde, Haji Mohamed Hussein, Mohamed Hirsi Nur (Siidii), Abdulqadir Sakhaawadiin, Osmaan Geedi Rage, Dheere Hagi Dheere, Dahir Haji Osman (Dhegaweyne), Yasin Hagi Osman, Ali Hasan Ali Maslah (Ali Verduro), Mohamed Ali Nur, Mohamed Farah Hilowle, X. Mohamed Abdulahi Hayesi, Hudow Ma'alin Abdullahi Salah and Mohamed Osman Baarbe. The party dominated Somali politics, and prime ministers and presidents came from it.

Technicals – the term was coined during the civil war and refers to Toyota pick-ups mounted with heavy machine guns used by Somali militias. The term 'technical' was coined by aid agencies that had to hire gunmen to protect food convoys. As they were not allowed to put expenses for hiring gunmen in their accounting books, they used the term 'technical assistants' as expenses paid for security, hence the word 'technicals' was coined.

Tumaals are part of a Gabooye caste-like group in Somalia. They are the blacksmiths. Refer to Gabooye.

Tuur, Abdirahman Ahmed Ali was one of the SNM leaders. He was from Habar Yonis, a sub-clan of the Isaaq clan. He was president of Somaliland from 1991 to 1995.

UCID – Ururka Cadaaladda iyo Daryeelka (Justice and Welfare Party) is a political party in Somaliland.

UDUB – Ururka Dimuqraadiga Umada Bahawday (United Democratic People's Party) was a political party in Somaliland.

Uffo – the Somali word for hurricane. The term was used by a self-help/voluntary professional group in Hargeisa that organized itself in 1982 to help improve social service provision, such as hospitals in the north-western region. Their detention and trial sparked a riot by students and public which was a turning point and precipitated political and civil unrests in northern regions of Somalia.

USC – United Somali Congress was a Hawiye-affiliated rebel movement formed in 1989 in Rome to oppose General Siyad Barre's government. Its leaders and founders included General Mohamed Farah Aideed, Ali Mahdi, Dr Ismail Jumale Osoble and Ali

M. Wardhiigely. The USC split into Ali Mahdi's Abgaal and General Aideed's Habargedir factions, which resulted in Mogadishu wars in 1991–2.

Wal Wal was a grazing area for Somali clans in the eastern Ogaden region. It is remembered for the Wal Wal incident in 1934 in which Italians, in order to fulfil their ambition of subjugating Ethiopia as an Italian colony, provoked an armed confrontation with Ethiopian troops at Wal Wal. Italy, which by then had exerted its authority over the Ogaden, had strengthened its position as colonial power in the Horn.

Wardhiigley, Ali Mohamed was a politician and one of the founders of the USC.

Warsangeli is a clan of the Harti confederation of the Daarood clan. The clan mainly inhabits the Sanaag region in northern Somalia.

WSLF - Western Somali Liberation Front was the main guerrilla and liberation front formed in 1976 to liberate the Ogaden region from Ethiopia. Supported by the Somali government, it played a crucial role during the first phase of the Ogaden conflict, liberating 60 per cent of the region in the summer of 1977 before the Somali government officially committed its forces.

Xeer – *see* Heer.

Yalahow, Muuse Sudi was a factional leader/warlord. He was from Daud, a sub-clan of the Abgaal. He was an associate of Ali Mahdi and was deputy of the Somali Salvation Alliance, Ali Mahdi's USC faction in the 1990s. He was involved in Hawiye factional fighting over the control of Mogadishu. He was one of the founders of the ARPCT which fought the ICU.

Yibirs – *see* Gabooye

Zenawi, Meles was the prime minister of Ethiopia. He was instrumental in leading the invasion and occupation of Somalia in 2006–8 by Ethiopian forces. He died in August 2012.

Notes

Introduction

1 Lewis, I. M. (1994a). *Blood and Bone: The Call of Kinship in the Somali Society*, Lawrenceville, NJ: Red Sea Press.
2 Samatar, Ahmed I. (1994a). The Curse of Allah: Civic Disembowelment and the Collapse of the State in Somalia, in Samatar, Ahmed I. (Ed.). *The Somali Challenge: From Catastrophe to Renewal*, pp. 95–146. Boulder, London: Lynner Reinner Publishers.
3 Stevenson, Jonathan (1995). *Losing Mogadishu: Testing U.S. Policy in Somalia.* Annapolis, MD: Naval Institute Press.
4 Samatar (1994a).

Chapter 1

1 Abdi, Mohamed M. (2007). *A History of Ogaden (West Somalia) Struggle for Self-Determination.* London: Lighting Source, p. 1.
2 Ibid.
3 Lewis, Ioan. M. (2002b). *A Modern History of the Somali: Nation and State in the Horn of Africa.* Athens: Ohio University Press, p. 25.
4 Ibid., pp. 24–7.
5 Ibid., p. 27.
6 Ibid.
7 Ibid., pp. 25–8; p. 312.
8 Ibid., p. 33.
9 Ibid., p. 40.
10 Lewis (2002b), pp. 40–9.
11 Hess, Robert L. (1966). *Italian Colonialism in Somalia.* London and Chicago: University of Chicago Press, pp. 13–38.
12 Ibid.
13 Ibid.
14 Ibid., p. 151.
15 Lewis (2002b), pp. 50–1.
16 Ibid., p. 50.
17 Ibid.
18 Ibid., pp. 54–5.
19 Okoth, A. (2006). *A History of Africa: African Societies and the Establishment of Colonial Rule, 1800-1915.* Nairobi: East African Educational Publishers, pp. 283–6.
20 Lewis (2002b), pp. 87–8.
21 Abdi (2007), pp. 187–91.
22 Laitin, David and Samatar, Said S. (1987). *Somalia: Nation in Search of a State.* Boulder and London: Westview Press, p. 55.

23 Rennell Rodd was the first secretary in the British Agency in Cairo who conducted the Anglo-Ethiopian treaty.

24 Lewis (2002b), pp. 56–62.

25 Ibid. +++

26 Adowa is a place in Ethiopia where Italian forces, invading from Eritrea in order to subjugate Ethiopia as colony, were defeated by Ethiopian forces in 1896.

27 Nelson, Harold D., ed. (1982). *Somalia: A Country Study*. Washington, DC: American University, pp. 14–16.

28 See map showing the division of the Somali nation by the imperial powers.

29 Lewis (2002b), pp. 61–2.

30 Laitin and Samatar (1987), p. 54.

31 Ibid.

32 Salihiya is one of the Sufi orders practised in Somalia.

33 Qadiriya is one of the Sufi orders practised in Somalia.

34 Lewis (2002b), pp. 63–70.

35 Isaaq is one of the major Somali clan families.

36 Lewis (2002b).

37 Nelson (1982), pp. 17–18.

38 Lewis (2002b), pp. 71–85.

39 Ibid.

40 Laitin and Samatar (1987), pp. 57–8.

41 Littlefield, Walter (1910). Mad Mullah Turns again to Fanatical Slaughter, *New York Times*, 10 April 1910. [Online]. Available at http://www.biyokulule.com/Mad_Mullah2 .htm. [Accessed 13 August 2011].

42 Ibid.

43 New York Times (1909a). Fears for Roosevelt, *New York Times*, 17 May 1909. [Online]. Available at http://www.biyokulule.com/Mad_Mullah2.htm. [Accessed 13 August 2011].

44 Bartholet, Jeffrey (2009). It's a Mad, Mad, Mad, Mad World, *Newsweek*, 12 October 2009. [Online]. Available at http://www.newsweek.com/2009/09/30/it-s-a-mad-mad-mad-mad-world.html. [Accessed 21 April 2011], p. 4.

45 Andrzejewski, B. W., Pilaszewicz, S. and Tyloch, W. (1985). *Literature in African Languages: Theoretical Issues and Sample Surveys*. Cambridge: Cambridge University Press, p. 350.

46 Littlefield (1910).

47 Bartholet (2009), p. 5.

48 Lewis (2002b), pp. 79–80.

49 Ibid.

50 Laitin and Samatar (1987), p. 59.

51 Bartholet (2009), p. 6.

52 Ahmed, Ali Jimale (1995). Daybreak Is Near, Won't You Become Sour? Going Beyond the Current Rhetoric in Somali Studies, in Ali Jimale Ahmed (Ed.), *The Invention of Somalia*. New Barkersville: ITC Kabel Ultra and the Red Sea Press, pp. 135–55, p. 138.

53 Nelson (1982), pp. 22–4.

54 Ibid.

55 Ibid.

56 Ibid., pp. 27–35.

57 Ibid.

58 Ibid.

59 Lewis (2002b), pp. 129–30.
60 Nelson (1982), p. 28.
61 Laitin and Samatar (1987), pp. 67–8.
62 Lewis (2002b), pp. 161–95.
63 Samatar, Ahmed I. (1988b). *Socialist Somalia: Rhetoric and Reality*. London and New Jersey: Zed Books.
64 The Constitution of the Somali Republic, article 6, Published in the Official Bulletin, No. 1 of 1 July 1960.
65 Lewis (2002b), p. 179.
66 Walz, Jay (1963). Premier Says Somalia Sought Soviet Weapons for Self-Defense, *New York Times*, 1 December 1963.
67 Ibid.
68 Lewis (2002b), pp. 183–94.
69 Ibid.
70 Abdi (2007), pp. 54–7.
71 Ibid.
72 Ibid.
73 Mohamoud, Abdullah A. (2006). *State Collapse and Post-Conflict Development in Africa, The Case of Somalia, (1960-2001)*. West Lafayette, IN: Purdue University Press, pp. 108–9.
74 Abdi (2007), p. 57.
75 Ibid.
76 Ibid.
77 Nelson (1982), pp. 232–3.

Chapter 2

1   Jackson, Donna R. (2007). *Jimmy Carter and the Horn of Africa: Cold War Policy Ethiopia and Somalia*. Jefferson, NC and London: McFarland and Company Inc., p. 68.
2   Lewis (2002b).
3   Selassie, Bereket H. (1980). *Conflict and Intervention in the Horn of Africa*. New York and, London: Monthly Review Press, pp. 22–47.
4   Ibid.
5   Ibid.
6   Ibid.
7   Ibid.
8   Samatar (1988b).
9   Ibid., p. 92.
10 Simons, Anna (1995). *Networks of Dissolution Somalia Undone*. Boulder, CO and Oxford: WestviewPress, p. 54.
11 Nelson (1982), pp. 243–4.
12 Ibid.
13 Ibid., p. 233.
14 Abdi (2007), pp. 87–94.
15 Ibid.
16 Selassie (1980), pp. 105–11.
17 Galaydh, Ali K. (1990). Notes on the State of the Somali State, *The Horn of Africa*, vol. XIII, no. 1&2, January–March, April–June 1990, pp. 1–28. Also, on online available at http://www.biyokulule.com/dr.per cent 20galaydh.htm. [Accessed 27 April 2011], p. 16.

18 Tareke, Gebru (2000). The Ethiopia-Somalia 1977 War Revisited. *International Journal of African Historical Studies*, vol. 33, no. 3. Boston University African Studies Center [Online]. Available at http://www.jstor.org/stable/3097438. [Accessed 9 December 2011], p. 640.

19 Abdi (2007).

20 Nelson (1982), p. 62.

21 Ibid., p. 244.

22 Ibid., p. 60.

23 Ibid.

24 Laitin and Samatar (1987), p. 141.

25 Ibid.

26 Galaydh (1990), p. 14.

27 Nelson (1982), p. 60.

28 Lewis (2002b), pp. 232–3.

29 Samatar (1988b), p. 132.

30 Wilson Centre (1977). Digital Archive International History Declassified- Transcript of Meeting Between East German Leader Erich Honecker and Cuban Leader Fidel Castro, East Berlin, 3 April 1977. [Online]. Available at http://digitalarchive.wilsoncenter.org/document/111844. [Accessed 6 April 2014].

31 Ibid.

32 Ibid.

33 Nelson (1982), pp. 244–5.

34 Laitin and Samatar (1987), p. 141.

35 Abdi (2007), pp. 87–94.

36 Nelson (1982), pp. 244–7.

37 Ibid.

38 Ibid., pp. 245–6.

39 Abdi (2007), p. 88.

40 Lewis (2002b), p. 236.

41 Nelson (1982), p. 218.

42 Arnold, Guy (2005). *Africa: A Modern History*. London: Atlantic Books, pp. 476–9.

43 Ibid.

44 Ibid., p. 479.

45 Farer, Tom K. (1976). *War Clouds on the Horn of Africa: A Crisis for Détente*. New York: Carnegie Endowment for International Peace, pp. 110–11.

46 Nelson (1982), 256–8.

47 Ibid., pp. 220–2.

48 Ibid.

49 Jackson (2007), pp. 41–55.

50 Arnold (2005), p. 497.

51 Ibid., p. 497.

52 Snow, Jon (1978). Interview with Somali President Siyad Barre, Channel 4 TV. [Online]. Available at http://www.youtube.com/watch?v=KBiPCCi4i9o. [Accessed 12 January 2011].

53 Bridges, Peter (2000). *Safirka: An American Envoy*. Kent, OH: The Kent State University, p. 66.

54 Lewis (2002b), p. 235.

55 Selassie (1980), pp. 130–4.

56 Ibid.

57 Maruf, Harun (2009). A Programme on the Rise and Fall of the Somali Revolutionary Regime Produced by VOA Somali Service, which Interviewed Senior Somali Politicians about the 40th Anniversary since the Military Government. [Online]. Available at http://www.voanews.com/somali/news/the-rise-and-fall-of-Siad-Barre-2009-20-19.html. [Accessed 11 October 2010].

58 Lewis (2002b), p. 241.

59 Rawson, David (1994). Dealing with Disintegration: U.S. Assistance and the Somali State, in Ahmed I. Samatar (Ed.), *The Somali Challenge from Catastrophe to Renewal?*. Boulder and London: L. Rienner, pp. 147–87, p. 152.

60 Farer (1976), p. 140.

61 Jackson (2007), pp. 78–80.

62 For more information on US foreign policy in the Horn during the Ogaden war, you may want to read: Woodruofe, Louise P. (2013). *Buried in the Sands of the Ogaden: The United States, the Horn of Africa, and the Demise of Détente*, Kent, OH: Kent State University Press.

63 Samatar (1988b), pp. 133–4.

64 Coldwar Channel (2009). Ogaden War 1977 Somalia Ethiopia. [Online]. Video clip available at: http://www.youtube.com/user/ColdWarWarriors#p/search/0/7CemACOk-p0. [Accessed 7 October 2010].

65 Jackson (2007), pp. 70–2.

66 Ibid.

67 Ibid., Woodroofe (2013).

68 Ibid.

69 Ibid., pp. 72–8.

70 Ibid., Woodroofe (2013).

71 Ibid.

72 Ibid., pp. 79–91.

73 Ibid.

74 Ibid.

75 Ibid., Woodroofe (2013).

76 Ibid.

77 Ibid., Woodroofe (2013).

78 Ibid., Woodroofe (2013).

79 Samatar (988b), p. 135.

80 Youtube (2016). Kulankii Siyaad bare iyo Fadal Castro ee Yamen iyo Gen Galaal oo ka waramaya (General Galaal talks about a meeting between Siyad Barre and Fidel Castro in Yemen). Published on youtube https://www.youtube.com/watch?v=0nb69LfnAYg [Accessed November 2016].

81 Lefebvre, Jeffrey A. (1991). *Arms for the Horn, U.S. Security Policy in Ethiopia and Somalia 1953-1991*. London: University of Pittsburgh Press, p. 202.

82 Nelson (1982), p. 252.

83 Selassie (1980), pp. 141–6.

84 www.urrib2000narod.ru.

85 Coldwar Channel (2009).

86 Nelson (1982), p. 246.

87 Abdi (2007), pp. 90–1.

88 Nelson (1982), p. 246.

89 Bridges (2000), p. 66.

90 Coldwar Channel (2009).

91 Nelson (1982), p. 252.

92 Jackson (2007), p. 135.
93 Coldwar Channel (2009).
94 Tareke (2000), p. 666.
95 Samatar (1988b), p. 74.
96 Laitin and Samatar (1987), p. 167.
97 Rawson, David (1994a). Dealing with Disintegration: U.S. Assistance and the Somali Statein Samatar, Ahmed I. (Ed.) *The Somali Challengefrom Catastrophe to Renewal?*, pp. 147–87, Boulder, London: L. Rienner, p. 152.

Chapter 3

1 Samatar (988b), p. 137.
2 Tareke (2000), p. 665.
3 www.urrib2000.com.
4 Nelson (1982), p. 253.
5 Selassie (1980), p. 11.
6 Nelson (1982), p. 245.
7 Tareke (2000), p. 665.
8 Biyokulule (2009a). Puntland: A Quisling Scheme, Roobdoon Forum, 01 August 2009, Secret Document Signed by Siyaad Barre, Africa Confidential, 26 September 1975, Vol. 16 No. 19, p. 8. [Online]. Available at http://www.biyokulule.com/view_content.php?articleid=2064. [Accessed 21 February 2011].
9 Nelson, (1982), p. 247.
10 Ibid., pp. 234–6.
11 Ibid., p. 252.
12 These figures were calculated by converting millions of Somali shillings into US dollars using the 1970s exchange rate of So.Sh 6.295 = 1 US dollar.
13 Nelson (1982), p. 295.
14 Ibid., p. 241.
15 Ibid., p. 128.
16 Lewis (2002b), pp. 246–8.
17 Samatar (1988b), p. 139.
18 Lewis (1994a), p. 226.
19 Nelson (1982), pp. 126–31; Samatar (1988b).
20 Ibid., pp. 126–31.
21 Ibid., p. 128.
22 Lewis (2002b), p. 247.
23 Ghalib, Jama (1995). *The Cost of Dictatorship: The Somali Experience*. New York: Lillian Barber Press, pp. 150–8.
24 Ibid.
25 Omar, Mohamed O. (1992). *The Road to Zero – Somalia's Self-Destruction Personal Reminiscences*. London: HAAN Associates, p. 151.
26 Samatar (1988b), p. 137.
27 Ibid., p. 138.
28 Ibid., p. 137.
29 Nelson, (1982), p. 265; Cumar, Daahir Cali (1997). *Qaran Duman iyo Qoon Talo-Waayey*. Nairobi, pp. 75–8.
30 Lewis (2002b), pp. 242–3.

31 Ghalib (1995), pp. 168–70.

32 Samatar (1988b), p. 138.

33 Ghalib (1995), p. 177.

34 Biyokulule (2010b). Zooming into the Past, Prime Minister Ali Samatar on Historical Account. [Online]. Available at http://www.biyokulule.com/Primeper cent 20Ministerper cent 20aliper cent 20samater.htm. [Accessed 7 October 2010].

35 Ibid., Biyokulule (2009a).

36 Compagnon, Daniel (1990a). The Somali Opposition Fronts: Some Comments and Questions, *Horn of Africa*, vol. XIII, no. 1 & 2, January–March, April–June 1990, pp. 29–54.

37 Biyokulule (2009a).

38 Ibid.

39 Ibid., Biyokulule (2010b).

40 Ibid., Biyokulule (2009a).

41 Maruf (2009).

42 Lewis (2002b), p. 246.

43 Majeerteen is a clan of the Daarood clan family, which is one of the four major family clans in Somalia. They were dominant during the civilian government (1960–9) and General Siyad Barre was reported to have been concerned about plots instigated by their Majeerteen officers in his regime.

44 Lewis (2002b); Ahmed (1995).

45 Lewis (1994a).

46 Lewis, Ion. M. (1982c). *A Pastoral Democracy – A Study of Pastoralism and Politics Among the Northern Somalis of the Horn of Africa*. New York: African Publishing Company.

47 Lewis, Iona.M. (1988d). *A Modern History of the Somalia: Nation and State in the Horn of Africa*. Boulder Col.: Westview Press, p. 168.

48 Ibid., (1982c), pp. 1–30.

49 Ibid.

50 Ibid.

51 Ibid.

52 Ibid.

53 Ibid., p. 82.

54 Lewis (1994a).

55 Ibid., p. 233.

56 Osman, Abdullahi A. (2007). The Somali Conflict and the Role of Inequality, Tribalism and Clanism, in Abdulahi A. Osman and Issaka K. Souare (Eds), *Somalia at the Crossroads – Challenges and Perspectives on Reconstituting a Failed State*. Adonis and Addey Publishers ltd., pp. 96–7, p. 98.

57 Samatar (1988b).

58 Samatar (1994a), pp. 95–146.

59 Ibid.

60 Ibid., pp. 42–61.

61 Ibid.

62 Ibid.

63 Ibid., (1988b), pp. 137–43.

64 Ibid.

65 Nelson (1982), p. 265.

66 Ibid., p. 237.

67 Youtube (2012). Cabdullaahi Yuusuf iyo Hareeri Wareysi Warfidiyeenka ShantaSoomaaliya (Video clip of interview of President Abdullahi Yusuf). Video clip

available at https://www.youtube.com/watch?v=TzPDuGG88q0. [Accessed 29 June 2017].

68 Lewis (2002b), p. 245.
69 Nelson (1982), p. 232.
70 Dool, Abdullahi (1998). *Failed States, When Governance Goes Wrong*. London: Horn Heritage, p. 231.
71 Laitin and Samatar (1987), pp. 96–8.
72 Ghalib (1995), pp. 126–31.
73 Nelson (1982), pp. 247–8.
74 Laitin and Samatar (1987), pp. 160–3.
75 Omar (1992), p. 143.
76 Maruf (2009).
77 Ibid.
78 Laitin and Samatar (1987), pp. 91–2.
79 Ibid.
80 Metz, Helen Chapin Metz (Ed.) (1992). *Somalia: A Country Study*. Washington: GPO for the Library of Congress. [Online]. Available at http://countrystudies.us/somalia /29.htm. [Accessed 20 April 2011].
81 Nelson (1982).
82 Ibid., pp. 272–5.
83 Ghalib (1995), p. 127.
84 Nelson (1982), pp. 271–5.
85 Dool (1998), pp. 18–19.
86 Ghalib (1995), p. 127.
87 Laitin and Samatar (1987), p. 98.
88 Brons, Maria H. (2001). *Society, Security, Sovereignty and the State: From Statelessness to Statelessness?* Utrecht: International Books; Charlbury: Jon Carpenter, pp. 176–8.
89 Lewis (2002b), p. 211.
90 Samatar (1988b), p. 113.
91 Ghalib (1995), pp. 127–8.
92 Lewis (2002b), p. 213.
93 Samatar (1988b), pp. 100–2.
94 Nelson (1982), p. 54.
95 Ibid., p. 120.
96 Ibid., pp. 52–4.
97 Ghalib (1995), p. 142.
98 Ibid.
99 Hashim, Alice Bettis (1997). *The Fallen State, Dissonance, Dictatorship and Death in Somalia*. Lanham and Oxford: University Press of America, pp. 79–80.
100 Nelson (1982), p. 54.
101 Ibid.
102 Ibid.
103 Ibid., p. 124.
104 Ibid, p. 281.
105 Ibid.
106 Laitin and Samatar (1987), pp. 83–8.
107 Hashim (1997), pp. 79–80.
108 Laitin and Samatar (1987), p. 86.
109 Nelson (1982), p. 99.

110 Ghalib (1995), p. 126.
111 Laitin and Samatar (1987), p. 89.
112 Africa Watch (1990). *Somalia: Government at War with Its Own People, Testimonies about the Killings and the Conflict in the North.* New York, Washington: Africa Watch.
113 Salwe, Abdisalam M. Issa (1994). *The Collapse of the Somali State.* London: HAAN Associates, pp. 67–8.
114 Ibid.
115 Nelson (1982), pp. 234–5.
116 Ibid., p. 266.
117 Jackson (2007), pp. 89–90.
118 Laitin and Samatar (1987), p. 90.
119 Jackson (2007), pp. 140–50.
120 Lefebvre (1991), p. 241.
121 Jackson (2007), p. 150.
122 Lefebvre (1991), p. 200.
123 Jackson (2007), p. 159.
124 Lefebvre (1991), p. 241.
125 Jackson (2007), p. 149.
126 Patman, Robert G. (2010). *Strategic Shortfall: The Somalia Syndrome and the March to 9/11.* Santa Barbara, Denvar and Oxford: Praeger, p. 5.
127 Ibid.
128 Ghalib (1995), pp. 180–8.
129 Ibid.
130 Wikileaks (2011). US Embassy Cable, Mogadishu. [Online]. Cables available at http://cab les.mrkva.eu/index.php?subject=somali&identifier=&keywords=&tags=&embassy=-1 &classification=-1&after=&before=&do=search&start=0. [Accessed 5 September 2011].
131 Barre, Mohamed Siad (1982). My Country and My People: The Collected Speeches of Major-General Mohamed Siad Barre, President, the Supreme Revolutionary Council. Mogadishu: Somali Ministry of Information and National Guidance.
132 Lewis (2002b), pp. 221–2.
133 Galaydh (1990), pp. 16–17.
134 Laitin and Samatar (1987), p. 94.
135 Galaydh (1990), p. 22.
136 Nelson (1982), pp. 247–8.
137 Compagnon, Daniel (1992b). Political Decay in Somalia: From Personal Rule to Warlordism, *Refuge*, vol. 12, no. 5 (November–December1992), pp. 8–13. [Online]. Available at http://pi.library.yorku.ca/ojs/index.php/refuge/article/viewFile/21676 /20349. [Accessed 19 April 2011], p. 9; Ruhela, Satya Pal (Ed.) (1994). *Mohammed Farah Aidid and His Vision of Somalia.* New Delhi: Vikas Publishing House PVT LTD., pp. 112–17.
138 Hashim (1997), pp. 79–80.
139 Lewis (2002b), p. 250.
140 Ghalib (1995), pp. 137–8.
141 Galaydh (1990), p. 18.
142 Ghalib (1995), pp. 137–8.
143 Ghalib (1995), p. 175.
144 Ibid., pp. 135–6.
145 Ruhela (1994), p. 70.
146 Laitin and Samatar (1987), p. 92.
147 Galaydh (1990), p. 23.

148 Ibid.
149 Tripodi, Paolo (1999). *The Colonial Legacy in Somalia: Rome and Mogadishu: from Colonial Administration and Operation Restore Hope.* Basingstoke: Macmillan Press, pp. 123–37.
150 Compagnon (1992b), pp. 8–9; Omar (1992), pp. 146–7.
151 Dhoodi Said, Saleban M. (2008). *Maxaa Burburiyey Soomaaliya? Maxaase Xalnoqon Kara? Qaybtii 1aad*, Minneapolis: The Somali Writers, p. 36.
152 Omar (1992), pp. 146–7.
153 Laitin and Samatar (1987), pp. 95–6.
154 Ibid.
155 Lewis (1994a), p. 205.
156 Ghalib (1995), pp. 165–6.
157 Ibid.
158 Ibid.
159 Detailed account of how SNM evolved from groups meeting in houses and pubs to a political opposition which would challenge Siyad Barre regime could be found on Chapter VIII, The Rise of the Somali National Movement: A Case Study in Clan Politics, in *Blood and Bone* Book, I. M. Lewis, 1994.
160 Ibid., p. 206.
161 Cumar (1997), p. 89.
162 Laitin and Samatar (1987), p. 99.
163 Simons (1995), p. 52.
164 Lewis (2002b), p. 249.
165 Laitin and Samatar (1987), p. 90.
166 Ghalib (1995), pp. 167–8.
167 Ibid.
168 Laitin and Samatar (1987), p. 98.
169 Wikileaks (2011).
170 Omar (1992), p. 152.
171 Laitin and Samatar (1987), p. 169.
172 Ruhela (1994), p. 114.
173 Salwe (1994), pp. 72–3.
174 Laitin and Samatar (1987), p. 169; Ghalib (1995), p. 171.
175 Ghalib (1995), p. 175.
176 Lewis (2002b), p. 254.
177 Salwe (1994), pp. 72.
178 Omar (1992), p. 190.
179 Laitin and Samatar (1987), p. 155.
180 Cumar (1997), p. 81.
181 Africa Watch (1990).
182 Ibid., pp. 44–62.
183 Ibid.
184 Ghalib (1995), pp. 160–7.
185 Ibid.
186 Ibid.
187 Africa Watch (1990), p. 65.
188 Ghalib (1995), p. 167.
189 Africa Watch (1990), pp. 124–5; Gersony, Robert (1989). *Why Somalis Flee A Synthesis of Conflict Experience in Northern Somalia by Somali Refugees, Displaced Persons and Others.* Washington: Department of State.

190   Ghalib (1995), p. 168.
191   Africa Watch (1990).+
192   Salwe (1994), p. 69.
193   Simons (1995), p. 69.
194   Salwe (1994), p. 70.
195   Lewis (1994a), p. 225.
196   Patman (2010), p. 5; Africa Watch (1990), p. 127.
197   Compagnon (1990a), pp. 38–9.
198   Africa Watch (1990), p. 127.
199   Mukhtar, Mohamed H. (2003a). *Historical Dictionary of Somalia*. Lanham, MD and Oxford: the Scarecrow Press, p. 233.
200   Africa Watch (1990), pp. 130–2.
201   Ibid.
202   Lyons, T. and Samatar, Ahmed I. (1995). *Somalia: State Collapse, Multilateral Intervention, and Strategies for Political Reconciliation*. Washington: The Brookings Institutions, p. 18.
203   Africa Watch (1990).
204   Ibid., pp. 140–1.
205   Africa Watch (1990); Gersony (1989).
206   Ruhela (1994), p. 124.
207   Africa Watch (1990), p. 44.
208   Reuters (2008a). Somali Pilot Returns to City He Refused to Bomb. [Online]. Available at http://uk.reuters.com/article/idUKL2735431920080627. [Accessed 16 January 2011].
209   Lyons and Samatar (1995), p. 18.
210   Africa Watch (1990), pp. 193–9; Gersony (1989); Salwe (1994), p. 71.
211   Dool (1998), pp. 236–7.
212   Dool (1998), p. 237; Hassan, Abdisalaam Sheikh (2004). *Taariikhda Soomaaliyeed iyo Tartanka Qabiilka*. Nairobi, pp. 67–74.
213   To read more about atrocities committed by all parties, read *Somalia: Government at war with its own people, Testimonies about the killings and the conflict in the north,* An African Watch Report, African Watch Committee, 1990, New York, Washington, and Why Somalis Flee A Synthesis of Conflict Experience in Northern Somalia by Somali Refugees, Displaced Persons and others, a report by Robert Gersony, August 1989.
214   Africa Watch (1990), p. 3.
215   Gersony (1989), p. 61.
216   Ibid.
217   Dool (1998), p. 246.
218   Somaliland247 Channel (2010a). Somaliland Genocide: War Crime by Somalia Government. General Morgan Ordering Shelling of Hargeisa and Commandeering the Operation. [Online]. Video clip available at http://www.youtube.com/watch?v =B0QcQ6S1L5g&NR=1&feature=fvwp. [Accessed 14 November 2010].
219   Somaliland247 Channel (2008b). Last SNM War Against Dictator Barre January 1991 Berbera. [Online]. Video clip available at http://www.youtube.com/watch?v =2YpGS_4wt_8&feature=related. [Accessed 26 July 2011].
220   Simons (1995), p. 78.
221   Dool (1998), pp. 251–3.
222   Drysdale, John (1994). *Whatever Happened Somalia?* London: HAAN Publishing, p. 12; Hassan (2004), pp. 72–5.
223   Osman (2007), p. 98.
224   Ghalib (1995), pp. 183–211.

225 Ibid., p. 201.
226 Nelson (1982), p. 253.
227 Wikileaks (2011).
228 Samatar, Said (1991a). *Somalia: a Nation in Turmoil*. London: Minority Rights Group, p 20.
229 Simons (1995), p. 79.
230 Ghalib (1995), pp. 203–6.
231 Lyons and Samatar (1995), p. 20.
232 Ghalib (1995), pp. 207–8.
233 Ramaas Media Group (2009). Jasira Massacre: Interview with Ibraahim Ali Barre Canjeex Xasuuqi Jasiira 1989 (Wareysi Ibraahim Cali Barre Canjeex). [Online]. Video clip available at http://www.youtube.com/watch?v=gVJFaNaOiVk. [Accessed 26 July 2011].
234 Ghalib (1995), pp. 203–6.
235 Biyokulule (2010c). The Somali Manifesto I. [Online]. Available at http://www .biyokulule.com/Somaliper cent 20Manifestoper cent 20I.htm. [Accessed 2 March 2011].
236 Omar, (1992), pp. 190–9.
237 Ghalib (1995), p. 196.
238 Ibid., Ghalib (1995), p. 207; Tripodi (1999), p. 133.
239 Drysdale (1994), p. 27.
240 Compagnon (1990a), p. 34.
241 Salwe (1994), p. 69.
242 Youtube (2012)..
243 Compagnon (1990a), p.40.
244 Ibid., p. 46.
245 Ibid., p. 40.
246 Mukhtar, Mohammed H. (1997b). Somalia: Between Self-Determination and Chaos, in Hussein M. Adam et al (Eds), *Mending Rips in the Sky: Options for Somali Community in the 21st Century*. Lawrenceville, NJ: Red Sea Press, p. 55; Afrah, Maxamed D. (1994a). The Mirror of Culture: Somali Dissolution Seen Through Oral Expression, in Ahmed I. Samatar (Ed.), *The Somali Challenge from Catastrophe to Renewal*. London: Lynne Rienner Publishers, pp. 233–51.
247 Dool (1998), pp. 219–26.
248 Compagnon (1990a), p. 42.
249 Ghalib (1995), p. 207.
250 Afrah (1994a), p. 248.
251 Dool (1998), pp. 228–30.
252 Bridges (2000), pp. 106–14.
253 Ibid.
254 Dool (1998), pp. 227.
255 Bradbury, Mark (2008). *African Issues: Becoming Somaliland*. London: Progressio, pp. 70–4.
256 Herring, Eric (1992). The Collapse of the Soviet Union: The Implications for World Politics, in J. Baylis and N. J. Regner (Eds), *Dilemmas of World Politics, International Issues in a Changing World*. Oxford: Clarendon Press, pp. 354–83.
257 Alagiah, George (2001). *A Passage to Africa*. London: Little, Brown and Company.
258 Clapham, Christopher (1996). *Africa and the International System, The Politics of State Survival*. Cambridge: Cambridge University Press, pp. 158–9.
259 De Maio, Jennifer L. (2009). *Confronting Ethnic Conflict, the Role of Third Parties in Managing Africa's Civil Wars*. Lanham, MD and Plymouth: Lexington Books, pp. 45–6.

260 Patman (2010), p. 18.
261 Tripodi (1999), pp. 124–37.
262 Ibid.
263 Ibid.
264 Africa Watch (1990), pp. 207–19.
265 Peterson, Scott (2000). *Me Against My Brother: At War in Somalia, Sudan, and Rwanda*. New York and London: Routledge, p. 16.
266 Rawson (1994), pp. 172–3.
267 Jackson (2007), p. 166.
268 Rawson (1994), p. 183.
269 Simons (1995), pp. 52-7.
270 Samatar (1988b).
271 Omar (1992), p. 151.
272 Rawson (1994), p. 178.
273 Lyons and Samatar (1995), pp. 26–8.
274 Sahnoun, Mohamed (1994). *Somalia: Missed Opportunity*. Washington: The United States Institute of Peace Press, p. 8.
275 Drysdale (1994), p. 25.
276 Frame, Iain et al. (2007). *Africa South of the Sahara. 37 Edition of the Europa Regional Surveys of the World*. London and New York: Routleg, p. 449.
277 Samatar (1994a), pp. 95–146.
278 Abdullahi, Mohamed Diriye (2001). *Culture and Customs of Somalia*. Westport: Greenwood Press, p. 39.
279 Ghalib (1995), pp. 210–11; Compagnon (1992b), pp. 8–13.
280 Lewis (2002b), p. 265.
281 Drysdale (1994), p. 26.
282 Lewis (2002b), p. 264.
283 Ghalib (1995), p. 211.
284 Kaha, Caasha (2000). *Gummaadkii Muqdisha & Hargeysa* (The massacre in Mogadishu and Haregeisa). London: Lower Shabelle Publishers, pp. 1–28. Kaha's book is the author's eye witness account of happened in Mogadishu in 1990–1 until she fled from the city. She described in full detail of atrocities committed by both sides.
285 Ibid.
286 Drysdale (1994), p. 27.
287 Samatar (1991a), p. 21.
288 Ruhela (1994), p. 64.
289 Ahmed (1995), p, 149.
290 For more information, read the book: Shire, Mohammed I. (2011). *Somali President Mohamed Siad Barre: His Life & Legacy*, London: Mohammed Ibraahim Shire. The author is the owner of www.jaallesiyaad.com, a website dedicated to former president's life history.

Chapter 4

1 Dool (1998), p. 261.
2 Bradbury (2008), pp. 78–9.

3 Dool (1998), pp. 259–61.

4 Lewis (2002b), pp. 262–4.

5 Lyons and Samatar (1995), p. 21.

6 Lewis (2002b), p. 263.

7 Amnesty International (1992). Somalia: A Human Rights Disaster. [Online]. Report available at http://www.amnesty.org/en/library/info/AFR52/001/1992/en. [Accessed 28 February 2011].

8 Hassan (2004), pp. 74–5; Dool (1998), pp. 256–61.

9 Keydmedia (2012). Top Secret Tape - Jen. Morgan 'Waa Dagaal Daarood iyo Hawiye'(General Morgan says: it is Daarood vs. Hawiye war). [Online]. Video available at http://www.youtube.com/watch?v=5Dae00I_qtQ&feature=youtu.be. [Accessed 9 January 2012].

10 Dool (1998), pp. 256–60.

11 Compagnon (1992b), p. 11.

12 Hassan (2004), p. 75.

13 Jowhar, Abdishakur (2007a). Ich Bin En Hawiye I am a Hawiye Citizen. [Online]. Available at http://www.hiiraan.com/op2/2007/apr/.aspx. [Accessed 28 February 2011].

14 For more analysis on historical clan narratives and the ugliness of clan cleansing, refer to Kapteijns, Lidwien (2013). *Clan Cleansing in Somalia The Ruinous Legacy of 1991,* Pennsylvania: University of Pennsylvania Press.

15 Lewis (2002b), p. 264.

16 Drysdale (1994), p. 24.

17 Hassan (2004), pp. 74–5.

18 Dool (1998), pp. 234–58.

19 Brons (2001), p. 213.

20 Ruhela (1994), pp. 130–54.

21 Ibid.

22 Ibid., pp. 167–71.

23 Ibid.

24 Ghalib (1995), pp. 213–14.

25 Silanyo, Ahmed M. (2010a). Ahmed Silanyo Speech in Minneapolis, US (Qudbadii Silanyo MN U.S. 2). [Online]. Video clip available at http://www.yout ube.com/watch?v=bmOxoyPdjOg&feature=related. [Accessed 20 February 2011]; Ghalib (1995), p. 214.

26 Frame (2007), p. 449.

27 Dool (1998), p. 106.

28 Bartamaha (2006). The Last Interview with Former Somali President Siad Barre. [Online]. Video clip available at http://www.youtube.com/watch?v=oilgkZqstBg &feature=related. [Also, available at www.bartamaha.com. [Accessed 28 February 2011].

29 Amnesty (1992).

30 Ibid.

31 Dool (1998), pp. 106–8.

32 Hassan (2004), pp. 76–7.

33 Dool (1998), pp. 106–8.

34 Lyons and Samatar (1995), p. 21.

35 Peterson (2000), p. 41.

36 Hassan (2004), pp. 78–82.

37 Drysdale (1994), p. 34.
38 Ibid.
39 Sahnoun (1994), p. 10.
40 Stevenson (1995), pp. 77–80.
41 Ibid.
42 Ruhela (1994), p. 169.
43 Compagnon, Daniel (1998c). Somali Armed Movements. in Christopher Clapham (Ed.), *African Guerillas*. Bloomington: Indiana University Press, pp.73–89.
44 Drysdale (1994), p. x.
45 Dowden, Richards (1992a). A Dirty Little War 5,000 Die in Civil War, *The Independent On Sunday*, 05 January 1992. [Online]. Available at http://www.biyokulule.com/January_per cent 201992per cent 282per cent 29.htm. [Accessed 23 February 2011].
46 Drysdale (1994), p. x.
47 Peterson (2000), pp. 22–3.
48 Drysdale (1994), pp. 36–8.
49 Tripodi (1999), pp. 134–5.
50 Peterson (2000), pp. 22–3.
51 Alagiah (2001), p. 91.
52 Lyons and Samatar (1995), p. 22.
53 The term 'technical' was said to have come from aid agencies who had to hire gunmen to protect food convoys and as they were not allowed to put expenses for hiring gunmen in their ledger account used the term 'technical assistants' as expenses paid for security in their books (Petterson, 2000: 31). Ammunition to gunmen was entered as 'nuts and bolts'.
54 Peterson (2000), p. 24.
55 Gebrewold, Belachew (2009). *Anatomy of Violence, Understanding the Systems of Conflict and Violence in Africa*. Farnham: Ashgate, p. 142.
56 Peterson (2000), pp. 25–6.
57 Ibid.
58 Stevenson (1995), p. 57.
59 Peterson (2000), p. 40.
60 The word mooryaan means different things in Somali: parasite worm living in the human body; the poor who sleeps next to stalls; the one who burrows – rummage to find food or cars (see the Mooryaans in Mogadishu p.198 Marchal, Roland).
61 Marchal, Roland (1997). Forms of Violence and Ways to Control it in an Urban War Zone: The Mooryaans in Mogadishu, in Hussein M. Adam et al. (Eds), *Mending Rips in the Sky: Options for Somali Community in the 21st Century*, Lawrenceville, NJ: Red Sea Press, pp. 197–200.
62 Ibid.
63 Ibid.
64 Stevenson (1995), p. 74; Marchal (1997), p. 201.
65 Sahnoun (1994), p. 17.
66 Peterson (2000), pp. 46–7.
67 Samatar (1994a), pp. 95–146.
68 Lyons and Samatar (1995), p. 23.
69 Menkhaus, Ken (2004). *Somalia: State Collapse and the Threat of Terrorism*. Oxford: Oxford University Press, pp. 40–7.

70 Stevenson (1995), pp. 10–14.
71 Menkhaus (2004), pp. 37–45.
72 Nduru, Moyiga (1996). No End in Sight to Banana War. [Online]. Available at http://www.netnomad.com/banana.html. [Accessed 21 November 2010].
73 Stevenson (1995), p. 9.
74 Peterson (2000), p. 20.
75 Drysdale (1994), pp. x–xxv.
76 Peterson (200), pp. 31–3.
77 Ibid.
78 Lyons and Samatar (1995), p. 23.
79 Lewis (2002b), pp. 265 and 287.
80 Lyons and Samatar (1995), p. 22.
81 Peterson (2000), pp. 29–30; Mukhtar, Mohamed Haji (1996c). The Plight of the Agro-pastoral Society of Somalia, *Review of African Political Economy*, December 1996, vol. 23, Issue 70, pp. 543–53; Cassanelli, Lee and Besteman, C. (1996). Explaining the Somali Crisis, in Lee Cassanelli and C. Besteman (Eds), *The Struggle for Land in Southern Somalia: The War Behind the War*. Boulder, CO: Westview Press; London: HAAN.
82 Peterson (2000), p. 30.
83 Lyons and Samatar (1995), p. 22.
84 Peterson (2000), p. 44.
85 Sahnoun (1994), p. 17.
86 Peterson (2000), p. 41.
87 Patman (2010), pp. 23–7.
88 Lyons and Samatar (1995), p. 30.
89 Ibid.
90 Sahnoun (1994).
91 Sahnoun (1994), pp. vii–viii; Peterson (2000), p. 46.
92 Sahnoun (1994), p. 20.
93 Sahnoun (1994), pp. 38–41.
94 Ibid., pp. 15–16.
95 Drysdale (1994), p. 4.
96 Sahnoun (1994), pp. 25–6.
97 Drysdale (1994), pp. 62–5; Peterson (2000), pp. 41–7.
98 Dowden, Richards (1992b). Bitter Tears as Sahnoun Leaves Mogadishu: UN Crisis Deepens after Dispute Between Secretary General and Envoy to Somalia, *The Independent*, and 30 October 1992. [Online]. Available at http://www.independent.co.uk/news/world/bitter-tears-as-sahnoun-leaves-mogadishu-un-crisis-deepens-after-dispute-between-secretarygeneral-and-envoy-to-somalia-1560394.html. [Accessed 8 September 2011]; Peterson (2000), p. 48.
99 Drysdale (1994), p. 4.
100 Ibid., pp. 74–84.
101 Ibid.
102 Ibid.
103 Ibid.
104 Ibid.
105 Ibid.
106 Ibid., pp. 4–7.
107 Peterson (2000), p. 48.

108 Maio (2009), p. 129.

109 Stevenson (1995), p. 50.

110 Peterson (2000), p. 45.

111 Ghali, Boutros Boutros (1996). *The United Nations and Somalia – 1992-1996*. New York: Department of Public Information, United Nations, pp. 30–40.

112 Drysdale (1994), p. 14.

113 Ibid., pp. 105–6.

114 Ibid.

115 PBS News Hour (1995a). Ambush in Mogadishu; Interview with Admiral Jonathan Howe. [Online]. Available at http://www.pbs.org/wgbh/pages/frontline/. [Accessed 28 August 2011].

116 Bush, George (1992a). President Bush's Speech. [Online]. Available at http://millerce nter.org/scripps/archive/speeches/detail/3984. [Accessed 28 February 2011].

117 Peterson (2000), pp. 51–61.

118 Ibid.

119 Lyons and Samatar (1995), p. 40.

120 Ghali (1996), p. 38.

121 Drysdale (1994), p. 109.

122 Peterson (2000), pp. 57–61.

123 Ibid.

124 Ibid.

125 Drysdale (1994), p. 109.

126 Neville, Leigh (2018). Day of Ranger: The Battle of Mogadishu 25 Years On. Oxford and Long Island City, NY: Osprey Publishing, p. 20.

127 Peterson, (2000), p. 60.

128 Ibid.

129 Ghali (1996).

130 Lyons and Samatar (1995), pp. 40–3.

131 Peterson (2000), pp. 61–7.

132 Ibid.

133 Ibid.

134 Ghali (1996).

135 Ibid., p. 50.

136 Peterson (2000), pp. 72–3.

137 Ibid.

138 PBS (1995a).

139 Ghali (1996), p. 376; Peterson (2000), p. 72.

140 Ibid., p. 50.

141 Peterson (2000), pp. 72–3.

142 Ibid.

143 PBS (1995a).

144 Ibid.

145 Peterson (2000), pp. 78–81.

146 Ibid.

147 Ibid.

148 Ghali (1996), pp. 50–1.

149 PBS (1995a).

150 Peterson (2000), p. 161.

151 PBS (1995a).

152 Peterson (2000), p. 95.

153 Takiff, Michael (2010). *A Complicated Man: The Life of Bill Clinton as Told by those who Know Him*, New Haven, CT and London: Yale University Press, p. 203.

154 Peterson (2000), pp. 93–4.

155 Ibid.

156 Stevenson (1995), pp. 83–9.

157 Ibid., pp. 67–8.

158 Peterson (2000), pp. 95–8.

159 Ibid.

160 Ibid., pp. 121–8.

161 PBS (1995a); Peterson (2000), p. 127.

162 Drysdale (1994), p. xiii; Peterson (2000), p. 118.

163 Peterson (2000), p. 120.

164 Ibid., p. 129.

165 Ibid., p. 131.

166 PBS (1995a).

167 Murphy, Ray (2007). *UN Peacekeeping in Lebanon, Somalia and Kosovo*. Cambridge: Cambridge University Press, pp. 190–2.

168 Human Rights Watch (1994a). World Report, 1994. [Online]. Available at http://www.hrw.org/legacy/reports/1994/WR94/Africa-08.htm#P356_163056. [Accessed 1 March 2011].

169 Peterson (2000), p. 127.

170 Ghali (1996).

171 Desbarats, Peter (1997). *Somalia Cover Up – A Commissioner's Journal*. Toronto: McClelland & Stewart Inc; Hussein, Shamis (1997). Somalia, A Destroyed Country and a Defeated Nation, in Hussein M. Adam et al. (Eds). *Mending Rips in the Sky: Options for Somali Community in the 21st Century*. Lawrenceville, NJ: Red Sea Press, pp. 165–92, p. 185.

172 Peterson (2000), pp. 111–15.

173 PBS (1995a).

174 Peterson (2000), pp. 127–8.

175 Ibid., pp. 137–41.

176 Bowden, Mark (1997). A Defining Battle [Online]. Available at http://inquirer.philly.com/packages/somalia/nov16/rang16.asp. [Accessed 1 March 2011].

177 Peterson (2000), pp. 137–8.

178 Ibid., p. 149.

179 Ibid.

180 Ghali (1996), p. 55.

181 Peterson (2000), p. 143.

182 Ibid., p. 99.

183 Lyons and Samatar (1995), p. 59.

184 Hughes, Dana (2014). Bill Clinton 'Surprised' at Black Hawk Down Raid, *ABC News*, 19 April 2014.

185 Takiff (2010), p. 204.

186 Ghali (1996), pp. 55–65.

187 Cohen, Jared (2007). *One Hundred Days of Silence, America and the Rwanda Genocide*. Lanham, MD and Plymouth: Rowman and Littlefield Publishers, p. 52.

188 Ibid.
189 Ghali (1996), pp. 55–9.
190 Peterson (2000), p. 147.
191 Stevenson (1995), p. 90.
192 Peterson (2000), p. 109.
193 Stevenson (1995), pp. 71–4.
194 Ibid., p. 86.
195 Peterson (2000), pp. 150–1.
196 Lewis (2002b), pp. 273–74.
197 Ibid.
198 Peterson (2000), pp. 150–1.
199 Keenadiid, Siciid Cusmnaan (2013). *Xusuusqor – Dagaalladii Sokeeye – Dis 30/1990-Juun 1994*. London: Anchor Print Group Ltd., p. 281.
200 Ibid., Peterson (2000), pp. 150–1.
201 Ibid., pp. 161–3.
202 Stevenson (1995), p. 70.
203 Peterson (2000), p. 153.
204 Lewis (2002b), pp. 267–82; Peterson (2000), pp. 164–9.
205 Lewis (2002b), pp. 267–82.
206 Ibid., pp. 275–6.
207 Peterson (2000), pp. 164–9.
208 Drysdale (199), p. 12.
209 Peterson (2000), pp. 152–3.
210 Ibid., p. 88.
211 Ghali (1996), pp. 83–4.
212 Peterson (2000), p. 34.
213 Ghali (1996), p. 84.
214 Dool (1998), pp. 272–3.
215 Ibid., p. 227.
216 Elmi, Afyare Abdi (2010). *Understanding the Somalia Conflagration: Identity, Political Islam and Peacebuilding*. New York: Pluto Press, pp. 21–3.
217 Ruhela (1994), pp. 169–86.
218 Ibid.
219 Ibid.
220 Ibid.
221 Ibid.
222 Ibid.
223 Ibid., pp. 173–4.
224 Ibid., p. 176.
225 Ibid., pp. 176–80.
226 Samatar (1994a), pp. 95–146.
227 Drysdale (1994), p. 86.
228 Stevenson (1995), pp. 82–9.
229 Ibid.
230 Takiff (2010), p. 203.
231 Stevenson (1995), pp. 62–3.

Chapter 5

1 Bradbury (2008), pp. 67–78.
2 Harti are Daarood sub-clans, such as Dhulbahante and Warsangelis who reside in Sanaag, Sool and Ceyn regions in the breakaway region of Somaliland. Majeerteens in the north-east regions of Somalia (Puntland) are also part of the Harti. The Gadabursi and Isse are part of the wider Dir clan family.
3 Bradbury (2008), pp. 67–78.
4 Ibid., pp. 90–3.
5 Dool (1998), pp. 232–3.
6 Bradbury (2008), pp. 74–85.
7 Ibid.
8 Ibid.
9 Ibid.
10 Ibid., pp. 50–3.
11 Ministry of National Planning & Coordination – MNPC (2004). *Somaliland in Figures 2004.* Hargeisa: Republic of Somaliland, p. 5.
12 Ibid., pp. 80–3.
13 Ibid.
14 Silanyo, Ahmed M. (1991b). A Proposal to the Somali National Movement on a Framework for Transitional Government, London, March, 1991. [Online]. Available at http://wardheernews.com/Articles_2010/October/Ahmed_Silanyo/13_Silanyos_proposal_91.html. [Accessed 20 February 2011].
15 Bradbury (2008), pp. 80–3.
16 International Crisis Group – ICG (2006a). Somaliland: Time for African Union Leadership, International Crisis Group Africa Report N°110, 23 May 2006. [Online]. Available at http://www.crisisgroup.org/~/media/Files/africa/horn-of-africa/somalia/Somalilandper cent 20Timeper cent 20forper cent 20Africanper cent 20Unionper cent 20Leadership.ashx [Accessed 21 February 2011].
17 Bradbury (2008), pp. 82–3.
18 Unionists from Northern Somalia – UNS (2011) The Consequences of Somaliland's International Recognition. [Online]. Available at http://www.wardheernews.com/Articles_2011/August/16_Consequencesper cent 20ofper cent 20Somaliland_unionist.pdf. [Accessed 20 August 2011]; Hirad, Abdalla (2006a). The Somaliland Mythology Indicted Calling the Spade a Spade Part I and II: The Charges. [Online]. Available at http://www.wardheernews.com/Articles_06/may_06/03_calling_the_spade_a_spade.html. [Accessed 20 February 2011].
19 UNS (2011); Bradbury (2008), pp. 82–3.
20 Ghalib (1995), pp. 218–20.
21 Northern Somalis for Peace and Unity – NSPU (2006). The Illusory 'Somaliland': Setting the Records Straight, report by Northern Somalis for Peace and Unity, Ottawa, 2006. [Online]. Availablae at http://wardheernews.com/Articles_06/may_06/Illusory __Somaliland pdf. [Accessed 20 February 2011].
22 Stevenson (1995), p. 123.
23 Bradbury (2008).
24 Ghalib (1995), p. 214; Silanyo (2010a).
25 Wikileaks (2011).

26 Youtube (2012). Cabdullaahi Yuusuf iyo Hareeri Wareysi Warfidiyeenka Shanta Soomaaliya – Interview with former Somalia President Abdullahi Yusuf by Abdisalam Hereri. Available at https://www.youtube.com/watch?v=TzPDuGG88q0 (Accessed 4 September 2012).

27 NSPU (2006); Ibid., ICG (2006a).

28 Lyons and Samatar (1995), p. 23.

29 Bradbury (2008), pp. 87–90; Brons (2001), pp. 248–9.

30 Bradbury (2008), pp. 87–8.

31 Brons (2001), p. 248.

32 Bradbury (2008), pp. 87–99.

33 Ibid.

34 Ibid.

35 Ibid.

36 Ibid., pp. 109–10.

37 Drysdale (1994), pp. 72–3.

38 Ibid., Hirad (2006a).

39 Bradbury (2008), pp. 97–101.

40 Ibid., pp. 112–20.

41 Ibid.

42 Ibid.

43 Ibid.

44 Ibid.

45 Ibid., p. 116.

46 Lewis (2002b), p. 255.

47 Dool (1998), pp. 236–7.

48 Ibid.

49 Bradbury (2008), pp. 124–7.

50 Ibid.

51 www.harowo.com.

52 NSPU (2006), pp. 12–13.

53 Bradbury (2008), pp. 131–6.

54 Ibid.

55 NSPU (2006).

56 Ibid., Hirad (2006a); Al-Jazeera TV (2010a). Somaliland vs. Somalia. [Online]. Video clip available at http://english.aljazeera.net/programmes/insidestory/2010/06/2010623123754251181.html. [Accessed 2 June 2011]. No Democracy in Somaliland . . . Abdi Ismail . . . Live on, a Dhulbahante diaspora & Isaaq MP disagree over Somaliland Independence.

57 UNS (2011).

58 Bradbury (2008), pp. 90–3.

59 Drysdale (1994); Bradbury (2008), pp. 105–8.

60 Menkhaus (2004), pp. 40–7.

61 Bradbury (2008), p. 121.

62 UNS (2011); Rooble, Faisal (2007). Local and Global Norms: Challenges to 'Somaliland's' Unilateral Secession, 2007, Volume XXV 2007. [Online]. Available at http://hornorafrica.newark.rutgers.edu and http://wardheernews.com/Articles_09/March/18_somaliland_faisal.pdf. [Accessed 19 November 2010]. NSPU (2006).

63 Ali, Ahmed Mohamed (2011). BBC Somali Service Interview with Abdirahman Faroole, Puntland President. [Online]. Available at http://www.bbc.co.uk/somali/. [Accessed 21 February 2011].

64 Biyokulule (2011d). Corporate Mercenaries in Somaliland! [Online] Available at http://www.biyokulule.com/view_content.php?articleid=3301. [Accessed 26 February 2011].

65 Youtube (2018). Dozens killed in fighting between Puntland and Somaliland forces. Available at https://www.youtube.com/watch?v=i06KCtlFKXc. [Accessed 18 September 2020].

66 Youtube (2020). Ugaaska Beelaha Gadabuursi oo sheegey in uu maalintii dhaweyd ka bad baadey isku day dil (Gadabursi clan leader survives assassination attempt). Available at https://www.youtube.com/watch?v=gRJNNyVSxh0. [Accessed 18 September 2020].

67 Lewis (2002b), pp. 286–9.

68 Biixi, Adam J. (2001). Building from the Bottom: Basic Institutions of Local Governance, in *Rebuilding Somalia: Issues and Possibilities for Puntland, War-Torn Societies Project (WSP) Somali Programme*. London: HAAN Associates, pp. 53–96, pp. 54–82.

69 Lewis (2002b), p. 288.

70 Shuke, Abdirahman (2004). Traditional Leaders in Political Decision Making and Conflict Resolution, in Richard Ford et al. (Eds), *War Destroys, Peace Nurtures: Reconciliation and Development in Somalia*. Lawrenceville, NJ: The Red Sea Press, pp. 147–68, p. 152.

71 Biixi (2001), p. 82.

72 Farah, Ahmed Yusuf (2004). Assessing Reconciliation Initiatives by the TNG after the Arte Peace Process, in R. Ford et al. (Eds), *War Destroys, Peace Nurtures: Reconciliation and Development in Somalia*. Lawrenceville, NJ: The Red Sea Press, pp. 117–46, p. 129.

73 Lewis (2002b), p. 288.

74 Biixi (2001), pp. 58–79.

75 The name Puntland comes from the mythological 'Land of Punt' in the Horn of Africa where ancient Egyptians used to trade with.

76 Ministry of Planning and Statistics – MPS (2003). Puntland Facts and Figures 2004, Puntland State of Somalia, 2003. [Online booklet]. Available at http://sitereso urces.worldbank.org/SOMALIAEXTN/Resources/PuntlandFigures.pdf. [Accessed 21 February 2011].

77 Ibid.

78 Biixi (2001), pp. 68–9.

79 International Crisis Group- ICG (2009b). Somalia: The Trouble with Puntland, International Crisis Group, policy briefing paper, Africa Briefing, 12 August 2009. [Online]. Available at http://www.crisisgroup.org/en/regions/africa/horn-of-africa/somalia/B064-somalia-the-trouble-with-puntland.aspx. [Accessed 21 February 2011], pp. 3–7.

80 Ibid.

81 Waldo, Mohamed Abshir (2010a). Federalism In Somalia: Birth of Puntland State and the Lessons Learned. [Online article]. Available at http://wardheernews.com/A rticles_2010/October/Waldo/10_Federalism in_Somalia_The_birth_of_Puntland_&_ the_lessons_learned.html. [Accessed 25 October 2010].

82 Nelson (1982), p. 32.

83 Ibid., ICG (2009b), pp. 2–5.

84 Harti regions were within the borders of the former British Somaliland Protectorate
    and remained so when it gained independence in 1960. Therefore Isaaqs claimed the
    region as part of the Somaliland colonial borders. However, some Harti clans never
    signed treaties with the British colonial administration to accept British rule as Isaaq
    clans had done, hence the dispute over these regions.

85 Ibid., ICG (2009b), pp. 2–5.

86 Ibid.

87 Waldo (2010a); Brons (2001), p. 271.

88 Brons (2001), p. 270.

89 Waldo (2010a).

90 Biixi (2001), p. 55.

91 Ibid., ICG (2009b), pp. 2–5.

92 Waldo (2010a).

93 Xinhua News Agency (2001a). Clan Elders Elect President in Somalia's Puntland
    Region, 14 November 2001. [Online]. Available at http://www.biyokulule.com/view
    _content.php?articleid=2942. [Accessed 21 February 2011].

94 Somaliland Times (2001a). Puntland's Looming Civil War. [Online]. Available
    at http://www.somalilandtimes.net/Archive/Archive/00001500.htm. [Accessed
    19 November 2010].

95 Biyokulule (2010e). Clan Wars with Religious Coloration. [Online]. Available at
    http://www.biyokulule.com/view_content.php?articleid=2942. [Accessed 12 August
    2010].

96 Somaliawatch (2002). 2001 Review of Puntland's Political Crisis by an Insider.
    [Online]. Available at http://www.somaliawatch.org/archivedec01/020102401.htm.
    [Accessed 20 November 2010].

97 Ibid., ICG (2009b), p. 5.

98 Somaliwatch (2002).

99 Ibid., ICG (2009b), p. 5; Compagnon (1990a), p. 39.

100 Ibid., ICG (2009b); Biyokulule (2010f). Zooming into the Past: What If Canada
    Would Have Sheltered Abdullahi Yusuf! [Online]. Available at http://www.biyokulule
    .com/view_content.php?articleid=2957. [Accessed 21 November 2010].
    BBC Monitoring Africa – BBCMA (2001). Puntland Administration Accused of Bad
    Governance, 28 February 2001. [Online]. Available at http://www.biyokulule.com/
    view_content.php?articleid=2957. [Accessed 22 November 2010].

101 Lewis (2002b), pp. 286–9.

102 Osman (2007), p. 98.

103 Shay, Shaul (2008). *Somalia between Jihad and Restoration.* New Brunswick, NJ:
    Transaction Publishers, pp. 78–9.

104 Garoweonline (2010a). IGAD is Misleading the World on Somalia, Garoweonline,
    10 October 2010. [Online]. Available at http://www.garoweonline.com/english/inde
    x.php?option=com_content&view=article&id=228:igad-is-misleading-the-world-on
    -somalia-&catid=49:editorial&Itemid=126. [Accessed 25 December 2010].

105 VOA (2011a). Renewed Mandate in Doubt as Puntland Breaks Away From Somali
    Government, 18 January 2011. [Online]. Available at http://www.voanews.com/en
    glish/news/africa/east/Renewed-Mandate-in-Doubt-as-Puntland-Breaks-Away-From
    -Somali-Government-114136594.html. [Accessed 21 February 2011]; Garoweonline
    (2009b). Somalia: Concern over Puntland Secession or Frustration with Progress?'

[Online]. Available at http://www.garoweonline.com/artman2/publish/Editorial_29 /Somalia_Concern_over_Puntland_secession_or_frustration_with_progress.shtm l. [Accessed 18 February 2011]; Garoweonline (2011c). Somalia: Puntland's Break with the T.F.G. and the International Crisis Group's Draft Report, 24 January 2010. [Online]. Available at http://www.garoweonline.com/artman2/publish/Somalia_27/ Somalia_Puntland_s_Break_with_the_T_F_G_and_the_International_Crisis_G roup_s_Draft_Report.shtml. [Accessed 18 February 2011].

106 Ibid., ICG (2009b), p. 3.
107 Ibid., p. 3.
108 Ali (2011).
109 Brons (2001), pp. 275–8.
110 Lewis (2002b), p. 264.
111 Cassanelli, Lee V. (1995a). Victims and Vulnerable Groups in Southern Somalia, 1 May 1995. [Online]. Report available at http://www.google.co.uk/#q=Victims+a nd+Vulnerable+Groups+in+Southern+Somalia,&fp=c7b1db55a5a734dc&hl=en. [Accessed 22 April 2011].
112 Mukhtar (1996c).
113 Somalimaitv (2011). Interview with Prof. Mohamed Haji Mukhtar (Wareysi ku Saabsan Taarkhida Somaliya, Prof. Mohamed Haji Mukhtar Part 1). [Online]. Available at http://www.youtube.com/watch?v=I3Nd3JQk8nY. [Accessed 13 February 2011].
114 Cassanelli (1995a).
115 Mukhtar (1996c).
116 Cassanelli (1995a); Osman (2007), p. 97; Brons (2001), p. 262.
117 Mukhtar (1996c).
118 Mukhtar (1996c); Osman and Souare (2007), pp. 12–13; Cassanelli and Besteman (1996).
119 Eno, Omar A. (1997). The Untold Apartheid Imposed on the Bantu/Jarer People, in Hussein M. Adam et al. (Eds), *Mending Rips in the Sky: Options for Somali Community in the 21st Century*, pp. 209–20. Lawrenceville, NJ Red Sea Press.
120 Hess (1966), pp. 85–100.
121 Mukhtar (1996c).
122 Osman (2007), p. 98.
123 Peterson (2000), p. 30.
124 Cassanelli (1995a).
125 Cassanelli and Besteman (1996).
126 Mukhtar (1996c).
127 Brons (2001), pp. 260–3.
128 Mukhtar (1996c).
129 Ibid.
130 Brons (2001), p. 262.
131 Ibid.
132 Ibid.
133 Mukhtar (1996c).
134 BBCMA (2001).
135 The Independent (1993). Profile: How to Turn a Warmonger into a Hero: General Aideed, Top Bad-guy on America's Hit List, *The Independent*, Saturday, 17 July 1993. [Online]. Available at http://www.independent.co.uk/opinion/profile-how-to-turn-a -warmonger-into-a-hero-general-aideed-top-badguy-on-americas-hit-list-1485338 .html. [Accessed 23 February 2011].

136　Lewis (2002b), p. 287.

137　Mukhtar (1996c).

138　AmaandhooreyChannel (2010a). Colonel Shaatigaduud Talking about RRA Struggle to Liberate Rahanweyn Lands from Habargedir Invaders (Halyeeyga Raxanwayn Shaatigaduud oo Ka Hadlaaya Halgankii RRA). [Online]. Video clip available at http://www.youtube.com/results?search_query=Halyeeyga+Raxanwayn+Shaatiguduud+oo+Ka+Hadlaaya+Halgankii+RRA&aq=f. [Accessed 14 November 2010].

139　Ibid.

140　AmaandhooreyChannel (2010b). Interview with Rahanweyn Girl who Took Part in the Liberation of the Bakool Region (Gabdhihii RRA Bakool Xureeyay). [Online]. Video clip available at http://www.youtube.com/watch?v=i4Cuws8xuLE&feature=related. [Accessed 14 November 2010]; AmaandhooreyChannel (2010c). General Jabiiq Urging RRA Militia to Fights General Aideed's Invading Militia (Halgamaa Wayn ee Jeneral Jabiiq oo Guubaabinaya Qaar ka Mid Ah Xaq u Dirirka RRA). [Online]. Video available at http://www.youtube.com/watch?v=AUtCRM3Anhc&feature=related. [Accessed 14 November 2010].

141　AmaandhooreyChannel (2010d). Somali Rahanweyn Leader, Cabdalla Deerow Meeting with RRA Fighters Encouraging them to Fight Hussein Aideed Habargedir Clan Militia. [Online]. Video clip available at http://www.youtube.com/watch?v=aY1iEi-t35c&feature=related. [Accessed 14 November 2010].

142　AmaandhooreyChannel (2010e). RRA Militiamen in a War Victory Traditional Dance (Ciidanka Wax Iska Caabinta Rahanweyn oo Baacsaday Huwantii Huseyn Caydiid) [Online]. Video clip available at http://www.youtube.com/watch?v=kJy-9_0DAfc&feature=related. [Accessed 14 November 2010].

143　Brons (2001), pp. 260–6.

144　Ibid., p. 266.

145　www.wikipedia.org wiki/Jubaland (1).

146　Ibid.

147　Menkhaus (2004), p. 43.

148　Biyokulule (2010g). The Mushrooming Cabbie Statelets. Roobdoon Forum. [Online]. Available at http://www.biyokulule.com/view_content.php?articleid=3139. [Accessed 24 February 2011].

149　VOA (2011b). Interview with Abdirazak H. Hussein, former prime minister (1964–67). [Online]. Available at http://www.voanews.com/somali/news/Marida-Makarafooka-Cabdirisaaq-Xaaji-Xuseen-120537379.html. [Accessed 3 May 2011].

150　Interpeace and Centre for Research and Dialogue – Interpeace (2009). History of Mediation in Somalia since 1988 [Online]. Available at http://www.interpeace.org/index.php/Publications/Publications.htm. [Accessed 17 February 2011].

151　Elmi (2010), p. 21.

152　Menkhaus (2004).

153　Interpeace (2009), pp. 24–36.

154　Ibid.

155　Drysdale (1994), pp. 115–20.

156　Stevenson (1995), p. 80.

157　Ibid.

158　Drysdale (1994), p. 127.

159　Ibid., p. 109.

160　Lyons and Samatar (1995), pp. 47–52.

161　Drysdale (1994), pp. 115–20.

162 Ibid., pp. 125–8.
163 Ibid.
164 Interpeace (2009), pp. 24–36.
165 Menkhause (2004), pp. 37–40.
166 Interpeace (2009), pp. 24–32.
167 Stevenson (1995), pp. 78–9.
168 Dool (1998), p. 227.
169 Stevenson (1995), pp. 71–86.
170 Interpeace (2009), p. 84.
171 Ibid., pp. 42–9.
172 Ibid.
173 Hirad (2006a); Wardheernews (2006). Faysal Ali Warabe and his Hate Message Comes to Washington DC, 8 September 2006. [Online]. Available at http://wardheer news.com/Editorial/editorial_35.html. [Accessed 24 October 2010].
174 Ibid.
175 Bradbury (2008), pp. 131–6.
176 Interpeace (2009), pp. 40–3.
177 Lewis (2002b), p. 275.
178 Interpeace (2009), pp. 39–51.
179 Elmi (2010), p. 98.
180 Interpeace (2009), pp. 39–51.
181 Ibid.
182 Ibid.
183 Ibid.
184 Ibid.
185 Ibid.
186 Ibid.
187 Ibid.
188 Farah (2004), p. 133.
189 Interpeace (2009), p. 46.
190 UN Secretary General – UNSG (2001a). Report on the Situation in Somalia to the Security Council, Document S/2001/963, 11 October 2001. [Online]. Available at http://www.un.int/wcm/webdav/site/somalia/shared/documents/statements/10867 58703.pdf. [Accessed 10 May 2011].
191 Menkhaus (2004), pp. 45–7.
192 Interpeace (2009), pp. 48–53.
193 Ibid.
194 Elmi (2010), pp. 22; 93–6.
195 Interpeace (2009), p. 48.
196 Menkhaus (2004), pp. 45–7. Situational spoilers are agents or factions which would do anything to disrupt reconciliation conferences and state building for their own parochial interests/reasons This has been the case throughout the Somali conflict. Once a government or a new state building initiative is proposed or constituted, existing or new factions would challenge it for different reasons.
197 Interpeace (2009), p. 49.
198 Ibid., p. 16.
199 Ibid.
200 Ibid., pp. 52–62.
201 Elmi (2010), pp. 23–7.

202 Khalif Farah, Hassan (2007). Interests and Role of External Actors in the Somali Peace Process, in A. O. Farah et al. (Eds), *Somalia: Diaspora and State Reconstruction in the Horn of Africa*. London: Adonis and Abbey Publishers Ltd., pp. 173–95.
203 Interpeace (2009), pp. 52–62.
204 Elmi (2010), pp. 23–7.
205 Khalif Farah (2007), pp. 179–88.
206 Interpeace (2009), p. 57.
207 Eno, Mohamed A. (2007). Inclusive but Unequal: The Enigma of the 14th SNRC and the Four-Point-Five (4.5) Factor, in Abdulahi A. Osman and Issaka K. Souare (Eds), *Somalia at the Crossroads – Challenges and Perspectives on Reconstituting a Flailed State*. London: Adonis and Addey Publishers Ltd., pp. 58–81, pp. 66–7.
208 Somalimaitv (2011).
209 Interpeace (2009), p. 57.
210 Eno (2007), pp. 58–81; Khalif Farah (2007), pp. 173–95.
211 Wikileaks (2011).
212 Osman and Souare (2007), p. 18.
213 Khalif Farah (2007), pp. 173–9; Elmi (2010), pp. 23–7.
214 Interpeace (2009), p. 60.
215 Wikileaks (2011).
216 Interpeace (2009), p. 60; Wikileaks (2011).
217 Hussein, Abdirazak H. (2005a). A Perilous Impasse in Somalia, 7 July 2005. [Online]. Available at www.wardheernews.com. [Accessed 1 December 2010].
218 Wikileaks (2011).
219 Elmi (2010), pp. 23–7.
220 Menkhause (2004).

Chapter 6

1 Shay (2008), pp. 37–47.
2 Bridges (2000), p. 102.
3 Abdi, Abdiaziz (2010). The Genesis of Islamism in Somalia. [Online article]. Available at http://wardheernews.com/Articles_2010/June/Abdiaziz_Abdi/22 The _Genesis_of_Islamism_in_Somalia.html. [Accessed 16 February 2011].
4 Shay (2008), p. 43.
5 Ibid.
6 Simons (1995), p. 79.
7 Menkhaus (2004), pp. 59–60.
8 Ibid.
9 Ibid.
10 Shay (2008), pp. 60–71.
11 Ibid., pp. 15–35.
12 Ibid., pp. 64–6.
13 Peterson (2000), pp. 150–1.
14 Shay (2008), pp. 43–6; Menkhaus (2004), pp. 59–65.
15 Shay (2008), pp. 37–58.
16 Ibid.
17 Ibid., pp. 93–123.

18 Menkhaus (2004), pp. 66–71.

19 Blomfield, Adrian (2002). U.S. Targets in Somalia Running for Cover, *The Daily Telegraph*, 10 January 2002. [Online]. Available at http://i.telegraph.co.uk/news/world news/africaandindianocean/somalia/1381012/US-targets-in-Somalia-running-for -cover.html. [Accessed 17 February 2011].

20 Menkhaus (2004), p. 68.

21 IRIN (2006a). Somalia: Islamic Courts Set up Consultative Council. [Online]. Available at http://www.irinnews.org/report.aspx?reportid=59444. [Accessed 29 November 2010].

22 BBC News Channel (2006a). 'Radical' Heads New Somali Body, *BBC News Channel*, 25 June 2006. [Online]. Available at http://news.bbc.co.uk/1/hi/world/africa/5113868 .stm. [Accessed 17 February 2011].

23 Sanders, Edmund (2006). Islamists Bring Order to Somalia, but Justice is Far from Uniform, *The Seattle Times*, 15 October 2006. [Online]. Available at http://seattlet imes.nwsource.com/html/nationworld/2003305401_somalia15.html. [Accessed 6 May 2011].

24 BBC News Channel (2006b). Profile: Somalia's Islamic Courts, 6 June 2006. [Online]. Available at http://news.bbc.co.uk/1/hi/5051588.stm. [Accessed 21 April 2011].

25 Yuusuf, Muuse (2007a), Tactical Retreat or the Demise of the UIC?, [Online]. Available at http://wardheernews.com/articles_07/jan_07/02_demise_ofper cent 20 _icu.html. [Accessed 1 December 2010].

26 International Crisis Group - ICG (2007c). Somalia: The Tough Part is Ahead, Africa Briefing Paper, no. 45, 26 January 2006. [Online]. Available at http://www.crisisgro up.org/en/regions/africa/horn-of-africa/somalia/B045-somalia-the-tough-part-is-a head.aspx. [Accessed 17 February 2011].

27 US Today (2006). Bin Laden Releases Web Message on Iraq. [Online]. Available at http://www.usatoday.com/news/world/2006-07-01-bin-laden-plans-message_x.htm. [Accessed 17 February 11].

28 Shay (2008), pp. 93–123.

29 Ibid.

30 Ibid.

31 Sii'arag, A. Duale (2006). Bravo Wardheernews! The Leading Light of the Emergent Somali Internet Portals, 19 November 2006. [Online article]. Available at www .wardheernews.com. [Accessed 30 November 2010].

32 Hassan, Olad M. (2006a). Islamic Leader Says Somali Regions in Kenya, Ethiopia Should be Part of Somalia. Associated Press, 18 November 2006. [Online]. Available at http://www.ap.org. [Accessed 6 May 2011].

33 Bryden, Matt (2006). Storm Clouds over Somalia As Rivals Prepare For Battle, *The Nation*, 8 December 2006. [Online]. Article available at http://www.crisisgroup.or g/en/regions/africa/horn-of-africa/somalia/storm-clouds-over-somalia-as-rivals-p repare-for-battle.aspx. [Accessed 22 April 2011].

34 Ibid.

35 Ibid.

36 Shay (2008), pp. 93–123.

37 New York Times (2006b). Militant Leader Emerges in Somalia - Africa & Middle East - International Herald Tribune, June 2006. [Online]. Available athttp://www.ny times.com/2006/06/25/world/africa/25iht-somalia.2047328.html. [Accessed 4 August 2011].

38 Bryden (2006).

39 Shay (2008), pp. 116–17.

40 Hassan, Mohamed Olad (2006b). Somalia Leader Escapes Attempt on Life. APNEWS [Online]. Available on HYPERLINK "https://apnews.com/article/063fd118eca80c867 54570c64a8fd046" https://apnews.com/article/063fd118eca80c86754570c64a8fd046. Accessed 29/12/2020.

41 UN Monitoring Group – UNMG (2006). Report of the Monitoring Group (S/2006913) to the Security Council on 17 November 2006. [Online]. Available at http://www.fas.org/asmp/resources/govern/109th/S2006913.pdf. [Accessed 10 May 2011].

42 Ibid.

43 Penketh, Anne (2006). The Big Question: What's Going on in Somalia, and is the Horn of Africa on the Brink of War? *The Independent*. [Online]. Available at http:/ /www.independent.co.uk/news/world/africa/the-big-question-whats-going-on-in -somalia-and-is-the-horn-of-africa-on-the-brink-of-war-427526.html. [Accessed 12 August 2011].

44 Lobe, Jim (2006). U.S.-Backed U.N. Resolution Risks Wider War, Inter Press Service New Agency, 28 November 2006. [Online]. Available http://ipsnews.net/africa/nota .asp?idnews=35635. [Accessed 5 May 2011].

45 Bryden (2006).

46 Pflanz, Mike (2006). Call for Jihad as Ethiopian Troops Go into Somalia, *The Telegraph*. [Online]. Available at http://www.telegraph.co.uk/news/worldnews /1531095/Call-for-jihad-as-Ethiopian-troops-go-into-Somalia.html. [Accessed 1 December 2010].

47 Rice, Xan and Goldenberg, Suzanne (2007). How U.S. Forged an Alliance with Ethiopia over Invasion, *The Guardian*, 13 January 2007. [Online]. Available at http:// www.guardian.co.uk/world/2007/jan/13/alqaida.usa. [Accessed 6 May 2011].

48 Ibid., ICG (2007c), p. 7.

49 Bush, George (2001b). Address to a Joint Session of Congress Following 9/11 Attack, Delivered on 20 September 2001. [Online]. Available at http://www.americanrhetoric .com/speeches/gwbush911jointsessionspeech.htm. [Accessed 2 December 2010].

50 Gulfnews.com (2006). Islamists Urge Muslims to Join Jihad on Ethiopia, Gulfnews .com, 24 December 2006. [Online]. Available at http://gulfnews.com/news/region /somalia/islamists-urge-muslims-to-join-jihad-on-ethiopia-1.271754. [Accessed 17 December 2010].

51 Reuters (2006b). Ethiopia Parliament Authorizes Action Against Somali Islamists, Reuters, 30 November 2006. [Online]. Available at http://nazret.com/blog/index.p hp/2006/11/30/ethiopia_parliament_authorizes_action_ag. [Accessed 2 December 2010].

52 Barnes, Cedric and Hassan, Harun (2007a). The Rise and Fall of Mogadishu's Islamic Courts, *Journal of Eastern African Studies* vol. 1, no. 2, pp. 151–60. [Online]. Available at http://www.tandfonline.com/doi/pdf/10.1080/17531050701452382 and http://www.chathamhouse.org.uk/files/9130_bpsomalia0407.pdf. [Accessed 4 August 2011], pp. 156–7.

53 de Vries, Lloyd (2007). U.S. Strikes In Somalia Reportedly Kill 31, CBSNEWS, 9 January 2007. [Online]. Available at http://www.cbsnews.com/stories/2007/01/08/ world/main2335451.shtml. [Accessed 2 December 2010].

54 Axe, David (2010). WikiLeaks Cable Confirms U.S.' Secret Somalia Op. WIRED. [Online]. Available at http://www.wired.com/dangerroom/2010/12/wikileaked-cable -confirms-u-s-secret-somalia-op/. [Accessed 15 February 2011].

55 Allahu Akbar means God is great, and saying it is seen as a slogan and moral boost.
56 Jowhar, Abdishakur (2006b). A War of Miscalculation. [Online]. Available at http:
    //www.hiiraan.com/comments2-op-2006-dec-a_war_of_miscalculation.aspx,
    26 December 2006. [Accessed 1 December 2010].
57 Kifle, Elias (2010). Wikileaks Dispatch Exposes Meles Zenawi as a Mercenary,
    Ethiopian Review. [Online]. Available at http://www.ethiopianreview.com/content/3
    0550. [Accessed 3 December 2010].
58 Prince, Rob (2010). Wikileaks Reveals U.S. Twisted Ethiopia's Arm to Invade
    Somalia, 8 December 2010. [Online]. Available at http://www.fpif.org/blog/wikil
    eaks_reveals_us_twisted_ethiopias_arm_toinvade_somalia. [Accessed 2 December
    2011].
59 Samatar, Abdi I. (2007a). Somalia: Warlordism, Ethiopian Invasion, Dictatorship, &
    America's Role. [Online]. Available at http://www.hiiraan.com/op2/2007/feb/somalia
    _warlordism,_ethiopian_invasion,_dictatorship,_americaper cent E2per cent 80per
    cent 99s_role.aspx. [Accessed 1 December 2010].
60 Yuusuf (2007a).
61 Ibid.
62 Barnes and Hassan (2007a), pp. 156–7.
63 Samatar, Said (2007b). The Islamic Courts and Ethiopia's Intervention in Somalia:
    Redemption or Adventurism? Paper presented to Chatham House on 25 April 2007.
    [Online]. Available at http://www.chathamhouse.org.uk/publications/papers/view/-/
    id/521/. [Accessed 6 May 2011].
64 O. Osman, Omarfaruk (2007). Ethiopia's Incursion of Somalia: A Blessing in
    Disguise. [Online article]. Available at http://www.hiiraan.com/print2_op/2007/jan/
    ethiopiaper cent E2per cent 80per cent 99s_incursion_of_somalia__a_blessing_in_di
    sguise.aspx. [Accessed 1 December 2010].
65 ICG (2007c), p. 10.
66 Byman, D. and Pollack, K. (2007). *Containing the Spillover from an Iraqi Civil War:
    Things Fall Apart.* Washington DC: Brooking Institution Press, pp. 165–76.
67 Hirad, Abdalla H. (2007b). The TFG's Victory over the UIC in Somalia: Triumph
    or New Menace for the Nation? – 05 January 2006. [Online]. Available at http://
    www.awdalnews.com - Articles&Opinions. [Accessed 1 December 2010]; Bahar, Ali
    (2007). Critical Period in Somalia: All Eyes on the Prize. [Online]. Available at http://
    www.hiiraan.com/op2/2007/jan/critical_period_in_somalia_all_eyes_on_the_prize_
    .aspx. [Accessed 18 October 2011].
68 Ibid.
69 Samatar (2007a); O. Osman (2007).
70 Ingiriis, Mohamed (2007). A Reality Check for Colonel Abdullahi Yusuf of TFG,
    3 March 2007. [Online article]. Available at http://www.benadir-watch.com
    /2007per cent 20News/0307_Reality_check_for_Yusuf.pdf. [Accessed 1 December
    2010].
71 Kifle (2010).
72 Gettleman, Jeffrey (2006a). Islamists in Somalia are Forced to Retreat - Africa &
    Middle East – *New York Times*, 26 December 2006. [Online]. Available at http://
    www.nytimes.com/2006/12/26/world/africa/26iht-somalia.4021189.html. [Accessed
    27 April 2011].
73 Adow, Mohammed (2006a). Why Ethiopia is on War Footing, *BBC News Channel*,
    21 July 2006. [Online]. Available at http://news.bbc.co.uk/1/hi/5201470.stm.
    [Accessed 2 December 2010].

74 New York Times (2006c). Ethiopian Premier Says His Troops Won't Stay in Somalia, *New York Times*, 3 January 2006. [Online]. Available at http://www.nytimes.com/20 07/01/03/world/africa/03somalia.html. [Accessed 1 December 2010].

75 Benadirwatch (2007). Full text of Somali Insurgent Statement Warning African Peacekeepers. [Online]. Available at http://www.benadir-watch.com/2007per cent 20News/0222_Warning_to_mercenaries.pdf. [Accessed 21 December 2010].

76 McGregor, Andrew (2007). The Leading Factions Behind the Somali Insurgency, 26 April 2007, The Jamestown Foundation. [Online]. Available at http://www.jame stown.org/aboutus/contactus/. [Accessed 1 December 2010].

77 Hoehne, Markus V (2007). Puntland and Somaliland Clashing in Northern Somalia: Who Cuts the Gordian Knot? 7 November 2007. [Online]. Available at http:// hornofafrica.ssrc.org/Hoehne/. [Accessed 30 April 2011].

78 Somaliland Times (2007b). We Will Not Negotiate On Independence, Somaliland Parliament Speaker, *Somaliland Times*, 6 April 2007. Available at http://www.soma lilandtimes.net/sl/2006/272/3.shtml. [Accessed 21 December 2010].

79 Garoweonline (2008d). Somalia's President 'likes to threaten everyone' Says Somaliland Boss, 2 January 2008. [Online]. Available at http://www.garoweonline.c om/artman2/publish/Somalia_27/Somalia_s_President_likes_to_threaten_everyon e_says_Somaliland_boss_printer.shtml. [Accessed 21 November 2011].

80 Garoweonline (2008e). Somaliland Separatist Will not be Allowed to Divide Somalia, Says President, 1 January 2008. [Online] Available at http://www.garoweonline.com/ artman2/publish/Somalia_27/Somaliland_separatists_will_not_be_allowed_to_divi de_Somalia_says_President.shtml. [Accessed 21 November 2011].

81 Samatar (2007b). A Keynote Speech at Horn of Africa Conference VI. [Online]. Available at http://www.youtube.com/watch?v=U0Una853S_E. [Accessed 22 December 2010].

82 Shafat, Abdifatah (2007). Somalis Condemn U.S. Ethiopian Involvement in Somalia, Afrika News. [Online]. Available at http://afrikanews.org/index.php?option=com_co ntent&task=view&id=45&Itemid=26. [Accessed 22 December 2010].

83 Human Rights Watch (2007b). Somalia: Shell Shocked, Civilians Under Siege in Mogadishu, 12 August 2007. [Online]. Available at http://www.hrw.org/en/reports/ 2007/08/12/shell-shocked. [Accessed 7 June 2011].

84 Ibid., p. 85.

85 McGreal, Chris (2007). Thousands Flee as Shelling by Ethiopian Tanks Kills Hundreds of Civilians in Somali Capital, *The Guardian*, Friday 27 April 2007. [Online]. Available at http://www.guardian.co.uk/world/2007/apr/27/warcrimes. [Accessed 5 May 2011].

86 Mire, Amina (2007a). Menacing Somalia: Unholy Trinity of U.S Global Militarism, Meles's Ethiopia and Thuggish Warlords, 13 June 2007. [Online]. Available at http://www.raceandhistory.com/historicalviews/2007/1306.html#34. [Accessed 23 December 2007].

87 Salad, Omar (2007). Somalia: Genocide/War Crimes and Humanitarian Disaster. [Online]. Available at http://www.hiiraan.com/op2/2007/apr/somalia_genocide_wa r_crimes_and_hummanitarian_disaster.aspx. [Accessed 2 December 2010]; Human Rights Watch (2007b), pp. 66–7.

88 Ibid., Human Rights Watch (2007b); New York Times (2008d). Ethiopian Soldiers Accused of War Crimes in Somalia. [Online]. Available at http://www.nytimes.c om/2008/05/06/world/africa/06iht-somalia.1.12610349.html. [Accessed 26 August 2011].

89 Hiiraan (2007a). Prime Minister Geedi Talks about an Assassination Attempt on his Life on 4 June 2007 (Ra'iisal Wasaare Geedi oo ka Warbixiyay Qaraxii Shalay lala Beegsaday Gurigiisa). [Online]. Available at http://www.hiiraan.com/news/2007/jun/wararka_maanta4- 1331.htm. [Accessed 17 December 2010].

90 Salad (2007); Ibid., ICG (2007c).

91 ICG (2007c), p. 3.

92 McGregor (2007); Ingiriis (2007).

93 Abdi I. Samatar (2007c). Somalia's Radical Hutus and the Bloodbath in Mogadishu. [Online]. Available at http://www.hiiraan.com/op2/2007/apr/somalia_s_radical_hutus_and_the_bloodbath_in_mogadishu.aspx. [Accessed 6 May 2011]; Salad (2007).

94 ICG (2007c), p. 10.

95 Samatar (2007c).

96 IRIN (2007b). SOMALIA: More Civilians Abandon Homes as Skirmishes Continue, 22 March 2007. [Online]. Available at http://www.irinnews.org/report.aspx?reportid=70868. [Accessed 19 December 2007].

97 Mire (2007a).

98 Wikileaks (2011).

99 Dool (1998), pp. 232–4.

100 Jowhar (2007a).-

101 Samatar (2007c).

102 Togane, Mohamud S. (2006b). Why The Daarood Will Never Return To Mogadishu Candidate Te-T-Te With Mohamed Dheere. [Online]. Available at www.togane.org/index.php/extended/why_the_Daarood_will_never_return_to_mogadishu_a_candidtte_tte_with_mohamed_d/. [Accessed 25 December 2010].

103 AFP (2007). Somali Opposition Alliance Begins Fight Against Ethiopia, AFP, 20 September 2007. [Online]. Available at http://afp.google.com/article/ALeqM5hIcARdyjMUukX3jKVh3Mje2M-wag. [Accessed 2 December 2010].

104 For analysis on origins, history and evolution of Al-Shabaab, refer to these books: (a) Harper, Mary (2019). *Everything You have Told Me Is True: The Many Faces of Al Shabaab*. London: Hurst & Company. (b) Hansen, Stig J. (2013). *Al-Shabaab in Somalia: The History and Ideology of a Militant Islamist Group, 2005-2012*. Oxford: Oxford University Press. (c) Maruf, Harun and Joseph, Dan (2018). *Inside Al-Shabaab: The Secret History of Al-Qaeda's Most Powerful Ally*, Bloomington: Indiana University Press.

105 McGregor (2007).

106 Associates Press AP (2007a). Somali Suicide Bombers – video released by Somali Islamist Insurgents, Associates Press. [Online]. Video clip available at http://www.youtube.com/watch?v=saZs3ZXYTsM. [Accessed 5 August 2011].

107 Biyokulule (2008h). Somalia's Mujahidin Youth Movement Spokesman Discusses Progress of Jihad, Jihadist Websites, 27 May 2008. [Online]. Available at http://www.biyokulule.com/view_content.php?articleid=1231. [Accessed 23 December 2010].

108 Page, Jacqueline (2010). Jihadi Arena Report: Somalia - Development of Radical Islamism and Current Implications, International Institute for Counter Terrorism, 22 March 2010. [Online]. Available at http://www.ict.org.il/Articles/tabid/66/Articlsid/814/currentpage/2/Default.aspx. [Accessed 23 December 2010].

109 Garoweonline (2008f). Cautious Welcome for UN-brokered Peace Deal in Somalia. [Online]. Available at http://www.garoweonline.com/artman2/publish/Somalia_27/

Cautious_welcome_for_UN-brokered_peace_deal_in_Somalia.shtml. [Accessed 5 August 2011].

110 VOA (2007c). A Discussion Programme about the Disagreement between President Yusuf and Prime Minister Geedi (Khilaafka Madaxweyne C/llaahi Yusuf iyo R/W Geedi) [Online]. Available at http://www.youtube.com/watch?v=guGwUo_O_vs&feature=related. [Accessed 5 August 2011].

111 Georgian, A. (2008). Interview with President Abdullahi Yusuf, France24 TV. [Online]. Video clip available at http://www.youtube.com/watch?v=cCT1Axm-bfg&feature=related. [Accessed 5 August 2011].

112 Nazret (2008) Somalia - Nur Hassan Hussein Adde's Charm Offensive. [Online]. Available at http://nazret.com/blog/index.php/2008/02/01/somalia_nur_hassan_hussein_adde_s_charm_?blog=15. [Accessed 5 August 2008].

113 Garad, Yuusuf (2008). Interview with President Abdullahi Yusuf, BBC Somali Section. [Online]. Available at http://www.youtube.com/watch?v=ciMuzRG5Zl8&feature=related; and http://www.bbc.co.uk/somali/ [Accessed 5 August 2011].

114 Adde, Nuur H. (2008). Press Conference by Prime Minister, Nuur Hassan Adde, Nairobi. [Online]. Video clip available at http://www.youtube.com/watch?v=Hh78XOI29zU&feature=related. [Accessed 5 August 2011].

115 Garoweonline (2010a).

116 Ibid.

117 Gettleman, Jeffrey (2007b). Ethiopian Premier Says His Troops Won't Stay in Somalia, *New York Times*, 3 January 2007. [Online]. Available at http://www.nytimes.com/2007/01/03/world/africa/03somalia.html. [Accessed 25 December 2010].

118 Kifle (2010).

119 Human Rights Watch (2007b).

120 Menkhaus (2004), pp. 37–40.

121 Page (2010).

122 Ibid.

123 For more information and analysis of AMISOM, you may want to read a book written by Williams, Paul D. (2018). *Fighting for Peace in Somalia: A History and Analysis of the African Union Mission (AMISOM), 2007-2017*. Oxford: Oxford University Press.

124 Ibid.

125 International Crisis Group – ICG (2010d). Somalia's Divided Islamists, International Crisis Group, Policy Briefing No. 74, 18 May 2010. [Online]. Available at http://www.crisisgroup.org/~/media/Files/africa/horn-of-africa/somalia/B74per cent 20Somaliasper cent 20Dividedper cent 20Islamists.ashx. [Accessed 28 December 2010].

126 Al-Jazeera TV (2008b). Somali Fighters Destroying Shrines. [Online]. Video clip available at http://www.youtube.com/watch?v=RPWI-p9Kl4g&feature=related. [Accessed 28 December 2010].

127 Jowhar.com (2010). Sheekh Indhoole ah iyo Caruurta Al-Shabab (A blind Sufi Cleric Being Tortured by Al-Shabaab. [Online]. Available at http://www.youtube.com/watch?v=frPbTNJi_lI. [Accessed 4 December 2011].

128 Adow, Mohammed (2011b). Somalia's Al-Shabaab Meet their Match, AljazeeraEnglish. [Online]. Available at http://www.youtube.com/watch?v=kTeqM7FVMOA. [Accessed 5 August 2011].

129 Gettleman, Jeffrey (2009c). For Somalia, Chaos Breeds Religious War, *New York Times*, 23 May 2009. [Online]. Available at http://www.nytimes.com/2009/05/24/world/africa/24somalia.html. [Accessed 28/12/2010].

130 Bloomfield, Adrian, *The Daily Telegraph*, 11 January 2020.

131 BBC (2017). Who Are Somalia's al-Shabab? Available at https://www.bbc.co.uk/news/world-africa-15336689. [Accessed 5 September 2020].

Chapter 7

1 Globalsecurity (2007). Somalia Civil War. [Online]. Available at http://www.globalsecurity.org/military/world/war/somalia.htm. [Accessed 4 December 2011].

2 *Kasmo* (2000), Wareysi: Aden Cabdulle Cusman (Somali newspaper), London, p. 2.

3 For analysis on Somalia as a failed state, refer to a book by Harper, Mary (2012). *Getting Somalia Wrong?: Faith, War and Hope in a Shattered State (African Arguments)*. London: Zed Books.

4 Hussein, Abdirazak H. (2011b). The Future Constitutional Structure of the Somali Republic: Federal or Decentralized Unitary State? [Online]. Available at http://www.hiiraan.com/op2/2011/apr/the_future_constitutional_structure_of_the_somali_republic_federal_or_decentralized_unitary_state.aspx. [Accessed 22 April 2011].

5 Little, Peter D. (2003). *African Issues Somalia: Economy Without State*. Oxford, Bloomington and Hargeisa: International African Institute in association with James Currey; Indiana University Press; Btec Books, pp. 165–7.

6 Ibid.

7 Ibid., pp. 139–47.

8 Ibid.

9 Ibid.

10 Ibid.

11 Ibid.

12 Ibid.

13 Ibid.

14 Ibid., pp. 123–5.

15 Ibid.

16 World Bank and United Nations Development Programme – WB/UNDP (2003). Socio-Economic Survey 2002, Report No. 1 Somalia Watching Brief 2003. [Online]. Available at http://info.worldbank.org/etools/docs/LICUS/194/175per cent 20-per cent 20Somaliaper cent 20-per cent 20Watchingper cent 20Brief-Macroeconomicper cent 20Dataper cent 20Collectionper cent 20andper cent 20Analysisper cent 20-per cent 20Socioeconomicper cent 20Survey.pdf. [Accessed 17 February 2011], p. 20.

17 Little (2003), pp. 83–138.

18 Ibid.

19 Ibid.

20 Ibid.

21 Chalmers, Caitlin and Hassan, Mohamed A. (2008). UK Somali Remittances Survey, supported by DFID and SendMoneyHome.org, London. [Online]. Available at http://www.diaspora-centre.org/DOCS/UK_Somali_Remittan.pdf. [Accessed 16 February 2011], p. 7.

22 UNDP (2009a). Somalia's Missing Million: The Somali Diaspora And Its Role In Development [Online]. Report available at website: http://www.so.undp.org. [Accessed 29 December 2010].

23 Ibid., Chalmers, Caitlin and Hassan (2008), p. 7.
24 Ibid.
25 UNDP (2009a), p. 19.
26 For more analysis on the role of remittance on Somalia, refer to a book by Lindley, Anna (2010). *The Early Morning Phonecall: Somali Refugees' Remittances*. New York: Berghahn Books.
27 Ibid., Chalmers, Caitlin and Hassan (2008).
28 Ibid., p. 25.
29 Little (2003), pp. 165–7.
30 Chalmers, Caitlin and Hassan (2008), p. 7.
31 UNDP (2011b). Cash and Compassion: The Role of the Somali Diaspora in Relief, Development and Peace Building.
32 WB (2006b). Somalia: From Resilience Towards Recovery and Development. [Online]. Available at http://siteresources.worldbank.org/INTSOMALIA/Resources/cem_01_06.pdf. [Accessed 10 May 2011].
33 Ibid., p. XI.
34 UNDP (2011b), p. 75.
35 Little (2003), pp. 165–7; WB (2006b), p. 61.
36 WB (2006b), p. 61.
37 CIA (2011). World Fact Book [Online]. Available at https://www.cia.gov/library/publications/the-world-factbook/geos/so.html. [Accessed 22 April 2011].
38 WB (2006b). p. 61.
39 Ibid.
40 UN webcast (2010). Press Conference by Mr. Abdulkareem Jama, Somali minister of information, post and telecommunications on the Situation in Somalia [Online]. Video clip available at http://www.unmultimedia.org/tv/webcast/2010/12/press-conference-mr-abdulkareem-jama-on-the-situation-in-somalia.html. [Accessed 17 December 2010].
41 Leeson, Peter T. (2007). Better Off Stateless: Somalia Before and After Government Collapse, Department of Economics, West Virginia University. [Online paper]. Available at http://www.peterleeson.com/Papers.html. [Accessed 16 February 2011].
42 WB (2006b), pp. 65–6.
43 Ismail, Jamal Abdi (2006). Africa Media Development Initiative, Somalia: Research Findings and Conclusion. [Online]. Available at www.bbcworldservicetrust.org/amdi and http://www.radiopeaceafrica.org/assets/texts/pdf/SOM_AMDI_Report_pp4per cent 201.pdf. [Accessed 28 December 2010], p. 19.
44 Ibid.
45 Ibid., p. 24.
46 National Union of Somali Journalists – NUSOJ (2010). The Untold Tales of Misery: Somali Journalists and their Precarious Work. [Online]. Available at http://www.nusoj.org/Somaliper cent 20Journalistsper cent 20andper cent 20theirper cent 20Precariousper cent 20Work.pdfwork [Accessed 1 January 2011], p. 3.
47 Ibid.
48 For a good coverage of media development in Somalia, see a report by Jamal Abdi Ismail, Africa Media Development Initiative, Somalia: Research Findings and Conclusion, BBC World Service Trust, available at www.bbcworldservicetrust.org/amdi.
49 Leeson (2007), p. 15; Ismail (2006).

50 UNESCO (1967). Somalia – Literacy and Adult Education by A., Rashid-Siddiqi, Paris, 1967, pp. 5–6.
51 Nelson (1982), p. 281.
52 WB (2006b), p. 91.
53 Ibid.
54 Ibid., p. 158.
55 Ibid., p. 92.
56 World Bank and United Nations – WB/UN (2006). Somali Joint Needs Assessment, Social Services and Protection of Vulnerable Groups Cluster Report, 14 September 2006. [Online]. Available at http://www.somali-jna.org/downloads/SSPVGper cent 20140906per cent 20ADper cent 20Finalper cent 20Draftper cent 20rec-socialper cent 20rev-I.pdf. [Accessed 27 December 2010], p. 58.
57 Nelson (1982), p. 281.
58 MNPC (2004), p. 76.
59 MPS (2003), p. 52.
60 Nelson (1982), p. 281.
61 WB (2006b), p. 94.
62 Cassanelli, Lee and Abdikadir, Farah Sheikh (2008). Somalia: Education in Transition, *Bildhaan: An International Journal of Somali Studies*. [Online]. Available at http://digitalcommons.macalester.edu/bildhaan/vol7/iss1/7/. [Accessed 22 July 2011], p. 102.
63 UNDP (2011b), p. 67.
64 Ministry of Education -MOE (2011). Somaliland Ministry of Education and Higher Education. [Online]. Available at http://moesomaliland.com/2011/index.php?option =com_content&view=section&layout=blog&id=18&Itemid=97. [Accessed 12 August 2011].
65 WB (2006b), p. 159.

Conclusion

1 WB (2020). Somalia to Receive Debt Relief under the Enhanced HIPC Initiative. Available at https://www.worldbank.org/en/news/press-release/2020/03/25/somalia -to-receive-debt-relief-under-the-enhanced-hipc-initiative. [Accessed 10 September 2020].
2 Teslik, Lee Hudson (2008). Iraq, Afghanistan, and the U.S. Economy. [Online]. Available at Council on Foreign Relations' website http://www.cfr.org/afghanistan/iraq -afghanistan-us-economy/p15404#p1. [Accessed 23 November 2011].
3 UNS (2011).
4 ABC (2010). General Muhammad Ali Samatar in Court Human Rights Violations. [Online]. Video clip available at http://www.youtube.com/watch?v=k0ySBgPkHV4. [Accessed 25 August 2011].
5 Ibid.; Universal TV (2010). TV Programme Debate about the Trial of General Mohamed Ali Samatar, former prime minister of Somalia. [Online]. Video clip available at http://www.youtube.com/watch?v=l7819M7khXI&feature=related. [Accessed 9 December 2011].
6 Ibid.

7 Togane, Mohamud S. (2005c). The Eedoar Botch the Case Against General Samatar. [Online]. Available at http://www.togane.org/index.php/extended/the_eedoar_botch _the_case_against_general_samatar/. [Accessed 22 October 2011].

8 Universal TV (2010).

9 Togane (2005c).

10 Abdulla, Ali H. (2010). Putting Surviving Members of the Defunct Somali Supreme Revolutionary Council (SRC) on Trial. [Online]. Available at http://www.hiiraan.com /op2/2010/mar/putting_surviving_members_of_the_defunct_somali_supreme_rev olutionary_council_src_on_trial.aspx. [Accessed 22 October 2011]. Togane (2005c).

11 Associated Press (2012a). Judge Awards $21 Million in Torture Lawsuit against Former Somali Prime Minister Samantar. [Online] Newspaper article available at http: //news.yahoo.com/judge-awards-21-million-torture-lawsuit-against-former-18125638 2.html [Accessed 29 August 2012].

12 Cali, Axmed Maxamed (2011). BBC Interview with Puntland President. (Wareysi BBCda la yeelay Abdirahman M. Faroole, Madaxweymaha Puntland). [Online]. Interview available at http://www.bbc.co.uk/somali/maqal_iyo_muuqaal/2011/09/1 10901_puntland_galmudug.shtml. [Accessed 4 September 2011]; Hiiraan (2011b). Speeches Made by Leaders of Puntland and Galmudug at the Roadmap Consultation Meeting in Mogadishu (Madaxda DKMG ah ee Soomaaliya iyo Madaxda Puntland iyo Galmudug oo Khudbadyo ka Jeediyay Shirka wadatashiga). [Online]. Available at http://www.hiiraan.com/news/2011/Sept/wararka_maanta4-14884.htm. [Accessed 4 September 2011].

Bibliography

Books

Abdi, Mohamed M. (2007). *A History of Ogaden (West Somalia) Struggle for Self-Determination*. London: Lighting Source.

Abdullahi, Mohamed Diriye (2001). *Culture and Customs of Somalia*. Westport, CT: Greenwood Press.

Afrah, Maxamed D. (1994). The Mirror of Culture: Somali Dissolution Seen Through Oral Expression. In Ahmed I. Samatar (Ed.), *The Somali Challenge from Catastrophe to Renewal?*, pp. 233–51. London: Lynne Rienner Publishers.

Afrax, Maxamed D. (2002). *Dal Dad Waayey iyo Duni Damiir Beeshay: Soomaaliya dib ma u Dhalan Doontaa?* Eldoret: Maji Matamu Printers.

Africa Watch (1990). *Somalia: Government at War with its own People, Testimonies about the Killings and the Conflict in the North*. New York and Washington, DC: Africa Watch.

Ahmed, Ali Jimale (1995). Daybreak is Near, Won't You Become Sour? Going Beyond the Current Rhetoric in Somali Studies. In Ali Jimale Ahmed (Ed.), *The Invention of Somalia*, pp. 135–55. New Barkerville: ITC Kabel Ultra and The Red Sea Press.

Alagiah, George (2001). *A Passage to Africa*. London: Little, Brown and Company.

Andrzejewski, B. W., Pilaszewicz, S. and Tyloch, W. (1985). *Literature in African Languages: Theoretical Issues and Sample Surveys*. Cambridge: Cambridge University Press.

Arnold, Guy (2005). *Africa: A Modern History*. London: Atlantic Books.

Barre, Mohamed Siad (1982). *My Country and My People: The Collected Speeches of Major-General Mohamed Siad Barre, President, the Supreme Revolutionary Council*. Mogadishu: Somali Ministry of Information and National Guidance.

Biixi, Adam J. (2001). Building from the Bottom: Basic Institutions of Local Governance. In *Rebuilding Somalia: Issues and Possibilities for Puntland, War-Torn Societies Project (WSP) Somali Programme*, pp. 53–96. London: HAAN Associates.

Bradbury, Mark (2008). *African Issues: Becoming Somaliland*. London: Progressio.

Bridges, Peter (2000). *Safirka: An American Envoy*. Kent, OH: The Kent State University.

Brons, Maria H. (2001). *Society, Security, Sovereignty and the State: From Statelessness to Statelessness?* Utrecht: International Books and Charlbury: Jon Carpenter.

Byman, D. and Pollack, K. (2007). *Containing the Spillover from an Iraqi Civil War: Things Fall Apart*. Washington, DC: Brooking Institution Press.

Cassanelli, Lee V. (1996). Explaining the Somali Crisis. In Lee Cassanelli and C. Besteman (Eds), *The Struggle for Land in Southern Somalia: The War Behind the War*, pp. 13–28. Boulder, CO: Westview Press and London: HAAN.

Clapham, Christopher (1996). *Africa and the International System, The Politics of State Survival*. Cambridge: Cambridge University Press.

Clausewitz, Isabelle (2005). *Clausewitz and African War Politics and Strategy*. London: Frank Cass.

Cohen, Jared (2007). *One Hundred Days of Silence, America and the Rwanda Genocide.* Lanham, MD and Plymouth: Rowman and Littlefield Publishers.

Compagnon, Daniel (1998). Somali Armed Movements. In Christopher Clapham (Ed.), *African Guerillas*, pp. 73–89. Bloomington: Indiana University Press.

Cumar, Daahir Cali (1997). *Qaran Duman iyo Qoon Talo-Waayey.* Nairobi: Daahir Cali Cumar

Cusmaan, Yuusuf Nuur (2013). *Xusuusqor – Dagaalladii Sokeeye – Dis 30/1990-Juun 1994 – Siciid Cusmaan Keenadiid.* London: Anchor Print Group Ltd.

De Maio, Jennifer L. (2009). *Confronting Ethnic Conflict, the Role of Third Parties in Managing Africa's Civil Wars.* Lanham, MD and Plymouth: Lexington Books.

Desbarats, Peter (1997). *Somalia Cover Up – A Commissioner's Journal.* Toronto: McClelland & Stewart Inc.

Dhoodi Said, Saleban M. (2008). *Maxaa Burburiyey Soomaaliya? Maxaase Xalnoqon Kara? Qaybtii 1aad.* Minneapolis, MN: The Somali Writers.

Dool, Abdullahi (1998). *Failed States, When Governance Goes Wrong.* London: Horn Heritage.

Drysdale, John (1994). *Whatever Happened Somalia?* London: HAAN Publishing.

Elmi, Afyare Abdi (2010). *Understanding the Somalia Conflagration: Identity, Political Islam and Peacebuilding.* New York: Pluto Press.

Eno, Mohamed A. (2007). Inclusive but Unequal: The Enigma of the 14th SNRC and the Four-Point-Five (4.5) Factor. In Abdulahi A. Osman and Issaka K. Souare (Eds), *Somalia at the Crossroads – Challenges and Perspectives on Reconstituting a Flailed State*, pp. 58–81. London: Adonis and Addey Publishers Ltd.

Eno, Omar A. (1997). The Untold Apartheid Imposed on the Bantu/Jarer People. In Hussein M. Adam and Richard Ford (Eds), *Mending Rips in the Sky: Options for Somali Community in the 21st Century*, pp. 209–20. Lawrenceville, NJ: Red Sea Press.

Farah, Ahmed Yusuf (2004). Assessing Reconciliation Initiatives by the TNG after the Arte Peace Process. In R. Ford, Hussein M. Adam and Edna Adan Ismail (Eds), *War Destroys, Peace Nurtures: Reconciliation and Development in Somalia*, pp. 117–46. Lawrenceville, NJ: The Red Sea Press.

Farer, Tom K. (1976). *War Clouds on the Horn of Africa: A Crisis for Détente.* New York: Carnegie Endowment for International Peace.

Frame, Iain and Europe Publications (2007). *Africa South of the Sahara. 37 Edition of the Europa Regional Surveys of the World.* London: New York: Routledge.

Gebrewold, Belachew (2009). *Anatomy of Violence, Understanding the Systems of Conflict and Violence in Africa.* Farnham: Ashgate.

Ghali, Boutros Boutros (1996). *The United Nations and Somalia –1992–1996.* New York: Department of Public Information, United Nations.

Ghalib, Jama (1995). *The Cost of Dictatorship: The Somali Experience.* New York: Lillian Barber Press.

Giorgetti, Chiara (2010). *A Principled Approach to State Failure, International Community Actions in Emergency Situations.* Boston, MA: Martinus Nijhoff Publishers.

Hansen, Stig J. (2013). *Al-Shabaab in Somalia: The History and Ideology of a Militant Islamist Group, 2005–2012.* Oxford: Oxford University Press.

Harper, Mary (2012). *Getting Somalia Wrong?: Faith, War and Hope in a Shattered State (African Arguments):* London: Zed Books.

Harper, Mary (2019). *Everything You have Told Me Is True : The Many Faces of Al Shabaab.* London: Hurst & Company.

Hashim, Alice Bettis (1997). *The Fallen State, Dissonance, Dictatorship and Death in Somalia*. Lanham, MD, New York and Oxford: University Press of America.

Hassan, Abdisalaam Sheikh (2004). *Taariikhda Soomaaliyeed iyo Tartanka Qabiilka*. Nairobi: Abdisalam Sheikh Hassan.

Herring, Eric (1992). The Collapse of the Soviet Union: The Implications for World Politics. In J. Baylis and N. J. Regner (Eds), *Dilemmas of World Politics, International Issues in a Changing World*. Oxford: Clarendon Press.

Hess, Robert L. (1966). *Italian Colonialism in Somalia*. London and Chicago: University of Chicago Press.

Hussen, Shamis (1997). Somalia, A Destroyed Country and a Defeated Nation. In Hussein M. Adam and Richard Ford (Eds), *Mending Rips in the Sky: Options for Somali Community in the 21st Century*, pp. 165–92. Lawrenceville, NJ: Red Sea Press.

Jackson, Donna R. (2007). *Jimmy Carter and the Horn of Africa: Cold War Policy Ethiopia and Somalia*. Jefferson, NC and London: McFarland and Company Inc.

Kaha, Caasha (2000). *Gummaadkii Muqdisha & Hargeysa (The Massacre in Mogadishu and Haregeisa)*. London: Lower Shabelle Publishers.

Khalif Farah, Hassan (2007). Interests and Role of External Actors in the Somali Peace Process. In A. O. Farah, Mammo Muchie and Joakim Gundel (Eds), *Somalia: Diaspora and State Reconstruction in the Horn of Africa*, pp. 173–95. London: Adonis and Abbey Publishers Ltd.

Laitin, David and Samatar, Said S. (1987). *Somalia: Nation in Search of a State*. Boulder, CO and London: Westview Press.

Lefebvre, Jeffrey A. (1991). *Arms for the Horn, U.S. Security Policy in Ethiopia and Somalia 1953–1991*. London: University of Pittsburgh Press.

Lewis, Ioan M. (1982). *A Pastoral Democracy – A Study of Pastoralism and Politics Among the Northern Somalis of the Horn of Africa*. New York: African Publishing Company.

Lewis, Ioan M. (1988). *A Modern History of the Somalia: Nation and State in the Horn of Africa*. Boulder, CO: Westview Press.

Lewis, Ioan M. (1994). *Blood and Bone: The Call of Kinship in the Somali Society*. Lawrenceville, NJ: The Red Sea Press.

Lewis, Ioan M. (2002). *A Modern History of the Somali: Nation and State in the Horn of Africa*. Athens: Ohio University Press.

Lewis, Ioan M. (2009). *Understanding Somalia and Somaliland, Culture, History and Society*. London: Hurst and Company.

Lindley, Anna (2010). *The Early Morning Phonecall: Somali Refugees' Remittances*. New York: Berghahn Books.

Little, Peter D. (2003). *African Issues Somalia: Economy Without State*. Oxford, Bloomington and Hargeisa: International African Institute in association with James Currey; Indiana University Press; Btec Books.

Lyons, T. and Samatar, Ahmed I. (1995). *Somalia: State Collapse, Multilateral Intervention, and Strategies for Political Reconciliation*. Washington, DC: The Brookings Institutions.

Marchal, Roland (1997). Forms of Violence and Ways to Control it in an Urban War Zone: The Mooryaans in Mogadishu. In Hussein M. Adam and Richard Ford (Eds), *Mending Rips in the Sky: Options for Somali Community in the 21st Century*, pp.193–207. Lawrenceville, NJ: Red Sea Press.

Marlow, David H. (1963). The Gaaljecel Barsana of Central Somalia: A Lineage Political System in a Changing World, Doctoral Thesis, Harvard University.

Maruf, Harun and Joseph, Dan (2018). *Inside Al-Shabaab: The Secret History of Al-Qaeda's Most Powerful Ally*. Bloomington: Indiana University Press.

Menkhaus, Ken (2004). *Somalia: State Collapse and the Threat of Terrorism*. Oxford: Oxford University Press.

Metz, Helen Chapin Metz, Ed. (1992). *Somalia: A Country Study*. Washington, DC: GPO for the Library of Congress. Available at: http://countrystudies.us/somalia/29.htm. [Accessed 20 April 2011].

Mohamoud, Abdullah A. (2006). *State Collapse and Post-Conflict Development in Africa, The Case of Somalia, (1960–2001)*. West Lafayette, IN: Purdue University Press.

Mubarak, Jamil A. (1996). *From Bad Policy to Chaos in Somalia: How an Economy Fell Apart*. Westport, CT and London: Praeger.

Mukhtar, Mohamed H. (2003). *Historical Dictionary of Somalia*. Lanham, MD and Oxford: The Scarecrow Press.

Mukhtar, Mohamed H. (1997). Somalia: Between Self-Determination and Chaos. In Hussein M. Adam and Richard Ford (Eds), *Mending Rips in the Sky: Options for Somali Community in the 21st Century*, p. 55. Lawrenceville, NJ: Red Sea Press.

Murphy, Ray (2007). *UN Peacekeeping in Lebanon, Somalia and Kosovo*. Cambridge: Cambridge University Press.

Nelson, Harold D., Ed. (1982). *Somalia: A Country Study*. Washington, DC: American University.

Neville, Leigh (2018). *Day of Rangers: The Battle of Mogadishu 25 Years on*. Oxford and Long Island City, NY: Osprey Publishing.

Ohls, Gary J. (2009). *Somalia from the Sea*. Newport, RI: Naval War College.

Okoth, A. (2006). *A History of Africa: African Societies and the Establishment of Colonial Rule, 1800–1915*. Nairobi: East African Educational Publishers.

Omar, Mohamed O. (1992). *The Road to Zero – Somalia's Self-Destruction Personal Reminiscences*. London: HAAN Associates.

Osman, Abdullahi A. (2007). The Somali Conflict and the Role of Inequality, Tribalism and Clanism. In Abdulahi A. Osman and Issaka K. Souare (Eds), *Somalia at the Crossroads – Challenges and Perspectives on Reconstituting a Failed State*, pp. 96–7. London: Adonis and Addey Publishers Ltd.

Patman, Robert G. (2010). *Strategic Shortfall: The Somalia Syndrome and the March to 9/11*. Santa Barbara, CA, Denvar and Oxford: Praeger.

Peterson, Scott (2000). *Me Against My Brother: At War in Somalia, Sudan, and Rwanda*. New York and London: Routledge.

Rawson, David (1994). Dealing with Disintegration: U.S. Assistance and the Somali State. In Ahmed I. Samatar (Ed.), *The Somali Challenge from Catastrophe to Renewal?*, pp. 147–82. Boulder, CO and London: L. Rienner.

Romersa, L. (1983). *Cesare Maria de Vecchi div al Cismon Il Quadrumviro Scomodo, Il Vero Mussolini nelle Memorie del piu Monarchio des Fascisti*. Milano: U. Mursia Editore.

Ruhela, Satya Pal, Ed. (1994). *Mohammed Farah Aidid and His Vision of Somalia*. New Delhi: Vikas Publishing House Pvt Ltd.

Sahnoun, Mohamed (1994). *Somalia: Missed Opportunity*. Washington, DC: The United States Institute of Peace Press.

Salwe, Abdisalam M. Issa (1994). *The Collapse of the Somali State*. London: HAAN Associates.

Samatar, Abdi I. (1989). *The State and Rural Transformation in Northern Somalia 1884 – 1986*. London and Madison: The University of Wisconsin Press.

Samatar, Ahmed I. (1988). *Socialist Somalia: Rhetoric and Reality*. London and New Jersey: Zed Books.

Samatar, Ahmed I. (1994). The Curse of Allah: Civic Disembowelment and the Collapse of the State in Somalia. In Ahmed I. Samatar (Ed.), *The Somali Challenge: From Catastrophe to Renewal*, pp. 95–146. Boulder, CO and London: Lynner Reinner Publishers.

Selassie, Bereket H. (1980). *Conflict and Intervention in the Horn of Africa*. New York and London: Monthly Review Press.

Shay, Shaul (2008). *Somalia between Jihad and Restoration*. New Brunswick, NJ: Transaction Publishers.

Shuke, Abdirahman (2004). Traditional Leaders in Political Decision Making and Conflict Resolution. In Richard Ford, Hussein M. Adam and Edna Adan Ismail (Eds), *War Destroys, Peace Nurtures: Reconciliation and Development in Somalia*, pp. 147–68. Lawrenceville, NJ: The Red Sea Press.

Simons, Anna (1995). *Networks of Dissolution Somalia Undone*. Boulder, CO and Oxford: Westview Press.

Stevenson, Jonathan (1995). *Losing Mogadishu: Testing U.S. Policy in Somalia*. Annapolis, MD: Naval Institute Press.

Takiff, Michael (2010). *A Complicated Man: The Life of Bill Clinton as Told by those Who Know Him*, pp. 201–7. New Haven, CT and London: Yale University Press.

Tripodi, Paolo (1999). *The Colonial Legacy in Somalia: Rome and Mogadishu: from Colonial Administration and Operation Restore Hope*. Basingstoke: Macmillan Press.

Williams, Paul D. (2018). *Fighting for Peace in Somalia: A History and Analysis of the African Union Mission (AMISOM), 2007–2017*. Oxford: Oxford University Press.

Woodroofe, Louise P. (2013). *Buried in the Sands of the Ogaden: The United States, the Horn of Africa, and the Demise of Détente*. Kent, OH: Kent State University Press.

Reports, Video Clips, News Items, Journals, Articles etc.

ABC (2010). General Muhammad Ali Samatar in Court Human Rights Violations. [Online]. Video clip available at http://www.youtube.com/watch?v=k0ySBgPkHV4. [Accessed 25 August 2011].

Abdi, Abdiaziz (2010). The Genesis of Islamism in Somalia. [Online article]. Available at http://wardheernews.com/Articles_2010/June/Abdiaziz_Abdi/22 The_Genesis_of _Islamism_in_Somalia.html. [Accessed 16 February 2011].

Abdulla, Ali H. (2010). Putting Surviving Members of the Defunct Somali Supreme Revolutionary Council (SRC) on Trial. [Online]. Available at http://www.hiiraan.com /op2/2010/mar/putting_surviving_members_of_the_defunct_somali_supreme_rev olutionary_council_src_on_trial.aspx. [Accessed 22 October 2011].

Abizaid, General (2010). General Abizaid Talks Iran, Iraq, Afghanistan With Abu Dhabi Crown Prince. [Online]. Available at http://91.214.23.156/cablegate/wire.php?id=07 ABUDHABI145&search=iran. [Accessed 2 December 2010].

Adde, Nuur H. (2008). Press Conference by Prime Minister, Nuur Hassan Adde, Nairobi. [Online]. Video clip available at http://www.youtube.com/watch?v=Hh78XOI29zU&fe ature=related. [Accessed 5 August 2011].

Adow, Mohammed (2006). Why Ethiopia is on War Footing, *BBC News Channel*, 21 July 2006. [Online]. Available at http://news.bbc.co.uk/1/hi/5201470.stm. [Accessed 2 December 2010].

Adow, Mohammed (2011). Somalia's Al-Shabaab Meet their Match, AljazeeraEnglish. [Online]. Available at http://www.youtube.com/watch?v=kTeqM7FVMOA. [Accessed 5 August 2011].

AFP (2007). Somali Opposition Alliance Begins Fight Against Ethiopia, AFP, 20 September 2007. [Online]. Available at http://afp.google.com/article/ALeqM5hIcA RdyjMUukX3jKVh3Mje2M-wag. [Accessed 2 December 2010].

Ali, Ahmed Mohamed (2011). BBC Somali Service Interview with Abdirahman Faroole, Puntland President. [Online]. Available at http://www.bbc.co.uk/somali/. [Accessed 21 February 2011].

AlJazeera TV (2010a). Somaliland vs. Somalia. [Online]. Video clip available at http:// english.aljazeera.net/programmes/insidestory/2010/06/2010623123754251181.html. [Accessed 2 June 2011]. No Democracy in Somaliland ... Abdi Ismail ... Live on, a Dhulbahante diaspora & Isaaq MP disagree over Somaliland Independence.

AlJazeera TV (2010b). Aljazeera Visits The SSC Peace Leaders. [Online]. Video clip available at http://www.youtube.com/watch?v=U62SpPVoQrI. [Accessed 25 January 2011].

AlJazeera TV (2008). Somali Fighters Destroying Shrines. [Online]. Video clip available at http://www.youtube.com/watch?v=RPWI-p9Kl4g&feature=related. [Accessed 28 December 2010].

Amaandhoorey Channel (2010a). Colonel Shaatigaduud Talking about RRA Struggle to Liberate Rahanweyn Lands from Habargedir Invaders (Halyeeyga Raxanwayn Shaatigaduud oo Ka Hadlaaya Halgankii RRA). [Online]. Video clip available at http:// www.youtube.com/results?search_query=Halyeeyga+Raxanwayn+Shaatiguduud+oo+ Ka+Hadlaaya+Halgankii+RRA&aq=f. [Accessed 14 November 2010].

Amaandhoorey Channel (2010b). Interview with Rahanweyn Girl who Took Part in the Liberation of the Bakool Region (Gabdhihii RRA Bakool Xureeyay). [Online]. Video clip available at http://www.youtube.com/watch?v=i4Cuws8xuLE&feature=related. [Accessed 14 November 2010].

Amaandhoorey Channel (2010c). General Jabiiq Urging RRA Militia to Fights General Aideed's Invading Militia (Halgamaa Wayn ee Jeneral Jabiiq oo Guubaabinaya Qaar ka Mid Ah Xaq u Dirirka RRA). [Online]. Video available at http://www.youtube.com/wa tch?v=AUtCRM3Anhc&feature=related. [Accessed 14 November 2010].

Amaandhoorey Channel (2010d). Somali Rahanweyn Leader, Cabdalla Deerow Meeting with RRA Fighters Encouraging them to Fight Hussein Aideed Habargedir Clan Militia. [Online]. Video clip available at http://www.youtube.com/watch?v=aY1iEi-t3 5c&feature=related. [Accessed 14 November 2010].

Amaandhoorey Channel (2010e). RRA Militiamen in a War Victory Traditional Dance (Ciidanka Wax Iska Caabinta Rahanweyn oo Baacsaday Huwantii Huseyn Caydiid) [Online]. Video clip available at http://www.youtube.com/watch?v=kJy-9_0DAfc&fe ature=related. [Accessed 14 November 2010].

Amaandhoorey Channel (2010f). Colonel Roobow Encouraging RRA Fighters to Fight General Aideed's Mooryaans (Gaashaanle Roobow Waa Halgamaa Wayn ee RRA Xiligii Huwanta Caydiid Ku soo Duushay Arlada Rahanweyn). [Online]. Video clip available at http://www.youtube.com/watch?v=K1KehzAiWjk&feature=related. [Accessed 11 May 2011].

Amnesty International (1992). Somalia: A Human Rights Disaster. [Online]. Report available at http://www.amnesty.org/en/library/info/AFR52/001/1992/en. [Accessed 28 February 2011].

Associated Press (2012). Judge awards $21 million in torture lawsuit against former Somali prime minister Samantar. [Online]. Newspaper article available at http://news .yahoo.com/judge-awards-21-million-torture-lawsuit-against-former-181256382.html. [Accessed 29 August 2012].

Associated Press (2007). Somali Suicide Bombers – video released by Somali Islamist Insurgents, Associates Press. [Online]. Video clip available at http://www.youtube.com/ watch?v=saZs3ZXYTsM. [Accessed 5 August 2011].

Axe, David (2010). WikiLeaks Cable Confirms U.S.' Secret Somalia Op. WIRED. [Online]. Available at http://www.wired.com/dangerroom/2010/12/wikileaked-cable-confirms-u -s-secret-somalia-op/. [Accessed 15 February 2011].

BBC (2017). Who Are Somalia's al-Shabab? Available at https://www.bbc.co.uk/news/wor ld-africa-15336689. [Accessed 5 September 2020].

BBC Monitoring Africa – BBCMA (2001). Puntland Administration Accused of Bad Governance, 28 February 2001. [Online]. Available at http://www.biyokulule.com/view :content.php?articleid=2957. [Accessed 22 November 2010].

BBC News Channel (2006a). 'Radical' Heads New Somali Body, *BBC News Channel*, 25 June 2006. [Online]. Available at http://news.bbc.co.uk/1/hi/world/africa/5113868 .stm. [Accessed 17 February 2011].

BBC News Channel (2006b). Profile: Somalia's Islamic Courts, 6 June 2006. [Online]. Available at http://news.bbc.co.uk/1/hi/5051588.stm. [Accessed 21 April 2011].

BBC News Channel (2006c). Ethiopia Admits Somalia Offensive, *BBC News Channel*, 24 December 2006. [Online]. Available at http://news.bbc.co.uk/1/hi/world/africa/6 207427.stm. [Accessed 21 April 2011].

BBC News Channel (2007). Somalia is Worst Refugee Crisis, 27 April 2007. [Online]. Available at http://news.bbc.co.uk/1/hi/world/africa/6598361.stm. [Accessed 23 December 2007].

BBC News Channel (2008). Seized Tanker Anchors off Somalia. [Online]. Available at http://news.bbc.co.uk/1/hi/world/africa/7735507.stm. [Accessed 06 December 2014].

BBC News Channel (2009). Somali Rage at Grave Desecration, 8 June 2009. [Online]. Available at http://news.bbc.co.uk/1/hi/8077725.stm. [Accessed 28 December 2010].

Bahar, Ali (2007). Critical Period in Somalia: All Eyes on the Prize. [Online]. Available at http://www.hiiraan.com/op2/2007/jan/critical_period_in_somalia_all_eyes_on_the_p rize_.aspx. [Accessed 18 October 2011].

Barnes, Cedric and Hassan, Harun (2007a). The Rise and Fall of Mogadishu's Islamic Courts. *Journal of Eastern African Studies*, Vol. 1, No. 2, pp. 151–60. [Online]. Available at http://www.tandfonline.com/doi/pdf/10.1080/17531050701452382 and http://www .chathamhouse.org.uk/files/9130_bpsomalia0407.pdf. [Accessed 4 August 2011].

Barnes, Cedric and Hassan, Harun (2007b). A Return to Clan-Politics or Worse in Southern Somalia? 27 March 2007, Social Science Research Council, New York. [Online]. Available at http://hornofafrica.ssrc.org/Hassan_Barnes/. [Accessed 28 April 2011].

Bartamaha (2006). The Last Interview with Former Somali President Siad Barre. [Online]. Video clip available at http://www.youtube.com/watch?v=oilgkZqstBg&feature=rela ted. [Also, available at www.bartamaha.com. [Accessed 28 February 2011].

Bartholet, Jeffrey (2009). It's a Mad, Mad, Mad, Mad World, Newsweek, 12 October 2009. [Online]. Available at http://www.newsweek.com/2009/09/30/it-s-a-mad-mad-mad-m ad-world.html. [Accessed 21 April 2011].

Benadirwatch (2007). Full text of Somali Insurgent Statement Warning African Peacekeepers. [Online]. Available at http://www.benadir-watch.com/2007per cent 20News/0222_Warning_to_mercenaries.pdf. [Accessed 21 December 2010].

Biyokulule (2009). Puntland: A Quisling Scheme, Roobdoon Forum, 01/08/09, Secret Document Signed by Siyaad Barre, Africa Confidential. 26 September 1975, Vol. 16, No. 19, p. 8. [Online]. Available at http://www.biyokulule.com/view:content.php?articleid=2064. [Accessed 21 February 2011].

Biyokulule (2010a). Zooming into the Past, Prime Minister Ali Samatar on Historical Account. [Online]. Available at http://www.biyokulule.com/Primepercent 20Minister percent20alipercent20samater.htm. [Accessed 7 October 2010].

Biyokulule (2010b). The Somali Manifesto I. [Online]. Available at http://www.biyokulule .com/Somalipercent20Manifestopercent20I.htm. [Accessed 2 March 2011].

Biyokulule (2010c). Corporate Mercenaries in Somaliland! [Online] Available at http:// www.biyokulule.com/view:content.php?articleid=3301. [Accessed 26 February 2011].

Biyokulule (2010d). Clan Wars with Religious Coloration. [Online]. Available at http:// www.biyokulule.com/view:content.php?articleid=2942. [Accessed 12 August 2010].

Biyokulule (2010e). Zooming into the Past: What If Canada Would Have Sheltered Abdullahi Yusuf! [Online]. Available at http://www.biyokulule.com/view:content.php?articleid=2957. [Accessed 21 November 2010].

Biyokulule (2010f). The Mushrooming Cabbie Statelets. Roobdoon Forum. [Online]. Available at http://www.biyokulule.com/view:content.php?articleid=3139. [Accessed 24 February 2011].

Biyokulule (2008g). Somalia's Mujahidin Youth Movement Spokesman Discusses Progress of Jihad, Jihadist Websites, 27 May 2008. [Online]. Available at http://www.biyokulule .com/view:content.php?articleid=1231. [Accessed 23 December 2010].

Blomfield, Adrian (2002). US Targets in Somalia Running for Cover, *The Daily Telegraph*, 10 January 2002. [Online]. Available at http://i.telegraph.co.uk/news/worldnews/afric aandindianocean/somalia/1381012/US-targets-in-Somalia-running-for-cover.html. [Accessed 17 February 2011].

Bowden, Mark (1997). A Defining Battle. [Online]. Available at http://inquirer.philly.com/ packages/somalia/nov16/rang16.asp. [Accessed 1 March 2011].

Bradbury, Mark (1994). The Somali Conflict: Prospect for Peace, paper commissioned by Oxfam. [Online]. Available at http://www.nzdl.org/gsdlmod?a=p&p=home&l=en&w =utf-8. [Accessed 20 November 2011].

Bryden, Matt (2006). Storm Clouds over Somalia As Rivals Prepare For Battle, *The Nation*, 8 December 2006. [Online]. Article available at http://www.crisisgroup.org/en/regions /africa/horn-of-africa/somalia/storm-clouds-over-somalia-as-rivals-prepare-for-battle .aspx. [Accessed 22 April 2011].

Bush, George (1992). President Bush's Speech. [Online]. Available at http://millercenter. org/scripps/archive/speeches/detail/3984. [Accessed 28 February 2011].

Bush, George (2001). Address to a Joint Session of Congress Following 9/11 Attack, Delivered on 20 September 2001. [Online]. Available at http://www.americanrhetoric .com/speeches/gwbush911jointsessionspeech.htm. [Accessed 2 December 2010].

Cali, Axmed Maxamed (2011). BBC Interview with Puntland President. (Wareysi BBCda la yeelay Abdirahman M. Faroole, Madaxweymaha Puntland). [Online]. Interview available at http://www.bbc.co.uk/somali/maqal_iyo_muuqaal/2011/09/110901_punt land_galmudug.shtml. [Accessed 4 September 2011].

Cassanelli, Lee V. (1995). Victims and Vulnerable Groups in Southern Somalia, 1 May 1995. [Online]. Report available at http://www.google.co.uk/#q=Victims+and+Vu

lnerable+Groups+in+Southern+Somalia,&fp=c7b1db55a5a734dc&hl=en. [Accessed 22 April 2011].

Cassanelli, Lee V. (1982). The Shaping of Somali Society, Reconstructing the History of a Pastoral People, 1600–1900. [Online]. Available at http://somaliswiss.wordpress.c om/2009/12/16/collecting-the-history-of-the-somali-clans-of-hawiye/. [Accessed 04 October 2010].

Cassanelli, Lee and Abdikadir, Farah Sheikh (2008). Somalia: Education in Transition, *Bildhaan: An International Journal of Somali Studies*. [Online]. Available at http://dig italcommons.macalester.edu/bildhaan/vol7/iss1/7/. [Accessed 22 July 2011].

Chalmers, Caitlin and Hassan, Mohamed A. (2008). UK Somali Remittances Survey, supported by DFID and SendMoneyHome.org, London. [Online]. Available at http:/ /www.diaspora-centre.org/DOCS/UK_Somali_Remittan.pdf. [Accessed 16 February 2011].

CIA (1994). World Fact Book. [Online]. Available at https://www.cia.gov/library/publica tions/the-world-factbook and http://www.fullbooks.com/The-1994-Edition-of-the-C IA-World-Factbook12.html. [Accessed 22 April 2011].

CIA (1995). World Fact Book, 1995. [Online]. Available at https://www.cia.gov/library /publications/the-world- factbook and http://permanent.access.gpo.gov/lps35389 /1995/wf950219.htm or http://www.umsl.edu/services/govdocs/wofact95/wf976.htm. [Accessed 29 December 2010].

CIA (2008). World Factbook 2008. [Online]. Available at https://www.cia.gov/library/pu blications/the-world-factbook or http://www.bartleby.com/151/so.html#Economy. [Accessed 29 December 2010].

CIA (2011). World Fact Book. [Online]. Available at https://www.cia.gov/library/publica tions/the-world-factbook/geos/so.html. [Accessed 22 April 2011].

Clayton, Jonathan (4 March 2005). "Somalia's Secret Dumps of Toxic Waste Washed Ashore by Tsunami". London: Timesonline.co.uk. [Online]. Available at http://www .thetimes.co.uk/tto/news/world/article1975917.ece. [Accessed 25 November 2014].

Coldwar Channel (2009). Ogaden War 1977 Somalia Ethiopia. [Online]. Video clip available at: http://www.youtube.com/user/ColdWarWarriors#p/search/0/7CemACOk -p0. [Accessed on 7 October 2010].

Compagnon, Daniel (1990). The Somali Opposition Fronts: Some Comments and Questions. *Horn of Africa*, Vol. XIII, No. 1 & 2 (January–March, April–June 1990), pp. 29–54.

Compagnon, Daniel (1992). Political Decay in Somalia: From Personal Rule to Warlordism. *Refuge*, Vol. 12, No. 5 (November–December1992), pp. 8–13. [Online]. Available at http://pi.library.yorku.ca/ojs/index.php/refuge/article/viewFile/21676/2034 9. [Accessed 19 April 2011].

Conciliation Resources - CR (2010). Wajid District: an Island of Peace. [Online]. Available at http://www.c-r.org/our-work/accord/somalia/wajid-district.php. [Accessed 17 November 2010].

Fatah, Ali (2007). Understanding Somali Opposition to the TFG: Clanism by other Names, Wardheernews, 24 September 2007. [Online]. Available at http://wardheer news.com/articles_07/September/Sept_24_Understanding_Somali_Opposition.pdf. [Accessed 24 December 2010].

Galaydh, Ali K. (1990). Notes on the State of the Somali State. *The Horn of Africa*, Vol. XIII, No. 1 & 2 (January–March, April–June 1990), pp. 1–28. Also, on online available at http://www.biyokulule.com/dr.per cent 20galaydh.htm. [Accessed 27 April 2011].

Garad, Yuusuf (2008). Interview with President Abdullahi Yusuf, BBC Somali Section. [Online]. Available at http://www.youtube.com/watch?v=ciMuzRG5Zl8&feature=rela ted; and http://www.bbc.co.uk/somali/. [Accessed 5 August 2011].

Garoweonline (2008a). Somalia's President 'likes to threaten everyone' says Somaliland Boss, 2 January 2008. [Online]. Available at http://www.garoweonline.com/artman2/ publish/Somalia_27/Somalia_s_President_likes_to_threaten_everyone_says_Somalila nd_boss_printer.shtml. [Accessed 21 November 2011].

Garoweonline (2008b). Somaliland Separatist Will not be Allowed to Divide Somalia, Says President, 1 January 2008. [Online]. Available at http://www.garoweonline.com/ artman2/publish/Somalia_27/Somaliland_separatists_will_not_be_allowed_to_divide _Somalia_says_President.shtml. [Accessed 21 November 2011].

Garoweonline (2008c). Cautious Welcome for UN-brokered Peace Deal in Somalia. [Online]. Available at http://www.garoweonline.com/artman2/publish/Somalia_27/ Cautious_welcome_for_UN-brokered_peace_deal_in_Somalia.shtml. [Accessed 5 August 2011].

Garoweonline (2009). Somalia: Concern over Puntland Secession or Frustration with Progress? [Online]. Available at http://www.garoweonline.com/artman2/publish/E ditorial_29/Somalia_Concern_over_Puntland_secession_or_frustration_with_pro gress.shtml. [Accessed 18 February 2011].

Garoweonline (2010). IGAD is Misleading the World on Somalia, Garoweonline, 10 October 2010. [Online]. Available at http://www.garoweonline.com/english/inde x.php?option=com_content&view=article&id=228:igad-is-misleading-the-world-on -somalia-&catid=49:editorial&Itemid=126. [Accessed 25 December 2010].

Garoweonline (2011). Somalia: Puntland's Break with the T.F.G. and the International Crisis Group's Draft Report, 24 January 2010. [Online]. Available at http://www.garo weonline.com/artman2/publish/Somalia_27/Somalia_Puntland_s_Break_with_the _T_F_G_and_the_International_Crisis_Group_s_Draft_Report.shtml. [Accessed 18 February 2011].

Georgian, A. (2008). Interview with President Abdullahi Yusuf, France24 TV. [Online]. Video clip available at http://www.youtube.com/watch?v=cCT1Axm-bfg&feature=rela ted. [Accessed 5 August 2011].

Gersony, Robert (1989). *Why Somalis Flee A Synthesis of Conflict Experience in Northern Somalia by Somali Refugees, Displaced Persons and Others*. Washington, DC: Department of State.

Gettleman, Jeffrey (2006). Islamists in Somalia are Forced to Retreat - Africa & Middle East – *New York Times*, 26 December 2006. [Online]. Available at http://www.nytimes .com/2006/12/26/world/africa/26iht-somalia.4021189.html. [Accessed 27 April 2011].

Gettleman, Jeffrey (2007). Ethiopian Premier Says His Troops Won't Stay in Somalia, *New York Times*, 3 January 2007. [Online]. Available at http://www.nytimes.com/2007/01/03 /world/africa/03somalia.html. [Accessed 25 December 2010].

Gettleman, Jeffrey (2009). For Somalia, Chaos Breeds Religious War, *New York Times*, 23 May 2009. [Online]. Available at http://www.nytimes.com/2009/05/24/world/africa /24somalia.html. [Accessed 28 December 2010].

Globalsecurity (2007). Somalia Civil War. [Online]. Available at http://www.globalsecurity .org/military/world/war/somalia.htm. [Accessed 4 December 2011].

Gulfnews.com (2006). Islamists Urge Muslims to Join Jihad on Ethiopia, Gulfnews.com, 24 December 2006. [Online]. Available at http://gulfnews.com/news/region/somalia/ islamists-urge-muslims-to-join-jihad-on-ethiopia-1.271754. [Accessed 17 December 2010].

Hassan, Harun (2007). Somalia: Mogadishu's Ghost Days. [Online]. Available at http://www.opendemocracy.net/democracy-africa_democracy/mogadishu_4507.jsp. [Accessed 1 December 2010].

Hassan, M. Olad (2006). Islamic Leader Says Somali Regions in Kenya, Ethiopia Should be Part of Somalia, *Associated Press*, 18 November 2006. [Online]. Available at http://www.ap.org. [Accessed 6 May 2011].

Hassan, Mohamed Olad (2006). Somalia Leader Escapes Attempt on Life. APNEWS [Online]. Available on https://apnews.com/article/063fd118eca80c86754570c64a8f d046. [Accessed 29 December 2020].

High Seas Task Force (2006). Closing the Net: Stopping Illegal Fishing on the High Seas. Governments of Australia, Canada, Chile, Namibia, New Zealand, and the United Kingdom, WWF, IUCN and the Earth Institute at Columbia University. [Online]. Available at www.iucn.org/dbtw-wpd/edocs/2006-024.pdf. [Accessed 27 September 2014).

Hiiraan (2007). Prime Minister Geedi Talks about an Assassination Attempt on his Life on 4 June, 2007 (Ra'iisal Wasaare Geedi oo ka Warbixiyay Qaraxii Shalay lala Beegsaday Gurigiisa). [Online]. Available at http://www.hiiraan.com/news/2007/jun/wararka_maanta4-1331.htm. [Accessed 17 December 2010].

Hiiraan (2011). Speeches Made by Leaders of Puntland and Galmudug at the Roadmap Consultation Meeting in Mogadishu (Madaxda DKMG ah ee Soomaaliya iyo Madaxda Puntland iyo Galmudug oo Khudbadyo ka Jeediyay Shirka wadatashiga). [Online]. Available at http://www.hiiraan.com/news/2011/Sept/wararka_maanta4-14884.htm. [Accessed 4 September 2011].

Hirabe, Ali Ahmed (2006). His Series of Articles and Columns Are Available at http://www.mudulood.com/PageDr.per cent 20AAHirabe.html. [Accessed 25 December 2010].

Hirad, Abdalla (2006). The Somaliland Mythology Indicted Calling the Spade a Spade Part I and II: The Charges. [Online]. Available at http://www.wardheernews.com/Ar ticles_06/may_06/03_calling_the_spade_a_spade.html. [Accessed 20 February 2011].

Hirad, Abdalla H. (2007). The TFG's Victory over the UIC in Somalia: Triumph or New Menace for the Nation?– 05 January 2006. [Online]. Available at http://www.awda lnews.com-Articles&Opinions. [Accessed 1 December 2010].

Hirad, Abdalla (2008a). The Woes and Worries of President Yusuf of Somalia, Maanhadal, 13 December 2008. [Online]. Available at http://www.maanhadal.com/articles. [Accessed 24 December 2010].

Hirad, Abdalla (2008b). Vultures Are Scavenging on the Remains of Somalia. [Online]. Available at http://www.wardheernews.com/Articles_09/Jan/25_ventures_hirad.html. [Accessed 24 December 2010].

Hoehne, Markus V. (2007). Puntland and Somaliland Clashing in Northern Somalia: Who Cuts the Gordian Knot? 7 November 2007. [Online]. Available at http://hornofafrica.ssrc.org/Hoehne/. [Accessed 30 April 2011].

Hughes, Dana (2014). Bill Clinton 'Surprised' at Black Hawk Down Raid, *ABC News*, 19 April 2014.

Human Rights Watch (1990). World Report, 1990. [Online]. Available at http://www.hrw.org/legacy/reports/1994/WR94/Africa-08.htm#P356_163056. [Accessed 1 March 2011].

Human Rights Watch (1994). World Report, 1994. [Online]. Available at http://www.hrw.org/legacy/reports/1994/WR94/Africa-08.htm#P356_163056. [Accessed 1 March 2011].

Human Rights Watch (2007). Somalia: Shell Shocked, Civilians Under Siege in Mogadishu, 12 August 2007. [Online]. Available at http://www.hrw.org/en/reports/2007/08/12/shell-shocked. [Accessed 7 June 2011].

Hussein, Abdirazak H. (2005). A Perilous Impasse in Somalia, 7 July 2005. [Online]. Available at www.wardheernews.com. [Accessed 1 December 2010].

Hussein, Abdirazak H. (2011). The Future Constitutional Structure of the Somali Republic: Federal or Decentralized Unitary State? [Online]. Available at http://www.hiiraan.com/op2/2011/apr/the_future_constitutional_structure_of_the_somali_repu blic_federal_or_decentralized_unitary_state.aspx. [Accessed 22 April 2011].

Immigration and Refugee Board – IRB (1997). Question and Answer Series, Somalia: Chronology of Events April 1995–January 1997, Research Directorate, Documentation, Information and Research Branch, Ottawa, Canada, February 1997.

Ingiriis, Mohamed (2007). A Reality Check for Colonel Abdullahi Yusuf of TFG, 3 March 2007. [Online]. Available at http://www.benadir-watch.com/2007per cent 20News/0307_Reality_check_for_Yusuf.pdf. [Accessed 1 December 2010].

International Crisis Group – ICG (2006). Somaliland: Time for African Union Leadership, International Crisis Group Africa Report No.110, 23 May 2006. [Online]. Available at http://www.crisisgroup.org/~/media/Files/africa/horn-of-africa/somalia/Somalilan dper cent 20Timeper cent 20forpercent20Africanpercent20Unionpercent20Leadership. ashx. [Accessed 21 February 2011].

International Crisis Group – ICG (2007). Somalia: The Tough Part is Ahead, Africa Briefing Paper, No. 45, 26 January 2006. [Online]. Available at http://www.crisisgroup .org/en/regions/africa/horn-of-africa/somalia/B045-somalia-the-tough-part-is-ahead. aspx. [Accessed 17 February 2011].

International Crisis Group – ICG (2009). Somalia: The Trouble with Puntland, International Crisis Group, Policy Briefing Paper, Africa Briefing, 12 August 2009. [Online]. Available at http://www.crisisgroup.org/en/regions/africa/horn-of-africa/ somalia/B064-somalia-the-trouble-with-puntland.aspx. [Accessed 21 February 2011].

International Crisis Group – ICG (2010). Somalia's Divided Islamists, International Crisis Group, Policy Briefing No. 74, 18 May 2010. [Online]. Available at http://www.crisisgro up.org/~/media/Files/africa/horn-of-africa/somalia/B74percent20Somaliaspercent20D ividedpercent20Islamists.ashx. [Accessed 28 December 2010].

Interpeace and Centre for Research and Dialogue – Interpeace (2009). History of Mediation in Somalia since 1988 [Online]. Available at http://www.interpeace.org/inde x.php/Publications/Publications.htm. [Accessed 17 February 2011].

IRIN (2006a). Somalia: Islamic Courts Set up Consultative Council. [Online]. Available at http://www.irinnews.org/report.aspx?reportid=59444, [Accessed 29 November 2010].

IRIN (2006b). Somalia: Fishermen Appeal for Help over Foreign Fishing Ships. [Online]. Available at http://www.irinnews.org/printreport.aspx?reportid=58369. [Accessed 12 October 2014].

IRIN (2007). SOMALIA: More Civilians Abandon Homes as Skirmishes Continue, 22 March 2007. [Online]. Available at http://www.irinnews.org/report.aspx?reportid= 70868. [Accessed 19 December 2007].

IRIN (2009). Somalia: Livelihoods - and Lives - at Risk in Puntland. [Online]. Available at http://www.irinnews.org/report/85825/somalia-livelihoods-and-lives-at-risk-in-pu ntland. [Accessed 27 September 2014].

Ismail, Jamal Abdi (2006). Africa Media Development Initiative, Somalia: Research Findings and Conclusion. [Online]. Available at www.bbcworldservicetrust.org/amdi

and http://www.radiopeaceafrica.org/assets/texts/pdf/SOM_AMDI_Report_pp4pe rcent201.pdf. [Accessed, 28 December 2010].

Jowhar, Abdishakur (2007). Ich Bin En Hawiye I am a Hawiye Citizen. [Online]. Available at http://www.hiiraan.com/op2/2007/apr/.aspx. [Accessed 28 February 2011].

Jowhar, Abdishakur (2006). A War of Miscalculation. [Online]. Available at http://www .hiiraan.com/comments2-op-2006-dec-a_war_of_miscalculation.aspx, 26 December 2006. [Accessed 1 December 2010].

Jowhar.com (2010). Sheekh Indhoole ah iyo Caruurta All Shabab (A blind Sufi Cleric Being Tortured by Al-Shabaab. [Online]. Available at http://www.youtube.com/watch ?v=frPbTNJi_lI. [Accessed 4 December 2011].

Kasmo (2000),Wareysi: Aden Cabdulle Cusman (Somali newspaper), London.

Keydmedia (2012). Top Secret Tape - Jen. Morgan "Waa Dagaal Daarood iyo Hawiye" (General Morgan says: it is Daarood vs. Hawiye war). [Online]. Video available at http://www.youtube.com/watch?v=5Dae00I_qtQ&feature=youtu.be. [Accessed 9 January 2012].

Kifle, Elias (2010). Wikileaks Dispatch Exposes Meles Zenawi as a Mercenary, Ethiopian Review. [Online]. Available at http://www.ethiopianreview.com/content/30550. [Accessed 3 December 2010].

Kipkorir, Donald (2008). Why Kenya and Ethiopia Ought to Annex and Divide Somalia, *Daily Nation*, 03 October 2008. [Online]. Available at http://www.hiiraan.com/op2/200 8/oct/why_kenya_and_ethiopia_ought_to_annex_and_divide_somalia.aspx. [Accessed 27 December 2010].

Leeson, Peter T. (2007). Better Off Stateless: Somalia Before and After Government Collapse, Department of Economics, West Virginia University. [Online paper]. Available at http://www.peterleeson.com/Papers.html. [Accessed 16 February 2011].

Lewis, I. M. (1990). The Ogaden and the Fragility of Somali Segmentary Nationalism. *Horn of Africa*, Vol. XIII, No. 1 & 2 (January–March, April–June 1990), pp. 55–61.

Littlefield, Walter (1910). Mad Mullah Turns again to Fanatical Slaughter, *New York Times*, 10 April 1910. [Online]. Available at http://www.biyokulule.com/Mad_Mullah2.htm. [Accessed 13 August 2011].

Lobe, Jim (2006). U.S.-Backed U.N. Resolution Risks Wider War, Inter Press Service New Agency, 28 November 2006. [Online]. Available at http://ipsnews.net/africa/nota.asp? idnews=35635. [Accessed 5 May 2011].

Maruf, Harun (2009). A Programme on the Rise and Fall of the Somali Revolutionary Regime Produced by VOA Somali Service, which Interviewed Senior Somali Politicians about the 40th Anniversary since the Military Government. [Online]. Available at http://www.voanews.com/somali/news/the-rise-and-fall-of-Siad-Barre-2009-20-19.html. [Accessed 11 October 2010].

McGreal, Chris (2007). Thousands Flee as Shelling by Ethiopian Tanks Kills Hundreds of Civilians in Somali Capital, *The Guardian*, Friday 27 April 2007. [Online]. Available at http://www.guardian.co.uk/world/2007/apr/27/warcrimes. [Accessed 5 May 2011].

McGregor, Andrew (2007). The Leading Factions Behind the Somali Insurgency, 26 April 2007, The Jamestown Foundation. [Online]. Available at http://www.jamestown.org/ aboutus/contactus/. [Accessed 1 December 2010].

Ministry of Education (2011). Somaliland Ministry of Education and Higher Education. [Online]. Available at http://moesomaliland.com/2011/index.php?option=com_cont ent&view=section&layout=blog&id=18&Itemid=97. [Accessed 12 August 2011].

Ministry of National Planning & Coordination – MNPC (2004). *Somaliland in Figures 2004*. Hargeisa: Republic of Somaliland.

Ministry of Planning and Statistics – MPS (2003). Puntland Facts and Figures 2004, Puntland State of Somalia, 2003. [Online booklet]. Available at http://sitereso urces.worldbank.org/SOMALIAEXTN/Resources/PuntlandFigures.pdf. [Accessed 21 February 2011].

Mire, Amina (2007a). Menacing Somalia: Unholy Trinity of U.S Global Militarism, Meles's Ethiopia and Thuggish Warlords, 13 June 2007. [Online]. Available at http://www.race andhistory.com/historicalviews/2007/1306.html#34. [Accessed 23 December 2007].

Mire, Amina (2007b). In Somalia, It's The Blood Money, Stupid! *The New World Black Magazine*. [Online]. Available at http://www.thenewblackmagazine.com/view.aspx?ind ex=894. [Accessed 22 December 2010].

Mohamed, Ahmed (2007). Somali PM Resigns after Feud with President, 29 October 2007 [Online]. Available at http://www.reuters.com/article/idUSL29233698._CH_.2400. [Accessed 24 December 2010].

Mukhtar, Mohamed Haji (1996). The Plight of the Agro-pastoral Society of Somalia. *Review of African Political Economy*, Vol. 23, No. 70 (December 1996), pp. 543–53.

National Union of Somali Journalists – NUSOJ (2010). The Untold Tales of Misery: Somali Journalists and their Precarious Work. [Online]. Available at http://www.nuso j.org/Somalipercent20Journalistspercent20andpercent20theirpercent20Precariousper cent20Work.pdfwork. [Accessed 1 January 2011].

Nazret (2008). Somalia - Nur Hassan Hussein Adde's Charm Offensive. [Online]. Available at http://nazret.com/blog/index.php/2008/02/01/somalia_nur_hassan_hu ssein_adde_s_charm_?blog=15. [Accessed 5 August 2008].

Nduru, Moyiga (1996). No End in Sight to Banana War. [Online]. Available at http://www .netnomad.com/banana.html. [Accessed 21 November 2010].

Netnomad.com (1996). Son of Somali Leader Succeeds His Slain Father. [Online]. Available at http://www.netnomad.com/aydiidson.html. [Accessed 25 February 2011].

New York Times (1909). Fears for Roosevelt, *New York Times*, 17 May 1909. [Online]. Available at http://www.biyokulule.com/Mad_Mullah2.htm. [Accessed 13 August 2011].

New York Times (2006a). Militant Leader Emerges in Somalia - Africa & Middle East - International Herald Tribune, June 2006. [Online]. Available at http://www.nytimes.c om/2006/06/25/world/africa/25iht-somalia.2047328.html. [Accessed 4 August 2011].

New York Times (2006b). Ethiopian Premier Says His Troops Won't Stay in Somalia, *New York Times*, 3 January 2006. [Online]. Available at http://www.nytimes.com/2007/01/03 /world/africa/03somalia.html. [Accessed 1 December 2010].

New York Times (2008). Ethiopian Soldiers Accused of War Crimes in Somalia. [Online]. Available at http://www.nytimes.com/2008/05/06/world/africa/06iht-somalia.1.12 610349.html. [Accessed 26 August 2011].

Northern Somalis for Peace and Unity – NSPU (2006). The Illusory "Somaliland": Setting the Records Straight, report by Northern Somalis for Peace and Unity, Ottawa, 2006. [Online]. Available at http://wardheernews.com/Articles_06/may_06/Illusory__So maliland pdf. [Accessed 20 February 2011].

NTVKenya (2009). Al-Shabaab Go for Arm and Leg. [Online]. Available at http://www .youtube.com/watch?v=fIXQW9FxcJk&feature=fvwrel. [Accessed 5 August 2011].

O. Osman, Omarfaruk (2007). Ethiopia's Incursion of Somalia: A Blessing in Disguise. [Online article]. Available at http://www.hiiraan.com/print2_op/2007/jan/ethiopia percentE2percent80percent99s_incursion_of_somalia__a_blessing_in_disguise.aspx. [Accessed 1 December, 2010].

Office of the Coordinator for Counterterrorism – OCOC (2010). Individuals and Entities Designed by the State Department under E.O. 13224, 7 December 2010.

[Online]. Available at http://www.state.gov/s/ct/rls/other/des/143210.htm. [Accessed 23 December 2010].

Page, Jacqueline (2010). Jihadi Arena Report: Somalia - Development of Radical Islamism and Current Implications, International Institute for Counter Terrorism, 22 March 2010. [Online]. Available at http://www.ict.org.il/Articles/tabid/66/Articlsid/814/c urrentpage/2/Default.aspx. [Accessed 23 December 2010].

PBS News Hour (1995a). Ambush in Mogadishu; Interview with Admiral Jonathan Howe. [Online]. Available at http://www.pbs.org/wgbh/pages/frontline/. [Accessed 28 August 2011].

PBS News Hour (2006b). Threat of War Rises in Somalia; Islamists Set Deadline for Ethiopian Withdrawal, December, 2006. [Online]. Available at https://www.pbs.org/ newshour/nation/africa-july-dec06-somalia_12-15. [Accessed August 2011].

PBS News Hour (2006c). Islamist Control of Mogadishu Raises Concern of Extremist Future for Somalia, 8 June 2006, *PBS News Hour*. [Online]. Available at http:// www.pbs.org/newshour/updates/africa/jan-june06/somalia_06-08.html. [Accessed 29 March 2011].

Penketh, Anne (2006). The Big Question: What's Going on in Somalia, and is the Horn of Africa on the Brink of War? *The Independent*. [Online]. Available at http://www.inde pendent.co.uk/news/world/africa/the-big-question-whats-going-on-in-somalia-and-is -the-horn-of-africa-on-the-brink-of-war-427526.html. [Accessed 12 August 2011].

Pflanz, Mike (2006). Call for Jihad as Ethiopian Troops Go into Somalia, *The Telegraph*. [Online]. Available at http://www.telegraph.co.uk/news/worldnews/1531095/Call-for-j ihad-as-Ethiopian-troops-go-into-Somalia.html. [Accessed 1 December 2010].

Prince, Rob (2010). Wikileaks Reveals U.S. Twisted Ethiopia's Arm to Invade Somalia, 8 December 2010. [Online]. Available at http://www.fpif.org/blog/wikileaks_reveals_us _twisted_ethiopias_arm_toinvade_somalia. [Accessed 2 December 2011].

Ramaas Media Group (2009). Jasira Massacre: Interview with Ibraahim Ali Barre Canjeex Xasuuqi Jasiira 1989 (Wareysi Ibraahim Cali Barre Canjeex). [Online]. Video clip available at http://www.youtube.com/watch?v=gVJFaNaOiVk. [Accessed 26 July 2011].

Reeve, Simon (2001). U.S. Returning to a Nightmare Called Somalia, *The San Francesco Chronicle*, 16 December 2001. [Online]. Available at http://www.sfgate.com/cgi -bin/article.cgi?file=/c/a/2001/12/16/MN115486.DTL#ixzz0xSNwEanX. [Accessed 26 November 2010].

Report of the Secretary-General on the Protection of Somali Natural Resources and Waters, United Nations Security Council Report No. S/2011/661, 25 October 201. [Accessed 25 November 2014].

Reuters (2008). Somali Pilot Returns to City He Refused to Bomb. [Online]. Available at http://uk.reuters.com/article/idUKL2735431920080627. [Accessed 16 January 2011].

Reuters (2006). Ethiopia Parliament Authorizes Action Against Somali Islamists, *Reuters*, 30 November 2006. [Online]. Available at http://nazret.com/blog/index.php/2006/11 /30/ethiopia_parliament_authorizes_action_ag. [Accessed 2 December 2010].

Rice, Xan and Goldenberg, Suzanne (2007). How US Forged an Alliance with Ethiopia over Invasion, *The Guardian*, 13 January 2007. [Online]. Available at http://www.guar dian.co.uk/world/2007/jan/13/alqaida.usa. [Accessed 6 May 2011].

Rice, Xan (2007). Somalia Air Strike Failed to Kill al-Qaida Targets, Says US, *The Guardian*, 11 January 2007. Available at: http://www.guardian.co.uk/international/ story/0,,1988300,00.html. [Accessed 23 December 2007].

Rooble, Faisal (2007). Local and Global Norms: Challenges to "Somaliland's" Unilateral Secession, 2007, Volume XXV 2007. [Online]. Available at http://hornorafrica.newark

.rutgers.edu and http://wardheernews.com/Articles_09/March/18_somaliland_faisal
.pdf. [Accessed 19 November 2010].

Said Samatar (1991). *Somalia: A Nation in Turmoil*. London: Minority Rights Group.

Said Samatar (2007). The Islamic Courts and Ethiopia's Intervention in Somalia:
Redemption or Adventurism? Paper presented to Chatham House on 25 April 2007.
[Online]. Available at http://www.chathamhouse.org.uk/publications/papers/view/-/id
/521/. [Accessed 6 May 2011]

Salad, Omar (2007). Somalia: Genocide/War Crimes and Humanitarian Disaster.
[Online]. Available at http://www.hiiraan.com/op2/2007/apr/somalia_genocide_wa
r_crimes_and_hummanitarian_disaster.aspx. [Accessed 2 December 2010].

Samatar, Abdi I. (2007a). Somalia: Warlordism, Ethiopian Invasion, Dictatorship, &
America's Role. [Online]. Available at http://www.hiiraan.com/op2/2007/feb/soma
lia_warlordism,_ethiopian_invasion,_dictatorship,_americaper cent E2per cent 80per
cent 99s_role.aspx. [Accessed 1 December 2010].

Samatar, Abdi I. (2007b). A Keynote Speech at Horn of Africa Conference VI.
[Online]. Available at http://www.youtube.com/watch?v=U0Una853S_E. [Accessed
22 December 2010].

Samatar, Abdi I. (2007c). Somalia's Radical Hutus and the Bloodbath in Mogadishu.
[Online]. Available at http://www.hiiraan.com/op2/2007/apr/somalia_s_radical_h
utus_and_the_bloodbath_in_mogadishu.aspx. [Accessed 6 May 2011].

Sanders, Edmund (2006). Islamists Bring Order to Somalia, but Justice is Far from
Uniform, *The Seattle Times*, 15 October 2006. [Online]. Available at http://seattlet
imes.nwsource.com/html/nationworld/2003305401_somalia15.html. [Accessed 6 May
2011].

Shafat, Abdifatah (2007). Somalis Condemn U.S. Ethiopian Involvement in Somalia,
Afrika News. [Online]. Available at http://afrikanews.org/index.php?option=com_co
ntent&task=view&id=45&Itemid=26. [Accessed 22 December 2010].

Silanyo, Ahmed M. (2010). Ahmed Silanyo Speech in Minneapolis, U.S. (Qudbadii Silanyo
MN U.S. 2). [Online]. Video clip available at http://www.youtube.com/watch?v=bmOx
oyPdjOg&feature=related. [Accessed 20 February 2011].

Silanyo, Ahmed M. (1991). A Proposal to the Somali National Movement on a Framework
for Transitional Government, London, March, 1991. [Online]. Available at http://war
dheernews.com/Articles_2010/October/Ahmed_Silanyo/13_Silanyos_proposal_91.h
tml. [Accessed 20 February 2011].

Sii'arag, A. Duale (2006). Bravo Wardheernews! The Leading Light of the Emergent Somali
Internet Portals, 19 November 2006. [Online article]. Available at www.wardheernews
.com. [Accessed 30 November 2010].

Slavin, Barbara (2007). U.S. Support Key to Ethiopia's Invasion, U.S. TODAY. [Online].
Available at http://www.usatoday.com/news/world/2007-01-07-ethiopia_x.htm.
[Accessed 2 December 2010].

Snow, Jon (1978). Interview with Somali President Siyad Barre, Channel 4 TV. [Online].
Available at http://www.youtube.com/watch?v=KBiPCCi4i9o. [Accessed 12 January
2011].

Somaliland Times (2001). Puntland's Looming Civil War. [Online]. Available at http://
www.somalilandtimes.net/Archive/Archive/00001500.htm. [Accessed 19 November
2010].

Somaliland Times (2007). We Will Not Negotiate On Independence, Somaliland
Parliament Speaker, *Somaliland Times*, 6 April 2007. Available at http://www.somalilan
dtimes.net/sl/2006/272/3.shtml. [Accessed 21 December 2010].

Somaliland247 Channel (2010). Somaliland Genocide: War Crime by Somalia Government. General Morgan Ordering Shelling of Hargeisa and Commandeering the Operation. [Online]. Video clip available at http://www.youtube.com/watch?v=B0Qc Q6S1L5g&NR=1&feature=fvwp. [Accessed 14 November 2010].

Somaliland247 Channel (2008). Last SNM War Against Dictator Barre January 1991 Berbera. [Online]. Video clip available at http://www.youtube.com/watch?v =2YpGS_4wt_8&feature=related. Accessed 26 July 2011].

Somalimaitv (2011). Interview with Prof. Mohamed Haji Mukhtar (Wareysi ku Saabsan Taarkhida Somaliya, Prof. Mohamed Haji Mukhtar Part 1). [Online]. Available at http://www.youtube.com/watch?v=I3Nd3JQk8nY. [Accessed 13 February 2011].

Somaliwatch (2002). 2001 Review of Puntland's Political Crisis by an Insider. [Online]. Available at http://www.somaliawatch.org/archivedec01/020102401.htm. [Accessed 20 November 2010].

SSC Times (2010). The Birth of a Resistance Movement: The Case of SSC", 23 January 2010. [Online]. Available at http://ssctimes.com/?p=685. [Accessed 25 January 2011].

Sudam, Mohamed (2006). Somali Leaders to End Rift, No Word on Government Move, Aden, Yemen (Reuters), Thu 5 Jan 2006. [Online]. Available at http://www.assatashakur .org/forum/afrikan-world-news/13848-somali-leaders-end-rift-no-word-govt-move .html. [Accessed 10 May 2011].

Tareke, Gebru (2000). The Ethiopia-Somalia 1977 War Revisited. *International Journal of African Historical Studies*, Vol. 33, No. 3. [Online]. Available at http://www.jstor.org/ stable/3097438. [Accessed 9 December 2011].

Teslik, Lee Hudson (2008). Iraq, Afghanistan, and the U.S. Economy. [Online]. Available at Council on Foreign Relations' website Available at http://www.cfr.org/afghanistan/ iraq-afghanistan-us-economy/p15404#p1. [Accessed 23 November 2011].

The Constitution of the Somali Republic, Published in the Official Bulletin, No. 1, 1 July 1960.

The Economist (2014). Swimming Against the Tide: The Battle Against Illegal Fishing off East Africa Coast. [Online]. Available at http://www.economist.com/node/7262034. [Accessed 12 October 2014].

The Huffington Post newspaper (2014). [Online]. Available at http://www.huffingto npost.com/2013/10/14/mohamedabdi-hassan-arrested_n_4097572.html. [Accessed 20 September 2014].

The Independent (1993). Profile: How to Turn a Warmonger into a Hero: General Aideed, Top Bad-guy on America's Hit List, *The Independent*, *Saturday*, 17 July 1993. [Online]. Available at http://www.independent.co.uk/opinion/profile-how-to-turn-a-warmonger -into-a-hero-general-aideed-top-badguy-on-americas-hit-list-1485338.html. [Accessed 23 February 2011].

The Saudi Gazette Newspaper (2009). [Online]. Available at http://www.saudigazette .com.sa/index.cfm?method=home.regcon&contentid=2009021028869 [Accessed 20 September 2014].

Togane, Mohamud S. (2008). Go Away from Country, Halganka 12 December 2008. [Online]. Available at http://www.togane.org/index.php/search/results/99f814d43a289 c55b84b01ed35cac182. [Accessed 25 December 2010].

Togane, Mohamud S. (2006). Why The Daarood Will Never Return To Mogadishu Candidate Te-T-Te With Mohamed Dheere. [Online]. Available at www.togane.org/ index.php/extended/why_the_Daarood_will_never_return_to_mogadishu_a_candidt te_tte_with_mohamed_d/. [Accessed 25 December 2010].

Togane, Mohamud S. (2005). The Eedoar Botch the Case Against General Samatar. [Online]. Available at http://www.togane.org/index.php/extended/the_eedoar_botch _the_case_against_general_samatar/. [Accessed 22 October 2011].

UNDP (2009). Somalia's Missing Million: The Somali Diaspora And Its Role In Development. [Online]. Report available at website: http://www.so.undp.org. [Accessed 29 December 2010].

UNDP (2011). Cash and Compassion: The Role of the Somali Diaspora in Relief, Development and Peace Building.

UNESCO (1967). Somalia – Literacy and Adult Education by A, Rashid-Siddiqi. Paris, 1967.

UN Monitoring Group – UNMG (2006). Report of the Monitoring Group (S/2006913) to the Security Council on 17 Nov 2006. [Online]. Available at http://www.fas.org/asmp/r esources/govern/109th/S2006913.pdf. [Accessed 10 May 2011].

Unionists from Northern Somalia – UNS (2011). The Consequences of Somaliland's International Recognition. [Online]. Available at http://www.wardheernews.com/Ar ticles_2011/August/16_Consequencespercent20ofpercent20Somaliland_unionist.pdf. [Accessed 20 August 2011].

United Nations Security Council – UNSC (1992a). Resolution no. 733 on Arms Embargo on Somalia, 23 January 1992.

United Nations Security Council – UNSC (1992b). Resolution no. 751 of 24 April 1992 Establishes the United Nations Operation in Somalia I (UNOSOM-I).

United Nations Security Council – UNSC (1992c). Resolution no. 767 of 27 July 1992 Urges Co-operation by Parties with the United Nations Operation in Somalia.

United Nations Security Council – UNSC (1992d). Resolution no. 775 of 28 August 1992 Authorises Increase in Strength of the United Nations Operation in Somalia.

United Nations Security Council – UNSC (1992e). Resolution no. 794 of 3 December 1992, Creation of the Unified Task Force in Somalia (UNITAF).

United Nations Security Council – UNSC (2008a). Resolution 5902 on 2 June 2008.

United Nations Security Council – UNSC (2008b). Resolution No. 1816 (2008).

United Nations Security Council – UNSC (1910). Resolution 1918, adopted unanimously on 27 April 2010.

United Nations Security Council – UNSC (2011). Resolution 1976, adopted unanimously on 11 April 2011.

United Nations Security Council – UNSC (2011). Resolution 2015 was unanimously adopted on 24 October 2011.

UN Secretary General – UNSG (2001). Report on the Situation in Somalia to the Security Council, Document S/2001/963, 11 October 2001. [Online]. Available at http://www .un.int/wcm/webdav/site/somalia/shared/documents/statements/1086758703.pdf. [Accessed 10 May 2011].

UN Secretary General – UNSG (1995). Report on Somalia to the Security Council, 28 March 1995, S/1995/231. [Online]. Available at http://www.un.int/wcm/webdav/site /somalia. [Accessed 10 May 2011].

UN Secretary General – UNSG (1994). Report on Somalia to the Security Council, on 17 August 1994, S/1994/977. [Online]. Available at http://www.un.int/wcm/webdav/s ite/somalia. [Accessed 10 May 2011].

UN Secretary General – UNSG (2007a). Monthly report of the Secretary-General on the Situation in Somalia, S/2007/115, 28 February 2007. [Online]. Available at http://www .un.org/Docs/sc/sgrep07.htm. [Accessed 17 December 2010].

UN Secretary General – UNSG (2007b). Report of the Secretary General on the Situation in Somalia, 27 June 2007, S/2007/381. [Online]. Available at http://daccess-dds-ny.un.

org/doc/UNDOC/GEN/N07/387/94/PDF/N0738794.pdf? Open Element. [Accessed 17 December 2010].

UN Webcast (2010). Press Conference by Mr. Abdulkareem Jama, Somali Minister of Information, Post and Telecommunications on the Situation in Somalia. [Online]. Video clip available at http://www.unmultimedia.org/tv/webcast/2010/12/press -conference-mr-abdulkareem-jama-on-the-situation-in-somalia.html. [Accessed 17 December 2010].

Universal TV (2010). TV Programme Debate about the Trial of General Mohamed Ali Samatar, former Prime Minister of Somalia. [Online]. Video clip available at http://www.youtube.com/watch?v=l7819M7khXI&feature=related. [Accessed 9 December 2011].

U.S. Government Accountability Office (2008). *Somalia: Challenges and Development Efforts, U.S. Government Accountability Office (GAO)*. New York: Nova Science Publishers.

USA Today (2006). Bin Laden Releases Web Message on Iraq. [Online]. Available at http://www.usatoday.com/news/world/2006-07-01-bin-laden-plans-message_x.htm. [Accessed 17 February 11].

VOA (2011a). Renewed Mandate in Doubt as Puntland Breaks Away From Somali Government, 18 January 2011. [Online]. Available at http://www.voanews.com/english /news/africa/east/Renewed-Mandate-in-Doubt-as-Puntland-Breaks-Away-From-Som ali-Government-114136594.html. [Accessed 21 February 2011].

VOA (2011b). Interview with Abdirazak H. Hussein, Former Prime Minister (964–67). [Online]. Available at http://www.voanews.com/somali/news/Marida-Makarafooka-C abdirisaaq-Xaaji-Xuseen-120537379.html. [Accessed 3 May 2011].

VOA (2007a). A Discussion Programme about the Disagreement between President Yusuf and Prime Minister Geedi (Khilaafka Madaxweyne C/llaahi Yusuf iyo R/W Geedi) [Online]. Available at http://www.youtube.com/watch?v=guGwUo_O_vs&feature=rela ted[Accessed 5 August 2011].

VOA (2007b). Transcript of VOA Somali Service Interview with Jendayi Frazer, Assistant Secretary of State for African Affair, VOA Somali service, November 2007. [Online]. Available at http://www.voanews.com/english/news/africa/a-13-2007-11-08-voa51.ht. [Accessed 3 May 2011].

VOA (2009a). Waste Dumping off Somali Coast May Have Links to Mafia, Somali Warlords. [Online]. Available at http://www.voanews.com/content/a-13-2005-03-15 -voa34/306247.html.

VOA (2009b). Discussion on the 40th Anniversary of the 1969 Revolution (Faaqidaad da-Todobaadka-iyo-Kacaankii-21-ka-October). [Online]. Available at http://www1 .voanews.com/somali/news/discussions. [Accessed October 2009].

Waldo, Mohamed Abshir (2010). Federalism in Somalia: Birth of Puntland State and the Lessons Learned. [Online article]. Available at http://wardheernews.com/Articles_20 10/October/Waldo/10_Federalism in_Somalia_The_birth_of_Puntland_&_the_lesson s_learned.html. [Accessed 25 October 2010].

Walz, Jay (1963). Premier Says Somalia Sought Soviet Weapons for Self-Defense, *New York Times*, 1 December 1963.

Wardheernews (2006). Faysal Ali Warabe and his Hate Message Comes to Washington, DC, 8 September 2006. [Online]. Available at http://wardheernews.com/Editorial/e ditorial_35.html. [Accessed 24 October 2010].

Wikileaks (2011). US Embassy Cable, Mogadishu. [Online]. Cables available at http://cab les.mrkva.eu/index.php?subject=somali&identifier=&keywords=&tags=&embassy=-

1&classification=-1&after=&before=&do=search&start=0. [Accessed 5 September 2011].

Wilson Centre (1977). Digital Archive International History Declassified-Transcript of Meeting Between East German Leader Erich Honecker and Cuban Leader Fidel Castro, East Berlin, 3 April 1977. [Online]. Available at http://digitalarchive.wilsonce nter.org/document/111844. [Accessed 6 April 2014]

World Bank – WB (2006). Somalia: From Resilience Towards Recovery and Development. [Online]. Available at http://siteresources.worldbank.org/INTSOMALIA/Resources/ cem_01_06.pdf. [Accessed 10 May 2011].

World Bank – WB (2020). Somalia to Receive Debt Relief under the Enhanced HIPC Initiative. Available at https://www.worldbank.org/en/news/press-release/2020/03 /25/somalia-to-receive-debt-relief-under-the-enhanced-hipc-initiative. [Accessed 10 September 20].

World Bank and United Nations – WB/UN (2006). Somali Joint Needs Assessment, Social Services and Protection of Vulnerable Groups Cluster Report, 14 September 2006. [Online]. Available at http://www.somali-jna.org/downloads/SSPVGper cent 20140906per cent 20ADper cent 20Finalper cent 20Draftper cent 20rec-socialper cent 20rev-I.pdf. [Accessed 27 December 2010].

World Bank and United Nations Development Programme – WB/UNDP (2003). Socio-Economic Survey 2002, Report No. 1 Somalia Watching Brief 2003. [Online]. Available at http://info.worldbank.org/etools/docs/LICUS/194/175per cent 20-per cent 20Somaliaper cent 20-per cent 20Watchingper cent 20Brief-Macroeconomicper cent 20Dataper cent 20Collectionper cent 20andper cent 20Analysisper cent 20-per cent 20Socioeconomicper cent 20Survey.pdf. [Accessed 17 February 2011].

Xinhua News Agency (2001). Clan Elders Elect President in Somalia's Puntland Region, 14 November 2001. [Online]. Available at http://www.biyokulule.com/view:content.p hp?articleid=2942. [Accessed 21 February 2011].

Xinhua News Agency (2002). Eyewitnesses Report Few Hundred Ethiopian Troops Moving Into Somalia, Beijing Xinhua in English, 7 January 2002. [Online]. Available at http:// news.xinhuanet.com/english/2002-01/07/content_228409.htm. [Accessed 12 May 2011].

Xinhua News Agency (2004). Somali President Calls for Deployment of AU's Stabilization Force, 19 November 2004. [Online]. Available at http://www.highbeam.com/doc/1P2 -16638384.html. [Accessed 12 May 2011].

YouTube (2007). General Aideed on Somaliland–Mentioning Isaaq Grievances as Reason for the Breakaway Decision. [Online video]. Available http://www.youtube.com/watch ?v=NKuhgW502xs. [Accessed 7 June 2011].

YouTube (2010a). Demonstrations in America against the Trial of General Mohamed Ali Samatar, former Prime Minister of Somalia (Banaanbax Lagu Diidan Yahay Dacwada Gen. Ali Samatar). [Online]. Video clip available at http://www.youtube.com/watch?v =krlX1P0qGYA&feature=related. [Accessed 25 August 2011].

YouTube (2010b). Sahro Ali Samatar. [Online]. Video clip available at http://www.youtube .com/watch?v=V9auz4Y3eLI. [Accessed 25 August 2011].

YouTube (2016). Kulankii Siyaad Barre iyo Fadal Castro ee Yamen iyo Gen Galaal oo ka waramaya (General galaal talks about a meeting between Siyad Barre ans Fidel Castro in Yemen. Published on youtube Available at https://www.youtube.com/watch?v=0nb6 9LfnAYg. [Accessed November 2016].

Youtube (2018). Dozens Killed in Fighting between Puntland and Somaliland Forces. Available at https://www.youtube.com/watch?v=i06KCtlFKXc. [Accessed 18 September 2020].

Youtube (2020). Ugaaska Beelaha Gadabuursi oo sheegey in uu maalintii dhaweyd ka bad baadey isku day dil (Gadabursi clan leader survives assassination attempt). Available at https://www.youtube.com/watch?v=gRJNNyVSxh0. [Accessed 18 September 2020].

Youtube.com/watch?v=NKuhgW502xs&feature=related. [Accessed 12 May 2011].

Yuusuf, Muuse (2007). Tactical Retreat or the Demise of the UIC?, [Online]. Available at http://wardheernews.com/articles_07/jan_07/02_demise_ofpercent20_icu.html. [Accessed 1 December 2010].

Yuusuf, Muuse (2008). Vultures Gather Again for Carrion. An Article by the Author of this Book. [Online]. Available at http://www.hiiraan.com/op4/2008/dec/8865/vultures_gather_again_for_carrion.aspx#sthash.SiyVrr5x.dpbs. [Accessed 26 October 2014].

www.africa.upenn.edu/Hornet/horn_sml.html.

www.harowo.com.

www.megavideo.com (2010). Shabab Releases Video of Man who Targeted former President, NTIS, US Department of Commerce, 18th April 2010. [Online]. Video available at http://www.megavideo.com/?v=466C63BC. [Accessed 19 December 2010].

www.raceandhistory.com/historicalviews/2007/1306.html#349999

www.somaliawatch.org/archivedec00/010122301.htm

www.urrib2000.narod.ru/Etiopia-e.htm

www.veengle.com/s/Biyooley.html: Astaanta Heesta Qaranka Ee Qowmiyada DM.

www.wikipedia.org wiki/Jubaland (1).

www.wikipedia.org/wiki/Ahmad_ibn_Ibrihim_al-Ghazi Ahmad ibn Ibrahim al-Ghazi (2).

www.wikipedia.org/wiki/Ogaden_War - Ogaden war (3).

www.wikipedia.org/wiki/Siad_Barre - Siad Barre (4).

www.wikipedia.org/wiki/Battle_of_Mogadishu. Battle of Mogaidhu (5).

www.wikipedia.org/wiki/List_of_universities_in_Somalia (6).

www.wikipedia.org/wiki/Rahanweyn_Resistance_Army (7).

www.wikipedia.org/wiki/World_Islamic_Front_for_Jihad_Against_Jews_and_Crusaders (8).

www.wikipedia.org/wiki/War_in_Somalia_per cent 282006per cent E2per cent 80per cent 932009per cent 29 (9).

www.wikipedia.org/wiki/Siad_Barre#cite_note-ReferenceA-22, Mogadiscio Domestic Service in Somali, 0448 GMT 1 May 1978 (10).

www.wikipedia.org/wiki/Maritime_history_of_Somalia#Antiquity (11).

Index

www.ingramcontent.com/pod-product-compliance
Lightning Source LLC
Chambersburg PA
CBHW050415280326
41932CB00013BA/1867